MONEY, BANKING, AND THE BUSINESS CYCLE

Also by Brian P. Simpson

Money, Banking, and the Business Cycle, Volume 2: Remedies and Alternative Theories

Markets Don't Fail!

Money, Banking, and the Business Cycle

Integrating Theory and Practice

Volume One

Brian P. Simpson

MONEY, BANKING, AND THE BUSINESS CYCLE
Copyright © Brian P. Simpson, 2014.

Softcover reprint of the hardcover 1st edition 2014 978-1-137-33531-9

All rights reserved.

First published in 2014 by
PALGRAVE MACMILLAN®
in the United States—a division of St. Martin's Press LLC,
175 Fifth Avenue, New York, NY 10010.

Where this book is distributed in the UK, Europe and the rest of the world,
this is by Palgrave Macmillan, a division of Macmillan Publishers Limited,
registered in England, company number 785998, of Houndmills,
Basingstoke, Hampshire RG21 6XS.

Palgrave Macmillan is the global academic imprint of the above companies
and has companies and representatives throughout the world.

Palgrave® and Macmillan® are registered trademarks in the United States,
the United Kingdom, Europe and other countries.

ISBN 978-1-349-46304-6   ISBN 978-1-137-33149-6 (eBook)
DOI 10.1057/9781137331496

Library of Congress Cataloging-in-Publication Data

Simpson, Brian P., 1966–
    Money, banking, and the business cycle : integrating theory and
practice / Brian P. Simpson.
        volumes ; cm
    Includes bibliographical references and index.

        1. Business cycles. 2. Monetary policy. 3. Banks and banking. I. Title.

HB3714.S56 2014
338.5'42—dc23   2013044047

A catalogue record of the book is available from the British Library.

Design by Newgen Knowledge Works (P) Ltd., Chennai, India.

First edition: April 2014

10 9 8 7 6 5 4 3 2 1

To Annaliese Cassarino, my wife, and Charles and JoAnn Simpson, my parents

CONTENTS

Exhibits

PREFACE

It took nine years to complete this book and get it published. It took me about six years to write a very rough first draft, about seven months to write the second draft, and about four months to complete the third draft. Securing a publisher, going through several more rounds of editing, and getting the book finalized for publication occupied the rest of the time. I did not realize how large a task it would be when I started it. It required far more research into more areas than I thought would be necessary. The project grew so much that it eventually became two volumes.

I wrote this book in part because people have a poor understanding of the business cycle. This lack of knowledge has been highlighted since the 2008–9 recession. Wrong explanations have been provided and bad policy prescriptions have been recommended and implemented. The world desperately needs to learn what is required to achieve financial stability in an economic system. The two volumes I have written on the business cycle will enable people to acquire the knowledge they need on this crucial subject. The first volume shows theoretically and empirically what causes the business cycle, and the second volume refutes alternative theories of the business cycle and provides government policy prescriptions, based on the theory in volume one, to solve the problem of monetary-induced recessions, depressions, and financial crises.

Portions of the two volumes of this work, such as the discussions on money, inflation, the causes of the business cycle, particular episodes of the cycle, the invalidity of Keynesian depression and business cycle theory, the invalidity of real business cycle theory, the nature of a free market in money and banking, the benefits of a gold standard, and other topics are appropriate for use as supplemental reading material in courses on "macroeconomics" and money and banking. The two volumes could also be used as the main textbooks either by themselves or with other, supplemental readings in courses on the business cycle. It would be well worth it to include the two volumes. They will help readers gain an integrated and comprehensive understanding of the business cycle and business cycle theory.

BRIAN P. SIMPSON
La Jolla, CA
January, 2014

Acknowledgments

There are a number of people and organizations whose help in bringing this project to completion I want to acknowledge. I thank the Social Philosophy and Policy Center—which before it merged with the Center for the Philosophy of Freedom at the University of Arizona was located at Bowling Green State University in Bowling Green, OH—for providing me with a visiting scholar position in the fall of 2008. I thank, in particular, Fred Miller, the executive director of the center. Before my position at the center I was not hopeful about completing the book because of the extensive amount of research I still needed to perform. I was able to complete much of the remaining research at the center.

I also thank National University for providing me with a sabbatical in the spring of 2012. While on sabbatical I was a visiting scholar at the Clemson Institute for the Study of Capitalism at Clemson University in Clemson, SC. I thank the Clemson Institute and its executive director, Brad Thompson, as well. I was able to complete far more work on the project than I thought I ever would while on sabbatical. It was not until I was finished with the sabbatical that I knew I would complete the book.

I also acknowledge my intellectual indebtedness to George Reisman and make a general reference to all of his works pertaining to the topics in this book. I have referenced his works extensively but since I owe so much of my knowledge of economics to this man, I underscore the importance of his influence on my thinking in economics and express my gratitude to him here.

In addition, I thank my beloved wife, Annaliese Cassarino, for all her support. In particular, I thank her for putting up with the long hours I worked to complete this project, especially in the final phases.

Despite the support of other people and organizations in completing this project, I alone am responsible for the views expressed in this book.

INTRODUCTION

W hat causes recessions, depressions, and financial crises? This is a question that has been asked by many economists, politicians, and other individuals, and there have been many answers given to it. In the following chapters I show that Austrian business cycle theory (ABCT) explains the causes of the business cycle in a comprehensive and logically consistent manner.

ABCT says that manipulations of the supply of money and credit in the economy create the cycle. These manipulations create distortions in the price, profit, and interest rate signals that are sent throughout the economy. Increases in the supply of money and credit, especially those that are greater than the expectations of businessmen, lead to expansions in the economy and what Austrian economists call "mal-investment." Decreases in the supply of money and credit (or even insufficient increases) lead to contractions and the elimination of mal-investment. ABCT says the expansion and contraction are not isolated events. The two come as a set, that is, expansion inevitably leads to contraction.

ABCT also says that the government is directly and indirectly responsible for manipulations of the supply of money and credit that cause the business cycle. The manipulations are a form of government interference in the monetary and banking system. I show how the government directly manipulates the supply of money and credit today through the control it exercises over the fiat-money monetary system it has created. This control gives the government the power to manipulate the supply of bank reserves and thus manipulate interest rates, spending, revenues, profits, and prices. I also show how government controls of the monetary system have made it possible in the past for the government to manipulate the supply of money and credit even without fiat money.

This book provides extensive theoretical and empirical support for ABCT. I not only provide a comprehensive theoretical exposition of ABCT, I defend ABCT from all the major criticisms leveled against it. The empirical support includes over 100 years of historical analysis of the US economy—from the beginning of the twentieth century to a few years beyond the "Great Recession." I also go back to eighteenth-century France to analyze the Mississippi Bubble. I show how ABCT can be applied to understand the business cycle across continents, throughout time, and in different types of economic systems.

The purpose of this book is to explain monetary-induced recessions, depressions, and financial crises. There can be other causes of economy-wide financial crises and recessions, some of which I discuss in the book (such as in chapter 3). However, these rarely occur and are easily explainable. The episodes that are difficult to explain are those that are induced by manipulations of the supply of money and credit.

Readers with a background in economics might find some of the topics familiar, such as what constitutes money, so-called fiscal and monetary policies, aggregate economic accounting (gross domestic product), the demand for money, inflation, and more. However, even when discussing familiar topics I often provide new insights and present little-known theories that even those with an extensive background in economics might not be aware of, such as a new measure of money, the use of gross national revenue (a largely unknown measure of aggregate spending), and a better understanding of inflation than is provided by the typical, mainstream discussions of the topic. It is necessary to include all essential topics involved in understanding the business cycle to provide a comprehensive treatment of the subject and clear up confusion created by mainstream economics on some of the basic economics pertaining to the issue. Readers familiar with specific topics can skip over them, although they should be careful when doing this so that they do not miss my enlightening perspective on familiar topics.

Let me say a little about the method of analysis used in this book. It involves applying economic theory to explain empirical data through a narrative analysis. I do not use econometric analysis. Such a tool is not epistemologically valid for understanding the world and attempting to form inductive conclusions. As a result, the use of econometrics has led to greater ignorance about economics. I merely make this assertion here. My analysis of econometrics will have to wait for a book I plan to write on epistemological and methodological issues in economics.

I also do not—at least primarily—analyze the records of government agencies and entities (such as the Federal Reserve) to determine how they might be attempting to influence the economy. I analyze the effects of their actions, such as how the money supply and interest rates are changing, to determine how or whether policies have changed and what influence they have had. In other words, my focus is not on what government officials say they are doing or will do but on the effects on the economy of what they actually do. I grant that looking at the records of certain governmental bodies can sometimes help one understand what that body is doing or intends to do (and I do this in some cases). However, my concern is what is actually happening in the economy regardless of what government officials might say about how they are trying to affect the economy.

I must emphasize that the use of empirical data in economics can be a very precarious activity. Measurement accuracy is often not that good (although this is not true for individual variables, such as the historical value of a particular interest rate like the federal funds rate). One cannot typically achieve the accuracy one is able to achieve in laboratory experiments. Furthermore, the accuracy of the data is not always as great as what it appears to be. For example, price data are often not accurate to the number of decimal places to which price indices are sometimes reported. If a price index changes from 229.098 to 229.177 (actual monthly values of the consumer price index), can one say anything more significant than that the price level remained constant? The accuracy of economic statistics often does not allow one to make more than ordinal categorizations, such as that the price level changed a little, changed a lot, or remained constant.

Economic data are generally based on statistical sampling, which is responsible for part of the inaccuracy. Adding to the difficulty is the fact that data are sometimes not available from one year to the next due to changes in the type of data being collected and reported. Moreover, data for similar variables are sometimes not compatible (or are compatible only with certain qualifications) due to different measurement techniques being employed. Furthermore, significant revisions are often made to the data as time goes by.

Price indices are subject to further problems. For example, they attempt to measure changes in the weighted-average price of a specific basket of goods and they therefore do not account for changes in the prices of goods that are not in the basket. In addition, it is hard to account for changes in preferences for goods in the basket. However, adjustments to the weights on each good in the basket are updated periodically to account for these changes. New goods are added to the basket and goods in the basket are taken out when necessary as well.

Given these qualifications, one can still use empirical data to analyze changes in the economy. It is just that it is difficult to make conclusions based on the data. This makes the fact that the data show a number of regular patterns all the more significant. It also emphasizes the importance of using deductive analysis to understand the business cycle.

One also has to keep in mind when performing economic analysis that while causal relationships do exist between economic variables there are no observable, quantitatively fixed responses between variables as there are in, say, physics. For example, it is true that minimum-wage laws cause unemployment, but one cannot legitimately conclude that if the minimum wage rises by a given dollar amount or percentage, unemployment will accordingly rise by a given number of people or percentage. It is not a part of the nature of economics that such observations can be made because one cannot hold all other variables constant in the economy (despite what econometricians might believe).

One should not take the above to imply that we cannot know economic reality or that *any* change in one variable can occur in response to a change in another variable. The laws of economics, like the laws of physics, are absolute. However, the ways in which those absolutes manifest themselves are different. Stated in a different way, we *can* know reality, and a part of that knowledge involves understanding what observations are capable of being made in a given field (like an astronomer knowing what observations are possible with a particular telescope).

Furthermore, there is no observable, fixed timing between changes in variables. The time to respond might be different for the same variables in different contexts (such as at different points in history or in different economies), although as with the magnitude of the response this should not be taken to mean that variables can adjust over *any* span of time. Too many other variables are changing in the economy to get the exact same timing in every case. More fundamentally, in economics we are dealing with a being of free will, which is a major factor preventing the ceteris paribus condition from holding and influences both the magnitude and timing of responses.

Let me say a few words about the nature of the business cycle and business cycle theory. This will help one better understand the reasons for the method of analysis used in this book. The business cycle is a complex phenomenon. It involves a multitude of facts, such as oscillations in interest rates, prices, wages, unemployment, output, spending, and more. To explain the business cycle, one needs a mechanism to integrate all these facts. These facts appear to be connected when one looks at the data, but one needs a unifying theory to connect them and make logical sense of them. One must apply many theories, including the law of demand, present value analysis, the uniformity of profit principle, capital theory, monetary theory, and more to integrate the facts of the business cycle into a logically consistent theory. Many of these theories are themselves derived from or encompass additional economic theories. For example, the law of demand is based on the law of diminishing marginal utility (or value), and monetary theory encompasses theories regarding inflation and the demand for money. All of these theories must be applied to the facts of the business cycle to develop a comprehensive business cycle theory. This is why business cycle theory must be developed deductively, not inductively. It is a process of applying already validated theory to explain a specific, concrete phenomenon. It is not merely a process of observing the fluctuations that take place during a multitude of business cycles across continents and centuries and generalizing about the causal factors involved. There are just too many changing elements involved to be able to do that.

It is important to understand that what I describe above as necessary to develop business cycle theory is not rationalism. Some people have a tendency to confuse deduction with rationalism. Deduction is the process of applying validated generalizations to make conclusions about other concrete phenomena and is an appropriate method of logic. The generalizations used in deductive reasoning are based on the facts, either directly or indirectly through inductive reasoning. Rationalism is an invalid form of deductive reasoning. It involves the attempt to explain phenomena using ideas not grounded in the facts of reality. An attempted explanation of the nature of the world based on the arbitrary premises of religious mysticism is a grand-scale example of rationalism.

While induction is not the primary method used in developing business cycle theory, it is still used in understanding the nature of the business cycle and validating business cycle theory. For example, induction is involved in identifying the common patterns of the cycle, such as the fluctuations in many variables that occur during the cycle (the rate of profit, interest rates, etc.) and the timing of the fluctuations of variables (for instance, that short-term interest rates tend to rise prior to recessions). Induction is also involved in making the generalization that government interference is the primary cause of the business cycle and the recessions, depressions, and financial crises that are a part of it. This generalization is made by using business cycle theory to explain a number of specific episodes of the cycle. In the end, induction cannot be escaped since any valid conclusions must ultimately be based on observations of the facts of reality, whether directly or indirectly.

While I do not consider all the inductive conclusions in this book fully validated, I have analyzed enough historical episodes of the business cycle across space and time, using the theory developed in the book, to be confident that I have identified the causes of the business cycle. The analysis of further episodes in history using the theoretical framework in this book will provide additional support for the validity of the theory. The types of episodes that need to be analyzed include pre–Federal Reserve episodes in America and episodes in other countries throughout the major periods of mankind's history (to the extent that data are available). Some of these episodes have already been analyzed, such as the depression of 1819–21 in the United States.[1] I also provide a brief analysis in this book of some of the episodes of the cycle in America in the twentieth century just prior to the creation of the Fed.

The main limitation one faces in a book that presents a complete analysis of the business cycle is space. Presenting a complete defense of business cycle theory would create a book that is far too long. Such a defense would include not only an extensive historical analysis but an exposition of the theory itself, a defense of the theory against criticisms, refutations of other theories, and a presentation of policy prescriptions that would essentially eliminate monetary-induced recessions, depressions and financial crises. That is why my treatment of the business cycle has been divided into two volumes. This volume focuses on the first three items. Part one of this volume focuses on an exposition of the theory and the foundational knowledge required to understand it, as well a comprehensive defense of the theory from criticisms. Part two focuses on the application of the theory to analyze historical episodes of the cycle.

The last two items are undertaken in volume two of my work on the business cycle. While I show in volume one the role of fractional-reserve banking in creating the cycle, in part two of volume two I show how government interference is responsible for the existence of the fractional-reserve checking system and thus responsible, at least indirectly, for the ability of banks to manipulate the supply of money and credit through this system. I show that the solution to the problem of financial crises, recessions, depressions, and the business cycle in general is to abolish the offending government interference. This means a free market in money and banking must be established to eliminate the business cycle.

In part one of volume two I refute several other theories of the business cycle, including Keynesian theories of the business cycle and real business cycle theory. After reading part one in volumes one and two, one will see not only that ABCT provides a comprehensive and logically consistent explanation of the business cycle but that it is the *only* theory that provides such an explanation. Both volumes in their totality enable one to see not only what causes the business cycle but also what the appropriate response to the cycle is. Let us begin this endeavor.

Part I

THEORY

1

Money, Banking, and Inflation

Introduction

Since the business cycle is an economy-wide, general phenomenon, money is a good candidate to help explain the cycle. Money is an asset readily acceptable in exchange in a given geographic area and is sought for the purpose of being re-exchanged. Virtually all transactions take place in the economy through the use of money. All prices are money prices. Profits are calculated in terms of money. Interest rates are also calculated based on monetary relationships. If one wants to understand the business cycle, one must begin here.[1] Further, the manner in which the banking system creates money is also important to an understanding of the business cycle. This topic will also be discussed in this chapter. Finally, it will be shown that inflation—and its role in the business cycle—can only properly be understood based on its relationship to increases in the money supply. As a part of the section on inflation, the problems with the popular definition of inflation—a sustained increase in the general price level—will be discussed.

Money

What Is Money?

It is changes in the money supply that drive the business cycle, so one needs to know what the money supply is composed of to understand how it changes and how it causes the business cycle.

The money supply today comprises coins, paper money, and checking deposits. In the United States, paper money is issued by the Federal Reserve, the central bank of the nation, and is known as Federal Reserve Notes. Checking deposits represent the largest component of the money supply today. Technically, they are not money but money substitutes, since they are claims to money held by the issuing bank. However, as long as the bank is not in financial trouble the checks circulate as the equivalent of money. When banks get into financial trouble, their checks might not be accepted in trade. In cases like these, the checking-account funds at such banks cease to be money because they are no longer a medium of exchange.[2] But this occurs infrequently and can be taken into account if necessary when measuring the money supply. It is proper to count checking deposits as a portion of the money supply under normal circumstances because they are generally accepted as a medium of exchange. As a part of the checking deposit component of the money supply, I include all accounts on which checks can be written. This includes personal and business checking accounts, money market deposit accounts (MMDAs), money market mutual funds (MMMFs), government checking deposits (at the federal, state, and local levels), and checking deposits of foreigners at US banks (whether foreign governments, banks, etc.). I discuss qualifications to some of these below. I also include certified checks, cashier's checks, money orders, and traveler's checks as a part of the checking deposit portion of the money supply.

Another category of money is standard money. While not a separate component of the money supply, standard money is important to have knowledge of if one wants to have a good understanding of money and be able to explain the business cycle. Standard money is money that has ultimate debt paying power and is not a claim to anything further. Today it consists of coins and paper money. It used to be gold when countries were on the gold standard. When countries were on the gold standard, paper money was merely a claim to the gold deposited in banks. Today, the coins and paper money that comprise the standard money are known as fiat money because they have been declared arbitrarily by the government to be money (i.e., to be legal tender). Fiat money has completely displaced gold today. It was not through a natural development of the free market that it displaced gold but through the use of government force (i.e., violations of the free market).[3]

The following example will help concretize the concept of standard money. When a man pays for his groceries with cash the transaction is complete. The man has paid everything he owes to the grocer. This is because cash is standard money. It has ultimate debt paying power. However, if the man writes a check to pay for his groceries the transaction is not complete. The grocer wants the funds deposited in the man's checking account; he wants the standard money. At this point, the grocer only has a claim to these funds in the man's account. Only after the grocer gives the check to his bank, his bank presents the check to the issuing bank, and the funds are transferred from the payer's to the grocer's checking account is the transaction complete. Now the standard money has been transferred to the grocer (or, at least, the appropriate debits and credits to each bank's balance sheet and each depositor's account have been made so that the balance sheets and accounts reflect the appropriate claims to standard money).

What Is Not Money?

Some bank accounts are very close to money but are not, in fact, money. These include savings and time deposits. Time deposits are interest earning deposits that have a stated maturity date and penalties for early withdrawal. These deposits may mature in, perhaps, as little as one month. However, their maturity date may also be years in the future. Savings deposits have no stated maturity date and no penalty for early withdrawal. Both time and savings deposits are accounts on which one cannot write checks and thus one temporarily gives up access to the funds in these accounts, even if the only delay is having to transfer the money electronically to one's checking account (in the case of savings accounts). Depositors are generally willing to temporarily give up access to these funds to earn interest (or a higher rate of interest). These accounts, at best, are highly liquid assets but are not money. One must be able to use the funds in an account as a medium of exchange in order for them to be money. The fact that these funds must be withdrawn as cash or transferred to an account from which they can be used as a medium of exchange dictates that they are not money. One cannot spend them until one has exchanged one asset for another—until one has exchanged a highly liquid asset for the liquid itself (i.e., money).

Above I said that MMDAs and MMMFs are a part of the money supply. Some might be confused by this statement because these accounts are typically designated as types of savings accounts. However, this is not a completely accurate designation. MMDAs (at banks) and MMMFs (at mutual fund companies) are accounts on which checks can sometimes be written but with some restrictions. For instance, the number of transfers (which includes checks written on the account) is limited on MMDAs. MMMFs typically have no restrictions on the number of transfers (including checks); however, a certain minimum amount must be transferred each time. The latter is also true of MMDAs.

Hence, these accounts are a part of the money supply, with some qualifications. They are a part of the money supply to the extent that depositors use them as a medium of exchange. It is generally believed that MMMFs are used more often as a medium of exchange than MMDAs, since the former accounts have fewer restrictions on them. Estimates have been made for the portion of MMMFs that have checking-writing capabilities on them. I use this to estimate the portion of MMMFs that should be included in the money supply. In the case of MMDAs, even though they generally have check-writing capabilities, because of their restrictions, it is generally believed that depositors do not use these as a medium of exchange as often. What portion of MMDAs to include in a measure of the money supply remains open to debate. I will have more to say about this below.

The last financial instrument I will discuss in this subsection is credit cards. They are not money. Credit cards give the holder electronic access to a loan; they enable the holder to borrow money and, of course, the loan must be paid off with money but the card itself is not money. The card, of course, does not change hands like money. In essence, the card gives the user temporary access to *someone else's money* (the card issuer's), which is borrowed to pay for goods purchased.

The economist Lawrence White has considered whether the signed charge slip handed over by the credit-card user to the seller at the time of purchase of the goods might be money. He says one might argue that "[w]ithin the retail sphere...an individual's debt instruments in the form of signed charge slips are generally acceptable...[and thus] qualify as a form of money." He goes on to reject this viewpoint because "the debt instrument in this case is not *acquired through trade in order to be spent* by anyone. The card holder...does not acquire it through trade. The merchant...does not intend to spend it." (Emphasis is in the original.) He also says that the reason why the debt instruments are not considered to be money is *not* because they are a form of debt, since checking deposits are debt to the issuing bank and yet they are money.[4]

While White comes to the right conclusion, he omits a crucial point along the way. The claim that the charge slip does not constitute money because it is not acquired in trade by the card holder and the merchant has no intention of using it in trade to purchase goods does not provide a complete answer. Money must not only be readily acceptable in exchange and sought for the purpose of being re-exchanged, it must be an asset to the user as well. Neither the credit card nor the charge slip is an asset to the card user. They are liabilities. Specifically, when the credit-card holder borrows via the credit card he incurs a debt, and debt incurred via a credit card is no more money than any other form of debt one incurs (whether a car loan, mortgage loan, a loan from issuing Treasury bonds, etc.).

Furthermore, in saying that one cannot claim that something is not money because it is a form of debt, since checking deposits are debt to the issuing bank and yet they are a form of money, White commits the same error: he fails to keep in mind the essential characteristic of money as an asset to the user. The checking deposit is not money to the bank because it is a liability to the bank. However, the checking deposit *is* money to the depositor because it is an asset to the depositor (that is readily acceptable in exchange). So we *can* say the credit card and charge slip are not money because they are forms of debt. They possess neither of the essential characteristics of money: they are not an asset to the user and they are not "acquired through trade in order to be spent by anyone." For something to be money it must possess both characteristics.

It must also be understood with regard to credit cards that their existence does not increase the amount of spending in the economy. If I take out a loan through the use of a credit card, as with any other loan, I am able to spend more money but the lender, at the same time, has less money and therefore is not able to spend as much.[5] As with all loans, they merely transfer money from the lender to the borrower and allow the borrower to temporarily spend more and make it so the lender is restricted in his spending but can earn interest as compensation.

Credit cards do not decrease the amount of money people hold either. Sometimes it is believed that people hold less money when they use credit cards because people hold less cash. They hold less cash because they use credit cards to purchase goods instead. However, the money represented by the reduced cash people hold does not disappear. To the extent that people are holding less cash, they are holding more money in other forms (viz., checking account balances). So credit cards do not reduce the amount of money people hold, they merely change the form in which people hold money.

Measures of the Money Supply

I have discussed the components of the money supply; however, this does not tell us what specific monetary measurements must be used to calculate the quantity of money in the economy at any point in time. There are a number of measures used today and some are more accurate than others. In determining what a valid measure of the money supply is, one must keep in mind the essential characteristic of money, namely, that it is a medium of exchange. Therefore, only those funds that are used as a medium of exchange should be included.

Up through the 1980s and early 1990s, the M1 measure of the money supply was the most accurate measure. This measure includes currency in the hands of the public plus traveler's checks and accounts designated as checking deposits by the Federal Reserve. Typically, an account is designated as a checking account if there are no limitations on check writing. Therefore, checking accounts include some, but not all, accounts on which one can actually write checks. For instance, they include traditional demand deposits and negotiable order of withdrawal accounts, but they do not include MMDAs and MMMFs. Since these latter deposits have grown significantly in recent decades and have at least some check-writing capabilities, M1 is no longer an accurate measure of the money supply.

M1's inaccuracy stems from the fact that it is too low as a measure of money. The next measure, M2, is too high. M2's main inaccuracy is that it includes some funds that are not, in fact, money, although it does also fail to include some funds that are money. M2 includes M1 plus savings deposits (which includes MMDAs), small-denomination time deposits (deposits less than $100,000), and "retail" MMMFs. Retail MMMFs are those opened with initial investments of less than $50,000 (typically by individuals). About 75 percent of these accounts have been estimated to have check-writing capabilities. About 20 percent of "institutional" MMMFs (MMMFs with initial investments of $50,000 or more) have been estimated to have check-writing capabilities.[6] M2 does not include institutional MMMFs at all. Not including the portion of institutional MMMFs that have check-writing capabilities on them results in M2 being too low of a measure of the money supply. The funds included in M2 that are not money are the savings deposits on which one cannot write checks (this includes the portion of MMDAs that checks cannot be written on), time deposits, and the portion of "retail" MMMFs on which checks cannot be written. In addition, the MMDAs and MMMFs included in M2 and on which checks can be written but that are not used as a medium of exchange by account holders are not money either. The net result of the inaccuracies of M2 is that it is larger than the money supply.

Money of zero maturity (MZM) is another measure of the money supply. MZM includes M2 minus small-denomination time deposits plus institutional MMMFs. Its drawback is the inclusion of savings deposits and the portions of MMDAs and MMMFs that are not used by account holders as a medium of exchange. All of the measures of the money supply I have discussed so far are easily obtainable because their values are reported by the Federal Reserve.

The most accurate measure of the money supply includes the following: M1 plus the portion of MMMFs and MMDAs that account holders use as a medium of exchange, the portion of "retail" sweep accounts not swept into MMDAs that depositors use as a medium of exchange, and the portion of "commercial" sweep accounts not swept into MMMFs that account holders use as a medium of exchange. Sweep accounts are accounts that allow banks to transfer funds back and forth between checking accounts and other accounts (such as MMMFs,

MMDAs, Eurodollar deposits, and repurchase agreements). Sweep accounts are used by banks to reduce the amount of legally required reserves they must keep on hand and to earn higher interest rates for themselves and their customers. In a sweep account, the funds reside in a checking deposit during the day (when checks might clear on the account) and are swept into interest-earning accounts (or accounts with higher interest rates) at night (when no activity takes place in the account). Sweep accounts reduce the reserves banks must keep on hand because checking accounts have legally imposed reserve requirements, while the accounts into which funds are swept have no reserve requirements. It is proper to include sweep accounts in the money supply because the funds are used, for the most part, like regular checking deposits.

Retail sweep accounts sweep funds from depositors' checking accounts into, typically, MMDAs. Commercial sweep accounts sweep funds from business demand-deposit accounts into such investments as MMMFs, Eurodollar deposits, and repurchase agreements. To the extent that swept funds into MMDAs and MMMFs are already included in the money supply through the sums in these accounts that depositors use as a medium of exchange, the swept funds should not be counted separately. If they were, they would be counted twice.

It is difficult to say exactly what portion of MMDAs and MMMFs are used as a medium of exchange. A significant number of MMDAs are probably used as a form of savings by depositors and have no checks written on them. Perhaps the best estimate of what portion of MMDAs are held as savings deposits are those MMDAs for which checks (or debit cards) are never ordered.[7] One could say the same for MMMFs. However, such data cannot be obtained. Given the data that exist, the most accurate statement I can make is that the money supply is closest to M1 plus MMMFs on which checks can be written, the portion of "commercial" sweep accounts not swept into MMMFs, and "retail" sweep accounts. An upper bound is this amount minus "retail" sweep accounts plus MMDAs. For convenience, I will label these monetary measures M1.5 and M1.6, respectively.

One must also add to all of the above measures the checking deposits of the US government, as well as dollar-denominated checking deposits of foreign official institutions and foreign commercial banks at US banks.[8] These are not included in any of the money supply variables discussed above. They are estimated separately by the Federal Reserve. They are small relative to the rest of the money supply.

As one can see, establishing a measure of the money supply is not easy. Some of the difficulty arises due to banking regulations that have made it harder for banks to provide financial services that customers demand. Hence, banks have had to devise roundabout mechanisms to provide the same type of service that, without the regulations, they could have provided in a much more straightforward and efficient manner. For instance, "commercial" sweep accounts arose at least in part because it was illegal for interest to be paid on business demand deposits. These sweep accounts made it possible for business checking-deposit funds to be placed in interest-earning assets. Of course, it would have been easier if banks could have simply paid interest on the business checking deposits themselves (and as of July 2010 they are now legally able to do this).

Some of the difficulty arises because many of the components of the money supply are either not measured or are difficult to measure. For instance, MMDAs have not been measured separately from savings deposits more generally since 1990. Moreover, even if they were counted separately, no one to my knowledge has measured the extent to which they are used as a medium of exchange.

Despite the difficulties, the money supply can be measured with enough accuracy for the purpose of explaining the business cycle. To explain the business cycle, one does not need an exact measure of the money supply. One only needs to know approximately how fast the money supply is changing.

To get an idea of the relative quantities of the different measures of the money supply, here are values of the measures I have discussed. The latest value for M1 is $2,556 billion as of September 2013. For M2, the latest value is $10,769.8 billion as of the same date. The value for MZM on this date is $11,985.6 billion. The latest value for M1.5 is $3,674.1 billion as of November 2010. The latest value for M1.6 is $5,780.9 billion as of that same date. The values for M1.5 and M1.6 with US government, foreign official institution, and foreign commercial bank checking deposits included are $3,698.5 and $5,805.3 billion, respectively.[9]

Since M1.5 and M1.6 are not calculated anywhere, they must be calculated by adding together data from different sources. I have not been able to update these values since November 2010 because I have not been able to obtain any "commercial" sweep data since that time. These data are not issued regularly. For a better comparison relative to M1.5 and M1.6, here are the values in November 2010 for M1, M2, and MZM: $1,828.3, $8,742.1, and $9,712 billion, respectively.

From these data, one can see just how inaccurate M1, M2, and MZM are as measures of the money supply. M2 and MZM are much too large, and although I will use M1 for my analysis of particular episodes of the business cycle that occurred far enough in the past, too many additional accounts with check-writing capabilities have been created recently and not included in M1. M1 started to become inaccurate as a measure of the money supply in the 1980s, and by the early to mid-1990s it was not accurate enough to use. It has only become worse since that time.

To avoid a possible misunderstanding, one final point must be stressed in connection with changes in the money supply. Such changes occur when changes in the cumulative total of all the components of the money supply occur, not simply when changes to one component occur. To illustrate what I mean, take the Y2K event that occurred due to the change in time from the year 1999 to 2000. It has been said by at least one economist that the money supply increased because the demand for money increased at that time. However, this is not true. Neither the money supply nor the demand for money increased. Why is this true?

Just prior to the year 2000, some people withdrew extraordinarily large amounts of money from their checking accounts to hold on to greater amounts of cash. They did this because they thought that with the date change computers might malfunction and they might not have access to the funds in their checking accounts until the problem was resolved. The question is: Does the withdrawing of funds from one's checking account to hold cash constitute an increase in the demand to hold money and cause the money supply to increase? The answer is "no." This merely represents a change in the type of money people hold; it does not represent an increase in the demand or supply of money. When people take money out of their checking accounts to increase the amount of cash they hold, for every additional dollar people hold in the form of cash they hold one less dollar in their checking accounts. Hence, there is no net change in the amount of money, only a change in the type of money people hold. This type of change constitutes a change in the components of the money supply with no net change in the money supply itself.[10]

Alternative Theories of Money

There are a number of views on what constitutes money. A few of them are discussed here to show why they are not valid and why money is as I describe it. This discussion should help one understand in a better fashion what is—and is not—money.

Some economists claim that if an asset can be "converted at par into money at any time on demand," it should be included in the money supply.[11] Based on this, savings deposits, US savings bonds, and even the cash surrender value of life insurance policies are said to be money. Likewise, funds in MMMFs and traveler's checks are not to be considered money because they cannot be converted at par into money at any time on demand.

Advocates of this theory claim that "demand deposits only function as money because they are...*money-substitutes*, i.e., they readily take the place of money, at par" and that the "distinguishing feature of a money-substitute...is that people believe it can be converted at par into money at any time on demand."[12] (Emphasis is in the original.) This claim is an instance of the logical fallacy of context dropping, first identified as a major logical fallacy by the novelist and philosopher Ayn Rand.[13] While it is true that a money substitute can be generally "converted at par into money at any time on demand," this occurs within the context of it being used as a medium of exchange. Being a medium of exchange is a crucial characteristic without which something can be neither money nor a money substitute.

So while it might be true that a savings deposit can be converted into money on demand, such a deposit is not a medium of exchange and thus is neither money nor a money substitute. One cannot directly use funds in one's savings account to purchase anything. If one does not believe this, try doing it at the grocery store. One will not be able to. One must first convert the savings deposit into another asset (whether a demand deposit, cashier's check, cash, etc.) before it can be used as a medium of exchange. Notice the crucial difference between a demand deposit and a savings deposit: a demand deposit does not need to be converted into anything to be used as money. It is already a medium of exchange. So while to be a money substitute it is crucial that the asset be convertible on demand at any time into money, it is also crucial that the asset be a medium of exchange.

Understanding that an asset must be a medium of exchange to be money makes it easy to reject many assets that are claimed to be money substitutes, but in fact are not. For example, savings bonds are not money substitutes because they cannot be used as a medium of exchange. Try taking a savings bond to the grocery store and exchanging it for a bag of groceries. It will not work. One must first cash the bond in, obtain money (or a money substitute), then exchange the proceeds received from cashing the bond in to obtain goods at the grocery store. The same is true of life insurance policies. The policy cannot be exchanged for any goods or services.

Advocates of the ideas being refuted here use analogies in an attempt to claim that savings deposits, savings bonds, and so forth are just "slower-moving" parts of the money supply because it is a little harder to convert them into money. These analogies are not valid. For example, it is claimed that checking deposits are like, in the days of a gold standard, gold coins kept in one's house (because they are easier to gain access to) and savings deposits are like gold coins locked away in a vault (because they are harder to gain access to). It is also claimed that demand deposits are like gold coins, and savings deposits, et cetera are like gold bars because the former are more active as money and the latter are less active.[14] The context that both these analogies drop is that, under a gold standard, *both gold coins and gold bars are money*, no matter where they exist, and one does not need to convert them into anything to use them as a medium of exchange. Savings deposits and so forth do need to be converted into money or a money substitute before they can be used as a medium of exchange.

In addition, Eurodollar deposits and repurchase agreements are not money. The former are a type of time deposit and the latter a loan. Neither of them is a medium of exchange. They must first be converted to a medium of exchange before they can be spent.

Also, it should be clear that traveler's checks are a part of the money supply since they are used as a medium of exchange. One does not need to first convert them into anything before they can be used to purchase goods and services. It should also be clear that MMMFs are a medium of exchange and thus are money substitutes and a part of the money supply. We see here that for an asset to be a money substitute it does not need to be convertible into money *at par*. Because MMMFs are equity claims on short-term investments, they are not convertible at par but at whatever the shares are worth at the time of conversion. Hence, they could lose value, although in fact that has rarely happened. The crucial characteristics for an asset to be a money substitute are that the asset should be capable of being converted into money on demand (not necessarily at par) and that it can be used as a medium of exchange.

Advocates of the "convertible on demand at par into money" theory of money confuse converting a highly liquid asset into money with converting a money substitute into standard money. This distinction is critical to make. The former case is one of converting an asset that is not money into money and the latter is a case of converting one form of money into another form of money. The advocates of this theory, in essence, see one characteristic of a money substitute and then classify any asset that has that characteristic as a money substitute, forgetting about the fact that to be a money substitute the asset must also be a medium of exchange.

One economist claims that MMMFs are not money because the asset that the check-writing customer relinquishes is not what the recipient of the check accepts. The check writer gives up ownership shares in a portfolio of assets. The assets include mostly short-term debt instruments and a small amount of checking deposits the MMMF uses to pay those who receive checks drawn on the fund. The recipient of the check receives ownership in a claim to bank reserves. As a result, it is argued that MMMF shares are "not directly spendable."[15]

The first thing to note here is that funds in MMMFs are, in fact, directly spendable to those who own shares in the funds. Account holders are able to write checks on the assets of the fund and these checks are readily accepted in trade as a means of payment. What happens behind the scenes to convert ownership shares in short-term investment assets into money to make the payments is irrelevant. The fund might have to sell some of its short-term assets to have the money available, but more than likely it will be able to make payments out of its checking account and be able to rely on inflows of money to replenish the account.

All of this is similar to what happens under fractional-reserve banking.[16] When depositors write checks they relinquish claims to funds in the account that are backed partially by reserves and partially by other assets (loans made by the bank), and the recipients of the checks receive ownership of claims to bank reserves. In order to have the funds available, the bank might have to sell some of the loans (if they are, say, Treasury bonds) or call some of the loans (if they are not marketable securities and the loans are callable), but in the typical case the bank will be able to manage its business so it can rely on its stock of reserves to transfer funds to recipients' banks and use inflows of money to replenish its reserves.

The main difference between checking deposits under fractional reserves and MMMFs is the relationship between the account holder and the manager of the account. The depositor has loaned funds to the bank and thus is a creditor to the bank, while the MMMF account holder is an owner of the assets managed by the mutual fund company. However, the results of the transactions on the accounts are the same: account holders use the accounts to directly gain access to money and make payments. So this argument for not including MMMFs in the money supply is not valid.

One last characteristic that some economists claim money must possess is the simultaneity of payments. That is, the entire stock of money consists only of those assets that can be spent at the same time.[17] This means checking deposits in a fractional-reserve banking system are not money (at least not the portion that is greater than the supply of bank reserves backing them).[18] This is clearly a problem. Checking deposits (including the portion above the supply of bank reserves) are so widely used as a medium of exchange that they cannot be excluded from the concept of money. At least one of these characteristics must go. Clearly, it is the requirement of the simultaneity of payments. The characteristic that best distinguishes the concept money from other concepts is that the asset be a generally accepted medium of exchange.

Banking

Banking is intimately tied to money, since people hold most of their money in banks or closely related financial institutions. To have a comprehensive understanding of the business cycle, one must understand the role of the banking system in creating the business cycle. Here I am not concerned with the productive role of bringing borrowers and lenders together that banks play in the division of labor. I am concerned only with their role in creating the business cycle. To understand this role, some basics of the banking system must be discussed.

A Bank's Balance Sheet

Banks have the ability to create money through the process of credit expansion and this contributes to the business cycle. The first step in understanding the money-creation process is to understand some of the components of a bank's balance sheet. A balance sheet is a two-column list that shows the financial position of a company on a specific date. One side of the balance sheet shows the assets of the company (what the firm owns) and the other side shows the liabilities and net worth of the company (what the firm owes to others and the amount the firm's owners have invested in the company, respectively). An example is shown in exhibit 1.1.

The identity pertaining to the balance sheet is that assets equal liabilities plus net worth. For our purposes, we will assume net worth is zero. We will focus only on assets and liabilities. So, in our case, assets will always equal liabilities.

The bank assets that are necessary to consider are reserves and loans. Reserves are funds a bank receives but does not lend out. Loans are funds the bank lends out to earn income. A bank cannot loan out all the funds it receives. It needs some funds to meet daily net withdrawals of cash and to provide a cushion to protect against running out of money in the face of larger than usual withdrawals. Reserves can be held in the form of vault cash or as deposits at the Federal Reserve.

Of course, banks will want to loan out some of the funds they receive to earn interest on them. Today, banks are legally required to keep some funds on hand as reserves to back deposits in checking accounts. When banks have less than 100 percent of their checking deposits on hand as reserves, this is known as fractional-reserve banking. This means checking deposits are only partially

Assets   Liabilities

Net worth

Exhibit 1.1 Example of a blank balance sheet.

Assets   Liabilities

Reserves Deposits

Loans

Exhibit 1.2   Bank balance sheet.

backed by standard money. When checking deposits are fully backed by standard money, it is known as 100-percent reserve banking.

The only liability necessary to consider is deposits. Deposits represent money owed to depositors. The bank merely holds on to the deposited funds or lends them out for depositors but must repay them to depositors if requested. An example of a bank balance sheet with the assets and liabilities discussed here is provided in exhibit 1.2.

The Process of Money Creation through the Banking System

This is the important aspect of the banking system's role in creating the business cycle. To get the process started, assume the government, through the Federal Reserve's ability to create money, creates $1,000 and gives it to someone, perhaps a Social Security recipient.[19] The recipient of the funds deposits them in his checking account at his bank, say Bank A. Bank A's initial balance sheet is shown in exhibit 1.3.

At this point, the banking system has not created any money. However, the bank can lend out some of the $1,000 in reserves it received. When the bank does this, money is created. For example, say the bank is legally required to hold reserves equal to 10 percent of all checking deposits and that it can loan out any reserves above this amount. Assuming the bank loans out all the funds that it is legally able to, after it makes the loan, Bank A's balance sheet will look as shown in exhibit 1.4.

Now, $900 of money has been created. The depositor of the original $1,000 can write checks on his entire $1,000 and the recipient of the loan can spend the proceeds of the loan. So now the money supply has increased to $1,900 (assuming this is the only money in existence). It consists of the original $1,000 created by the government and the $900 loaned out by Bank A. But the process does not stop here.

If the recipient of the $900 loan deposits the money into his checking account at his bank, say Bank B, more money can be created. Now Bank B can lend out 90 percent of the funds it receives. So it can make an $810 loan. This increases the money supply by that amount. Now the money supply is $2,710. This is because the holder of the original deposit can spend his $1,000, the recipient of the $900 loan can spend this money, and the recipient of the $810 loan can spend this money. The process can continue as long as the proceeds of the loans are deposited into a bank. If every bank that receives funds lends

Assets   Liabilities

$1,000 (R) $1,000 (D)   R = Reserves
                              D = Deposits

Exhibit 1.3   Bank A's initial balance sheet.

Assets   Liabilities

$100 (R) $1,000 (D)   L = Loans

$900 (L)

Exhibit 1.4   Bank A's balance sheet after making a $900 loan.

out 90 percent of the funds and only holds 10 percent on reserve, the banking system can create a total of $9,000 of additional money and the total money supply would be $10,000. Ten thousand is the result of the summation of an amount that starts at $1,000 and declines by 10 percent each time it is added. The money supply now consists of $1,000 of standard money and $9,000 of fiduciary media.

Fiduciary media are transferable claims to standard money, payable by the issuer on demand, and accepted in commerce as the equivalent of standard money, but for which no standard money exists.[20] Fiduciary media constitute all checking deposits not backed by standard money but backed by debt. For example, in exhibit 1.4 fiduciary media come into existence when Bank A makes the $900 loan. At this point, the $1,000 checking deposit is no longer balanced by the $1,000 in reserves but by only $100 in reserves and a $900 loan. Here the depositor still has access to his $1,000 and could technically use it all to make payments. However, if he tried to withdraw any more than $100 or make a payment with more than that amount, the bank could not cover the withdrawal or payment (unless it is able to successfully call the loan). The bank is counting on the depositor to not withdraw the greater portion of his funds.

This is exactly the position the US banking system was in until 2008. Most of the money in the United States had been fiduciary media. Banks are only required to have a minimum of 10 percent of checking deposits over a certain amount on hand as reserves. Since about 1990 until the 2008 financial crisis and recession, commercial banks in the United States retained about 7 percent reserves relative to checking deposits. Since the financial crisis the ratio has soared to a maximum of over 150 percent! The ratio rose because the Federal Reserve injected massive amounts of reserves into banks. As the recovery takes place, I expect these ratios to fall toward their previous levels (as they have already begun to do).

The process of money creation described above also works in reverse if the loans are repaid and the money is not lent out again or if borrowers default on loans. In either case, the money supply shrinks. In the above example, the money supply could potentially shrink down to the amount of standard money in existence: $1,000. One gets an idea here of how volatile the money supply can be under a fractional-reserve banking system. The money supply can expand dramatically and has the potential to contract drastically. The fractional-reserve banking system plays a major role in creating the business cycle. Just what that role is will be discussed extensively in subsequent chapters.

INFLATION

To understand the business cycle, it is important to have a good understanding of inflation. To this end, I discuss a number of definitions of inflation in this section. Only one of these definitions provides a sound understanding of what, in fact, is inflation. The widely accepted view of inflation today is that it refers to a sustained rise in the general price level. This means not just a rise in some prices but a rise in the average price level. If the prices of some goods fall they must be more than offset by a rise in the prices of other goods to cause the average price level to rise. This is contemporary economists' version of inflation.

This definition of inflation is not sound because it is not a definition based on the essential characteristic of the concept. A proper definition identifies the essential or fundamental characteristic(s) of a concept. The fundamental characteristic explains all the other characteristics of the concept or the largest number of other characteristics. For instance, the concept "horse" is defined as a large, solid-hoofed, herbivorous mammal domesticated since a prehistoric period and used as a beast of burden, a draft animal, or for riding.[21] This definition identifies the characteristics that best distinguish a horse from other animals. It helps to explain such things as what types of food a horse might eat, that it is used by man for various purposes, among other things.

An essential characteristic is the one that makes something the kind of concrete that it is. Using the essential characteristic to define a concept makes it easiest to retain the concept and use it appropriately. For instance, it makes it as easy as possible for one to remember the concretes that are subsumed under a concept. If one uses a nonessential characteristic to define a concept, it leads to confusion about what that concept identifies and to false conclusions based on that confusion. For example, if one defined a horse based on a nonessential characteristic, such as that it is an animal with a tail, it would lead to confusion as to what is a horse. It would be more difficult to distinguish it from other animals with a tail, such as dogs, cats, pigs, and buffalo, but that are fundamentally different.

Even if a horse did not have a tail, it would still be the same essential animal. It would still possess other characteristics that distinguish it from other animals and that require their classification under separate concepts. There would be differences between horses and other animals in the types of food they eat, what they are used for by man, what type of habitat they require for their survival, what animals they are capable of mating with, what diseases they are prone to contracting, et cetera. The fundamental differences between horses and other animals make it necessary that they be classified separately so their separate natures can be studied and understood. Their distinct natures also require a definition based on their different essential characteristic(s) so that no confusion arises when identifying and discussing the animals.

It may be hard to imagine what confusion would arise with regard to identifying animals because the differences are often self-evident: one need merely point to the right animal and say, "By a horse I mean this." Nonetheless, it is still important to have properly defined concepts that identify animals so we do not have to go through the difficulty of finding pictures of horses and other animals to point at so we can distinguish them from each other.

With regard to abstract concepts, such as inflation, it is far more important to have valid definitions. One cannot define inflation ostensively, as one can a specific animal. Because inflation embraces complex phenomena, without a definition to properly distinguish it from other phenomena it can lead to confusion and false conclusions on a large scale.[22] Let us begin to see why the contemporary economists' definition of inflation leads to confusion and false conclusions. More will be discussed on this topic throughout the book, especially chapter 2.[23]

Inflation has its roots in the concept "inflate." To inflate means to cause to expand or increase abnormally. The question to ask with regard to the contemporary economists' definition of inflation is this: Is there something at a more fundamental level expanding or increasing abnormally? In other words, is there something causing prices to rise?

There are two basic reasons why prices can rise: due to a lesser supply of goods or greater spending in the economy. In fact, the general price level can be represented in a simple equation

$$P = D \, / \, S$$

where P is the general price level, D is the monetary spending for goods and services in the economy during any time period (i.e., the demand for goods and services in the economy), and S is the supply of goods produced and sold in the economy during that same period. Over roughly the past century in America, prices have not been rising due to a general decrease in the supply of goods. Prices have been rising in America despite the fact that the supply of goods has increased dramatically in the last century. So it is not a decrease in the supply of goods that is causing prices to rise. This leaves an increase in spending.

During roughly the last century the amount of spending in the economy has increased to an even greater extent than the supply of goods. This means that even though there are more goods to purchase, people are engaging in an even greater amount of spending to purchase those goods. This has caused the general level of prices to rise. In connection with the general price level equation above, this means that despite the fact that S has increased during the past century in America, D has increased even more, so P has risen. So rising spending is the cause of rising prices. But is there anything more fundamental at work driving prices?

During the earlier parts of the last century, America moved from a gold-based monetary system to a fiat-paper monetary system controlled by the government. It is much easier to increase the supply of money under a fiat monetary system than under a gold standard. One need merely crank up the printing press or, today, make entries on a computer screen. The US government has certainly not hesitated to do this to finance its spending for things such as wars and welfare. As a consequence, the supply of money has increased dramatically and has done so more dramatically to the extent we have moved off of gold and toward a fiat money system. The supply of money in existence during the last century has increased at maybe a 5- or 6 percent annual rate, while the supply of goods has risen at perhaps a 3 percent annual rate.

What happens when people have more money? They do not wallpaper their walls with the extra money or bury it in mason jars in their backyard. They spend it. When people have more money, they can (at least initially) afford to purchase more goods. It is the greater supply of money that has driven spending higher in the economy, which, in turn, has caused the general price level to rise. This is the most fundamental economic causal factor of rising prices.

A good definition of inflation does not focus on prices. It focuses on increases in the money supply because that is what drives prices. Hence, a good definition of inflation is an undue increase in the money supply or, equivalently, an increase in the money supply by the government.[24] The definition of inflation based on rising prices provides no reason why prices rise. The definition based on money helps explain many things associated with inflation, including rising prices.

The good definition also helps explain what happened to prices in earlier centuries. During the nineteenth century, America was on a gold standard and the money supply tended to rise at a slow and steady pace, equal to the increase in the supply of gold discovered. It is very difficult to increase the supply of gold because it must be dug out of the earth. This explains why prices tended to remain constant during the period, and the constant prices can be explained by the general price level equation: the slow and steady increase in the money supply caused D to increase at the same rate as S. Let me repeat the claim about prices since it will be hard for readers living in the early twenty-first century to comprehend that fact, since they are so used to prices rising from year to year. The general level of prices at the beginning of the nineteenth century was about the same as the general price level at the beginning of the twentieth century. Today people think a 3-, 2-, or 1 percent annual rate of increase in prices is low. In nineteenth-century America, the rate was *zero percent for one-hundred years*. That means, for instance, that goods whose prices followed the general trend, such as, perhaps, a loaf of bread, cost the same in the year 1800 as in the year 1900. In contrast, a loaf of bread was probably about 50 times more expensive in the year 2000 than in the year 1900. Constant prices over an extended period of time are unfathomable in today's fiat-money environment but were the norm under the gold standard.

Even more unfathomable from today's perspective, but easily explainable based on a proper understanding of inflation, was the fact that prices tended to remain constant in Britain for a quarter of a millennium—that's 250 years!—from approximately the mid-1600s until World War I. Again, this can be explained by the general price level equation based on the amount of spending increasing at the same pace as the supply of goods. The slow and steady rise in spending is explained based on a slow and steady rise in the money supply because Britain was on a gold standard during the great majority of this period.[25]

The definition of inflation given above based on an increase in the money supply can be refined. It is now possible to see what constitutes an "undue" increase in the money supply. The most precise definition of inflation is an increase in the supply of money at a rate more rapid than the increase in the supply of gold or precious metal money.[26] Having a proper understanding of inflation is crucial to understanding the causes, effects, and cures of the business cycle. This will become apparent in subsequent chapters.

I must stress here that no price index provides a good assessment of inflation. The use of price indices to assess the state of inflation is based on the belief that rising prices are the essential characteristic of inflation. However, rising prices are only one of the major symptoms of inflation—they are an effect of inflation—they are not the phenomenon itself. There can be rising prices without inflation. If the supply of goods decreases and the money supply and amount of spending remain constant, based on the general price level equation, prices will rise. Alternatively, prices will also rise if the amount of spending falls at a slower rate than the supply of goods.

Even the price of gold does not provide a good estimate of inflation. The price of gold can change due to shifts in demand to or from gold that have nothing to do with inflation (such as due to changes in the industrial demand for gold or the demand for gold jewelry). Also, the price of gold can lag behind inflation (of the money supply) if people do not see the connection between the increase in the money supply and inflation because of the bad economic ideas they have been taught regarding inflation by contemporary, mainstream economists. At best, the gold price provides an assessment of what people's expectations are for inflation. If the price of gold rises, it means people expect greater inflation. If it falls or remains flat, people expect less or steady inflation. These are true to the extent there is more, less, or steady demand for gold as an inflation hedge.

It is important to understand that expectations for inflation are not inflation itself. Humans are not omniscient and expectations can be wrong. Based on the widespread use of the bad definition of inflation, people's expectations about inflation are often wrong. For example, they were wrong during the late 1990s when many people believed inflation was low due to the fact that prices were rising at a relatively slow pace (at least based on today's standards). However, inflation was actually quite high during this time period because the money supply was being increased at a dramatic pace. This fueled the inflationary boom that occurred during this period and portended a bust once the inflation stopped or slowed sufficiently. This was something many economists missed, in part, because of the invalid definition of inflation to which they subscribe. In fact, some economists believed the business cycle was dead during the long expansion from the recession of the early 1990s to the recession in 2001. They would have thought otherwise had they had a proper understanding of inflation.

Substituting a symptom of inflation for inflation itself is like substituting a symptom of a disease for the disease itself. This can lead to incorrect remedies for a patient. For example, if a doctor merely observes a patient sneezing and prescribes allergy medicine based on that information, the doctor could be prescribing an incorrect remedy. Sneezing could be a symptom not only of allergies, but a cold, the flu, or just dust in the air.

The same is true of rising prices. Rising prices are themselves just effects and can be caused by different factors, so identifying rising prices as the fundamental characteristic of inflation—the one responsible for all the other or the largest number of other characteristics associated with inflation—can lead to proposing incorrect remedies because it takes the focus off the actual causal factor with regard to inflation and places the focus on a mere effect. By making rising prices the defining characteristic of inflation, it leads people to believe that, in essence, if we just stop prices from rising inflation and all its harmful effects will be stopped.

For example, during the 1970s President Nixon imposed universal maximum price controls to stop "inflation." He thought just by preventing prices from rising he would stop "inflation." However, all he did was add the negative effects of price controls (such as shortages) to the negative effects of inflation (such as the business cycle). As long as the money supply was being increased at a rapid rate, inflation and all its ill effects were not stopped. All that preventing prices from rising did was cover up one of the symptoms of inflation.

Furthermore, putting the focus on rising prices leads to a whole host of invalid explanations for inflation. For example, according to contemporary economists there is demand-pull inflation, cost-push inflation, wage-push inflation, wage-price spiral inflation, profit-push inflation, et cetera. However, if prices rise according to these theories, there must be an increase in the money supply to make it possible. So these theories provide no explanation for inflation.

For instance, according to the demand-pull theory prices are supposed to rise because there is increased demand by consumers for consumers' goods that "pulls" prices up. However, how do consumers have the ability to bid prices up? If they do not have any more money available to pay higher prices, prices will not be bid up. They need more money to bid them up. So this is not an explanation of rising prices. It is just a result of the increase in the supply of money and spending. Consumers can afford to bid the prices of goods up because they have more money and thus can spend more.

As another example, the so-called profit-push variant of inflation says prices rise because businesses want to earn higher profits so they raise their prices to do so. However, if buyers cannot afford the higher prices, such an attempt will lead to growing stocks of unsold inventory. In the end, sellers will be forced to lower prices back down to their original levels. So this provides no explanation for rising prices. More money and spending in the economy make it so businesses can afford to raise their prices and buyers can still buy the same amount or a greater quantity of goods at the higher prices. So it comes back to the money supply again.[27]

One other definition of inflation that must be addressed here to prevent people from embracing an invalid definition is the following: inflation occurs when there is an increase in the money supply that is greater than the increase in the demand for money.[28] This definition creates confusion because it is similar to the valid definition of inflation, in that it includes the essential characteristic of inflation (viz., the increase in the money supply). However, it also includes an additional characteristic: the demand for money. The demand for money refers to the desire people have to hold on to money balances relative to their spending, and an increase in the demand for money occurs when people attempt to build up their money balances.[29] It is alleged by proponents of this definition that as long as the demand for money increases at least as fast as the money supply, then no inflation exists. All it will do is add to the money balances people hold and no greater amount of spending will occur. Prices will not be affected by the additional money as well.

While it is true that if the demand for money increases at the same rate as the supply of money that spending will not rise in the economy, one must consider here what causes the demand for money to change. If one looks back not too far in history, one can get an idea. During the massive inflation in Weimar Germany in 1922–23, the money supply was increased at astronomical rates. This caused spending and prices to increase astronomically as well. Because of this, the value of the mark rapidly decreased. As a result, people held on to fewer marks relative to the amount of spending in which they engaged. People hold on to less of the medium of exchange in this type of situation because it is declining in value relative to expectations. They would rather hold on to assets that are increasing in value instead of the rapidly depreciating money. During the Weimar inflation, the mark lost its value so rapidly that people quickly spent the money on goods (any goods) to avoid holding on to worthless pieces of paper.

What is seen above is that a rapid (and accelerating) increase in the money supply in Weimar Germany *caused* the demand for money to decrease. This is something that occurs in general; that is, accelerating changes in the supply of money (both positive and negative) generally cause changes in the demand for money. For instance, during the Great Depression the money supply declined in America along with spending and prices. As a result, the value of the dollar increased and people held on to more money relative to their spending because it was increasing in value. Here, a change in the money supply also changed the demand for money, but in the reverse direction. Here a decrease in the money supply caused an increase in the demand for money. Likewise, after World War II the money supply in America rose at an accelerating pace until the late 1970s. During this time the demand for money generally fell. It was only once the rise in the money supply began to slow significantly in the late 1970s and early 1980s that the demand for money increased. Here we see that changes in the money supply exerted a similar influence on changes in the demand for money: in the former case an accelerating increase in the money supply caused the demand for money to decrease and in the latter case a deceleration of the rise in the money supply caused the demand to increase.

The money supply is particularly susceptible to rapid changes under a fiat monetary system. Hence, under such a system changes in the demand for money are largely an effect of changes in supply. Because of this, the demand for money is a nonessential characteristic of inflation and does not belong in the definition.

There are other factors that can affect the demand for money. For example, universal maximum price controls can increase the demand for money. During World War II, the US government imposed such controls. In an attempt to deal with the shortages that maximum price controls cause, it also imposed rationing. Hence, spending was limited to the artificially low prices imposed by the government multiplied by the limited number of goods individuals were allowed to purchase. Since the government also inflated the money supply rapidly to pay for the war, this mathematically implied that the demand for money increased.[30] Therefore, one should not see this as a contradiction to the claim above that when the money supply is increased rapidly the demand for money decreases. There was another causal factor at work in this case that prevented the increase in the money supply from having its normal effect. Specifically, the government was forcibly preventing people from spending money.

The memory of past experiences can also have an effect on the demand for money. For example, the demand for money remained high long after the Great Depression due to the horrible experiences people had of not having enough money to purchase necessities during the depression. Bad experiences like this can make people more financially conservative and thus make them hold on to more money relative to their spending.[31] This is another reason why, sometimes, an accelerating increase in the money supply does not cause the demand for money to decline: people refuse to spend the additional money because of their memory of a bad financial experience. Hence, when the government inflates the money supply at an accelerating pace at the onset or in the midst of a recession, as it did during the recession of 2001 and again during the recession of 2008–9, and the demand for money does not decline, one should not see this as a contradiction of the proposition that the demand for money declines when the money supply is inflated in an accelerating manner. There is simply another causal factor at work, affecting the demand for money, in these cases. Changes in the money supply are only one causal factor—albeit a powerful one—affecting the demand for money.

The last point I will make about inflation in this chapter is that the government is responsible for inflation. It causes inflation both directly and indirectly. It does so directly by creating standard money, which it does through the Federal Reserve. It needs a fiat paper money system to be able to do that. One cannot increase the supply of gold arbitrarily. The government causes inflation indirectly by making it possible, through various regulations and controls, for banks to lend out reserves backing checking deposits. I show elsewhere how the government makes fractional-reserve banking possible.[32] In the next chapter I turn to a discussion of how the government directly creates inflation.

2

How Does the Government
Cause Inflation?

Introduction

In this chapter I show how the government creates inflation through so-called monetary policy. I also show the role "fiscal policy" has, if any, in causing inflation. The chapter also discusses how the government creates money ex nihilo and looks at some of the effects of inflation, particularly on profits and interest rates.

"Monetary Policy"

What Is "Monetary Policy"?

How does the government use "monetary policy" to create inflation? How is the money that banks multiply through the fractional-reserve banking process created? In other words, where does the standard money come from that banks multiply? The answer: the Federal Reserve.

The Fed is the central bank of the United States. It is known as the central bank because it is a banker's bank and the US government's bank. Banks and the US government have deposits at the Fed. The Fed was created in 1913 and was supposed to make the financial system more sound. However, it is no accident that the worst economic disaster in US history occurred only 16 years after the creation of the Fed: the Great Depression. The Fed has lowered the stability of the financial system and is increasing the potential for much larger disasters than the Great Depression.[1]

The Fed affects the economy through so-called monetary policy. "Monetary policy" encompasses manipulating the money supply and interest rates and regulating the banking system. It is a euphemism for inflation. The Fed is an institution that was created in order to inflate the money supply. This has been the history of the Fed. It was created in order to have a more "elastic" money supply. It has been used to finance government spending by creating a market for government debt. Financing government spending has been the purpose behind the creation of central banks in general.[2] As a natural result of this process, the Fed causes inflation. How does it do this?

The Fed causes inflation mainly through so-called open-market operations. These operations involve buying and selling government debt in the market for such debt. When the Fed buys government bonds, ceteris paribus, it increases the money supply. When it sells government bonds that it has accumulated, ceteris paribus, it decreases the money supply.

When the Fed buys government debt, say $1 million in bonds from a bank, it transfers money to the seller and the Fed receives the bonds. The bank now has more money to use for whatever purposes it wishes. This new money can be spent or lent out. Either way the amount of standard money in the economic system has increased by $1 million. If the Fed sells government debt to someone, money is transferred from the buyer to the Fed and is therefore taken out of the economic system. The buyer now has less money and a correspondingly greater value of bonds.

The Fed uses so-called open-market operations to manipulate the federal-funds rate (FFR). The FFR is a short-term (overnight) interbank lending rate. The Fed does not set this rate. Banks do. However, the Fed can push the rate up by selling government debt and down by buying government debt. If the Fed buys government debt, the supply of bank reserves increases. The greater reserves represent an increase in the supply of loanable funds. As with an increase in the supply of a good or service, an increase in the supply of loanable funds pushes the price of such funds down. The price of loanable funds is the interest rate. Interest is the sum one receives for lending money and the amount one pays to borrow money. Therefore, the purchase of government debt lowers interest rates. It provides banks with more funds to lend and thus gives them an incentive to lower the FFR so they can lend out the greater supply of reserves they have available.

This effect can be seen in exhibit 2.1. Exhibit 2.1 shows supply and demand curves in the loan market. The supply of loans is the amount of money that lenders are willing and able to offer for people to borrow at various interest rates. The quantity of loans supplied varies directly with interest rates—namely, the higher the interest rate, the more funds lenders are willing to loan—because, ceteris paribus, lenders stand to make more money as the interest rate rises and

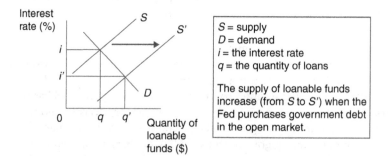

Exhibit 2.1   The effect in the loan market of an open-market purchase of government debt by the Fed.

less as the interest rate falls, so they are correspondingly willing to lend more or less money.

The demand for loans is the willingness and ability to borrow money. The quantity of loans demanded varies inversely with the interest rate because, ceteris paribus, it becomes more costly to borrow as the interest rate rises; hence, individuals are not willing or able to borrow as much. Likewise, it becomes less costly to borrow as interest rates fall, so people tend to borrow more.

When the Fed purchases government debt in the open market, it shifts the supply of loanable funds to the right, increasing the quantity of loans made from q to q' and decreasing the interest rate from i to i'. The reverse is true if the Fed sells bonds. This takes money out of the buyer's bank account and transfers it to the Fed. This decreases the reserves banks have available to lend out and thus decreases the supply of loanable funds, which raises the interest rate. In exhibit 2.1, this would be equivalent to a shift in the supply of loanable funds from S' to S, a decrease in the loans made from q' to q, and an increase in the interest rate from i' to i. The Fed can accurately target a specific FFR. From experience it knows how much government debt needs to be bought or sold to lower or raise the interest rate or maintain a specific interest rate.

One might ask, where does the Fed get the money to purchase government debt? The answer: from nowhere. The Fed has the power to create money out of nothing—ex nihilo. It creates money merely by making computer entries in banks' accounts at the Fed. The Fed can also destroy money in a similar manner but it has used its power to create money to a far greater extent.

Although the Fed mainly uses so-called open-market operations to cause inflation, it also uses other methods. For example, the Fed lends money to banks at the discount rate (DR). This rate is directly set by the Fed. When it lowers this rate, it encourages more bank borrowing from the Fed and thus tends to increase the supply of reserves banks possess. When the Fed raises this rate, it discourages bank borrowing from the Fed and thus decreases the supply of reserves banks possess. This will, respectively, increase or decrease the money supply in the economic system through the fractional-reserve process. However, this mechanism has only a small effect on the money supply since only a small amount of bank reserves are borrowed from the Fed at the DR. The Fed typically only wants banks to borrow at this rate if they cannot obtain the funds elsewhere.

The loans made at the DR are short-term loans. During the 2008 financial crisis, the Fed began making longer-term loans not only to banks but to non-bank financial institutions, such as insurance companies and brokerage firms. These loans might range from a few months to several years and change the money supply in the same manner as loans at the DR (when lending directly to banks) or buying government bonds (when lending to non-bank financial institutions).

Another method the Fed started using to manipulate the money supply during the 2008 financial crisis is buying and selling assets other than government debt that are held by banks and financial institutions. These assets include mortgage-backed securities. These purchases and sales change the money supply in the same way as buying and selling government debt.

Also during the 2008 financial crisis the Fed began paying interest on reserves banks hold at the Fed. If the Fed wants to reduce the money supply, it pays higher interest rates and banks tend to hold more reserves at the Fed. Banks also therefore lend less and create less money by creating less fiduciary media. Likewise, if the Fed wants to increase the money supply it lowers the interest rate on reserves, banks hold fewer reserves, lend more, and create more money by creating more fiduciary media.

Additionally, the Fed sets reserve requirements on bank deposits. To the extent it changes these requirements on checking deposits, it can affect the money supply. Currently banks are legally required to keep 10 percent on reserve for checking deposits over about $50 million. If the Fed lowers the reserve requirement, this gives banks a greater ability to lend out reserves, since they do not have to keep as many funds on reserve backing checking deposits. This is a way for the Fed to attempt to increase the money supply. If the Fed raises the reserve requirements on checking deposits it can reduce the money supply because banks now have to keep more on hand as reserves backing checking deposits. However, it does not often change the reserve ratio and has not done so for about two decades.

One last point to make is that although much of the lending the Fed engages in affects short-term interest rates, the Fed is still able to influence long-term rates. It can do this even if all its lending is in the short-term loan market. This influence exists because if the Fed changes the returns that lenders can earn in the short-term loan market, it makes the risk-reward relationship either more or less attractive in the long-term loan market, depending on whether it is targeting lower or higher short-term interest rates. For example, if the Fed pushes short-term rates down, ceteris paribus, lending becomes relatively more profitable in the long-term loan market. Hence, some lenders switch their lending to the long-term loan market, the supply of loanable funds increases in this market, and long-term interest rates fall. In this way, the Fed affects interest rates in all loan markets. However, since the financial crisis the Fed has actually been purchasing more long-term government debt, which directly affects long-term rates.

The Effects of "Monetary Policy"

By engaging in these activities, the Fed manipulates the money supply and interest rates. I showed that when the Fed takes action to increase the money supply (such as by purchasing government debt) it puts downward pressure on interest rates and when the Fed decreases the money supply it raises interest rates. However, this relationship between changes in the money supply and interest rates is a short-run relationship. In the long run, the relationship is the opposite. There is a distinction between the short-run and long-run effects of changes in the money supply on interest rates. A greater rate of inflation, ceteris paribus, leads to lower interest rates in the short run but higher interest rates in the long run. Likewise, a lower rate of inflation, ceteris paribus, leads to higher interest rates in the short run but lower interest rates over the long run. How are these opposites results brought about?

Let us focus on an increasing money supply. A greater supply of money is brought about by a greater supply of reserves and this greater supply of reserves constitutes a greater supply of loanable funds. This has an immediate downward effect on interest rates, as shown in exhibit 2.1, because the extra funds are immediately available for banks to loan out. However, in the long run, more money leads to more spending in the economy. More spending, in turn, leads to greater revenue and profits for businesses.

The new money increases profits in the economy largely due to the historical nature of costs. Costs that are deducted from revenues to determine profits are based on spending that occurred in the past. For instance, the depreciation cost of a 30-year-old factory is based on spending for the factory that occurred 30 years in the past. Likewise, the depreciation cost of a 5-year-old machine with a useful life of 10 years is based on spending for that machine that occurred 5 years ago. Further, the cost of goods sold of a product that takes a year to build (such as, perhaps, a residential home) reflects spending from the previous year. While some products and services used by businesses in their productive processes are expensed immediately (such as advertising and electricity), many are not expensed immediately but are expensed in later periods. This means the value of these assets, and thus the cost associated with them that is deducted from sales revenue, was determined in the past (when they were purchased).

Therefore, if the money supply and spending are increasing in the economy, any costs in the present period that were determined by spending from the past were determined in periods when spending was lower. Likewise, spending in the present period for those goods whose costs were determined by spending in the past reflects a greater total amount of spending due to the increase in the money supply. As a result, when costs that reflect a lesser supply of money and spending (from previous periods) are subtracted from revenues that reflect a greater amount of money and spending (from the present period), there is an addition to profits due to the rise in the amount of money and spending. This addition represents an amount added to profits and the rate of profit that would not have existed had the money supply and volume of spending not increased.[3]

For example, if with no change in the amount of money and spending in the economy an asset that was purchased one year ago for $1,000 is sold for $1,050, a $50 profit or 5 percent rate of profit is earned. However, if due to the inflation of the money supply an increase in the volume of spending occurs of 10 percent during the time between the purchase and sale of the asset, the asset that was purchased for $1,000 now sells for $1,155 (= $1,050 × 1.1). Now the profit is $155 and the rate of profit is 15.5 percent. Note that this appears to represent a real increase in the rate of profit to the extent that prices rise by less than 10 percent, which is likely if the increase in money and spending is unexpected.[4] I say this merely appears to be an increase in the real rate of profit because the additional profits are purely nominal, since they result from an increase in the supply of money and spending. Once prices adjust appropriately, the purely nominal nature of the profits is revealed. Nonetheless, for a while they can appear to be real since it might take a while for prices to "catch up."

The example above is an extreme case but the amplification of the rate of profit still occurs with more modest increases in the supply of money and spending. The amplification remains even if the amount of spending does not increase to the same extent as the supply of money. The amplification occurs to the extent that there is any increase in the amount of spending between the time when the asset is purchased and sold or during the time the asset is used up in the production of a product. If all assets are used up immediately in the production of a good, or purchased and sold immediately, no increase in spending relative to costs will occur because replacement assets will have to be purchased continuously as the amount of spending increases. However, to the extent it takes time to use up an asset or purchase and sell an asset, spending can increase and there will be no corresponding increase in costs with respect to that asset since its cost was fixed at the time of purchase. The cost of that asset will increase only at the time a replacement for it is purchased.

For example, if the asset above purchased for $1,000 was immediately sold for $1,050, then the rate of profit would be 5 percent. In this case, if the supply of money and spending increase 10 percent each time the asset is purchased and sold, then both revenues and costs increase at a 10 percent rate. So in the second round of purchasing and selling, the asset is purchased for $1,100 and sold for $1,155 and the rate of profit is still 5 percent (= $100 \times $55 / $1,100$). It is with a delay between the purchase and sale of an asset (or some delay between when the asset is purchased and when it is completely used up in the production of goods; that is, its useful life is greater than zero) that increases in the supply of money and spending increase the rate of profit, as in the original example above. This is the typical case.

Greater profits give businesses a greater ability and incentive to borrow and invest. Therefore, over time as the new money and spending raise the rate of profit, they increase the demand for loanable funds (i.e., increase the amount of borrowing) and increase interest rates. In terms of the supply and demand for loanable funds, the long-term effect described here shows up as an increase in the demand for loanable funds. Exhibit 2.2 reproduces exhibit 2.1 but also shows the effect of an increase in demand. Here demand shifts from D to D', with the effect that the interest rate rises above the original level of i (to i'')

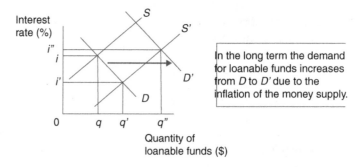

In the long term the demand for loanable funds increases from D to D' due to the inflation of the money supply.

Exhibit 2.2 The long-term effect in the loan market of a greater inflation rate (of the money supply) on interest rates.

Another way to think about this issue is to consider that businesses are both huge borrowers and lenders. Therefore, if the rate of profit rises, ceteris paribus, they have a greater incentive to borrow more to invest in their own business and earn the higher rate of profit. They also have less incentive to lend funds in the loan market, since the higher rate of profit will induce them to invest more of their funds instead of lending them at the relatively lower interest rate. Both of these facts—more borrowing and less lending—raise interest rates. In terms of supply and demand in the loan market, this would be equivalent to a long-term decrease in the supply and increase in the demand for loanable funds. So not only will D shift to D' in the long term, S' will start to shift back to S.

In fact, as spending and income rise over time due to the greater amount of money, borrowers in general (both businesses *and* consumers) have a greater ability to pay higher interest rates. Hence, competition for the limited supply of loanable funds will push interest rates up. However, these things—the higher profit and rate of profit, as well as the greater ability of borrowers in general to pay higher interest rates—come about over time, only after the initial downward pressure on interest rates from the increased supply of loanable funds is experienced. It takes time for new money to be spent and re-spent throughout the economy and increase revenue, profit, and income, but the new money is available immediately for banks to lend.

Once businesses get used to the increase in spending, revenues, and profits, interest rates will level off at a higher point than prior to the existence of the inflation of the money supply. For example, if the average annual rate of profit prevailing in the economy is 5 percent and the average level of annual interest is 3 percent with no inflation, the rate of profit might rise to 6 percent and the rate of interest might initially fall to 2.5 percent when the rate of inflation is 5 percent.[5] However, this relationship cannot last because there is a greater incentive for businesses to borrow and invest more to earn the higher rate of profit, a greater incentive for businesses to lend less, and a greater ability of borrowers in general to pay higher interest rates due to the increase in the volume of spending and incomes caused by the inflation. All of this would eventually cause the rate of interest to rise toward the higher rate of profit. Perhaps the interest rate would settle at 4 percent.[6]

To keep the interest rate at the artificially low level of 2.5 percent, the Fed would have to resort to an even greater rate of inflation, perhaps 10 percent per year. This would initially increase the supply of loanable funds relative to the demand for such funds and thus keep the interest rate low. However, to the extent that the volume of spending increases at a greater rate, due to the greater rate of inflation (of the money supply), the rate of profit will rise even higher, perhaps to 7.5 percent. This will create an even larger gap between interest rates and the rate of profit and place even more pressure on the interest rate to rise. This, in turn, will create the need for even greater inflation to maintain the artificially low interest rate.

As one can see, to keep the interest rate at an artificially low level relative to the rate of profit, it takes successively larger increases in the money supply. At some point, the inflation must be stopped or slowed or it will lead to a massive inflation (so-called hyperinflation), drastically rising prices, and the breakdown of the monetary system. So far the Fed has slowed the rate of inflation in America at various points and has not yet allowed it to reach massive levels. The reduction in inflation reduces the rate of profit through the same, but reverse, process by which the rate of profit was raised and the interest rate decreased.

One can see based on this how the Fed causes inflation and how this affects the rate of profit and the interest rate. I will show in the next chapter how this relates to the business cycle.

"FISCAL POLICY"

The Nature of "Fiscal Policy"

So-called fiscal policy refers to changes in taxes and/or government expenditures to achieve certain economic goals, such as changing the amount of spending in the economy. "Fiscal policy," like "monetary policy," is really just a euphemism for inflation. It is generally used to attempt to increase the amount of spending in the economy, but this can only be brought about through a policy of inflation. The government cannot change the amount of spending in the economy merely by changing taxes or its own spending. Nevertheless, a distinction is made between so-called expansionary fiscal policy and contractionary fiscal policy. The government engages in so-called expansionary fiscal policy when it lowers taxes and/or increases its own spending. It does this in an attempt to increase the amount of spending in the economy. It engages in so-called contractionary fiscal policy when it raises taxes and/or decreases its spending. It does this in an attempt to decrease spending in the economy.

To see the effects that changes in government spending have on total spending in the economy, one must consider how the spending is financed. There are only three ways in which the federal government can finance its spending: (1) it can tax the public, (2) it can borrow from the public, and (3) it can inflate (i.e., print money). If the government taxes or borrows from the public to finance its spending, total spending in the economy does not change. For instance, if the government decides to spend $100 billion more on, say, roads and bridges and decides to tax the citizens another $100 billion in the same time period to finance the additional spending, the government merely spends funds that it has taken from the citizens. Therefore, the government's ability to spend has increased by $100 billion but at the same time the public's ability to spend has decreased by $100 billion. This does not change the total amount of spending in the economy by even one penny. It merely changes who is doing the spending. Government officials spend more and taxpayers spend less. The pattern of spending changes as well, from what taxpayers would have bought to roads and bridges. Of course, the same is true, mutatis mutandis, for a decrease in spending and taxes. If the government decreases spending on roads and bridges by $100 billion and at the same time decreases taxes by $100 billion, spending does not decrease by one penny. Taxpayers spend more money and the government spends less.

The exact same thing is true if the government finances additional spending by borrowing more from the public or uses surplus funds, due to decreased spending, to pay down debt owed to the public. If the government spends $50 billion more to purchase, say, military hardware and finances the spending by issuing $50 billion in bonds that are purchased by the public (i.e., citizens and businesses), no more spending exists in the economy. The government spends more and, to the same degree, the public has and spends less. Money is simply transferred from the citizens of a country to their government through the lending. Again, who spends the money and what the money is spent on changes but the total amount of spending in the economy stays the same.

The same is true if the government decreases its spending and uses the surplus (assuming it had a balanced budget to begin with) to pay down debt it owes to the public. The government spends less but dollar-for-dollar the public spends more. If the government already has a budget deficit to start, it does not change the essence of the example. Assuming it finances the deficit by borrowing from the public, and it decides to reduce its spending to reduce the deficit, then the government merely reduces the amount of money it needs to borrow from the public by reducing its spending. Again, though, there is no net change in spending. The government spends less and the public spends more.

Even when a government borrows from foreigners, the same is generally true, namely, there is no change in spending in the economy. For instance, if the US government borrows $10 billion from Japanese investors, the Japanese have to buy dollars in the foreign currency markets to lend to the US government because the US government borrows in dollars, not yen. Here the borrowing is still a transfer from US citizens (or foreigners holding dollars) to the US government, only indirectly. In essence, money is first transferred from US citizens or foreigners holding dollars to the Japanese investors and then lent to the US government. The same results obtain: the US government spends more and US citizens or foreigners who were holding dollars spend less (at least in the United States). Likewise, no change in spending generally occurs, mutatis mutandis, if the government decreases its spending and pays down debt owed to foreign creditors. In the case of the Japanese investors, as long as they spend or lend the dollars in America or they purchase yen or other foreign currencies from someone who plans on spending or lending the dollars in America—and one of these will most likely occur since dollars for the most part cannot be spent or lent elsewhere—the amount of spending in America does not change.[7]

The only way the amount of spending changes with regard to borrowing from and paying back foreigners is if the amount of money in the US economy changes in connection with the additional or reduced amount of borrowing. For instance, if the United States is on a commodity money standard (such as a gold standard) and the US government's borrowing from foreigners is in the form of gold shipped to the United States, it increases the supply of gold (i.e., the supply of money) in the US economy and increases the amount of spending correspondingly. The same occurs, mutatis mutandis, if the US government ships gold abroad to pay off its foreign debts. However, this change in spending does not occur due to the borrowing as such but due to the change in the money supply as a result of the borrowing.

Even under a fiat money system, borrowing from and paying back foreigners can lead to changes in the money supply. This occurs if a nation attempts to establish a fixed exchange rate between its own currency and the currency of another nation. In this case, if the US government borrows from foreigners and has to issue an additional quantity of money into the foreign currency markets to maintain the fixed exchange rate, in response to the foreign lenders' purchases of dollars in that market, this increases the money supply in the United States and thereby the amount of spending. The same, of course, is true, mutatis mutandis, if the US government pays down debt owed to foreigners and has to purchase dollars in the foreign currency markets to maintain the fixed exchange rate as a result. Here, say, the Japanese investors mentioned above who receive dollars from the US government in exchange for their bonds might use the dollars to purchase yen. If this creates an imbalance between the supply and demand for dollars in the foreign currency markets (increasing the supply of dollars relative to the demand), the US government will have to intervene and purchase the dollars to absorb the additional supply. This, of course, will reduce the supply of money in the economy and the amount of spending.

The key to remember here is that the amount of spending in the economy changes due to changes in the money supply, not merely due to changes in the amount of spending, taxation, or borrowing by the government. Hence, so-called fiscal policy, by itself, does not affect the amount of spending in the economy. It only affects who does the spending.

To increase the amount of spending in the economy, the government must inflate the money supply. To decrease the amount of spending, it must deflate the money supply.[8] If the government increases its spending by any amount, say $10 billion, and creates more money to do so, more money exists in the economy and therefore more spending can take place. The government creates the money through the Federal Reserve and the process discussed above in connection with so-call monetary policy where the Fed buys government bonds. When the Fed does this, it is a case of the government lending to (and borrowing from) itself. In essence, the Fed (one government entity) buys bonds from the Treasury (another government entity) with newly created money that the Fed issues (which only it has the power to do).[9] This process occurs indirectly due to the statutory requirements in the Federal Reserve Act, the law that created the Fed. That is, the Fed does not directly purchase bonds from the Treasury. The Treasury sells the bonds to the public and the Fed buys them from the public. Nonetheless, the result is the same. When the Fed buys bonds (i.e., inflates), the effect is more money and spending in the economy. One could imagine the Fed buying the exact same amount of bonds the Treasury sells to the public at the exact same time. In this case, the government spends more money while the public's ability to spend is not diminished.

Likewise, when the government decreases its spending and, in essence, destroys the surplus funds, the money supply and spending decrease. To do this the government must use the surplus funds to pay back debt it owes to itself (i.e., debt that the Treasury owes to the Fed). Indirectly, the Fed sells bonds it owns to the public and the Treasury pays back debt it owes to the public, which decreases the money supply and spending.[10]

What the Fed specifically creates and destroys are the reserves that banks use to back their checking deposits. The changes in reserves brought about by the Fed will be multiplied through the banking system, as described in chapter 1, to bring about changes in the money supply and spending. So changes in the money supply and spending come from the banks themselves through fractional-reserve banking. However, the source of standard money is the Fed. Moreover, the fractional-reserve banking system itself has its source in the government—specifically, government regulation of the banking system.[11] So in the end all changes in the money supply and spending under a fiat-money, fractional-reserve monetary and banking system come from the government.

The Effects of "Fiscal Policy"

Since "fiscal policy" does not cause inflation or greater spending in the economy, what are the effects of this "policy"? To answer this question, we need to look at the effects of taxes and government spending on the economy.

Increased government spending beyond its appropriate bounds of protecting individual rights has detrimental effects on the economy.[12] If the government inflates the money supply to finance the additional spending, it has all the detrimental effects of inflation, including the business cycle.[13] If the government taxes the public more to finance its spending, it diverts funds from productive activities and discourages production. To the degree that profits and income are taxed away from productive individuals (whether wage earners or businesses), it decreases the incentive and ability to engage in productive activities, since people keep less of what they earn and have less to use for their own productive activities.

To the extent the taxes are so-called progressive income taxes, and fall to a larger degree on the rich, it harms the productive capability to an even greater extent than if the taxes to finance the additional spending take the same proportion of everyone's income, from the rich and poor alike. In a capitalist society (or even a heavily regulated capitalist society like we have today in the United States), the rich tend to be the most productive people in the economic system. To earn large incomes in a capitalist society, one must produce or provide some good or service for which there is a large demand and do so efficiently. This raises the productive capability of the economy. By taking away more funds from the most productive individuals, one prevents them from reinvesting those funds into their productive activities and restricts the increase in the productive capability. Even worse, if the rich are taxed more to provide welfare to the poor, one ends up taxing the most productive individuals in the economic system to give money to the least productive individuals in the economy. In addition to violating the rights of wealthy individuals, the detrimental effects on the standard of living of transferring funds from the productive to the unproductive should be obvious.

Moreover, to the degree that the rate of economic progress is lower, this prevents the economy from expanding as rapidly and prevents the standard of living of people from rising as quickly. Even a small reduction in the rate of economic progress can have large effects on the standard of living over a significant period of time. This is similar to the compounding effect of earning interest on one's savings. For instance, if an economy progresses at a 3 percent rate annually (i.e., the ability to produce wealth increases by 3 percent each year), the goods and services produced will double about every 23 years. However, if due to the detrimental effects of progressive taxes the rate of economic progress falls to only a 2 percent annual rate, it will take about 35 years for the productive capability to double. Hence, any one-time increase in the incomes of poor people due to the redistribution of income will be offset each subsequent year by a lower rate of economic progress, which will eventually lead to a lower standard of living for the recipients of the welfare than they could have otherwise achieved.

Furthermore, to the extent the taxes reduce the consumption of individuals, they inhibit the ability of individuals to derive the greatest possible satisfaction from their income. By reducing their incomes, the taxes forcibly prevent individuals from pursuing their rational self-interests by preventing them from consuming some goods that they deem would be beneficial to them. Instead, individuals are forced to finance government consumption and diminish their own.

The last sentence highlights another point that must be made in connection with increased government spending: the government is a consumer from an economic standpoint. Economically consumptive spending is spending engaged in without the intention of producing and selling a product or service. It is the type of spending individuals engage in when they buy, for example, food, clothing, and shelter to further their lives. This type of spending stands in contrast to economically productive expenditure: expenditures made for the purpose of producing a good or service and making a subsequent sale (i.e., they are expenditures made for the purpose of earning money). Businesses make economically productive expenditures. They purchase inputs, including capital goods and labor, and use those inputs to produce output, which they sell. Economically productive expenditure is regenerating or self-sustaining. For instance, if a firm spends $1,000 to purchase inputs and produce a product that it sells for $1,100, the business has spent the money, but by producing and selling the product it is able to get the funds back with a profit.

Consumptive spending is not self-sustaining. For instance, when an individual spends money on food, the money is gone and the food is eventually consumed. The purchase and consumption of food does not provide the means to replace the expended funds, as is true with the spending engaged in by businesses.

Note here that it is the purpose of the spending that is important, not the activity itself. Consider the difference between a family preparing a meal at home and a restaurant preparing a meal. The very same food ingredients might be used to make the meals; however, at the end of the meal the restaurant owner is paid and therefore has the means to replace the resources used up in the course of preparing the meal, and if he is a successful businessman he has made a profit as well. Therefore, the restaurant owner is able to replace the raw food ingredients used to prepare the meal, the labor, the portion of the useful life of the oven, flatware, linen, table, chairs, building, and so forth. The same is not true with the family. It has no means to replace what has been used up in the course of preparing and consuming the meal. Someone in the family must actually engage in an economically productive activity (and earn an income) to replace what has been used up.

One sees in this example that even though both the family and the restaurant are *physically* productive in making the meal, both of them are not *economically* productive. In a division of labor society, in order to produce wealth and sustain one's productive capacity (i.e., in order to be economically productive), one must sell his product for money to be able to replace what he has used up in the course of his productive activity.[14]

The distinction between economically productive activity or spending and economically consumptive activity or spending is crucially important to make. Economically productive activity underlies the productive capability, and therefore the standard of living, in the economy. Economically consumptive activity, beyond a certain amount, undermines the productive capability and standard of living in the economy. To see this, think of what would happen if individuals were to consume with all the money they possess and engage in no economically productive expenditures. This means, eventually, all businesses would cease to exist. Every penny that a business possesses would be used for consumption by the owners and would not be used to replace the assets used up in production. As materials are used up, machines require maintenance and replacement, and factories become run-down, the productive capability would fall dramatically, since none of these assets would be repaired or replaced. Repairing or replacing these assets requires productive expenditure. After all business assets are used up that had existed prior to people engaging in no productive spending, nothing would be produced for sale. At this time, the only production that would take place would be that for personal consumption. In other words, the division of labor and all the productive gains it makes possible would cease to exist.[15]

Of course, we do need to consume a certain portion of the wealth we produce in order to survive and enjoy our lives. It would be irrational to die of starvation in the midst of abundance. However, the greater the productive spending in the economy relative to consumptive spending, the higher will be the productive capability and, ultimately, the standard of living. Most spending in a progressing economy constitutes economically productive spending. This is the case in the United States today. That is, spending by businesses is greater than spending by consumers in a progressing economy. This is true despite the fact that spending by consumers makes up a larger portion of gross domestic product (GDP) than spending by businesses. GDP does not measure all spending in the economy. It only measures spending on final goods (goods in the hands of the final user). It fails to account for spending on intermediate goods (goods purchased for resale by businesses, such as inventory). I discuss in chapter 5 the deficiencies of GDP and the virtues of a better measure of spending.

The standard of living will ultimately be higher with greater productive spending relative to consumptive spending because if one consumes a smaller percentage of a more rapidly growing amount of wealth, eventually the smaller percentage will constitute a larger amount in absolute terms. Think of the difference between two brothers who initially have the same level of income, perhaps $500,000 each annually due to inheritance. One saves and invests a large proportion of his income (i.e., engages in economically productive activities) while one consumes all the income he has available to him at restaurants, night clubs, and on parties. The first brother will initially not be able to live as extravagantly, since he will be forgoing current consumption to engage in economically productive activity. However, as his investments and income grow, he will eventually be able to consume more than the profligate brother because his total income will be larger. If he is eventually able to achieve an income of, say, $2 million annually through his saving and investing, while his brother's income is maintained at the much smaller original level, the frugal brother will be able to consume as much as the profligate brother by consuming just 25 percent of his own income. If he consumes more than 25 percent, he can live a more luxurious lifestyle and still save and invest the great bulk of his income to further increase it.

The same is no less true of a nation since a nation merely comprises a large number of individuals. To the degree that the individuals in a nation decide to save and invest, they can increase their incomes and eventually consume more than they would have been able to had they consumed all of their incomes.

As I said at the beginning of this discussion, the government is a consumer. It does not spend for the purpose of making subsequent sales (for the purpose of making money). Of course, some amount of government spending is necessary for the protection of individual rights. This protects the freedom people need to engage in economically productive activity and further their lives and happiness by raising their standard of living. However, when the government goes beyond its appropriate bounds of protecting individual rights, the consumption in which it engages generally undermines the productive capability and standard of living.

As long as the government does not do things with the grossest inefficiency and incompetence, even as it goes beyond its appropriate bounds it might be able to contribute to the productive capability of citizens in certain cases, perhaps by building a bridge or road that makes it easier to transport goods. However, this is still not economically productive activity. It is not an economically productive activity so long as the road or bridge is not a self-sustaining toll road or bridge. The fact that tax revenue needs to be raised to support these projects confirms that the expenditures necessary to finance these projects are not economically productive. The projects cannot sustain themselves, hence, the government must resort to periodic taxation of those who have engaged in economically productive activity to maintain the roads and bridges and eventually replace them.

In addition, economically productive activity precludes money or wealth obtained through the threat and use of force, such as confiscatory taxation. Using force to obtain money or wealth, whether by a criminal or the government, is neither economically productive nor consumptive activity. Such activities fall under a third category: economically destructive activity. It not only consumes wealth but undermines the ability to produce wealth by taking wealth from productive individuals and decreasing the incentive and ability to produce.

We have looked at the effects of financing government spending through inflation and taxes. What about financing government spending by borrowing from the public? This also diverts funds from economically productive spending to economically consumptive spending. Such borrowing raises interest rates and makes it harder for businesses and individual consumers to obtain loans. To the extent that funds are borrowed by the government that could have been borrowed by businesses to engage in economically productive activity, consumption increases at the expense of production and therefore the productive capability and standard of living fall.

What about the government reducing taxes through so-called fiscal policy? What effects does this have? Decreased taxes are beneficial because they make it possible for the full incentive of the profit motive to exist. To the degree taxes are lower, rights are protected and people have greater freedom to use the money they earn to engage in economically productive activities. It makes it possible for the most productive individuals in the economy to keep the money they earn and reinvest it in their economically productive pursuits. This raises the productive capability and standard of living of everyone.

However, for tax cuts to have a beneficial effect they must be permanent and they must be made in conjunction with at least equivalent reductions in government spending. If a tax cut is made only for a few months or years, while this is better than no tax cut at all, it does not provide a long-term incentive to produce and it does not enable individuals to accumulate greater amounts of money and capital over the long term to increase their productive activities. Furthermore, if spending is maintained at the pre-tax-cut level, the government will have to either borrow from the public or inflate to make up the difference. This will lead to all the negative effects of these methods of financing government spending and more than offset any beneficial effects of the tax cuts.[16]

Sound government fiscal policies involve eliminating inflation and reducing government spending to the point where the only activity on which the government spends money is the protection of individual rights. If this is done, the rate of economic progress and standard of living will be as high as possible for all individuals, including both the rich and poor alike.

Why Many Economists Believe Changes in Government Spending Change Total Spending in the Economy

Economists' Poor Understanding of Inflation and the Quantity Theory of Money

The belief held by many economists that mere changes in government spending can cause changes in total spending in the economy (without inflation) is based, in part, on their erroneous view of inflation. They do not understand what inflation is because of their acceptance of the invalid definition of inflation that focuses on rising prices. This, in conjunction with a rejection of the significance of the quantity theory of money, prevents economists from understanding how government spending affects total spending in the economy.

The quantity theory of money states

$$D = M \times V = \Sigma\,(P \times Y)$$

where D is the total spending in the economy during some time period, M is the quantity of money in existence during that time period, V is the velocity of circulation of money over that time, P is the price of each good sold, and Y represents the quantity of each good sold. The product of P and Y is summed across all prices and goods. I have already discussed the quantity of money. The total spending in the economy in any period of time is just the spending generated by the quantity of money that exists. How much spending a given quantity of money can generate in a specific period of time depends on how fast the money is spent and re-spent. That is, the spending generated by a specific quantity of money depends on the velocity of circulation of money.

One can think of the summation of P multiplied by Y as the price of each good multiplied by the number of units of the good sold at that price. This operation would be performed for all goods sold. One can also think of it as the weighted-average price multiplied by the total number of units of goods sold during a given period. This is another way of calculating the total spending in the economy. However, the importance of the quantity theory of money equation is contained in the first expression of total spending in the economy: $M \times V$.

I have discussed velocity implicitly in my discussion of the demand for money in the previous chapter. The demand for money and the velocity of circulation are inversely related. The velocity of circulation of money is the average number of times the supply of money is spent and re-spent during a certain time period. For instance, if there is $30 trillion of spending in an economy in one year and the quantity of money is $6 trillion, the velocity of circulation of money is 5 and, therefore, the average dollar must have been spent and re-spent five times during the year. To understand what this means, think of it in terms of the purchases that individuals might make. If I use $20 to purchase groceries at the grocery store, that constitutes a velocity of circulation of 1 for the $20. However, during the year the grocer might use the $20 to purchase inventory from a wholesaler, the wholesaler might spend the $20 at a food manufacturer to replenish his inventory, the food manufacturer might use the $20 to purchase, say, flour from a miller, and the miller might spend the $20 to purchase wheat from a farmer. So the $20 passes between hands five times, which in this case is the same as the average number of times the entire money supply is used to purchase goods in the economy during the year.

Velocity is the means by which one measures the demand for money. Velocity increases as the demand for money decreases and decreases as the demand for money increases. If the quantity of money remains constant, it is impossible for everyone in the economic system, at the same time, to increase or decrease the quantity of money he actually holds. If I decide to hold on to an extra dollar of money that I receive from someone, then there is one less dollar for others to hold on to. If I decide to decrease the amount of money I hold by one dollar and use it to purchase something, then whoever receives the money simultaneously holds on to an extra dollar. So a change in the demand for money, by itself, does not actually change the average money balance held in the economy. If there is a given amount of money in the economy, someone must be holding on to it in his hand, his wallet, his pocket, her pocketbook, his checking account, underneath his mattress, or wherever. For every extra dollar I hold, someone else holds a dollar less. For every dollar less I hold, someone must hold a dollar more.

When everyone attempts to hold greater or fewer dollars, it does not result in a change in the quantity of money being held, but a change in the velocity of circulation. For instance, if everyone attempts to hold on to all the money he receives, and does not spend any of it, it would result in the amount of spending in the economy falling to zero and the velocity of circulation falling to zero, since no money would ever change hands. However, people would still be holding the same amount of dollars as they did during the period prior to the cessation of spending.

If everyone attempted to hold no dollars, people would spend every dollar they receive as soon as they receive it. However, this would mean as soon as you receive a dollar and get rid of it by spending it, someone else would be receiving it. Likewise, someone else would be spending another dollar that you might receive as soon as you spent your previous dollar. People would be passing dollars like hot potatoes. However, at any given moment, the same total number of dollars would be held in aggregate. Just as if a number of hot potatoes were actually being passed around a group of people, at any given moment someone must be holding the potatoes. The same is true in the economy. If we take a snapshot at any particular point in time to see who is holding the money, every dollar would be held by someone. If everyone attempted to hold on to no money, the amount of spending in the economy would increase dramatically. In fact, it would approach infinity because velocity would approach infinity.

As one can see, when velocity increases (i.e., the demand for money decreases) the amount of spending rises relative to the amount of money and as velocity falls (i.e., the demand for money increases) the amount of spending decreases relative to the amount of money. In this way, velocity can be used to measure the demand for money. Further, because velocity is inversely related to the demand for money, the same factors that affect the demand for money affect velocity, only in the opposite direction.

Based on the quantity theory of money equation, one can see the only way to affect the amount of spending in the economy is either to change the quantity of money or the velocity of circulation of money. However, as discussed in chapter 1, since in a fiat-money monetary system changes in the quantity of money are one of the main determinants of the demand for money (and thus velocity), it really comes down to changes in the quantity of money as the driver of spending. This means additional government spending must be financed with inflation to increase total spending, and reductions in government spending must be accompanied by deflation to reduce total spending in the economic system.

Unfortunately, as I said at the beginning of this subsection, economists often reject the significance of the quantity theory of money. For example, they dismiss the quantity theory of money equation as merely a tautology because it simply offers us two ways to calculate total spending. They say that the quantity theory of money is not true because it assumes velocity is constant. They also say that the equation does not provide us any meaningful information. That is, the identity has to be true given the definitions of the variables involved.

Nonetheless, the quantity theory of money does provide us with valuable information. It is a conceptual method of representing total spending in the economy and helps us understand the components of spending. It can therefore help us understand what affects spending. Moreover, while it is true that some economists do assume velocity is constant (or at least relatively so), that is not an inherent feature of the quantity theory of money any more than a physicist assuming mass remains constant is an inherent feature of Newton's second law of motion (Force = Mass × Acceleration). The assumption that velocity remains constant is false. The significance of the quantity theory stems from the fact that it focuses economists' thinking on two variables (money and velocity) that affect spending in the economy and thus on the ways these variables, and the factors that affect them, can affect spending in the economy. This is extremely important in understanding the nature of economic activity and, more specifically, the nature of the business cycle.

The "Keynesian Multiplier"

A widespread and pervasive fallacy in economics today that has contributed to the belief that changes in government spending, by themselves, cause changes in spending in the economy is the so-called Keynesian multiplier. This fallacious idea leads many economists to believe that replacing the same amount of spending by taxpayers with government spending increases total spending in the economy while the opposite action decreases total spending in the economy. Why does the "Keynesian multiplier" lead to this belief?

John Maynard Keynes was an early twentieth-century British economist who believed that the rate of return on additional investment at full employment would be too low to induce businesses to engage in investment spending and maintain that level of employment. He also believed that if wages fell to achieve full employment, spending would also fall and thus full employment, even if it could be achieved, could not be maintained. Based on this, he believed that chronic unemployment was an inevitable feature of a capitalist society. There are many fallacies in this idea alone, of which the easiest to see is that lower wages in the economy do not represent a lesser total ability to spend if correspondingly more wage earners are employed.[17] Today, Keynes's intellectual heirs, in part because they recognized the fallaciousness of his ideas, have retreated to claiming that wages and prices are inflexible in the downward direction and even if they would eliminate unemployment if they did fall, they either will not fall or will not fall quickly enough.

The solution in either case, according to Keynes and his followers, is to increase spending (specifically consumption) in the economy. Keynes himself thought war was a good means of increasing spending and consumption in the economy because here spending would involve the purchase of war goods and those goods would be consumed on the battlefield, which would necessitate the production of replacement goods. If, according to Keynes, we were not fortunate enough to be involved in a war, then destructive forces of nature such as earthquakes and useless activities such as pyramid building could suffice to allegedly increase spending and provide an outlet for the "excess" labor that would be employed and "excess" production that would take place at full employment.

Another alleged source of extra spending during peacetime is to have government budget deficits. We have seen that government budget deficits, by themselves, do not lead to more spending in the economy. They only lead to more spending in the economy if they are financed by inflation. It is Keynesian economists who are the culprits of putting forward the fallacy that budget deficits always lead to more overall spending in the economy. Why do they claim this even though it is not true?

Enter the "Keynesian multiplier."[18] The "multiplier" is derived in part from the so-called marginal propensity to consume (MPC), which is the fraction of additional income that people use for consumption expenditures. For instance, if my current income is $50,000 per year and I receive an additional $1,000 in annual income, my MPC would be 0.75 if I consume with 75 percent or $750 of the additional income.

The "multiplier" is also based on the belief that what is saved is not spent. That is, there are two options a man has with regard to the income he receives: he can consume with it or he can save it. If he chooses to consume with it, the money is spent to purchase goods and services. If he chooses to save it, the money does not generate any spending; it is a "leakage" from the economy according to Keynesians.

In the example above, with the additional $1,000 in income that I receive, the 25 percent that is not consumed is saved and thus does not generate any spending in the economy. Obviously, an implication of this is that the more people consume the more spending that exists in the economy and the more people save the lower is spending. Why is this true?

To see the answer, let us look at an extension of the example of the additional $1,000 in annual income that I receive. If I receive the additional $1,000 in income and we make the further assumption that the MPC for all individuals in the economy is 0.75, then we can see that the additional $1,000 in income generates total additional spending in the economy of $3,000. This is the case because if my MPC is 0.75, then, according to Keynesians, I spend $750 of the additional income and save the rest. Hence, the $250 saved in the economy disappears and does not generate any spending. However, the $750 consumed is used by me to purchase goods and services from other individuals in the economy. So other individuals receive an additional $750 in income from the additional $1,000 I have obtained. This represents an increase in spending of $750 generated by my original increase in income of $1,000.

However, the process does not stop here according to Keynesians. Those who are the recipients of my $750 of consumption spending will consume with 75 percent of what they receive. Hence, the $750 they receive will generate an additional $562.50 of spending. Of course, the process does not stop at this point because the recipients of the $562.50 in additional spending will consume with

75 percent or $421.88. The process will go on, with each successive round of consumption being 25 percent less than the round before. The additional amount of spending that can be generated by such a process is finite and is equal to the original amount of additional income that I received divided by one minus the MPC (or, equivalently, divided by the marginal propensity to save or MPS, which in this case is 0.25). After one subtracts from this amount the original $1,000 one gets the additional spending allegedly generated by my original increase in income of $1,000 (i.e., $1,000 / (1 − 0.75) − $1,000 = $3,000). So the total spending generated by the original $1,000 is $4,000: the $1,000 of spending represented by my receipt of the additional income plus the $3,000 of additional spending generated by the subsequent consumption by me and everyone else.

In a similar manner, if everyone's MPC is 0.9, the additional spending generated by an additional $1,000 of annual income that I or anyone else might receive is $9,000. So the $1,000 here creates a total of $10,000 in spending. If the MPC is 0.25, the additional spending is $333.33 for a total in spending generated of $1,333.33. As one can see, the greater the proportion of consumption out of additional income, the greater the total amount of spending generated by such an increase in income. Likewise, the less the consumption (i.e., the greater the MPS) the less the total amount of spending that will be generated by additional income according to Keynesians.

The "Keynesian multiplier" is labeled as such because it shows how an initial increase in income can allegedly be "multiplied" into even greater increases in total spending in the economy. The "multiplier" is the ratio of the total spending generated by additional income to the initial increase in income (also equal to 1 / (1 − MPC)). For instance, when the MPC = 0.75 (or, conversely, the MPS = 0.25), the "multiplier" is 4 (= 1 / (1 − 0.75)) and when the MPC = 0.25 (MPS = 0.75) the "multiplier" is 1.33 (= 1 / (1 − 0.25)).

How does this relate to changes in government spending causing changes in total spending in the economy? As I stated above, the government is a consumer. The government consumes with 100 percent of the funds it receives, so its MPC is 1. However, taxpayers typically save with at least a small portion of the money they receive. Say, for instance, the MPC of the average taxpayer is 0.9. This means that an additional amount of funds received by the government will allegedly generate more spending than if the same amount is received by taxpayers.

For example, if the government receives $1,000, since it consumes with all the funds it receives, this generates $1,000 in new spending in the economy. Assuming additional rounds of spending take place only between taxpayers (i.e., non-government entities) and the prevailing MPC among taxpayers is 0.9, the $1,000 spent by the government will allegedly generate an additional $9,000 in spending (i.e., $1,000 / (1 − 0.9) − $1,000), for a total additional amount of spending of $10,000 ($1,000 by the government and $9,000 by taxpayers). However, if the additional $1,000 initially ends up in the hands of taxpayers, only $9,000 in additional spending is allegedly created, which is $1,000 less than if the government originally receives the funds.

This also has implications for government borrowing from the public. When the government borrows from the public, the source of its borrowing is people's savings. For instance, if I decide to purchase a $10,000 Treasury bond, this $10,000 constitutes savings to me. My act of saving allegedly prevents additional spending from taking place. Fortunately, according to Keynesians, at the same time that I save, the government borrows the money and consumes with it, which generates additional spending. In fact, my lending money to the government is better than lending money to another individual (perhaps to help buy a car or a home), according to "Keynesian multiplier" theory, because the government's MPC is 1 while individuals' MPCs are less than 1. So when the government borrows and spends it prevents people's savings from "leaking" from the economy and allegedly helps to generate more spending than if the savings were borrowed by other individuals.[19]

When the government engages in equal amounts of taxing and spending, it also creates additional spending according to Keynesians. If the government increases its spending by, say, $1,000 and finances this spending by collecting an additional $1,000 of taxes, total spending in the economy will increase according to Keynesians. This allegedly occurs because of the difference in the MPCs between the government and taxpayers. While it is true, according to Keynesians, that taxpayers will have $1,000 less money, if taxpayers' MPC is 0.9, 10 percent of these taxes will be paid with funds that would have been saved and 90 percent will be paid with funds that would have been consumed. Remember, though, that the funds that would have been saved by taxpayers would generate no spending, according to Keynesians. So 10 percent of the funds taken from taxpayers would allegedly generate no spending while all the funds will generate spending by the government when it consumes with the funds. Hence, by taxing the citizens and spending an equivalent amount, the government can allegedly increase total spending in the economy.

For example, when the government taxes citizens $1,000, taxpayer spending is allegedly only reduced by $9,000 since only 90 percent of the funds used to pay the taxes come from consumption spending. This is the reverse of an increase in total spending caused by an increase in income. Here we have a decrease in spending caused by a decrease in (after-tax) income. However, at the same time the government's additional $1,000 of consumption expenditures allegedly generate an addition to total spending in the economy of $10,000 (the $1,000 of spending by the government plus the $9,000 in additional spending generated by citizens, assuming they have an MPC of 0.9). So the net gain in total spending in the economy by taxing and spending equal amounts is allegedly $1,000, which is the amount equal to what was taken in taxes and spent by the government. This goes by the name of the balanced-budget multiplier.

By taxing citizens and spending an equal amount or by borrowing and spending the same amount the government can allegedly increase the total amount of spending in the economy. So it appears the government does not have to inflate the money supply to increase the total amount of spending in the economy or deflate it to decrease spending. By virtue of the "Keynesian multiplier," spending can allegedly be changed without resorting to the printing press or the destruction of money.

Notice I say that spending can *allegedly* be changed through the "Keynesian multiplier." In fact, spending cannot be changed through this means. It can only be changed in the manner I have stated previously: through changes in the quantity of money and the velocity of circulation of money, but fundamentally by the former since changes in velocity under a fiat-money monetary system are largely determined by changes in the supply of money. The reason why changes in total spending cannot be achieved through the "Keynesian multiplier" is because such a multiplier does not exist. Why does it not exist?

The multiplier hinges on the idea that savings "leak" from the economy, that is, savings do not get spent. However, this is not true. Saving is the use of revenue or income by businesses or individuals for purposes other than spending on consumers' goods to be consumed in the present.[20] Savings do get spent. The example above of the government borrowing from me illustrates this point. The $10,000 of savings is used to finance the borrowing and spending of the government, so my savings are spent.

In general, this is the case. For example, when individuals save money by putting it in their savings account, the money is lent out by the bank to individuals to buy homes, cars, or make purchases on their credit cards or it is lent to businesses to make purchases. In one way or another, the savings are spent. The down payment on large consumers' goods (such as homes and cars) is also financed by savings. In addition, if an individual saves money by buying a share of stock, the money is either transferred to the corporation if it is a share sold in an initial public offering or it is transferred to another shareholder if the share is bought in the secondary market. Either way the money is spent: either by the corporation or the other shareholder. The same is true, mutatis mutandis, if an individual saves by buying a corporate bond. In all of these cases, the money is spent.

There is something, at first glance, that looks like the "Keynesian multiplier" but in fact is very different and actually does exist. This is the velocity of circulation of money. When new money is created and the money is spent and re-spent in the economy (whether it is consumed or saved), the amount of spending generated by an increase in the quantity of money is determined by multiplying the amount of money by the velocity of circulation. However, in order to generate additional spending, some amount of new money must be created. The additional spending is not generated by the "marginal propensity to consume."

Even Keynesians must rely on increases in the money supply to generate new spending. In the original example above in which I receive $1,000 of additional income, the $1,000 must represent an increase in the money supply for this to generate additional spending. Keynesians call this type of increase in income an "autonomous" increase (i.e., emanating from outside the system). Such income, "emanating from outside the system," can only come from an increase in the money supply. If my income is increased at the expense of the money someone else has available to spend, then my income and the money I have available to spend are $1,000 greater and someone else has $1,000 less to spend. Hence, I can spend $1,000 more and someone else must spend $1,000 less. So no net change in income and spending has taken place in the economy.

However, if the money supply increases by $1,000, it is possible for my income to increase by $1,000 while the money available to everyone else remains constant. Now I can spend $1,000 more and everyone else can still spend the same, so income and spending increase in the economy. While it is true that a change in velocity could cause the change in income and spending (if velocity increases enough to increase the amount of spending and therefore revenue and/or wages by $1,000), remember that changes in velocity are largely dependent on changes in the supply of money in a fiat-money system, so it is not a fundamental factor in causing changes in spending and income.

Not only do all savings generally get spent in the economy but savings are the source of most spending in the economy. All money spent by businesses for factors of production comes from savings and is investment. Either the owners have forgone current consumption to use their money to buy inputs for the business or the business has borrowed from individuals who have forgone current consumption so the business can purchase inputs with the proceeds of the loan. Either way all spending by businesses comes from savings.

Spending by businesses for goods and services represents the largest amount of spending in a progressing economy. Spending by businesses generally represents about 60 to 65 percent of all spending in the economy. Spending by consumers (including individual consumers and the government) for goods and services represents only about 35 to 40 percent of all spending. For example, in the United States in 2010 total spending for goods and services produced (including labor) was $34.7 trillion. Of this, spending by businesses was $20.8 trillion, spending by individual consumers was $10.2 trillion, and spending by the government was $3.7 trillion.[21] The year 2010 is the latest year for which I have been able to obtain data on total spending.

In 2010, spending by businesses represented only 60 percent of spending in the economy. Spending by businesses was low in that year. It had not yet recovered fully from the 2008–9 recession. This is seen by comparing total spending for 2010 with the same value for 2008. In 2008, total spending was $37.9 trillion (the high-water mark for total spending based on the available data), spending by businesses was $24.4 trillion, and spending by individual consumers and the government was $13.5 trillion.[22] Here, spending by businesses represented 64 percent of total spending. This is more typical. Notice the large change in spending by businesses relative to consumption spending between 2008 and 2010. This is a typical phenomenon. That is, spending by businesses is generally more volatile than spending by consumers during the business cycle.

My statistics on spending by businesses and consumers in the economy may appear to contradict spending in the economy as measured by GDP, since spending by all consumers (including individuals and the government) represents about 85 to 95 percent of GDP. The reconciliation of this difference lies in the fact that, as I stated previously, GDP does not measure total spending in the economy. It measures only the spending that takes place for final goods and services, which is mainly consumer spending.

Very little spending by businesses constitutes spending on final goods and services. The main form of spending by businesses that constitutes spending on final goods is spending on plant and equipment. Businesses do not buy these inputs to resell them. Hence, when businesses buy them they are in the hands of their final users. A small amount of spending by businesses associated with inventory is also included in GDP, which is known as net spending for inventory and consists of the difference between how much businesses spend to purchase inventory during a time period and how much inventory businesses sell. However, since most inventory of businesses is typically sold to buyers in any given time period, most of the inventory does not constitute a final good to businesses during the period. Therefore, most of the spending by businesses that is associated with inventory is not included in GDP. In fact, sometimes net spending on inventory is negative, since more inventory can be sold than purchased.

For example, if a business adds $800 worth of goods to inventory during the year but sells $700 of the inventory during the year, only the spending constituted by the net increase in inventory will be added to GDP (viz., $100). This is the only part of the inventory that constitutes a final product to the business at the end of the year. The other $700 of goods added to the inventory of the business was sold to someone else, so it is not a final product to the business in question. It is a final product only to the last person to purchase the product (as a brand-new, freshly produced product).

So my figures that show the greater proportion of spending by businesses in the economy, relative to consumption spending, are correct despite their differences with the relative proportions of business spending versus consumption spending in GDP.

Another way to see that most spending in the economy is spending by businesses is to think of the spending that takes place at each stage of production for goods. For example, a farmer produces wheat that is purchased by a miller and used to make flour that is purchased by a baker, which is used to make bread and the bread is then sold to a consumer (the final user). Ignoring any purchases by the farmer, for the sake of simplicity, the miller might pay, say, $90 for the wheat, the baker $95 for the flour, and the consumer $101 for the bread. Total spending here is $286, which is made up of $185 of spending by businesses (the miller and the baker) and only $101 of spending by the final user. So about 65 percent of all spending is by businesses and about 35 percent by the final user, and the example does not include some spending by businesses (such as spending by the farmer). Spending by businesses represents a larger portion of spending in the economy because there is spending by businesses at multiple stages as a product goes through its various stages of production. Only the last round of spending for any good constitutes spending by the final user. (For those who think I am committing the "double-counting error," please see chapter 5 where I show that when measuring gross spending this error is, in fact, not an error at all.)

So either way you look at it, spending by businesses makes up the great majority of spending in the economy and thus savings are the source of most spending in the economy since all spending by businesses comes from savings. In fact, not only are savings the source of most spending in the economy, they are indirectly the source of virtually all consumptive spending. For instance, the spending by consumers to purchase food, clothing, shelter, et cetera comes largely from the wages paid by businesses. Wages paid by businesses are paid for out of money that has been saved and not consumed. Further, spending by governments that is financed by taxes comes directly or indirectly from businesses. It either comes from taxes on the profits of businesses, taxes on wages, or taxes such as property taxes, sales taxes, et cetera that are paid directly by businesses or with income earned from businesses. So the source of virtually all spending in the economy, directly or indirectly, is businesses. The only spending that businesses are not directly or indirectly the source of is spending with newly created fiat money.

Savings are also the source of a rising aggregate quantity demanded in real terms. Greater savings and the investment they finance increase the production and supply of goods and thus shift the aggregate supply curve to the right. This causes, ceteris paribus, the price level and output to move down and to the right along the aggregate demand curve.

In fact, as discussed above, an increase in savings ultimately leads to an increase in consumption. A greater rate of savings temporarily reduces the amount of consumption; however, since it leads to a greater rate of capital accumulation and technological advancement, it also leads to a greater rate of economic progress. This, in turn, eventually leads to greater consumption as the supply of goods and services available to consume eventually increases to the point where a smaller relative amount of consumption constitutes a greater absolute amount of consumption because the total supply of goods and services available for production and consumption is greater. In other words, a piece of pie representing a smaller percentage of the total pie can be bigger than a piece of pie representing a larger percentage of the total pie if the pie in the former case is larger than the pie in the latter case by a great enough amount.[23]

One issue that must be addressed in connection with the claims Keynesian economists make about savings is the effect of interest rates. Keynesians sometimes say the problem is that changes in interest rates will not ensure that the supply of savings equals the amount of borrowing and investing by businesses. The claim is that savings, borrowing, and investing respond to things other than interest rates, such as the amount of income people want to earn from their savings, so changes in interest rates will not bring them in line.[24] There are a number of problems with this claim that I want to address here.[25]

First, while the greatest use of savings is for investment, it is not the only use. Savings also finance some consumption. For example, savings finance the down payments on large consumers' goods purchases (such as cars, homes, and major appliances). In addition, savings do not just finance lending, they finance equity investments as well. For example, savings finance the equity investment that an individual makes in his business that he owns as a sole proprietor. So investment does not equal savings and total lending does not equal savings. Neither has to equal savings because savings exist in forms beyond investment and lending.

Supply and demand analysis in the loan market can shed light on this issue as well. Just as the supply and demand for goods and services can be affected by factors other than their prices, so too can the supply and demand for loans be affected by factors other than the prices of loans. This is what distinguishes shifts of supply and demand curves from movements along the curves. However, the fact that other factors can affect the supply and demand for loans does not deny the effect that a change in the price of a loan has. Ceteris paribus, a change in the interest rate will affect the amount of money people want to borrow and lend. Just as, ceteris paribus, a change in the price of any good or service will affect the amount of that good or service people want to buy and sell. The fact that other factors do not always remain equal just means the interest rate must be free to adjust to these changing factors to ensure that the supply of loanable funds is equal to the demand for borrowing (including both for investment and consumption).

The key is to ensure that the freedom of borrowers and lenders (and their financial intermediaries) is protected so they have the ability to adjust the interest rates they are willing to pay or receive according to their own personal circumstances and the facts of the market. This means that laws such as usury laws must be abolished and restrictions on how lenders can choose borrowers must be abolished as well, such as the Community Reinvestment Act of 1977.

Ultimately, Keynesians are attempting to deny the influence of the interest rate to get the results they want. They want to create the image that the market will fail to equilibrate the supply and demand for loans so they can rationalize government interference in the market, such as manipulations of the market through so-called fiscal policy. However, as I have stated, the only proper fiscal policy for the government to follow is one based on financial responsibility. It is the same type of advice that any responsible parent would give to his child when teaching the child how to manage his money. Live within your means. Even better, live below your means and save for the future. In the case of the government, limit your spending only to activities that protect individual rights so individuals who earn income can save for their future.

Keynesians also say that, in some cases, borrowing and lending will cease. People would rather hold on to their money than lend or invest it. That is, a so-called liquidity trap is created where people do not lend or invest their savings but hoard money.

There are cases when people save in the form of retaining money balances. This should not be seen as detrimental to the economy, as Keynesians would like people to think. In fact, saving in the form of retaining money balances is beneficial: it is generally engaged in by individuals to restore their liquidity when they have become unduly illiquid. This process typically occurs as a part of the business cycle, which will be explained in detail in chapter 3. However, the discussion above in this chapter on the effect of "monetary policy" on interest rates and the rate of profit can help one understand the phenomenon in question.

When the Fed increases the money supply to cause a temporary decline in interest rates and an increase in spending, revenues, and the rate of profit, individuals can eventually become inordinately illiquid, as seen by the increase in the velocity of circulation of money or, correspondingly, the decrease in the demand for money during these periods. People often engage in far more spending, relative to their money holdings, by taking on more debt during these inflationary expansions. This occurs because the Fed makes it easier to borrow during these periods through low interest rates. This enables individuals to more easily pur-chase homes, cars, and other large consumers' goods, while at the same time making it easier for businesses to build up inventory and expand their opera-tions. In fact, not only is it easier for businesses to borrow to make purchases, it becomes more profitable to make purchases because businesses can sell accumu-lated inventory into a rapidly growing revenue stream due to the Fed's expan-sionary policy. So businesses have both the means and incentive to reduce money balances, relative to their spending, to expand their operations.

Once the inflationary expansion stops or merely slows sufficiently, loans become harder to obtain or refinance due to rising interest rates and revenue streams either stop rising or do not rise as quickly as expected. The rate of profit declines as well, especially relative to expectations. Once this occurs, businesses and individuals realize they must build up their money balances to pay off their bills and prepare for the tougher-than-expected financial times ahead. As a result, the demand for money increases, as it typically does during a recession or depression.

It is important to note here that the scramble for liquidity is not the cause of the recession or depression. It is an effect. Businesses and individuals are respond-ing to something. They are responding to the change in "monetary policy" by the Fed.

This is not, fundamentally, a case of savings not being spent. It is a case of government interference in the economy in the form of an inflationary expansion causing individuals and businesses to artificially lower their demand for money and thus creating the need for individuals to raise their demand for money after the expansionary policy changes to a contractionary policy (or merely a less expansionary policy). If one wants to get rid of the fluctuations in the demand for money, one needs to get rid of the government interference causing them.

Furthermore, as I previously stated, it is important to note that the restora-tion of liquidity is beneficial to the economy. It puts the economy on a more sound financial footing because individuals have higher money balances relative to their purchases. This means it is less likely that they will get into financial trouble and become insolvent or go bankrupt.

In addition, the process of restoring liquidity only temporarily reduces the rate of profit. Eventually, it raises the rate of profit. This is true, for among other reasons, because as spending declines in the economy, due to the increased demand for money, and the value of goods and services declines as a result, the value of capital goods also declines. This increases the potential return to be earned on capital goods as spending eventually increases (as it does in the recovery from a recession or depression). In other words, once people become sufficiently liquid and the demand for money moves down toward more normal levels, the increase in spending this generates leads to a higher rate of profit than would otherwise exist without the previous decline in asset values. So the process of restoring liquidity tends to sow the seeds for recovery and thus is self-limiting.[26]

My reference to hoarding in connection with this topic highlights the real issue behind the Keynesians' claim that savings do not contribute to spending in the economy. Implicitly, the Keynesians are equating saving with hoarding. When a person saves by stuffing money under his mattress or burying it in a mason jar in his backyard, it is true that these funds are not spent. However, very little savings take place in this form. As I have said, saving takes place in the form of financing investment and large consumer purchases (among a few other things). Saving in the form of hoarding mainly occurs due to government interference that causes the demand for money to fluctuate.

In fact, it is the fallacy of composition to believe that net saving at the level of the economy as a whole can take place in the form of hoarding. Only individuals can save by hoarding. An economy cannot. Ceteris paribus, when one person saves by hoarding money another person must decrease his money holdings. Economy-wide saving can only take the form of increasing assets other than money (such as plant and equipment).

The only way all people in the economy can hold on to more money is if the supply of money increases. However, an increase in the money supply does not lead to more savings in real terms—in terms of the physical assets individuals possess—and therefore does not improve the standard of living. Only savings in the form of more productive or consumptive physical assets can raise the standard of living on an economy-wide level.

Hoarding actually reduces the savings in an economy stated in terms of money if the money supply remains constant. If everyone attempts to build up his money balances, spending decreases in the economy and prices decrease as well. Therefore, the value of assets other than money declines. Also, to the extent that large numbers of individuals sell assets to increase their money balances, the supply of goods on the market increases and reduces the selling prices that people are able to get for them. In the end, people have the same amount of money and the same assets (although they have changed hands) but the monetary value of the assets has decreased.

CONCLUSION

In this chapter we have seen what tools the government uses to cause inflation. The Federal Reserve uses so-called monetary policy to create inflation. We have seen that so-called fiscal policy is not an inflationary (or deflationary) tool unless the government resorts to the creation or destruction of money (through "monetary policy"). We have also seen the fallacy behind the "Keynesian multiplier" and the confusion this creates on the issue of inflation.

So inflation is created by the government. This is different from what is often thought today. One often reads in the paper or hears on the evening news (or, unfortunately, even from many economists) that the government must combat inflation, as if inflation is an evil force that comes from outside the government and with which the government must do battle. This is a false view of inflation. The only battle government officials must engage in to stop inflation is with their own desires to spend. They need the discipline to be financially responsible and stop spending more than they bring in through tax revenues.

3

What Causes the Business Cycle?

Introduction

When one discusses the fluctuations known as the business cycle, it is important to remember that one is talking about general, or economy-wide, fluctuations and not fluctuations that are specific to one geographic region or industry within an economy. One is talking about fluctuations in output, unemployment, prices, revenues, profits, and interest rates, among other variables, that occur across the economy. The fluctuations that constitute the business cycle occur across a number of years. In the post–World War II United States, the average cycle has lasted almost six years. Expansions in the post–World War II United States have generally lasted almost five years while the contractions have lasted almost one year on average.

Fluctuations are always taking place within an economy. Some industries and geographic regions expand while others contract. For instance, as technological advancement takes place in an economy, the more technologically advanced products replace their less advanced substitutes. Hence, the industries in which the technologically advanced products are produced expand, while the industries in which their less technologically advanced substitutes are produced contract. This has occurred in many industries throughout the history of capitalism. One notable example is the expansion of the automobile industry and the contraction of the horse breeding, buggy making, and blacksmithing industries. These types of industry-specific fluctuations are not what one seeks to explain within the context of business cycle theory. If one is going to explain the type of phenomena that have come to be known as business cycles, one must explain economy-wide fluctuations and therefore one must look at factors that can have an effect on the entire economy. One must look at what can cause a large number of people—acting in a large number of widespread geographic regions and industries—to act in such a manner that it creates short-run economic expansions and contractions. It is these factors I discuss in this chapter.[1]

Although when I refer to the business cycle I am talking of general fluctuations, one should not be misled to think that every single region, industry, and firm in the economic system must experience an expansion or contraction at the exact same time during the cycle. Some areas of the economy may lag behind other areas. In fact, some firms, industries, or regions might do particularly well in a contraction and poor in an expansion. For example, discount stores such as Wal-Mart might continue to expand their businesses during a contraction as incomes decline and people look for less expensive goods to purchase. The point one must remember, when I write of economy-wide fluctuations, is that a large portion of the economy is experiencing an expansion or contraction at the same time or at about the same time. The general trend is one of expansion followed by contraction. This does not imply, however, that some areas of the economy will not go against the trend. But the fact that some regions are going against the trend, lagging behind it, or leading it does not deny that there is a trend. They can only do this if some trend exists.

One must also recognize that I am not saying specific and general fluctuations take place completely independently of each other. I am saying that a fluctuation specific to a geographic region or industry will not cause geographic regions and industries in general to fluctuate in the same direction if the same forces acting on the specific area within the economy are not acting on the economy in general. For instance, if one area of the economy experiences a downturn due to a decrease in demand for the goods that it produces, this downturn will not spread throughout the economy if, at the same time, the rest of the economy experiences an exactly offsetting increase in demand that caused the decrease in demand experienced in the area with the downturn. Here, the area experiencing the downturn will be less profitable and the rest of the economy will be more profitable. This type of fluctuation occurs due to a shift in demand from one area to another. This type of fluctuation does not produce an economy-wide fluctuation because, on net, the two fluctuations cancel each other out. Although it is important to understand these fluctuations, business cycle theory is not concerned with them. Business cycle theory is concerned with *net* fluctuations in the entire economy. With net fluctuations of the entire economy, it is not the case that demand has merely *shifted* from one area of the economy to another. It is the case that *aggregate demand has decreased or increased*, although we will see that shifts within the economy do occur as a part of the cycle, specifically between capital goods industries and consumers' goods industries.

There are other types of fluctuations that business cycle theory does not seek to explain because the sources of these fluctuations are either obvious and/or cause fluctuations only in a specific area of the economy. These include fluctuations due to seasonal cycles, widespread cultural practices, and natural disasters. Seasonal cycles cause easily predictable patterns in business for specific industries and geographic regions. For instance, cold, mountainous regions experience an upturn in business during the winter months with the arrival of ski season and a downturn during the summer months, while beach areas do better during the summer months and worse during the winter months. In addition, retail stores experience an upswing in business during the fourth quarter of the year due to Christmas. They likewise do less business during the rest of the year. Furthermore, tropical locations experience a dramatic downturn in tourist business as a hurricane approaches and arrives. However, many industries in the area hit by the hurricane experience a boom in business. Such industries as the hardware supply business and the construction industry generally see substantial increases in business after hurricanes as people rebuild what was damaged or destroyed. In fact, some industries, such as the grocery and hardware industries, even experience a rise in business before the pending storm, as people stock up on food and water and cover the windows of their homes and businesses with plywood to brace for the storm.

With these types of cases, no detailed study is needed to determine the cause of the fluctuations. Only the most rabid skeptics would deny the causes of these fluctuations. What I am concerned with here is fluctuations whose causes are not easily identifiable. I am concerned with the types of fluctuations that economists have spent much effort trying to explain and for which there are many theories. Nonetheless, only one theory provides a comprehensive explanation of the cycle. The theory I discuss here is the only one that makes sense logically and explains all the facts of the cycle. The only valid theory of the business cycle is Austrian business cycle theory (ABCT), as put forward by writers such as Ludwig von Mises, George Reisman, Friedrich Hayek, and Murray Rothbard, among others.[2] In another volume, I discuss other theories of the business cycle to show why they are deficient.[3]

THE EXPANSION

Why the Economy Expands

When one thinks of the characteristics of the business cycle, the first thing that typically comes to the minds of most people is the extraordinarily profitable times that exist during the expansion and the unprofitable period that exists during the contraction (the recession or depression). Why is it that profitability in an entire economy can go through such dramatic swings? What is the driving force behind this general trend in profitability that occurs during a cycle?

There are many other variables that fluctuate during the business cycle. For example, unemployment tends to fall during the expansion and rise during recessions and depressions. Likewise, short-term interest rates tend to fall just prior to and sometimes during the expansion and rise just prior to and during the contraction. Business revenues tend to rise more rapidly during the expansion and fall or rise more slowly during the contraction. The same question arises: What causes all of these variables to change? Further, what could cause so many variables to move simultaneously?

Since the business cycle is an economy-wide phenomenon and swings in profitability, interest rates, unemployment, and revenues are among its central features, to find a cause one must look for something that is capable of affecting these variables throughout the entire economy (i.e., something that is not specific to one industry or geographic region). When looking for this causal factor or factors, one is naturally led to money. Virtually all transactions take place in the economy through the use of money. In other words, money is one side of virtually every transaction. Monetary calculations are calculations that anyone acting within the context of a division of labor society must make. Whether one is determining the costs one will incur or the revenues or income one will make, these calculations are made with money.

Furthermore, all prices that people deal with in a division of labor society are prices stated in terms of money. Whether it is individual consumers deciding whether to purchase food, clothing, shelter, et cetera, or businesses determining what quantity of capital goods to purchase or how much money to charge for the products they are selling, the prices of all of these goods are stated in terms of money. In addition, the differences between the prices at which businesses buy inputs and sell outputs determine the profits they will earn. Therefore profits are also calculated in terms of money. Wage rates, which are the prices of the various types of labor, are also stated in terms of money. Interest rates are also calculated using money. No person who participates in an advanced division of labor economy can avoid coming into contact and being affected by money. No other instrument is capable of having such a wide effect on an economy. Not only are changes in the money supply capable of producing the appropriate effect on the economy, but, as I show in later chapters, changes in the money supply occur at the right time throughout history to cause the business cycle. It is here, then, that the discussion of the causes of the business cycle must begin.

The business cycle is caused by changes in the supply of money in the economy. Specifically, the business cycle is initiated by rapid increases in the money supply. As discussed in chapters 1 and 2 in connection with the demand for money and the quantity theory of money, changes in the money supply tend to cause changes in the amount of spending in the economy: the more money the more spending, and the less money the less spending. This is true because money is what everyone uses to purchase goods. Hence, if people have more of that which they use to purchase goods in their wallets or pockets, they will not simply accumulate a growing stock of it but will tend to increase their spending on goods since they can afford to pay more for the goods. Likewise, if they have less of that which they use to buy goods, they will decrease their spending on goods since they cannot afford to spend as much for the goods.

If the money supply increases at a slow and steady pace, spending increases but this has a minimal effect on the economy. When spending increases at a slow and steady pace from year to year, it is easy for businessmen to incorporate such changes into their expectations and adjust their plans to the slow but steady increase in the amount of spending. A slow but steady increase provides no extra inducement for businessmen to produce more goods (i.e., to expand their productive activities, which constitutes the expansion phase of the cycle). As long as the increase in spending is slow and steady, businessmen will come to expect the increase from year to year and raise their prices, raise the wages they offer to pay workers, the amount they borrow, as well as make other adjustments that are consistent with the change in spending.

When the increase in money and spending is not slow and steady, but rapid and accelerating, changes in the amount of money and spending can have dramatic effects on the types and amount of goods produced in the economy. More money and spending in the economy mean more spending for the goods sold by businesses. This is the case because a large portion of spending in the economy is spending for the goods and services produced and sold by businesses. This means that business revenues and profits increase in response to an increase in the supply of money and spending. This is also true of the situation in which the amount of money and spending increase at a slow and steady pace. However, the difference between slow and steady increases versus rapid and accelerating increases is that the latter tend to occur at rates that outstrip the expectations of businessmen. As a result, businesses become unexpectedly profitable. The consequence of this is that businesses expand their activities to take advantage of the larger-than-expected profits.

The easiest way to begin to understand the nature of the business cycle is to consider a simple example using changes in the money supply, spending, revenues, profits, and prices. Further below I discuss additional features of the cycle and make certain modifications to the simple example to better describe what is happening during the cycle. By the end of the chapter, one will have a complete picture of the nature of the business cycle.

To start, let us see what happens if the money supply and spending increase at a slow and steady pace. For instance, what happens if the amount of money and spending increases at a constant, 2 percent rate from year to year and has been doing so for many years? Here, revenues would also tend to increase at a 2 percent annual rate and the new money and spending would also add a significant component to the rate of profit.[4] However, the increase in profitability would not provide businesses with an incentive to expand. If the money supply and spending increase at a constant rate, the change would be easily predictable. Hence, businessmen would come to expect the 2 percent increase and adjust their prices, borrowing, and budget allocations, among other things, accordingly. Because of the adjustments businesses would make in response to the increased money and spending, the increased money and spending would have no real effect on the economy. That is, the increases in revenues and profits would only be nominal; they would not represent real increases. Businesses would raise their prices 2 percent each year. This means no more goods could be purchased with the increased revenues and profits that businesses are earning. No more goods could be purchased because no more goods would be produced and sold in response to the increased money and spending. The same quantity of goods would be sold but at prices that are 2 percent higher each year.[5]

For example, assuming the money supply and spending had been increasing for many years at a 2 percent annual rate, if the average price level in the economy at some point during this time was $1, business revenue in the economy at the same time was $1,000, and costs of production at this time were $950, which implies economy-wide profits of $50, all of these variables would increase at a 2 percent annual rate. That is, profits would rise to $51 based on revenues of $1,020 and costs of $969. However, since the average price level would rise to $1.02, no more goods could be purchased with the additional revenues or profits. The same amount of goods can be purchased with $1,020 or $51 when prices are $1.02, on average, as can be purchased with $1,000 or $50 when the average price level is only $1.[6] There is no change in the amount of goods produced and sold (i.e., no real changes in the economy).

However, if spending begins to increase at a more rapid rate from year to year, it can have real effects on the economy. It can eventually cause production to temporarily increase in the economy. For instance, imagine that the money supply and spending begin to increase at a 4 percent annual rate. Initially, businessmen will expect only a 2 percent increase in money, spending, revenues, and profits and, as a result, will only raise prices by 2 percent. In this case, the 4 percent increase in spending has the appearance of a real increase in revenues and profits.[7] This is the case because revenues and profits that rise by 4 percent can purchase approximately 2 percent more goods if prices rise by only 2 percent. Hence, businesses are more profitable in real terms, and unexpectedly so.

For example, if revenues, costs, and profits rise from their same initial values as given above to $1,040, $988, and $52, respectively, but the average price level only rises from its same initial value as given above to $1.02, now the revenues and profits earned by businesses buy approximately 2 percent more goods relative to the lower level of revenues and profits earned in earlier years. That is, $1,040 and $52 buy approximately 2 percent more goods when prices are $1.02, on average, than $1,000 or $50 buy when prices are $1 on average.[8] The increases in revenues and profits have the appearance of being real increases in these variables and arise due to the fact that spending increased at a rate greater than what businessmen had come to expect. Businessmen did not raise prices enough to completely offset the increase in spending.

The 4 percent increase in money and spending would probably have no effect if these variables continued to rise at this same rate indefinitely. It would take businessmen a while to adjust to the new increase in money and spending; however, once the adjustment is made, revenues, costs, and profits would increase at a 4 percent annual rate, but prices would increase at this rate as well (ignoring any increases in the supply of goods due to economic progress). Hence, the increase in money and spending would provide no incentive to businesses to produce any more goods

However, if money and spending increase by 4 percent for only one year and increase by, say, 7 percent the next year, this may begin to have real effects on the economy. Businessmen would not even have adjusted to the 4 percent rise in spending and now spending increases by 7 percent. At this point, businessmen may have expected spending to rise at a rate more rapid than 2 percent and, if they were particularly quick to adjust, may have even expected a 4 percent rise. But at the very moment they are expecting this rise, spending, revenues, and profits rise by a greater amount. Thus, the rise in these variables would, again, outstrip businessmen's expectations. Businesses would, for a second year in a row, be more profitable than expected.

If businesses are extraordinarily profitable in one year, they might not respond by, expanding their output. However, being unexpectedly profitable for two years in a row might inspire some businesses to begin to increase production. At first, the expansions in output might be small: perhaps workers are put on overtime or more workers are hired to use up any excess capacity the business has. Nonetheless, increases in production would begin to take place to earn the higher-than-expected profits.

While some businesses might hold off on expanding after only two years of unexpectedly high profits, a third year of such profits would convince more businesses to expand. Imagine that just this happens. Before businesses can even fully adjust to the 7 percent rise in spending, in the subsequent year, spending rises by 12 percent. This would induce more businesses to expand production and expand it in a more substantial way. Now some businesses would not only put workers on overtime and hire workers, some might even add equipment to their factories or build or rent extra space to take advantage of the increased profitability.

It might even be the case that businessmen accurately predict that spending will increase by more than 7 percent. Businessmen are intelligent individuals and after a rise in the rate of increase in spending from 2- to 4- to 7 percent, they might expect, perhaps, a 10 percent rise in spending.[9] However, if the rise in spending continues to outstrip their expectations, businesses will still have an incentive to expand. If they raise prices by 10 percent in expectation of the rise in spending, the 12 percent increase will still represent a real increase in spending. Whatever businessmen's expectations are, as long as the increase in spending outstrips them, it provides an incentive to expand. If increases in money and spending continue to outstrip businessmen's expectations for a number of years, the incentive to expand their activities will be greater and the extent to which they actually expand will be greater.

This is the nature of the expansion. It occurs, in essence, due to money, spending, revenues, and profits increasing at a rate greater than expected by businessmen. The inflation of the money supply distorts economic signals. The unexpectedly good times give businesses the incentive to expand and they eventually do just that. The expansion can be larger or smaller depending on how rapidly the money supply and spending increase and for how long they increase. The longer and more rapid the increase in money and spending, the more businesses will expand in response. They might not react immediately to the increases in money and spending but eventually, since the demand for their products has risen and they can make higher profits based on this rising demand, they will expand.

Although the essence of the expansion phase of the business cycle—the increased profitability that outstrips businessmen's expectations and inspires them to produce more—has been captured above, the incentive to expand is even more powerful than what I have portrayed. I purposely left out a more complex feature of the business cycle in order to make the introduction to this cycle theory more easily understandable. I will now incorporate this more complex feature to show what effects it has on the economy.

This more complex feature of the business cycle is nothing significantly different, in terms of essentials, than what I have presented above. It merely amplifies the incentive to expand. This more complex feature is the way profits increase in the economy due to an increase in money and spending. More rapid increases in the amount of money and spending cause the revenues that businesses receive to rise relative to costs due to the historical nature of costs, as discussed in chapter 2.

Recall that the costs of businesses are determined based on past spending by businesses. For example, for a long-term asset, such as a factory, the purchase price might be depreciated over, say, a 30-year period. Hence, some of the money that was spent on this asset does not show up as a cost until 30 years have passed. The same is true for shorter-term assets. For example, materials used to produce goods might not show up as costs until a year into the future, when the products they have been used to help produce are finally sold. Until they are expensed, the value of these assets is accumulated on the balance sheet as inventory or work in progress. On average for all goods and services that businesses buy, there is a significant amount of time that passes by between when businesses spend money on the goods and services and when they are expensed.

For instance, suppose that one-fifth of spending by businesses is on buildings (factories and office space) that have a useful life of 30 years, two-fifths of all spending by businesses is on equipment that has a useful life of 5 years, and two-fifths of spending is immediately expensed. This means that, on average and assuming straight-line depreciation, a dollar of spending by businesses does not show up on the income statement as an expense for 8 years. This is the weighted average of the different useful lives of all the assets businesses purchase, with a useful life of zero being used for assets that are immediately expensed. In other words, 8 years = 30 years $\times$ 0.2 + 5 years $\times$ 0.4 + 0 years $\times$ 0.4.

Because of this lag, revenues tend to rise at a more rapid rate than costs due to an accelerating increase in the money supply. This causes the profits that businesses earn to increase at an accelerating pace as well. Further, the rate of profit businesses earn on capital invested also increases, since the value of the capital businesses possess is based largely on purchases made in the past, when the amount of spending in the economy was lower.

For example, imagine an economy where the supply of money is initially $1,000 and the annual spending generated by this money for the goods and services produced by businesses (i.e., revenues) is also $1,000. Further, suppose also that the economy-wide costs incurred by businesses are $900 annually. This means profits are $100 annually. In addition, assume that each dollar a business spends takes five years to show up as an expense on the income statement. This means the useful life of the assets of businesses is also 5 years. This useful life could be thought of as a weighted average useful life made up of a large number of assets with a variety of useful lives. However, we do not need to be concerned with the individual useful lives of assets to show the effects of an increase in money and spending on profitability. All that matters is that there is some useful life of the assets businesses purchase that is greater than zero. I use assets with only one useful life to make my example less complicated. But the principle would remain the same whether one employed 50 or even 100 assets with different useful lives.

There are just a couple other assumptions before I start my example. I assume all spending in the economy takes place at the beginning of the year. Finally, assets purchased by businesses start depreciating, using straight-line depreciation, immediately when they are purchased.

To get this example started, assume that the initial values for the variables have remained constant for many years. This implies that the average value of the capital employed by businesses in each year is $2,250. This is the case because if businesses spend $900 each year on assets with a useful life of 5 years and have done this for a large number of years, it means they have in their possession five sets of assets at the beginning of each year. They have assets just purchased that still have the entire 5-year useful life left, they have 1-year-old assets with four years of useful life left, and so on until we get to 4-year-old assets with one year of useful life left. Since these assets are depreciated using straight-line depreciation, they lose one-fifth of their value each year. Since $900 of these assets is purchased each year, the depreciation expense for businesses for the assets purchased each year is $180.

Based on the above, at the beginning of each year, the assets that are newly purchased have a book value of $900, the 1-year-old assets have a book value of $720 (i.e., $900 – $180), the 2-year-old assets have a book value of $540 (i.e., $900 – [2 × $180]), and the 3- and 4-year-old assets have a book value of $360 and $180, respectively. Once the assets reach an age of 5 years (their useful life), they have a book value of zero and are discarded (they are assumed to have no salvage value). Hence, at the beginning of each year, businesses in the economy have assets with a book value of $2,700 (= $900 + $720 + $540 + $360 + $180). At the end of each year these assets are now worth $1,800, since they have depreciated another $180 each. So the average value of the assets employed by businesses during the year is $2,250 (= [$2,700 + $1,800] / 2). This value is given in exhibit 3.1 as the average capital for year 1. Values for the amount of money, spending on the goods produced by businesses (i.e., revenue generated by businesses), the amount of spending by businesses, total costs, profits, and the return on capital are also given in exhibit 3.1. One can see in exhibit 3.1 that the return on capital (what I have been calling the rate of profit) is 4.44 percent in year 1 (= 100 × profits / average capital invested = 100 × $100 / $2,250).

Imagine now that the money supply and spending increase by 2 percent the next year, year 2 of exhibit 3.1. This means that spending in the economy is now $1,020 and spending by businesses is now $918. However, notice that costs do not rise by 2 percent in year 2. This is because costs are still made up largely of assets purchased in the four years prior to year 2. In the four prior years, assets with a five-year lifespan were purchased and their combined depreciation expense for year 2 is $720 (= $180 × 4). However, at the beginning of year 2, assets with a value of $918 are purchased. The depreciation cost associated with these assets in year 2 is $183.60 (= $918 / 5). Hence, the total costs in year 2 are $903.60 (= $720 + $183.60). So costs only rise by the more modest amount of 0.4 percent, which is less than the 2 percent increase in money and spending and is due to the influence on costs of purchases made by businesses in the past, when the money supply and spending were lower.

Based on the rise in spending, revenues, and costs, profits rise to $116.40 in year 2. However, the average capital employed also rises: to $2,266.20. Notice the capital employed rises in value by an amount less than 2 percent, since the value of the capital is based largely on the purchases made in the previous four years. At the beginning of the year the value of the capital is $720 + 540 + 360 + 180 = $1,800 (the value of the capital purchased in the previous four years) plus $918 (the value of the newly purchased capital) or $2,718. At the end of the year the capital depreciates by $180 multiplied by four (for the four sets of assets purchased at $900) plus $183.60 for the assets newly purchased at $918 and is worth $1,814.40. So the average value of the capital for year 2 is $2,266.20 and the return on capital has risen to 5.14 percent based on the large rise in profits and the small increase in the average capital invested during the year.

Here one can see the effect an increase in the money supply and spending has on profits and the rate of profit in the economy. A 2 percent increase in spending has increased the rate of profit from 4.44 percent to 5.14 percent. This increase in profitability appears as if it is a real increase in profitability to the extent that prices do not rise (which is likely in year 2) or do not rise as much as the increase in the rate of profit. This rise in the rate of profit could provide an incentive for businesses to produce more.

In my example in exhibit 3.1, I assume there is only a one-time rise in the money supply and spending. In each year after year 2, the money supply and spending remain equal to what they were in year 2. Such a one-time rise would not provide businessmen an incentive to expand their businesses, since businessmen would see their revenues remaining constant, costs and the value of capital employed rising, and profits and the rate of profit falling in years 3–6 until, once again, the return on capital is 4.44 percent. The value of the average capital employed and costs continue to rise as long as the more expensive assets (costing $918 when new) continue to replace the less expensive assets (costing only $900 when new). By year 6, all assets costing $900 have been fully used up and depreciated. From this time forward only assets costing $918 are employed. Because of this, all the variables (including money and spending, spending by businesses, costs, profits, and the average value of capital employed) have risen by 2 percent from their original values in year 1 and the rate of profit has fallen back to its original value in year 1. So we can see more clearly why the one-time increase in the money supply and spending might not inspire businesses to produce more. Its effect is fleeting. It diminishes as costs rise to reflect the rise in spending by businesses.

Looking at exhibit 3.2, one can see the effect of a continuous rise in money and spending of 2 percent per year.[10] Notice here that profits start out rising more quickly than the rise in money and spending (16.4 percent from year 1 to year 2). However, their rise diminishes until in year 6 they rise by only 2 percent

Year	Money and spending or revenue	Business spending	Cost	Profit	Average capital	Return on capital
1	$1,000	$900	$900	$100	$2,250	4.44%
2	1,020	918	903.60	116.40	2,266.20	5.14
3	1,020	918	907.20	112.8	2,278.80	4.95
4	1,020	918	910.80	109.20	2,287.80	4.77
5	1,020	918	914.40	105.6	2,293.20	4.60
6	1,020	918	918	102	2,295	4.44

Exhibit 3.1   One-time increase in money and spending of 2 percent.
Note: Year 1 is the first year selected after many years of constant money and spending.

Year	Money and spending or revenue	Business spending	Cost	Profit	Average capital	Return on capital
1	$1,000	$900	$900	$100	$2,250	4.44%
2	1,020	918	903.60	116.40	2,266.20	5.14
3	1,040.40	936.36	910.87	129.53	2,295.32	5.64
4	1,061.21	955.09	921.89	139.32	2,334.03	5.97
5	1,082.43	974.19	936.73	145.70	2,378.91	6.12
6	1,104.08	993.67	955.46	148.62	2,426.49	6.12

Notes: Year 1 is the first year selected after many years of constant money and spending. Figures may be slightly off due to rounding.

per year, the same as the rise in money and spending. This is due to the fact that costs start out rising at a slower rate than the amount of money and spending, but the annual rise in costs increases until year 6 when it reaches its maximum rate of 2 percent per year, in line with the rise in money and spending. The book value of the capital employed each year follows a similar pattern as that of costs, rising at a more rapid rate each year until reaching a maximum rate of increase of 2 percent per year in year 6. The rate of profit increases continuously until settling at its new steady-state rate of 6.12 percent.

This shows that a constant rate of increase in the supply of money and volume of spending adds a permanent component to the rate of profit. However, this increase in the rate of profit would probably not provide businesses with an incentive to expand their activities. It reaches some maximum value and approaches that maximum value at a diminishing rate. The fact that revenues are increasing at a constant rate and costs are increasing at an accelerating rate until year 6 would also tend not to provide any incentive for businesses to expand.

The situation is very different in the example shown in exhibit 3.3. This example shows the money supply and spending increasing at an accelerating rate. At first they are increasing at an exponentially accelerating rate (i.e., 2 percent in year 2, 4 percent in year 3, and 8 percent in year 4). Then the acceleration of the rate of increase slows a bit in years 5 and 6, as it rises to only 10 and 11 percent, respectively, in those years. Next the acceleration rises dramatically in year 7, as the rate of increase in money and spending increases to 25 percent. Finally, in year 8 the rate of increase slows (i.e., decelerates) dramatically, as the money supply and spending increase by only 10 percent.

In this situation, profits tend to rise in an accelerating manner up through year 7. They increase by 16.4 percent in year 2 and by over 64 percent in year 7. This provides a strong inducement for businesses to expand their activities. Because of the accelerating nature of spending and the increasing rate of profit it produces, both variables would probably tend to outstrip businessmen's expectations. Businessmen would want to expand to take advantage of the unexpectedly large profits they could earn in their businesses. Further, the longer the accelerated increase in spending occurs, the more powerful is the incentive to expand their activities. Perhaps businesses could restrain themselves if prof

Year	% Δ in money and spending or revenue	Money and spending or revenue	Business spending	Cost	Profit	Average capital	Return on capital
1	–	$1,000	$900	$900	$100	$2,250	4.44%
2	2%	1,020	918	903.60	116.40	2,266.20	5.14
3	4	1,060.80	954.72	914.54	146.26	2,311.85	6.33
4	8	1,145.66	1,031.10	940.76	204.90	2,415.29	8.48
5	10	1,260.23	1,134.21	987.60	272.63	2,585.31	10.55
6	11	1,398.86	1,258.97	1,059.40	339.46	2,820.78	12.03
7	25	1,748.57	1,573.71	1,190.54	558.03	3,269.53	17.07
8	10	1,923.43	1,731.08	1,345.81	577.62	3,732.43	15.48

Exhibit 3.3 Accelerating increase in money and spending.

Notes: Year 1 is the first year selected after many years of constant money and spending. Figures may be slightly off due to rounding. % Δ ≡ percent change.

increased for only one or two years in this way, thinking, perhaps, that the dramatic increases will not last very long. However, the longer the increase in money and spending occurs at an accelerating pace, the more permanent the increased profitability appears and the more tempting those profits become. Ceteris paribus, businessmen want to earn the highest rate of profit possible, and when the rate of profit is increasing in this manner, businessmen face very real and strong incentives to expand to take advantage of it. Hence, businesses will have a particularly strong incentive to expand should the accelerating increase in money and spending occur for an extended period of time. As I have said, the expansion may start slowly enough (such as by businesses putting workers on overtime and hiring new workers); however, if it goes on long enough it will occur at a more dramatic pace (such as by businesses building new factories, renting more office space, buying more equipment, etc.).

Finally, in year 8, I show the increase in money and spending slowing. If the government wanted to attempt to keep the expansion going, it would have to continue the acceleration of the inflation to keep profits increasing at a pace that outstrips businessmen's expectations. However, the government will typically take action to slow the rate of inflation at some point for fear of causing so-called hyperinflation and causing prices to rise in a dramatic fashion, as well as the breakdown of the monetary system, if the inflation is not stopped. Since government officials are not typically so irresponsible to cause hyperinflation (at least not in most of the industrialized countries), they stop or slow the inflation. This brings on the contraction phase of the cycle, which I discuss in detail below.

The example in exhibit 3.3 assumes that the velocity of circulation of money is 1 and that it remains constant. This is unrealistic. Velocity would be much larger than 1 and would change as the amount of money and spending change. However, neither of these changes the essential results of my example. In fact, a changing velocity during the cycle amplifies the effect of changes in the supply of money on spending and makes the results on spending, profit, and the rate of profit shown in exhibit 3.3 more pronounced.

The first thing to point out here is that different velocities do not change the effect of the historical nature of costs. So if in the examples in exhibits 3.1–3.3 I had chosen a constant velocity of 2, 8, 9, or whatever instead of 1, the results would have been essentially the same. All that would have changed is the amount of spending, costs, profits, and the average monetary value of the capital. The rate of profit would not have changed.

Changes in spending that occur due to changes in velocity affect revenues and costs in the same way that changes in the money supply affect changes in spending. As long as the effect of the historical nature of costs exists, it does not matter what has changed to generate the change in spending by businesses. Of course, as I discussed in chapters 1 and 2, velocity is largely dependent on changes in the supply of money in a fiat-money system.

This brings me to the factor regarding velocity that would amplify the results shown in exhibit 3.3. It is likely that velocity would increase through year 7 and decrease in year 8. Perhaps in year 2 it might remain the same, in year 3 it might rise from 1 to 1.1, year 4 to 1.2, year 5 to 1.4, year 6 to 1.6, and year 7 to 2. In year 8, due to the drop in the money supply, the velocity may decrease to 1.2.[11]

Recall the discussions in chapters 1 and 2 on why velocity increases (the demand for money decreases) as the money supply and spending increase. First, people want to hold on to less money as it decreases in value when prices rise. In addition, to the extent that businesses can sell their products into a rising revenue stream to obtain money, they do not have to operate with as much money on their balance sheets. Also, in a fractional-reserve banking system it is much easier to borrow and thus operate with lower money balances when the money supply is rising, since most of the new money comes into existence in the form of new credit. All of these (and more) drive spending up even further than the increase in money during the expansion and will cause the crash to be even greater during the contraction (the start of which is shown in year 8 in exhibit 3.3) due to the opposite causes having the opposite effects on velocity.[12]

Note that a decrease in velocity in year 8 is not unrealistic even though the money supply increases. It is changes in the supply of money and credit relative to expectations that is the key factor. If businessmen expect a much larger increase in the supply of money and credit during year 8 due to the large increase in year 7, the small increase in the supply of money and credit that actually occurs during year 8 can have a significant negative effect on velocity.

The effects of the changes in velocity are shown in exhibit 3.4. Exhibit 3.4 is the same as exhibit 3.3 except for the changes in velocity. Notice the much larger increase in spending, revenues, costs, profits, capital, and the rate of profit through year 7. Notice also the dramatic drop in spending, revenues, profits, and the rate of profit in year 8 due to the drop in velocity. However, costs continue to rise in year 8 due to the effects of past spending on costs. One could think of year 8 as the beginning of a recession, where profits might turn negative in year 9 (if I showed it) due to a further drop in velocity and in the rate of increase in the money supply.

The examples discussed so far, especially in exhibits 3.3 and 3.4, have a number of features that might not be true of what would actually occur in reality.

Year	% Δ in money	Money	Velocity	Spending or revenue	Business spending	Cost	Profit	Average capital	Return on capital
1	–	$1,000	1	$1,000	$900	$900	$100	$2,250	4.44%
2	2%	1,020	1	1,020	918	904	116	2,266	5.12
3	4	1,061	1.1	1,167	1,050	934	233	2,398	9.72
4	8	1,146	1.2	1,375	1,237	1,001	374	2,668	14.02
5	10	1,260	1.4	1,764	1,588	1,139	625	3,186	19.62
6	11	1,399	1.6	2,238	2,014	1,362	876	3,950	22.18
7	25	1,749	2	3,497	3,147	1,807	1,690	5,513	30.65
8	10	1,923	1.2	2,308	2,077	2,013	295	5,680	5.19

Exhibit 3.4   Accelerating increase in money and spending with change in velocity.

Notes: Year 1 is the first year selected after many years of constant money and spending. Figures may be slightly off due to rounding. % Δ ≡ percent change.

For example, I mentioned that a velocity of 1 is not realistic but that it does not matter. In addition, the increases and decrease in spending shown might be more dramatic and occur over a shorter period of time than in real life. Also, for some years profits are higher than they ever would be in reality relative to revenues. Furthermore, spending by businesses would tend to fluctuate more than spending in general, since investment spending tends to fluctuate more than consumer spending in the economy. Moreover, spending for the goods produced by businesses (i.e., spending that generates revenue) is not the only spending in the economy. There is also spending for labor, spending for used assets (used cars and existing homes), and spending for assets other than goods (such as stocks, bonds, foreign currency, etc.). Incorporating these features would make the examples much more complicated but would not fundamentally alter the results. None of the differences between reality and my examples deny the validity of what I am demonstrating here. In fact, incorporating some of these features, such as more dramatic fluctuations in spending by businesses, would further accentuate the results and reinforce the phenomenon that I am demonstrating here.

The incentive to expand in the examples discussed so far exists due to the increasing money supply and spending (and velocity) and the historical nature of costs. The increase in profits and the rate of profit these cause provide a strong incentive for businesses to expand their activities. Notice that even if businesses raise their prices to some extent, the incentive to expand is still there because the historical nature of costs and velocity amplify the rate of profit. These latter factors keep profits and the rate of profit rising at rates at which they can easily outstrip businessmen's expectations for a long period of time, especially if the money supply and spending are increasing at an accelerating rate.

To the extent that prices rise at a slower rate than the addition to the rate of profit, the additional profits appear to be real. So in exhibit 3.4 if prices rise less than 0.68 percent in year 2, less than 4.6 percent in year 3, less than 4.3 percent in year 4, 5.6 percent in year 5, 2.56 percent in year 6, and 8.47 percent in year 7, the increased rate of profit in each year will appear to be real to some extent.

This is not unlikely and will provide a strong incentive for businesses to expand their activities.

The incentives of the business cycle discussed here arise because of the nature of revenue, the value of capital, and costs. The timing of how spending affects these is different based on how they are determined. The value of capital and costs are determined largely by past expenditures. However, revenues are determined by spending in the present. This effect does not arise when the increase in spending is slow and steady. It only arises when the increase is rapid and accelerating.

Furthermore, the effect does not disappear if the cost of long-term assets is not determined through depreciation but is determined by immediately expensing the purchase price of these assets (i.e., in the year in which they are purchased). If this type of accounting method is used, a firm would have a large expense in the year it purchased an expensive, long-term asset and would probably incur a large loss in that year. However, during the time until a replacement asset is purchased the firm would experience larger profits because it would not have the depreciation expense of this long-term asset on its income statement. Further, if the money supply and spending grow, its revenues would grow relative to its costs until a replacement asset was purchased. So profits would still grow due to the increased money and spending and the rate of profit would be higher over the life of the asset, regardless of how the purchase price of the asset is expensed.

I started my explanation of the expansion phase of the business cycle discussing how revenues and profits increase relative to prices. I did this as a simple way of describing what takes place during the cycle. However, prices, while important, are not the crucial variable of the business cycle. Money, spending, revenues, and profits are the crucial variables. The rise in these variables can generate the expansion even if prices fully adjust in response. This is true because the increasing money supply makes it easier to borrow due to the process of credit expansion (discussed below). Moreover, the rising revenues and incomes make debt taken on in the past easier to pay off.

It is believed by some that prices must actually rise to generate the expansion. The belief is that selling prices for businesses must rise relative to the prices at which businesses buy to create the expansion. However, this is not necessary. The rise in money, spending, revenues, and profits can generate the expansion phase of the cycle even if prices remain constant. Historically, inflation has been fairly high during certain periods and generated an expansion even though prices did not rise rapidly or remained fairly constant, such as in the 1920s in the United States.

The rise in some prices during the expansion phase might increase profitability in certain industries. For example, rising housing prices increase profitability in home building and stimulate the construction industry. Some prices might rise as a reflection of the increased profitability in the economy during the expansion, such as stock prices. The rise in some prices might dampen the increase in profits, such as a rise in input prices for businesses (like wages). The point to emphasize is that prices are not the crucial variable to watch and understand in regard to the business cycle. It is profitability that drives the cycle, and money and spending drive profitability on an economy-wide basis during the cycle.

It is true that spending also drives prices; however, when inflation is occurring in an accelerating manner, profits tend to rise at a faster rate than spending due to the historical nature of costs. This means that prices will generally rise at a slower rate than profits and the addition to the rate of profit due to the increased spending. The rate of change of prices will also lag behind during the expansion because it takes time for businessmen to adjust their expectations and adjust prices appropriately when faced with accelerating increases in money and spending.

Of course, just because I say the focus should be on movements in profits during the business cycle, and not prices, does not mean one cannot get large movements in prices during the cycle. Such movements can occur but are of secondary importance. As long as the prices at which businesses sell their output are greater than the prices at which they buy their inputs (and margins are not declining), more spending will generate more profits and create an incentive to expand. In fact, increases in money and spending, by their very nature, tend to bring about a profitable relationship between the selling and buying prices of businesses because businesses are selling into a rising revenue stream when money and spending are increasing rapidly, and this tends to push the selling prices up relative to the buying prices of businesses.

Finally, every business will not face the same incentive to expand. Some businesses will face more of an incentive than others and, as I have stated, some might even go against the trend. It depends on where the new money is spent in the economy. Spending can be concentrated in different areas of the economy. For instance, in the late 1990s much of the increase in spending during that period was concentrated in the stock market and in computer-related industries. This made that expansion phase particularly acute in the financial industry (such as at brokerage firms) and in the computer technology industries (such as at computer hardware manufacturing firms and Internet companies). As another example, the large increases in spending that occurred for several years after the September 11 terrorist attacks in 2001 were concentrated in the housing market. Hence, the construction industry and home remodeling related industries expanded rapidly. I discuss historical episodes of the cycle in great detail in later chapters. These particular episodes are discussed in chapter 6.

Also, for reasons I discuss below in this chapter, capital goods industries generally expand more rapidly than consumers' goods industries. Likewise, capital goods industries at earlier stages of production (i.e., farther removed from consumers' goods industries) tend to expand more rapidly than capital goods industries at later stages of production. This means, for instance, mining companies tend to expand more than steel companies, which, in turn, tend to expand more than automobile manufacturers, which tend to expand more than automobile dealerships. Similarly, agricultural businesses tend to expand more than food manufacturers, which, in turn, tend to expand more than food wholesalers and retailers. Likewise, industries that are more interest rate sensitive, such as the construction industry and brokerage industry (the latter due to the interest rate sensitivity of the stock market), tend to expand more during the boom phase than those industries that are less interest rate sensitive.

When spending increases in the economy, it does not usually increase in all industries at the same time or to the same degree. Where the new money is spent and re-spent can depend on many factors. For instance, it can depend on how sensitive the prices of the goods of an industry are to changes in interest rates or it can depend on whether an industry has recently suffered a severe contraction (and thus individuals may be less likely to purchase the goods or services produced in that industry or invest in that industry due to the recollection of the recent hard times associated with that industry). Where the spending is concentrated will dictate how much some industries expand relative to others.

The Effect of Changing Interest Rates

If the above were the only incentives businessmen had to expand their business activities in response to an increase in the supply of money and spending, the increase in business activity that occurs would be much less than it actually is. However, there is another very powerful incentive that an increase in the money supply causes, which provides businesses with a further incentive to expand. This is the effect that increases in the money supply have on interest rates. As discussed in chapter 2 and mentioned above in this chapter, because most new money comes into existence in our economy in the form of additional supplies of credit, downward pressure is placed on interest rates, especially relative to the rate of profit. This process occurs, as discussed in chapter 1, through the fractional-reserve checking system. When interest rates are held artificially low, this gives businessmen the means and incentive to expand their activities by using additional supplies of debt to do so.

The decrease in interest rates provides the means and incentive for businesses to expand because interest rates are a cost of financing business operations. The lower interest rates decrease the cost of borrowing and make it less expensive to finance business activities with debt. The lower interest rates also make some projects look profitable that would have been unprofitable at higher interest rates. So, at the same time the higher rate of profit makes business activities particularly profitable and gives businesses, in general, an incentive to expand, lower interest rates provide the same type of incentive.

It is important to remember that the incentive provided by interest rates arises because *the interest rate falls relative to the rate of profit*. Interest rates might rise in absolute terms during the expansion phase. However, to the extent that the rate of profit rises more, the change in interest rates still provides an incentive to expand, since the cost of financing business activities is lower relative to the returns, in general, that can be earned on those activities.

As discussed in chapter 2, the rate of profit and the interest rate are competing returns that businesses can choose between. So the artificially high rate of profit and low rate of interest provide a twofold incentive to expand: the high rate of profit itself provides businesses an incentive to expand and the low rate of interest (relative to the rate of profit) provides businesses an incentive to borrow more to expand and to withdraw more of their funds from the loan market and use them to expand their own business activities.

It is important to have increases in the supply of loanable funds that outstrip the demand for such funds to keep interest rates low. In other words, one must get increases in the supply of loanable funds that continuously outstrip businessmen's expectations for changes in such funds. This means one must get accelerating increases in the supply of loanable funds, due to accelerating increases in the money supply, to offset the increased borrowing and reduced lending on the part of businesses in response to the falling rate of interest and rising rate of profit. So keeping the rate of profit artificially high and interest rates artificially low both require an accelerating increase in the money supply.

Conclusion to the Expansion

The essence of the expansion phase of the business cycle is that profits are artificially increased by rapid increases in money and spending. These increases provide temporarily real increases in the rate of profit. The longer these artificial profits persist, the greater is the incentive for businesses to expand to take advantage of the high profits.

At the same time, due to the fractional-reserve nature of the banking system, when inflation is artificially raising the rate of profit it is also reducing interest rates. This also provides a temporary but real incentive for businesses to expand by reducing the cost of financing an expansion using debt. So businesses have a dual incentive to expand, and the greater and more prolonged the increase in money and spending, the more businesses will expand and the more widespread throughout the economy the expansion will be.

Generally, economists who subscribe to ABCT do not place much (or any) emphasis on changes in the rate of profit generating the cycle. They place far more focus on changing interest rates. While the effect of interest rates is important, much more emphasis needs to be placed on the rate of profit. This is the more important variable. The rate of profit is the primary reason why businessmen and entrepreneurs invest. The interest rate is secondary, providing an added inducement to invest (and shift investments, as will be discussed below) by lowering the cost of funds and increasing the incentive of a business to invest its funds in its own business activities. For further discussion on this topic, see the section in chapter 4 on interest rates. The emphasis on the rate of profit is an advance in ABCT by George Reisman. See the references to his works at the beginning of this chapter for his exposition on this topic.

ABCT says that, by their very nature, the artificial expansions created by increases in the supply of money and credit lead to contractions. This brings me to the next phase of the business cycle.

THE CONTRACTION

To induce the contraction phase of the business cycle, one merely needs a decrease in the rate of inflation of the money supply or, if the inflation of the money supply is rapid enough during the expansion, only a slowing or insufficient increase in the rate of acceleration of the inflation of the money supply is required. As is illustrated in year 8 of exhibits 3.3 and 3.4, if the inflation of the money supply slows sufficiently, this will cause the rate of increase in spending and profits to slow, especially relative to the expectations of businessmen, or cause outright decreases in these variables. As this occurs, and businessmen realize they will not earn the high rates of profit they had come to expect, they will contract their activities. This means they reduce their purchases of materials, lay off workers, reduce their borrowing, and/or sell off or close facilities, among other things. In other words, when the rate of profit that businessmen had come to expect fails to materialize, businesses retrench and contract their activities to prepare for the tougher than expected times ahead. Businesses must decrease their investments so they can build up money balances and prepare to pay down debts they have taken on during the expansion and pay their bills in general in the more restrictive financial environment of the contraction.

As the slowing of the inflation of the money supply causes the rate of profit to fall short of businessmen's expectations, it also causes interest rates to rise in the short term. Interest rates rise in the short run during the contraction because the supply of loanable funds fails to increase sufficiently relative to the demand for such funds. In the long run, as discussed in chapter 2, interest rates fall due to a slowing of the inflation of the money supply because of the falling spending and rate of profit and the corresponding decrease in the demand for borrowing and increase in the desire to lend on the part of businesses that these bring about.

In the short term, the increase in the demand for loanable funds outstrips the increase in the supply because businessmen continue to borrow large amounts as determined by their expectations, which were formed during the expansion. They will reduce their borrowing only after they incorporate the new information regarding the slowing spending and reduced profitability into their expectations. The increase in interest rates raises the costs businesses incur and provides them with a further incentive to contract their activities and restrict their borrowing. Therefore, as in the expansion, two forces provide incentives in the same direction. In the expansion, an increase in the rate of profit and a decrease in interest rates both provide an incentive for businessmen to expand their economic activities. In the contraction, a decreasing rate of profit and rising interest rates induce businessmen to contract their activities.

It cannot be stressed too much that a contraction can be created merely by a decrease in the rate of inflation of the money supply (or by a slowing or insufficient increase in its acceleration) and not only by a decrease, or deflation, of the money supply. Although actual decreases in the money supply and spending can cause a contraction (or make it worse), they are not required to cause a contraction. Furthermore, as with the expansion, the focus in the contraction is not on prices. Prices can fall, remain constant, or even rise during a contraction, although they do tend to fall or, at least, their rate of increase falls. The key, however, is that contractions are induced when the money supply and spending create rates of profit in the economy that are below the expectations of businessmen and increase the supply of loanable funds at a slower rate than the increase in the demand for such funds.

All of the above will be borne out in later chapters that discuss historical examples of the business cycle. In those chapters the changes in the rate of profit, interest rates, liquidity of businesses, and more will be shown during both the expansions and contractions.

The contraction can vary from being mild to extremely severe. It can mean just a mild financial tightening or a credit crunch (an example of which occurred in 1966), a mild recession (such as the one in 2001), a major recession (such as the 2008–9 recession), or a depression (like the Great Depression). In the most severe contractions many businesses and banks go bankrupt, mass unemployment occurs, and the money supply and spending shrink dramatically along with velocity. Contractions can last from a few months to years, depending on how the government responds to the contraction. It will be shown in later chapters on the historical episodes of the cycle that if the government engages in greater interference in an attempt to reduce the severity of or hasten the end of the contraction, the contraction will tend to be longer and more severe.

Another Important Feature of the Business Cycle

There is another feature of the business cycle that ABCT can explain. It explains trends that occur in specific industries or areas within the economy during the business cycle. Particularly, it explains the different incentives given to capital goods industries versus consumers' goods industries by the accelerating increases in the money supply that create the expansion phase of the cycle. These incentives can be seen best within the context of the structure of production that Austrian economists discuss.[13] This structure makes distinctions between those industries that produce goods that are closer to final consumption and those industries that produce goods that are farther removed from final consumption. Since the distinction between capital goods and consumers' goods is consistent with the identification of the various stages of production, I will use the comparison between these types of goods when discussing the structure of production.

Capital goods industries are affected more dramatically than consumers' goods industries by increases in the money supply because of the different effects that changing interest rates have on the two types of industries. Due to the greater period of time that must pass before goods produced by capital goods industries exit the productive process and are finally consumed, any change in the discount rate (i.e., the rate of interest) will have a greater effect on these industries relative to consumers' goods industries. This occurs because of the compounding effect that discount rates have over time. Ceteris paribus, an equal decrease in the discount rate for both capital goods and consumers' goods industries increases the present value (PV) of investments in capital goods industries relative to investments in consumers' goods industries.[14] This relative increase in PV occurs due to the relative increase in profitability in capital goods industries. This is why capital goods industries expand relative to consumers' goods industries during the expansion phase of the cycle and contract relative to consumers' goods industries during the contraction phase of the cycle. The increase or decrease in profitability is more dramatic in the capital goods industries due to the compounding effect, so the expansion or contraction is more dramatic.

For example, the PV of a $150 profit to be received five years in the future with a 10 percent discount rate (i.e., rate of interest) is $93.14.[15] The PV of the same profit to be received one year in the future with the same discount rate is $136.36. If the discount rate is reduced due to monetary and credit expansion to 5 percent, the PV of the $150 profit to be received five years in the future rises to $117.53 and the PV of the same profit received one year in the future (with the same discount rate) rises to $142.86. Note that the PV for the five-year investment rose by about 26 percent while the PV for the one-year investment rose only about 5 percent. This means that the longer-term investment increased in value relative to the shorter-term investment and thus the longer-term investment would provide a much stronger relative incentive to invest in it. In other words, the industries with longer-term investments would expand relative to industries with shorter-term investments.

The situation does not change fundamentally if a weighted average cost of capital (WACC) is used—which is typical for businesses making investment decisions—that comprises the cost of debt (the interest rate) and the "cost" of equity (the desired return on equity).[16] The WACC still moves in the same direction as the interest rate, but only by an amount corresponding to the portion of the investment financed by debt. Using a WACC only changes the magnitude of the change of the discount rate due to changes in the interest rate, not the direction. Of course, it is true that some projects may be financed with all equity but to the extent that debt financing is used, lower interest rates will affect the WACC.

Another way of thinking about this issue is to remember that to the extent the products a firm produces are farther removed from final consumption, a decrease in the interest rate will have a much greater effect on that firm. This causes the structure of production, or the average period of production (which is essentially the same thing), to change. The average period of production is the average time it takes for a good to go through the entire productive process, from the most remote stage in the capital goods industries to its final stage of production. Anything that decreases interest rates (i.e., the discount rate) tends to increase the average period of production or, equivalently, lengthen the structure of production. Anything that increases interest rates tends to decrease the average period of production or shorten the structure of production.

During the expansion, the structure of production or average period of production lengthens because of the artificially low interest rates. The low rates make it look like there are additional savings available in the economy to justify the lengthening of productive processes. The lengthier productive processes are preferable because they are more productive, but they require greater savings and investment due to the increased capital intensity they represent. Nonetheless, during the expansion, interest rates are low not due to greater savings but due to credit expansion. When interest rates rise in conjunction with the contraction, it is revealed that no additional savings are actually available to lengthen productive processes. Hence, the structure of production must shorten to reflect the actual availability of savings.

Other Issues Related to the Business Cycle

In this chapter I have referred to the increase in profits and the rate of profit during the expansion phase of the business cycle. However, I have said that this increase is not real but only appears to be real. If taken in isolation, the rise in profits during the expansion does, indeed, appear to be real. Profits and the rate of profit rise while prices do not rise to the same extent. However, to determine whether the increased profits during the expansion are real, one cannot consider the expansion alone. One must consider it along with the contraction. The expansion and contraction are not independent events. They come as a set. Profits are wiped out during the contraction and, in fact, often turn into losses. If one considers the higher profits of the expansion with the lower profits or outright losses of the contraction, one will see that the higher profits during the expansion are offset by the lower profits or losses during the contraction.

The higher profits during the expansion are merely nominal increases in profits that, at least temporarily, appear to be real because of the relative movement of profits and the rate of profit to prices during the expansion. Profits and the rate of profit increase relative to prices. This is due to the effect that increases in the money supply and spending have on profits and the rate of profit that has been discussed in this chapter. However, during the contraction, the opposite occurs due to decreases or insufficient increases in the money supply and spending. As a consequence, profits and the rate of profit fall relative to prices.

During the expansion and contraction, nominal profits change due to changes in the money supply and spending. To get real changes in profits one needs changes in production. Increases in production come about from things that improve our ability to produce wealth and thus that improve our ability to progress economically. These include savings, capital accumulation, and technological advancement, which increase the number of tools and machines and the quality of the tools and machines available to assist us in production. Greater economic progress also comes from greater knowledge and skills that individuals gain concerning the production of wealth. More fundamentally, progress comes from the protection of private property rights, so people have the freedom to produce and are able to keep what they produce without fear of having it stolen by criminals or confiscated by the government. This gives individuals the ability and incentive not only to produce more goods but to produce those goods that people judge to be worth purchasing, since producers will be able to profit from their productive activities and keep the profits they earn. The protection of property rights depends on the existence of capitalism, which is the political and economic system based on the protection of individual rights, including property rights. And finally, economic progress depends, most fundamentally, on the degree of rationality that exists in a culture. That is, it depends on the degree to which people use reason to assess the facts and make logical connections between them. For instance, it depends on whether people use the scientific method to understand natural phenomena and apply the knowledge they gain to the production of wealth or whether they go by faith and emotions, both of the latter representing an abandonment of reason. It also depends on whether people use reason to understand which political and economic system is consistent with the production of wealth and human life itself.[17]

The business cycle is not a necessary feature of economic progress. Rapid rates of economic progress do not inevitably lead to contractions; prosperity does not lead to poverty. It is inflationary expansions that inevitably lead to recessions and depressions. More specifically, recessions and depressions are a necessary feature of fiat money and fractional-reserve banking, both of which are created by government interference in the monetary and banking system.[18] We can have rapid rates of economic progress without the business cycle. However, this requires that an economy possess the characteristics discussed above that make rapid rates of economic progress possible.

The increase in production during the expansion phase of the cycle is a temporary phenomenon due to the acceleration of inflation and the temporary effects this creates. When considered along with the contraction, any temporary gains in production from the expansion are *more than offset* by decreases in production during the contraction. I say more than offset because the business cycle is a net burden on the productive capability of an economic system. The factors that cause the cycle undermine the ability to produce wealth. Specifically, the inflation that causes the business cycle decreases the productive capability by causing mal-investment, overconsumption, the withdrawal of wealth from the economy by the government or by those to whom the government gives the newly created money, and a number of other factors that are detrimental to production. All of these lead to capital decumulation in the economy.[19] Based on these negative effects of inflation, even if an economy is progressing forward, if it suffers from bouts of the business cycle, no matter how mild, it is progressing at a slower rate than it otherwise would.

I mentioned above in this section that the expansion and contraction phases of the cycle come as a set. The expansion comes before and leads to the contraction. Inflation causes businesses to expand their productive activities excessively and expand them in the wrong areas. They are induced to do so because of the artificial profitability and low interest rates that are created by inflation. The artificially high rate of profit and low interest rates require a continuously accelerating inflation. If the government attempted to keep the expansion going indefinitely, it would lead to so-called hyperinflation and the breakdown of the monetary system, as prices begin to skyrocket and the monetary unit becomes worthless. So the expansion either ends when the government fails to increase the money supply sufficiently or when the monetary system breaks down. Either way, contraction necessarily follows expansion.

Furthermore, the longer and bigger the expansion, the more devastating will be the contraction. The contraction is, in fact, a correction of the mal-investments made during the expansion. A brief discussion here of mal-investment will help concretize why the contraction must follow the expansion.[20] Mal-investments are investments that look like they are profitable due solely to the existence of inflation. Once the inflation disappears, the unprofitable nature of the mal-investments is revealed. As discussed above, because of the distortion of the rate of profit and interest rates, some areas of the economy look like they are more profitable than others. For example, interest-sensitive industries, such as the construction industry, tend to expand more than other industries during the expansion because interest costs make up a much larger portion of the total costs in this industry than in other industries. Hence, when interest rates fall, costs fall more in this industry than other industries. Ceteris paribus, this means this industry looks more profitable and will induce more new investment than other industries. Much of the investment in the construction industry from 2001 to 2006 was inflationary induced mal-investment and the consequent recession starting in 2008 was a part of the correction process.

When the expansion ends, many of the construction projects that were taken on at the lower interest rates and are not yet finished have to be scaled back or completely abandoned because they are no longer profitable at the higher interest rates and lower rate of profit. In essence, divestment out of the mal-investments caused by the inflationary expansion occurs during the contraction. Because interest rates and the rate of profit were distorted from their long-term values, investment in industries must shift to realign the size of industries with the long-term values of these variables. In other words, while interest rates and the rate of profit have changed in the short term due to the inflation of the supply of money and credit, time preference in the economy has not changed. Hence, the structure of production must revert back to its original composition of consumers' and capital goods so that it is consistent with people's unchanging time preference.[21]

Mal-investment can occur in many ways beyond just excessive investment in construction. It can take the form of investing in gold or other commodities as protection against the negative effects of inflations. It can take the form of investing more than one otherwise would in the stock market to take advantage of temporarily high rates of return caused by inflation, as occurred during the latter 1990s in the United States. It can take the form of businesses investing more than they normally would in inventory to take advantage of high rates of profit that they can earn by selling into a rising revenue stream that is caused by inflation. There are many more ways in which mal-investment can occur.

Contraction following expansion is the typical sequence of events of the business cycle. However, this does not mean that variations on the sequence cannot occur. A contraction can be induced by a deflation or slowing of inflation after a significant period in which inflation occurs at a constant rate. This might appear at first glance to violate the sequence discussed above. However, it does not. The inflationary expansion comes first, followed by a period of constant inflation and no further expansion due to the inflation, and then followed by the ending or slowing of inflation, which leads to the contraction. The basic sequence is still the same: expansion then contraction. It is just a variation on the basic sequence.

Essentially, the key to generating the fluctuations in business activity that have come to be known as business cycles is that the rate of inflation of the money supply changes erratically. It requires that one type of inflation becomes expected and that, at some point, those expectations go unfulfilled and inflation continues at a lower-than-expected pace or outright deflation occurs. Either way, the abrupt change in the rate of inflation of the money supply brings an expansion in business activity followed by a contraction.

Even though the above variation of greater inflation followed by a period of constant inflation and then followed by a slowing of inflation or outright deflation is possible, it tends not to be the norm. The tendency is for inflation to accelerate once it starts and lead to an abrupt end once it slows or to the breakdown of the monetary system. The acceleration occurs due to the desires of politicians to keep the expansion going and to finance government spending through inflation. This latter allows the government to avoid explicit taxation, which is more easily recognized as a violation of the rights of citizens and is a more difficult means of obtaining funds from people, since the money is taken from them, in essence, right in front of their eyes. Inflation, in contrast, takes money from people behind their backs through the devaluation of the monetary unit and the loss of purchasing power of incomes and savings this causes.

So far I have only discussed the business cycle as it pertains to a single, national economy. However, this theory can accommodate open economies. All economies around the world today have fiat money and fractional-reserve banking systems, so they are completely capable on their own of generating the cycle. However, the major central banks around the globe often act in unison or cooperate with each other in the policies they set and thus establish similar policies. Hence, it is no accident that multiple countries often experience expansions and contractions at the same time.

Furthermore, if there is trade between countries then what happens in one country will affect other countries. If there is direct investment (such as a business based in one country establishing foreign subsidiaries in other countries), exports and imports, or borrowing and lending between countries, then events that occur in one country can impact other countries. So if many banks in country A lend to many individuals and businesses in country B, and country B experiences a contraction in which many individuals and businesses go bankrupt and cannot repay loans, banks in country A can be affected negatively by the contraction in B, which can cause a reduction in the supply of money and credit in A and induce a recession or depression there as well.[22]

Finally, it must be emphasized that government interference is responsible for the existence of the business cycle, and therefore government interference is responsible for recessions and depressions and all the other ill effects of the cycle. I have shown in chapter 2 how the government is responsible for inflation through so-called monetary policy. I demonstrate elsewhere why this is a form of government interference.[23] As a part of the discussion on government interference that I provide elsewhere, I also show how government interference is responsible for the existence of fiat money and fractional-reserve banking. It is these two institutions that ultimately make the regular fluctuations that have come to be known as the business cycle possible, although both of them need not exist together to create the cycle. I am not saying here that there would be no fluctuations in economic activity without the government interference in the monetary and banking system that is responsible for the existence of fiat money and fractional-reserve banking. However, the number and severity of the fluctuations would be dramatically reduced, and monetary induced fluctuations would be almost nonexistent without such interference.

Another way of saying the above is that the business cycle is not a feature of the free market. The free market (or laissez-faire capitalism) leads to rapid rates of economic progress without the business cycle. It does so because it makes possible all the things discussed above that cause economic progress. Government interference into the market reduces the ability to progress forward. One way in which it does this is through the inflation that generates the business cycle.[24]

A HYPOTHETICAL EXAMPLE OF THE BUSINESS CYCLE

To gain a better understanding of the business cycle, it will help to see an example of how events progress throughout the cycle. The example I provide here is a hypothetical one of how certain key variables change throughout the cycle. This will help one see the essence of the changes during the cycle. In later chapters I show changes in key variables during real-life episodes of the business cycle.

To see what happens during the cycle, imagine that initially the money supply and spending are increasing at a constant 3 percent annual rate and have been doing so for many years. Further, assume the rate of profit prevailing in the economy is 6 percent and the interest rate is 4 percent. These can be thought of as averages throughout the economy. In addition, the interest rate can be assumed to be a short-term interest rate, since this is the relevant interest rate for the business cycle. Short-term interest rates fluctuate much more with the cycle than long-term rates. Long-term rates take longer to adjust since they tend to be affected much more by long-run changes in the economy. As we know, the business cycle is a short-run phenomenon, so the factors that cause it will not have as great an effect on long-term rates.

The initial conditions I have described are shown in exhibit 3.5. In the exhibit, I show the short-term interest rate in two contexts. The first is the short-term interest rate in the present: the "Short-term interest rate in the short run." The second is the short-term interest rate projected into the future if the rate of inflation in the present year is maintained indefinitely: the "Short-term interest rate in the long run (if current rate of inflation is maintained)." Let me emphasize it to make sure it is understood: the two separate columns devoted to interest rates in exhibit 3.5 show the same interest rate. They just show this interest rate under two different scenarios. The differences between these values highlight the difference between the short-run and long-run effects of inflation on interest rates in an economy with a fractional-reserve banking system. Finally, I show the percent change in real output from year to year in exhibit 3.5 (i.e., the change in the physical supply of goods and services produced from year to year, not merely the change in the monetary value of the physical supply of goods and services).

Year	% Δ in money supply	Rate of profit	Short-term interest rate in the short run	Short-term interest rate in the long run (if current rate of inflation is maintained)	% Δ in real output
1–20	3%	6%	4%	4%	3.5%
21	8	8	3	9	4
22	8	9	3.5	9	5
23	13	10	2.5	14	6
24	18	12	2.5	19	6
25	18	12.5	3.5	19	4
26	6	9	9	7	2
27	6	0	8	7	−1.5
28	6	7	7	7	1
29	6	9	7	7	3

Exhibit 3.5 Hypothetical example of the business cycle.

Note: % Δ ≡ percent change.

So the economy has been progressing along at a 3.5 percent annual rate for 20 years. Since the rate of change of the money supply and spending has been constant for 20 years, no monetary-induced distortions in the rate of profit and interest rates have been created for a long period of time and therefore no monetary-induced business cycles have existed either. However, if the money supply begins to increase at a more rapid rate, as I show in year 21 with an 8 percent annual increase, this causes spending, revenues, profits, and output to increase at a more rapid rate and causes the rate of profit to increase as well. This is the start of the business cycle. Notice that the more rapid increase in money and spending also causes interest rates to decrease in the short run, as the short-term interest rate dips to 3 percent.

If the Fed were to engage in a monetary policy that maintained the 8 percent increase in the money supply, profits would eventually stabilize at a higher nominal level, short-term interest rates would rise, and businesses would become used to the more rapid increase in money and spending and incorporate it into their expectations. If this were to occur, any temporary stimulus from the inflation would disappear. So the Fed needs to accelerate the inflation to keep the expansion going; it needs to accelerate the inflation to keep interest rates unexpectedly low and the rate of profit unexpectedly high. The Fed does this in year 23 by engaging in a policy that increases the money supply at an even faster rate: 13 percent annually. Here the rate of profit increases further, while the short-term interest rate declines further. This provides further stimulus to expand, and output expands by 6 percent during the year.

By year 24 it may be difficult to keep output expanding at this rate, and the acceleration in the rate of change of the money supply in that year fails to create an increased rate of expansion of the economy. In year 25, the rate of expansion actually declines with the same rate of inflation as in year 24. Notice also that in year 24 the current interest rate does not decline in absolute terms but does so relative to the rate of profit. This is important to note. A stimulus to expand can be provided merely by changes in the interest rate relative to the rate of profit, not just by absolute changes in either of these variables. The widening gap between these variables creates strong upward pressure on the interest rate, as businesses look to borrow more to invest in their businesses and lend less. This is why I show the interest rate rising relative to the rate of profit in year 25.

The Fed would have to continue the acceleration of inflation in an attempt to keep the expansion going. Whatever the Fed does, the expansion would end sooner or later: sooner if the Fed slows the inflation or deflates the money supply and later, with the breakdown of the monetary system, if the Fed continues the acceleration. Assuming those in charge of the Fed are semi-responsible, we can imagine that they engage in a monetary policy that slows the inflation before the breakdown of the monetary system occurs, which they do in year 26. In that year, the rate of increase in the money supply is slowed to 6 percent. This brings on a decrease in the rate of profit and a dramatic increase in the current interest rate. This latter occurs because borrowers seek to borrow larger amounts based on expectations formed during the expansion, and the supply of loanable funds does not keep pace due to the lower rate of inflation. Hence, the expansion slows further and eventually, in year 27, turns into an outright contraction. As I have said, the economy can contract without actual deflation but merely with a slowing of inflation or even an insufficient increase in inflation. In addition, profits can be pushed down even further if the demand for money increases sufficiently (i.e., velocity falls), causing spending and revenues to decline further relative to costs, as businesses (and individuals in general) retrench and build up money balances to prepare for the tougher-than-expected times ahead.

If the Fed decides to begin inflating more rapidly again, the whole process will start anew, although it would take some time for the new inflation to create another expansion given the recent experience of the contraction. Such an experience would cause people to be more financially conservative for a number of years. However, if the 6 percent annual rate of increase in the money supply is maintained indefinitely, eventually the rate of profit and annual increase in production would recover, although the latter would be slightly below what it was during years 1–20 due to the inflation in years 26 and beyond. I have indicated this slowing in the rate of economic progress with a rate of expansion of the economy in year 29 of 3 percent, which is slightly below the 3.5 percent annual rate of progress in years 1–20. This slower rate of economic progress would exist because of the negative effect that inflation has on production, even if it is a constant rate of inflation.[25]

If inflation is eliminated, the economy would eventually return to its original rate of economic progress (barring no other changes in the economy). If this occurs, the loss due to inflation would be limited to what occurred when inflation existed in the economy (i.e., the net loss in production during the business cycle). If inflation remains constant (regardless of the rate at which it remains constant), the rate of profit would eventually settle out at a level that is slightly higher than the rate of interest, and the interest rate in the short run would eventually equal the interest rate if the current rate of inflation is maintained.[26]

Of course, in any particular episode of the cycle the changes might not occur exactly as I show them. For example, interest rates over the long run and the rate of profit in the long run would most likely not change in a one-for-one manner with the money supply, although there is a tendency for this to be approximately true.[27] In addition, the changes I show might be a bit more dramatic than they would be in real life (given the changes in the money supply) and might occur over a shorter period as well, but this is just for purposes of illustration. It is important that the changes occurring can be easily seen when illustrating the cycle, and I do not want exhibit 3.5 to be too long. What I show are the essential changes taking place during the cycle. This is what is important to illustrate to understand how the business cycle unfolds.

CONCLUSION

As one can see, the business cycle is created by manipulations of the money supply. These manipulations are caused by the government. Government interference is responsible for the fiat-money, fractional-reserve monetary and banking system and the inflation created through this system. Eliminating the government interference responsible for fiat money and fractional-reserve banking will eliminate these institutions and, as a consequence, virtually eliminate monetary-induced business cycles. Eliminating fiat money and fractional reserves entails moving to a 100-percent reserve gold-based monetary and banking system.[28]

I show in chapters 5–9 what the business cycle looks like in real life by showing the movements in the relevant variables during actual episodes of the cycle. This gives one the opportunity to see the causes (and effects) of the cycle in action, so to speak. However, in the next chapter I turn to a defense of the business cycle theory presented in this chapter. It shows that criticisms of this theory are not valid.

4

In Defense of Austrian Business Cycle Theory

Introduction

The business cycle theory expounded in the previous chapter has its roots in Austrian business cycle theory (ABCT). ABCT was originated by Ludwig von Mises and developed further by Friedrich Hayek. The theory I present also incorporates many important truths identified by George Reisman.[1] Others have contributed to the development and defense of ABCT as well. In terms of essential characteristics, there are no differences between what I present here and ABCT, so I will refer to them synonymously.

Many criticisms of ABCT have been made over the last several decades by various people. All of them are invalid. The theory provides the only comprehensive and logically consistent explanation of the cycle. It is the only theory that is consistent with all the facts of the cycle. Nonetheless, since many criticisms have been made, they need to be addressed. I will not address all of the criticisms in this chapter. Many of the criticisms are shown to be invalid in other chapters, such as the claim that ABCT does not explain the contraction phase of the cycle (chapter 3) and the claim that the theory is not based in reality (chapters 3 and 5–9).[2] In addition, some of the criticisms are devoid of intellectual content or are incoherent and therefore require no response.[3]

The only criticisms of ABCT I will address in this chapter are those that are not addressed elsewhere in this book and that raise serious questions about the validity of ABCT. One criticism, on whether ABCT is consistent with what contemporary economists call rational expectations, requires significant treatment to show that this, in fact, is not a valid criticism. Others pertain to claims that ABCT is too complex and that ABCT commits errors in regard to its use of interest rates. Still others criticize ABCT for allegedly requiring full employment at the start of the expansion to generate the harmful effects of the cycle. And there are many more. I address the "rational expectations" criticism last, since it requires a more lengthy treatment. I start with the claim that ABCT is overly complex.

Complexity

The charge that ABCT is too complex says that there are simpler theories that explain the same phenomenon (i.e., the boom-bust business cycle). Therefore, based on the principle of Occam's razor (that in choosing between two competing theories, each of which does an equally good job explaining the same phenomenon, the simpler one should be accepted), ABCT must be rejected. Occam's razor is a valid principle. One does not want to create needless complexity in attempting to understand the world. This will only make it harder to do so, since people will have to retain concepts, ideas, propositions, et cetera that they would otherwise not have to. Each individual has only a limited mental capacity and creating needlessly complex theories goes against the requirements of cognition. The distinctive feature of human beings, the one that raises them above the lower animals, is their conceptual faculty. This faculty makes it possible for humans to retain an enormous amount of information by *condensing* and classifying knowledge.[4] Creating needlessly complex theories undercuts this process.

Notice the emphasis is on the rejection of *needlessly* complex theories. A good theory will not be needlessly complex but it will not be overly simplified either. What determines whether a theory has the appropriate level of complexity? The answer: the nature of reality. The nature of the phenomenon being analyzed determines whether a theory explaining it will need to be complex or simple. If a phenomenon is complex (for instance, if it has many parts to explain and understand or deals with abstract issues), it will require a complex theory to explain it. However, if a phenomenon is simple, it will require a simple theory. For example, explaining addition is much simpler than explaining how to solve differential equations. The steps involved in the latter are more complex and the concepts used are more abstract, so one would expect any theory describing the latter to be more complex than a theory describing the former. But this would not make an explanation of how to solve differential equations overly complex because the nature of what is being explained is complex. Occam's razor only applies to two competing theories that explain the same phenomenon. It does not apply to two theories that explain different phenomena.

The business cycle is an enormously complex phenomenon.[5] It is a series of events that occur over many years and can encompass large geographic areas. It can involve millions—even billions—of people, perhaps tens of thousands of different types of goods, millions of businesses, and thousands of industries. It affects consumers and producers, prices, unemployment, interest rates, output, revenues, profits, and many other variables. To be able to understand the causal nature of something that affects so many variables across significant periods of time and widespread geographic areas requires an enormous act of integration. This can only be done at a very abstract level. This is why any valid business cycle theory will be complex. Such a theory must explain, or at least be consistent with, what is occurring throughout the entire economy during the cycle.

The charge of ABCT being too complex would only be valid if there was another theory that did an equally good job explaining the cycle and was less complex. However, there is no such theory. ABCT is the only theory that is consistent with all the facts of the business cycle and explains the cycle in a logical fashion. I have given my explanation of the cycle based on ABCT in chapter 3. I show elsewhere that other theories put forward in an attempt to explain the cycle do not in fact do so. They are either inconsistent with one or more facts of the business cycle and/or are invalid logically.[6]

INTEREST RATES

A number of economists have criticized ABCT's use of interest rates in explaining the cycle. They include the claim that ABCT exaggerates the importance of interest rates in influencing the volume of investment and the claim that ABCT says businesses use changes in interest rates to predict how the demand for goods will change (specifically, to predict shifts in demand from consumers' goods to capital goods during the cycle) but that interest rates are not good predictors of demand. The claims also include that inflation affects short-term interest rates more than long-term interest rates, so investment should not be affected much by changes in interest rates due to inflation because investment depends more on changes in long-term rates. In addition, they include the claim that changes in interest rates can be caused by things other than changes in the quantity of money (such as changes in investment and savings) and the claim that businessmen will think the interest rate is high during the inflationary expansion, not low, and that this will lead to greater investment in projects of shorter duration, not longer duration as ABCT states. Finally, they include the claim that ABCT identifies the wrong relationship between interest rates, inflation, and/or investment. In regard to this last assertion, it is said that ABCT says more inflation causes lower interest rates and less inflation causes higher interest rates when the opposite is allegedly true. Also in regard to this last assertion, it has been said that the greater inflation necessary to decrease interest rates might decrease investment since changes in inflation mean inflation will be more volatile and this can affect investment negatively. More inflation and lower interest rates leading to less investment is the opposite of what ABCT says should occur.[7] Let us take a look at these criticisms.

With regard to the claim that ABCT overemphasizes the effect of changes in interest rates on the volume of investment, while it might be true that some supporters of the theory have done this, not all of them have done this.[8] Supporters of ABCT also emphasize changes in relative prices of goods at various stages of production as a factor influencing businesses to produce more of some goods and less of others. However, the theory as presented in this book does not give as great a role to interest rates and relative prices as other supporters of the theory. The one thing that is emphasized in this book—more than anything else—that affects businesses directly is the rate of profit.

One cannot deny the influence the rate of profit has on investment. People invest to make money and the more money they can make, the more they will tend to invest, ceteris paribus. So the rate of profit, not the interest rate, is the primary factor influencing changes in investment; the interest rate is only a secondary factor.

This can also be seen in the primacy of production over borrowing. We need to produce wealth to survive and we borrow in support of our productive activities. It is *not* the case that we need to borrow to survive and production is engaged in merely to aid us in our borrowing.

The primacy of the rate of profit over the interest rate is true even in the case in which a person borrows money to open a business and engage in some productive enterprise (and even if the newly formed business is, however unlikely, completely financed by borrowing). Here it appears as if the borrowing comes before production. However, before money is available for a creditor to lend, the creditor first had to produce something and earn an income (or obtain the money from someone who did).

Any valid business cycle theory must recognize the primacy of the rate of profit over the interest rate. Hence, this criticism only applies to some supporters' versions of ABCT. It is not a criticism of the theory as such and certainly does not apply to the version of ABCT that is presented in this book.

What about the claim that ABCT allegedly says that businesses use interest rates to predict demand but that interest rates are not very good predictors of demand?[9] This is not a completely accurate statement. Although changes in interest rates can be predictors of demand for goods that require debt financing to purchase (such as homes), ABCT does not fundamentally rely on interest rates as predictors of demand. Changes in spending, which lead to changes in profits, are the main predictor of demand for ABCT.

The main influence of changes in interest rates on businesses is through costs. Changes in interest rates mean the costs of production of businesses will change and can cause changes in the kinds of investment activities that are profitable to businesses. For instance, lower interest rates raise the profitability of long-term investments relative to short-term investments because interest costs loom larger for long-term investments. As a part of this effect, lower interest rates also raise the profitability of investments farther from final consumption relative to the profitability of investments closer to final consumption; that is, they raise the profitability in capital goods industries relative to the profitability in consumers' goods industries and in capital goods industries that are farther removed from final consumption relative to capital goods industries that are not as far removed from final consumption.

Another critique is that ABCT postulates that businessmen make the most costly errors to generate business cycles.[10] Austrian economists state that low interest rates will induce businessmen to take on projects of longer duration during the expansion phase of the cycle but, it is claimed, they do not consider the equally likely scenario that businessmen might invest in projects of shorter duration. Additionally, it is claimed that lower interest rates might not create a significant response from businesses or might lead to no response or even a response to contract their activities. The alleged reason for all of these reactions is that businessmen do not understand inflation but they know it can have negative consequences on their businesses, such as creating greater investment risk due to potentially more volatile inflation with greater rates of inflation. Therefore, they might respond in the opposite manner one would expect with lower interest rates or they might not respond as much as one would expect or at all.

The first question to ask here is: If businessmen do not understand inflation very well, how do they understand the connection between inflation and interest rates? How do they know that low interest rates can be caused by inflation? What businessmen understand about the expansion phase, regardless of their knowledge of the relationship between inflation and interest rates, is that interest rates are low relative to the rate of profit. As I have said, it may be that businesses are cautious at first and do not expand their activities dramatically at the first sign of lower interest rates and a higher rate of profit. If businessmen have been fooled in the past into expanding rapidly at the first sign of low interest rates, high rates of profit, and rapidly rising spending, they will err on the side of caution. If the expansion phase does not last very long, businesses will not expand their activities very much and will not have to make large adjustments when it comes to an end.

However, as the money supply is inflated at accelerating rates for longer periods of time, more dramatic effects will be felt by businesses. Businessmen will, in a step-by-step process, begin to take on longer and more costly investments. This is only natural because interest costs tend to be more significant the longer and greater the investment project. Therefore, lower interest rates tend to have the greatest effect on these projects. Likewise, the profits that can be earned are larger the longer the rate of profit is kept artificially high.

Businessmen do not jump right into the longest-term projects at the first sign of inflation. However, over a long period of sustained and accelerating inflation the incentives become greater and steer businesses toward longer-term projects.[11] This is why a more dramatic and longer-lived inflation creates a business cycle that has larger swings in output.

The case of businessmen responding by shortening the duration of their investments or contracting their investments with lower interest rates, due to the added risk that greater inflation represents in the form of potentially more volatile inflation, goes against all logic and facts. If risk increases due to more volatile inflation, interest rates will rise not fall. They will rise in response to the added risk of losing one's principal when making investments. Creditors will require the added return to compensate for the additional risk.

If one actually did get a contraction or a shortening in the duration of investments due to the added risk, it would not be a case of getting a contraction or a shortening in the duration of investments due to lower interest rates, but due to higher interest rates. The case of postulating added risk and lower interest rates is a case of wanting to have one's cake and eat it too. Ceteris paribus, one can have added risk *or* lower interest rates, but not both.

Additionally, lower interest rates do not lead to contractions. I have shown theoretically in the previous chapter how lower interest rates lead to expansions, not contractions, when produced by the inflation of the supply of money and credit. I will show empirically in the following chapters their association with expansions.

I must emphasize here that I am referring to the *cause* of a contraction. I am not referring to how the central bank might act to lower interest rates after the start of a recession or how it might act to lower interest rates after it has sensed it has driven interest rates too high and thus led the economy to the brink of a recession. I am also not referring to how interest rates might move during an extended and/or severe contraction. The Great Depression provides an example of the latter because interest rates fell during that depression. However, they did so due to the dramatic decrease in the money supply, spending, and profitability during that depression. The lower interest rates did not cause the Great Depression but were an effect of the dramatic change in the money supply during the Great Depression. Higher interest rates caused the Great Depression (at least in part). This will be seen in chapter 8, where I discuss the Great Depression in detail.

In addition, if businesses do not respond to the inflation or do not respond as significantly as they might otherwise because of additional risk, this is also not due to lower interest rates. Again, if there is added risk then interest rates will either not fall due to the inflation or will not fall as much as they otherwise would have. Here again it is the forces causing interest rates to rise (which either partially or fully offset the downward pressure inflation puts on interest rates in the short run) that are causing businesses to not respond or respond less significantly to the inflation.

This discussion highlights the fact that other forces can be at work in the economy and these forces can counteract the forces that cause the business cycle. It is also true that other factors can be at work in the economy that act in concert with the forces causing the business cycle. We will see examples of the latter in the discussion of the Great Depression and in the discussion of the recession of 2008–9 in chapter 6. However, the fact that there can be other forces acting in the economy does not deny the validity of ABCT. The forces at work in the economy causing the business cycle that ABCT identifies do exist. The evidence presented throughout this book is proof of this statement.

One of the other factors at work in the economy can be volatile inflation. It is certainly true that more volatile inflation creates greater risk in the economy for businessmen, and investors in general, due to the uncertainty in the demand for goods (among other things) that it generates. Moreover, there is evidence that greater rates of inflation tend to be associated with more inflation volatility.[12] However, the criticism related to this topic contains a misunderstanding of ABCT. The focus of ABCT is not volatile inflation but accelerating inflation. During the expansion, accelerating, not volatile, inflation leads to more spending, higher profits, and lower interest rates, especially relative to the expectations of businessmen. To the extent inflation is accelerating *and* volatile, two opposing forces are acting in the economy and different results will be brought about depending on which one is dominant. If accelerating inflation is dominant, one will get an inflationary expansion. If volatile inflation is dominant, one will not get an inflationary expansion. ABCT does not deny that one can have volatile inflation and that this has an effect on the economy. But the fact that one can have volatile inflation and that this may dominate in some instances does not deny that accelerating inflation can exist and can dominate (and even be present without volatile inflation).

Another criticism claims that ABCT says businessmen confuse increases in the money supply with increases in savings. Both can cause changes in interest rates and, it is claimed, businessmen must confuse changes in interest rates due to "monetary policy" with changes in interest rates due to changes in savings for them to react appropriately and create a cycle. However, this allegedly can only be plausible if savings are volatile, and savings are not volatile.[13] Since savings are stable, presumably businessmen will know that the changes in interest rates are not due to real factors. They will know it is due merely to monetary factors and therefore they will not respond to the changes, according to this claim.

This criticism attributes greater knowledge to businessmen than they actually possess. ABCT does not depend on businessmen confusing increases in savings with increases in the money supply. It depends on businessmen thinking the rate of profit will be held high and interest rates will remain low for a significant period of time (long enough for them to want to attempt to make money from the distorted economic data). Businessmen do not need to know what causes changes in these variables, and many of them probably do not (especially if they accept the validity of contemporary, mainstream economics). The key is that, as discussed in connection with the previous criticism, these variables move in the right direction for a long enough period of time to provide the appropriate incentives. Again, this book provides ample evidence that they do.

The next criticism of ABCT concerns the claim that inflation tends to affect short-term interest rates more than it affects long-term rates. Based on this, it is claimed that the decrease in interest rates due to an accelerating inflation should not have a significant effect on investment, since long-term interest rates tend to drive investment, and in particular should have very little effect on long-term investment.[14]

There are a number of issues to consider in connection with this criticism. First, to the extent that some interest rates are affected, whether long term or short term, the ability and incentive to borrow to finance investments will be changed and this will have at least some effect on investment. ABCT does not predict exactly what the length of maturity of the investments of the business cycle will be. It only says that as interest rates fall there will tend to be relatively more investment in areas of the economy farther removed from final consumption. Likewise, as interest rates rise there will be relatively more investment in areas closer to final consumption. Nowhere does it specify how far removed investment will be from final consumption.

In addition, while it is true that inflation has a smaller effect on long-term than on short-term interest rates, this does not deny that it has some effect on long-term interest rates. For example, as discussed in chapter 2 in connection with the effects of the Federal Reserve's policies on interest rates, to the extent that short-term rates fall relative to long-term rates there will be an incentive for borrowers to shift their borrowing more toward short-term debt instruments. This will put at least some downward pressure on long-term rates. There will be an opposite incentive for lenders. They will want to switch their lending toward the higher interest long-term debt instruments, which will also tend to bring long-term rates down. The long-term rates might not come down as much as the short-term rates, but there is an incentive for long-term rates to move in the same direction as short-term rates. The two rates do tend to follow each other (at least eventually).

Further, to the extent that the profitability of long-term investments is more sensitive to fluctuations in interest rates than the profitability of short-term investments, it does not take as much of a decrease in long-term interest rates to make long-term investments look more profitable relative to short-term investments. This can be seen in a simple example.

A business is considering two investment projects. The two projects have the same total costs and all costs are incurred at the beginning of the projects. However, project A has an expected payoff of $1,000 at the end of one year and project B has an expected payoff of $1,275 at the end of five years. If the one-year interest rate (i.e., the rate expected to prevail over the next year for one-year debt instruments) is 5 percent and the five-year interest rate is 6 percent, the two projects will have the same present value (PV), which is $952, and be equally profitable if these respective interest rates are used as the discount rate. If the short-term interest rate was to suddenly fall so that the one-year rate is 4.5 percent, the PV of project A increases to $957. This represents a 0.5 percent decrease in the short-term interest rate. In order for the PVs of the two projects to remain equal, the five-year interest rate must fall by only 0.1 percent. Here we see that a decrease of only 0.1 percent in the five-year rate is needed to maintain the profitability of project B in the face of a 0.5 percent decrease in the short-term rate. This occurs due to the compounding effect.

So the fact that long-term rates are not affected as much by inflation as short-term rates does not deny the validity of ABCT. In fact, it may be that long-term rates are not affected as much, at least in part, precisely because it takes less of a fall in these rates to preserve the profitability of long-term investment projects relative to short-term projects. The key is that some change in interest rates occurs (and, more importantly, some change in the rate of profit occurs) and this provides some impetus for capitalists and businessmen to expand or contract their enterprises.

The next criticism related to interest rates is the claim that changes in interest rates could occur for reasons other than changes in the money supply, such as changes in time preference (which would lead to changes in the amount of savings) or changes in borrowing. If interest rates change for other reasons, all the same effects one gets during the business cycle might not occur. So why should one expect changes in interest rates due to credit expansion and contraction to create the business cycle?

It is true that interest rates change for many reasons. However, when interest rates change for these other reasons, this is not a part of the business cycle. During the expansion, it is the increased quantity of money that leads to more spending, revenues, and profits and lower interest rates. All of these provide the incentive for businesses to expand. Likewise during the contraction, when money, spending, revenues, and profits are declining (or rising more slowly) and interest rates are rising, the incentive for businesses to cut back on their business activities is in place.

If interest rates change due to time preference, such as a decrease in time preference, some of the same results are obtained as in the business cycle; however, there are also many differences. A lower time preference prevailing in the economy, for example, means people are looking more toward the future and will save more. This tends to lower interest rates and increase the funds available to borrow and invest. As in the expansion phase of the business cycle, this will make it possible for businesses to expand their activities, including taking on more capital-intensive projects and more long-range projects (i.e., projects farther removed from final consumption). These possibilities exist thanks to the fact that individuals are now thinking more long range and are willing to wait longer to obtain payoffs from investments.

However, unlike during the business cycle, these changes tend to be long-term changes: changes that people do not make on a whim and a wish but make after considering their financial future and determining it would be better if they saved more. Hence, these changes tend to be more permanent and stable, whereas changes during the business cycle are short term and unstable. Changes during the business cycle do not occur due to a fundamental shift in the time horizon of people's thinking; that is, they do not occur due to, as one economist has claimed, "violent fluctuations in time preferences."[15] Fluctuations during the business cycle occur due to the creation of more money and the cessation or slowing of its creation. Such fluctuations often are violent.

Furthermore, changes in borrowing have effects different from changes in the quantity of money, even though both can cause changes in interest rates. For instance, a decrease in borrowing will cause interest rates to fall. Lenders will lower interest rates to get rid of the excess supply of loanable funds. However, this just means less borrowing and lending will occur. It will not create an expansion (or contraction). Only the type of financing used in the economy (debt vs. equity) will change, and there are limits to how much this can change since, as I have stated previously, the rate of profit and interest rates are intimately related. To the extent they move farther apart (in my example here, interest rates are falling relative to the rate of profit), it changes the incentives businesses have to borrow and invest in their own projects to earn a profit or lend their money to earn interest. These incentives work to keep the rate of profit and interest rates from getting too far apart. As interest rates fall relative to the rate of profit, there will be more of an incentive for businesses to borrow and invest in their own business activities and less incentive to lend their money.

In addition, in this situation the rate of profit will probably fall to some extent because a desire to engage in less borrowing signals a desire to take on less financial risk. This means less risky investment projects will probably be taken on to the extent the desire to be exposed to less financial risk indicates a desire to take on less risk in general. Less risk being taken on implies corresponding lower overall rates of return, which helps to keep the rate of profit in line with interest rates.

It has also been claimed that interest rates might change due to a change in investment on the part of businesses. For instance, the interest rate might fall due to businesses engaging in less investment. Lower interest rates are said to come about due to businesses borrowing less as a result of the decline in investment. In this case, it is claimed, lower interest rates could signal to businessmen that there are fewer good investment opportunities and thus cause further decreases in investment. If businessmen mistake low interest rates during the expansion to mean there are fewer investment opportunities, it might lead to less investment during the expansion instead of more, as ABCT says will occur. This means the expansion will actually be a contraction![16]

First, it must be made clear that less investment does not necessarily lead to lower interest rates. It would only lead to lower interest rates if, as a result of the decreased investment, the overall demand for loanable funds (i.e., borrowing) in the economy declined. If there is a shift in the economy from investment spending to consumption spending, interest rates might not decline if borrowing to consume simply replaces borrowing to invest. Moreover, there is a key variable missing from this discussion, which brings me to my second point.

The interest rate is not the appropriate variable to use to determine whether there are fewer investment opportunities. The appropriate variable to consider is the rate of profit. During the expansion phase of the cycle, the rate of profit rises, which signals more (or, at least, better) investment opportunities. Interest rates pertain to the lending and borrowing of money and it may be the case that there are fewer profitable *lending* opportunities if they fall. However, lower interest rates make *investment* opportunities on the part of businesses more profitable, not less, from the two perspectives I have discussed previously: they lower the cost of borrowing to invest and raise the attractiveness of investing over lending (since during the expansion phase they are lower relative to the rate of profit). It is rising interest rates (relative to the rate of profit) that decrease the investment opportunities of businesses because they raise the cost of financing those investments if debt financing is used.

Furthermore, there is a fundamental distinction between interest rates changing due to a change in borrowing, lending, or time preference and interest rates changing due to changes in the money supply. Changes in the money supply make possible changes in the amount of spending and related variables. They make possible an inflationary expansion or deflationary contraction of the economy. This is not true when interest rates change for any other reason. If interest rates change due to a change in borrowing, for instance if they fall due to decreased borrowing, as I said, this merely changes the type of financing occurring in the economy. More equity financing of investment spending is used and less debt financing but no total change in spending occurs.

Likewise, if interest rates fall due to decreased time preference and increased savings, there is no change in total spending. Here there will be a shift in spending away from consumers' goods and toward capital goods, in conjunction with the lower time preference and greater focus on the future, but no total change in spending. Further, with lower time preference the rate of profit will fall along with interest rates. So the rate of profit moves in the opposite direction relative to when the money supply is inflated and interest rates are pushed lower temporarily as a result. Lower time preference means more focus on spending for capital goods and production and less on consumers' goods and consumption.

This means the economy becomes more capital intensive. As a result, costs rise relative to revenues in the economy as productive expenditures increase and bring the rate of profit down.[17] In fact, the declining rate of profit is what causes interest rates to fall. However, do not think, as Keynesians might, that the lower rate of profit will be inadequate to induce sufficient investment. Investors do not need as much inducement because their time preference is lower.

So, changes in interest rates due to changes in the supply of money and changes in interest rates due to other factors must be kept distinct in one's mind. The former are a part of the business cycle but the latter are not. The former are consistent with changes in total spending in the economy and the latter are not. The latter are consistent with shifts in spending and/or financing (among other things not related to the business cycle). The latter occur independently of the business cycle. This turns out to be not a criticism of ABCT but the recognition of two separate and distinct ways in which interest rates change.

Another criticism is that ABCT says more inflation leads to lower interest rates and less inflation leads to higher interest rates, but the real relationship is the opposite.[18] This criticism only tells half of the story. It fails to distinguish between the short-run and long-run effects of inflation on interest rates.

It is true that ABCT says that greater inflation leads to lower interest rates and less inflation leads to higher interest rates. However, this only occurs in the short run due to the fractional-reserve nature of the monetary and banking system. This short-run relationship exists because most of the new money in this system comes into existence in the form of an additional supply of credit. In the long run, as the new money is spent and re-spent and begins to drive up spending, revenues, and profits, the greater inflation drives interest rates up. This is also a part of ABCT and was first discussed in chapter 2.

The short-run relationship between interest rates and inflation is seen in the policies followed by the Federal Reserve and all central banks. That is, to immediately target lower interest rates, for example, the Fed could buy government bonds, lower the required reserve ratio, and/or lower the discount rate, all of which tend to increase the money supply. It could do the exact opposite to immediately target higher interest rates. The Fed is quite good at achieving its targets using it policies. How could the Fed be so good at achieving its targets, given the policies it uses to do so, if interest rates were not inversely related to inflation (at least in the short run)? The fact is that it can *because* of the inverse relationship between these two variables in the short run.

In the long run, if the Fed wants to continuously target lower interest rates it must pursue a policy of continuously accelerating inflation. This is the only way it can continuously attempt to exploit the short-term relationship between inflation and interest rates. However, if it pursues such a policy indefinitely it will eventually lead to so-called hyperinflation and the breakdown of the monetary system. Therefore, over the long run the Fed must eventually reverse course on its interest rate target. It must do so precisely because the long-term, direct relationship between inflation and interest rates begins to assert itself.

The final criticism to be addressed in this section is the claim that businessmen will believe that interest rates are high during the inflationary expansion and this will shorten the structure of production, not lengthen it as ABCT predicts. The claim here is that prices increase at a slower pace during the initial phases of an inflation when compared to the latter phases of the inflation. Hence, during the initial phases the relatively slow rise in prices will not reduce real interest rates very much (relative to nominal interest rates). However, as prices begin to rise at a more rapid rate, and even accelerate, during the latter stages of the inflation, businessmen will realize that their initial estimates of real interest rates were high. This is allegedly the case because the nominal level of interest rates that prevailed during the initial phases of the inflation, when contrasted with the higher price increases during the latter stages of the inflation, creates real interest rates that are lower than if those same nominal rates are compared to the rate of price increase that existed during the earlier stages of the inflation. Since businessmen use the slower rate of price increase during the earlier stages of the inflation to estimate the real interest rates during those stages, it is claimed they will overestimate the level of real interest rates. This estimation will allegedly be corrected only after the inflation begins to cause prices to rise at a faster pace.[19]

Assuming prices and interest rates move during the business cycle as this critique requires, the problem with this criticism is that the wrong rates are being compared to determine whether real interest rates are low or high in the initial phase of the inflation. What is important is that during the initial phase of the inflation, real interest rates are kept low relative to the real *rate of profit*. The rates to compare are the difference between real (or nominal) interest rates and the real (or nominal) rate of profit *before* the start of the inflation and the difference in those same variables during the *initial phase* of the inflation. If one compares these variables, one will see that the real rate of profit is higher compared to real interest rates during the initial phase of the inflation than it is prior to the inflation. Thus, there is an incentive for businessmen to expand their activities and take on debt to do so. The only question for businessmen at this point is: How long will this relationship persist?

The refutation of this criticism assumes that the movement in prices and interest rates is as stated in the criticism. However, there is some question as to whether they will always move as this criticism requires. There is no need for prices to follow a specific pattern during the various stages of the cycle. For example, prices can move fairly slowly throughout the expansion, as they did during the 1920s prior to the Great Depression and as they did during the expansion phase of the cycle in the latter 1990s. As I have stated, the variables that follow a specific pattern that is universal to the cycle are interest rates and the rate of profit.

Prices, Net Investment, Full Employment, "Forced Savings," and Statist Premises

There are a number of other criticisms of ABCT that I will address in this section. First is the focus on prices. It is claimed that changes in relative prices are necessary to create the expansion and some of the associated characteristics (such as mal-investment).[20] However, as I explained in chapter 3, it is not prices that need to move. Prices did not change dramatically in the 1920s prior to the Great Depression and yet an inflationary expansion occurred. It is the inflation of the money supply that is important and the consequent changes in spending, revenues, profits, interest rates, and the rate of profit. To the extent that the interest rate is the price of borrowing and lending, one may consider this an example of prices changing, but prices in general need not change. They need not rise during the expansion and fall during the contraction, as some state is necessary, although they often do. Prices often do change in this manner because they are merely one of the effects of inflation and deflation.

Businesses base their decisions on such variables as profits and interest rates, not merely prices. Of course, prices affect these variables and their effects will be taken into account. However, changes in profits and interest rates can occur without changes in prices. For example, if spending and production both increase and prices remain constant, a business can make more money on the production of a good to the extent it has a positive profit margin. Likewise, as spending and production shrink, with no change in prices and a positive profit margin, profits shrink.

One criticism claims that net investment must be negative for the structure of production to shorten but that the only time we have seen negative net investment is during the Great Depression, so ABCT must not be applicable to most episodes of the cycle. How does ABCT explain the shortening of the structure of production if what it claims should occur only occurs in one out of many cases?[21] First, the structure of production could shorten without negative net investment. One could have a shift of net investment from industries farther removed from final consumption to those closer to final consumption. Nonetheless, the important variable to focus on during the cycle is output, not net investment. I show in chapters 5–9 that the change in output is negative during every contraction. In fact, since contractions are determined based on what happens to output, this variable, by definition, must decrease to have a contraction.

In addition, most episodes of the cycle are too mild to get absolute changes in the structure of production (as is indicated in this criticism by the fact that net investment is rarely negative during the contraction). Fluctuations in output are generally too small to get absolute changes in the structure of production. Hence, the structure of production might not actually shrink during the contraction but might only increase by a lesser amount than it otherwise would have.

This means, during the contractions in the mild episodes of the cycle, real net investment will only decline and not actually be negative. Real net investment and real consumption decline along with output. The fact that real net investment is rarely negative during the contraction does not invalidate ABCT; it is perfectly consistent with ABCT. It just means that in many contractions gross investment has not decreased enough to turn net investment negative. In other words, when output shrinks the productive assets in existence do not always decrease. In many cases, only their rate of increase decreases.

Another claim is that ABCT only predicts mal-investment and the consequent adjustments if the inflationary expansion starts in an environment in which resources are fully employed.[22] If there is unemployment or presumably unused resources of any kind, mal-investment will not occur and thus there will be no need for an adjustment period (i.e., recession) to occur either. In fact, according to this criticism, inflation could help put resources to work (or, at least, put them to work faster than they otherwise would be if the inflation had not existed). This criticism is not valid and has been addressed by Austrian economists.[23] Let me say just a few words here.

Resources are virtually never fully employed. Even in a free market some amount of unemployment will exist and factories will not be utilized 100 percent.[24] This is consistent with the plans of businessmen and workers. For example, workers might remain unemployed as they hold out for a better job. A factory owner might use less than 100 percent capacity during the off-season when demand is low.

Just because resources are not being used at present does not mean they are being wasted. One has to consider the overall plans of the owners of the resources to determine if they are being wasted. It might make sense to hold resources idle for a time to wait for better opportunities. However, putting idle resources to use based on distortions of market data caused by inflation is a waste. Among other things, it can prevent businessmen from responding (or responding in a more timely fashion) to real changes in demand due to, for instance, changes in the preferences of buyers.

Inflation will create the boom and the bust—and the attendant mal-investment—regardless of whether there are fully employed or unemployed resources. It does so because resources are employed that would not otherwise be employed or are employed for purposes for which they would not otherwise be employed (at least temporarily) due to the inflation. This is what happens when profits and interest rates are distorted. Activities look profitable that would not otherwise be profitable, and resources are pulled from other activities or taken from the supply of idle resources to engage in the temporarily profitable activities. When the profits disappear, the resources employed will have to be shifted to different activities, be idled once again, or scrapped altogether. This is mal-investment even in the case of idle resources being temporarily put to use to the extent the owner of the resources would have determined, without the distorting incentives created by inflation, that the best use of the resources would have been to idle them until better opportunities for the resources were identified.

One might ask here: What if resources are unemployed due to a recession or depression? Can't inflation help get the resources employed in a quicker fashion? The important question to consider here is: What caused the recession or depression? The answer: inflation. Remember, boom and bust come as a set. To say that inflation is the cure for a recession or depression is to say that the cause of recessions and depressions is the cure. This is contradictory. In fact, more inflation will only lead to continued distortions of economic signals, more mal-investment, and, ultimately, more recessions and depressions. The cure to recessions and depressions (and the unemployed resources to which they lead) is to free up the market. One needs to free up labor markets, the monetary and banking system, and other markets.[25]

Next is the topic of "forced savings." "Forced savings" has a number of definitions from various writers. At least one criticism says that, based on ABCT, the crisis results from a process of "forced savings." Here it is claimed that the lengthening of the structure of production is the manner in which "forced savings" occur. As interest rates and the rate of profit change during the expansion, there is a shift from consumption to production and from the production of goods less remote from final consumption to goods more remote from final consumption. The savings are said to be "forced" because the shift from consumption to production occurs due to changes in incomes and consumers' goods prices. Because of distortions in the prevailing economic data, people end up saving more and consuming less. Their mix of saving and consumption is different than it otherwise would have been.[26] The claim by those who criticize ABCT based on "forced savings" is that such savings do not inevitably lead to a crisis and that such savings do not always exist during the cycle.[27] The basis for this claim is not important for my purposes here. One can show that the "forced savings" criticism is not valid without a discussion of the basis for this claim.

One major problem with the "forced savings" criticism is that so-called forced savings are only one of the *effects* of the boom-bust cycle; they are not a cause. The manipulations of the supply of money and credit, and the resulting changes in the rate of profit and interest rates, cause the changes in the structure of production, changes in prices if they occur, and more. So-called forced savings are merely one aspect of this.

If "forced savings" do not occur, it is not a blow to ABCT. One still gets malinvestment, overconsumption, and the other ill effects of the cycle. One still gets the expansion and contraction based on the temporarily distorted data caused by inflation. It is the distortion of economic data that is the fundamental problem and the main driver of the cycle. If data were not distorted, inflation would not cause many of the problems that it does.

In fact, the distortion of data does not create savings on net.[28] Inflation leads to greater consumption and capital decumulation (i.e., a decrease in overall savings in the economy). Inflation causes both mal-investment *and* overconsumption, not "forced savings" (at least not on net).[29]

The final criticism that I will address in this section is the one based on a statist premise.[30] The claim is that Austrians are essentially looking for ways to blindly apply their allegedly irrational individualist and free-market views to the business cycle. Hence, when Austrians develop business cycle theory the claim is that they have an "agenda" and are nihilistic, while the statists have "simple and down-to-earth" explanations.[31]

This criticism stems from the belief that the state should control people's lives (at least to some extent) and thus play a role in manipulating the economy, whether through so-called monetary and fiscal policies or through other means. There are a number of questions with which the statist should be confronted on these issues. For example, why is it assumed that the individualist has an irrational agenda? Why is it not considered that the individualist rejects the statist approach because the statist views are wrong and destructive?

It must be admitted that this criticism does contain an element of truth: the extension of free-market ideas to business cycle theory is just an overall part of an agenda to apply individualism to a wider sphere. However, neither the application of individualist views nor the individualist views themselves are irrational. Individualism is not only valid morally and politically, it is valid economically. Collectivism is invalid morally, politically, and economically. I do not say this based on some prejudice I have for individualism and the free market. I say this based on a logical analysis of the facts.[32] The application of individualist ideas to the business cycle is merely an objective extension of individualist ideas to the economic sphere.

The validity of ideas is based on whether they agree with the facts of reality and make sense logically. This ultimately determines whether they can lead to success when put into practice. Altruist and collectivist ideas—the ideas underlying statism—have failed in reality. They fail because they are inconsistent with the requirements of human life and have led to death and destruction on a massive scale as a result. Individualism succeeds in reality. It does so because it is consistent with the requirements of human life and thus has led to the flourishing of human life when put into practice. The failure of socialism and success of capitalism in history is just some of the evidence to support these claims.[33]

It is the statist agenda that is irrational. The assumption that individuals must be controlled through the use of force by the government to achieve allegedly beneficial results must be rejected. Only then can economic analysis (or any analysis pertaining to the realm of human action) be objective. If one discounts a possible solution to a problem simply because it is individualist, one is not being objective.

Moreover, individualists should not concede the idea that we need "value free" scientific analysis. No objective analysis can or should be value free. The mere statement, in fact, is a contradiction, since it professes a value. Those who defend the scientific method defend profound values such as honesty, integrity, observation, the freedom of inquiry, et cetera. The key is to have one's analysis free of emotion. One's analysis must be grounded in the facts and proven through a logical analysis of the facts.

As stated by the great economist George Reisman, "the advocacy of capitalism...should be no more remarkable, and no more grounds for objection, than the advocacy of health by medical doctors."[34] If the statists performed their analysis free of their emotional attachment to altruism and collectivism, they would reject statism. They need to reject the underlying altruist and collectivist premises that lead them to a prejudice against individualism and for the statist agenda that flies in the face of not only a sound and objective analysis of the facts, but of human life itself.

"RATIONAL EXPECTATIONS"

The most potentially damaging criticism of ABCT is the claim that the theory is not consistent with what contemporary economists call rational expectations.[35] This attack says that if the government regularly creates the business cycle through a manipulation of the supply of money and credit, businessmen should be able to learn from these repeated episodes and not make the same mistakes over and over again. They should not get repeatedly fooled by the government's manipulation of money and credit. They should not be repeatedly duped into expanding, only to have to eventually rid themselves of the investments they engaged in during the expansion. According to this argument, by learning from the repeated episodes of the business cycle, businessmen should even be able to prevent the government from continuously creating such a cycle by counter-acting the effects of the government's actions. In fact, according to this argu-ment, entrepreneurial individuals should be able to profit from the government's actions by using the theory to position themselves appropriately based on which phase of the cycle is approaching. At a minimum, businessmen should be able to use ABCT to make themselves immune from the government's actions if, indeed, ABCT is correct.

The "rational expectations" argument against ABCT is potentially the most damaging because rationality is a fundamental characteristic of human beings. If the theory cannot be defended against this argument, it would be proper to abandon it. Fortunately, ABCT can be defended and its abandonment is not necessary.

In this section, I show that ABCT is fully consistent with "rational expecta-tions," as the term is used by contemporary economists. I also show that the concept of "rationality" that contemporary economists use is not a very good one because it is defined based on nonessential characteristics of the concept. Because of this deficiency, I present a better view of what rationality is and show that ABCT is consistent with that as well.[36]

Why Austrian Business Cycle Theory Is Consistent with "Rational Expectations"

In order to understand why ABCT is consistent with "rational expectations," one must first understand what exactly is meant by that term. "Rational expecta-tions," as contemporary economists use the term, means that people's expecta-tions of the future are not systematically wrong and that people use all available information, including the best economic theory, when forming their expecta-tions. It says people can learn about changes taking place in the economy and correct any mistakes they made in the past.[37] Even though this does not provide a very good understanding of what it means to form expectations rationally, ABCT does not imply that businessmen make systematic errors, that they do not correct their mistakes, that they do not use all available information, or that they do not understand the best economic theory.

The first thing that can be said in defense of ABCT is that the same econo-mists who use "rational expectations" theory to argue against ABCT also often recognize that ABCT is not a very well-known or widely accepted theory among economists. If this is true, it is hard to believe that many businessmen, who are taught business cycle theory by economists, know about the theory. How could they use a theory they have never even heard of to protect themselves or profit from the cycle?[38] One cannot be said to be acting inconsistently with "rational expectations" if one does not have the knowledge necessary to correct one's actions. In fact, to the extent there are other theories of the business cycle, that do not accurately explain the cycle, prevalent among economists and thus prevalent among businessmen, the errors businessmen commit in connection with the cycle will be made worse (if they act on these theories).

There is reason to believe the business cycle theory that is prevalent among businessmen is loosely based on ABCT, even though it does not go by that name. Therefore, this argument in defense of ABCT is not a strong one. I make it here only to point out the inconsistency between the claim that ABCT is not that well known or widely accepted and the claim that businessmen should be able to use the theory to circumvent the government created fluctuations.

Even if businessmen do have knowledge of ABCT (or something equivalent), and thus are in a position to use it to their advantage, one must remember that being rational does not imply being omniscient.[39] Businessmen do not have a crystal ball they can use to predict the future. They cannot know every move that a central bank, private banks, or the demand for money will make. They cannot predict the exact lag between a change in the money supply and a change in the volume of spending or in which parts of the economy the new money will be spent first. All that can be said is this: if businessmen are continuously faced with revenues and profits that are rising and interest rates that remain low relative to the rate of profit, sooner or later they will expand their business activities. Further, the longer and more rapid the increase in the money supply and spending, the more likely businesses will expand and the greater that expansion will be. ABCT does not imply that businessmen expand in response to inflation because they are too stupid to see that inflation is the cause. As shown in chapter 3, inflation creates real, but temporary, distortions in the economic data that give businessmen real incentives to expand. This is confirmed by real-life businessmen.[40]

ABCT does not imply that businessmen do not form their expectations rationally because the government does not manipulate the money supply to create a consistent pattern of expansions and contractions. For instance, the government does not create a contraction with the same amplitude once every five years. If this was the case, businessmen could exploit this pattern and incorporate it into their expectations. Recessions do not occur at an unchanging frequency; they occur in an erratic manner because of the erratic manner in which the government manipulates the money supply. Therefore, no businessman should be able to know what the government is going to do to the money supply tomorrow, next week, next year, or in the next decade. Uncertainty in both the duration and magnitude of the changes in the supply of money and credit is what helps to generate the cycle (or, at least, make a particular cycle more severe).

The business cycle does not stem from the errors and lack of information and knowledge of businessmen. It stems from the nature of the monetary and banking system that exists. It occurs due to the nature of fiat money and fractional-reserve banking. Fiat money gives the government the ability to easily manipulate the money supply. It gives the government the power to increase the money supply at a rapid rate, thus creating an expansion, and then decrease it or slow its increase, thus creating a contraction. In addition, as discussed in chapter 2, fractional reserves create the effects in the loan market that provide further incentives to businessmen to expand or contract their activities. The fractional-reserve nature of the banking system also makes possible potentially large and rapid swings in the money supply due to the creation and destruction of fiduciary media.

It is important to realize that one does not need both fiat money and fractional-reserve banking at the same time to create the business cycle. Both are sufficient by themselves to create the cycle. However, the two together are capable of creating much wider swings in the cycle, although fractional-reserve banking provides a much stronger influence in creating the cycle than does fiat money.

Under a system of fiat money and fractional-reserve banking, the actions of businessmen cannot be expected *not* to create the business cycle. This is the case because if the money supply is increased at a rapid rate, the incentives to expand are in place and it will only be a matter of time before businesses begin to expand. As I stated in the previous chapter, they may not expand if the supply of money and volume of spending increase for only a short period of time or at only a very low rate, but the longer and more rapid the increase, the higher the profits are that can be earned, the lower interest rates will be relative to the rate of profit, and thus the more likely it is that businesses will expand their activities. In other words, the incentives to expand their activities in response to rapid increases in the money supply exist whether businessmen know about and believe in ABCT or not, whether they can use the theory to their advantage or not, and whether they know how the money supply is changing and affecting the economy or not.[41]

This brings me to the actual role of expectations in the business cycle. As I have said, businessmen are not omniscient, and it is difficult for them to know exactly how an increase in the money supply will affect the demand for their products from year to year. However, as I discussed in chapter 3, when the increase is fairly slow and constant, businessmen can easily take it into account and it will not cause them to expand. They will simply adjust their prices and borrowing accordingly. Here, because the increase in money, spending, and credit is slow and steady, the rate of profit will not be continuously increased, businessmen's expectations will tend to accurately reflect the changes in these variables, and the actions they take based on these expectations will tend to be in line with what is actually occurring in the long run, so no cyclical expansion and contraction take place.

It is only when the increase in demand for their products, due to an increase in the money supply, is greater than expected that the incentive to expand will be present. It may be that businesses do not expand immediately when spending for their products is greater than expected. They may adjust their prices and make other appropriate adjustments initially to adapt to the changing conditions without expanding. However, if spending for their products repeatedly outstrips their expectations, and the rate of profit continuously remains high relative to interest rates, sooner or later businessmen will expand in response to these incentives. In essence, when businessmen *expect* to be able to profit from the increase in money and spending, they will expand their activities.[42]

One can do this without making systematic errors, while using all the information one has available, and while employing the best-known economic theory. In fact, using all available information and employing the best-known economic theory (which would include employing ABCT) can help one profit more from the cycle. So ABCT is consistent with so-called rational expectations (at least the legitimate aspect of "rational expectations"). However, forming one's expectations in a manner consistent with so-called rational expectations theory will not prevent the business cycle from occurring.

It is true that businessmen do make errors during the business cycle due to uncertainties associated with the size and duration of the expansion and due to the readily available supply of money and credit during the expansion, but these errors are not systematic and businessmen cannot, ultimately, be blamed for such errors or for the existence of the business cycle. Responsibility for the cycle, and the errors businessmen make in connection with it, must ultimately be placed on the institutions of fiat money and fractional-reserve banking and the economists and government officials who support such institutions. It is economists and government officials that have created the system within which businessmen must act. Businessmen are merely reacting to the incentives provided by a system that is fundamentally flawed.

The system is flawed because it is not based on freedom and freedom is a fundamental requirement of human life. Fiat money must be forcibly imposed on an economic system. In free competition with gold, fiat money would disappear. Further, fractional-reserve banking arises due to regulation of the banking system (i.e., violations of the rights of bank owners and their customers).[43] As a result, a system with fiat money and fractional-reserve banking is inconsistent with the freedom people need to produce and trade the wealth on which their lives depend. Moreover, because of the violations of freedom, such a system creates an environment in which periodic financial and economic disasters are inevitable.

In putting the ultimate blame on economists and government officials who support the current system, I am not denying that businessmen are responsible for the decisions they make and errors they commit. However, the system within which they act encourages and rewards errors. This must be recognized when evaluating their actions.

If anyone is making systematic errors, not using all available information, and not using the best economic theory, it is the government officials and economists who support the institutions of fiat money and fractional-reserve banking. They repeatedly commit the error of supporting a monetary and banking system based on these institutions despite the flaws that are inherent in the system and in spite of the fact that these flaws have been recognized by better economists since the nineteenth century. If contemporary economists and politicians acted in accordance with "rational expectations," when faced with the repeated episodes of boom and bust that such a system creates, they would learn from their mistakes and correct their errors. They would take the necessary actions to abandon the current system and replace it with its opposite, the only system that renders monetary-induced fluctuations virtually impossible: a 100-percent reserve gold-based monetary and banking system.[44]

A Better Understanding of Rationality

The arguments made in defense of ABCT so far in connection with so-called rational expectations are based on the definition of "rational expectations" as used by contemporary economists. However, this definition is not a very good one because it does not get to the most important characteristic of rationality. As a result, contemporary economists' concept of rationality is the source of much confusion in economics, including the source of much of the confusion regarding the validity of ABCT.

As I stated in chapter 1, a good definition must be based on the most fundamental, or essential, characteristic(s) of a concept. Aristotle was the first philosopher to recognize the importance of defining concepts based on their essential characteristics.[45] For example, Aristotle identified man's defining characteristic as his rational faculty. What Aristotle was referring to when he wrote of man's rational faculty was his reasoning mind.[46] Reason is the tool that identifies and integrates the material provided by man's senses.[47] It allows him to think at the conceptual level (i.e., in terms of concepts, principles, and ideas). It is the faculty that separates man from the lower animals.

Rationality enables one to do many things. For instance, one who possesses a rational faculty is capable of using reason, understanding economics, following a recipe, building a skyscraper, committing errors, discovering and correcting mistakes, applying one's knowledge to a particular problem, using concepts, using logic, understanding causes and effects, thinking and acting based on a consideration of the facts of reality, choosing to act rationally or irrationally, thinking in terms of principles, and much more. However, the essential characteristic of rationality is, as Aristotle identified, to use reason or, equivalently, to base one's thoughts and actions on the facts of reality and a logical analysis of those facts. These are the characteristics of rationality that make it possible for man to think in terms of principles, follow a recipe, understand causal relationships, et cetera. In contrast, to act on one's emotions, or on ideas not based on facts and logic, is to act contrary to reason and rationality; it is to act irrationally.

Acting rationally also makes it possible for one to use all available information, understand and use the best economic theory, and not commit systematic errors. However, these things are just effects of acting rationally; they are effects of going by facts and logic. They are not the essential characteristics of rationality. Therefore, to define rationality based on the use of all available information, the comprehension of the best economic theory, and the absence of systematic error—which is what contemporary economists do—is to take effects, or nonessential characteristics, of rationality and make these the essence of rationality. As one would expect, this leads to a great deal of confusion with regard to the application of rationality to economics.

For instance, as long as businessmen form their expectations using reason, their expectations are rational. In many cases, it can be rational to base one's expectations on past experience alone (if that is the only information one has available or is the only information that one believes to be relevant). Therefore, what economists call adaptive expectations can be rational.

A person can also make mistakes and still be rational. In addition, one can still be rational even if one does not understand the best economic theory (if one does not have the intellectual capacity or time to comprehend it). Likewise, one can still be rational even if one does not use all available information (if one does not have time to seek it out or if one thinks it is irrelevant). The focus of the concept "rationality" is on the process one employs to gain and use knowledge, not on the outcome of that process. Of course, a rational person will use his mind to his fullest capacity to understand and apply relevant ideas and information to his life and career. He will also take the necessary steps to correct any mistakes he might make and therefore tend to eliminate errors.

Some readers may think that differences between definitions are just semantic differences, that definitions are arbitrary statements of what a concept is, and that differences in definitions do not play a significant role in intellectual life or in economics. Such a belief is grossly mistaken. Definitions are not arbitrary. The definition of a concept helps to distinguish one concept from all other concepts and helps one to determine what concretes in reality to subsume under a particular concept. A definition can improve or undermine one's conceptual understanding of what something is. Good definitions help us achieve a clearer understanding of what something is; they make it easier to analyze the world at the conceptual level. Poor definitions hamper our ability to understand the world. The poor understanding of "rational expectations" and how they apply to the business cycle is just one example of the misunderstanding to which bad definitions lead. The misunderstandings to which the poor definitions of inflation have led and the sound understanding to which the good definition of inflation has led, which were discussed in chapter 1, provide another example.[48]

If definitions were truly arbitrary, one could literally define something to be anything one wanted. For instance, a horse could be defined as a doughnut-shaped flotation device. If such a method of definition was taken seriously, it would lead to confusion and false conclusions on a massive scale. Fortunately, those who claim that definitions are arbitrary usually do not act consistently on that belief. However, to be in a position in which we must rely on the inconsistencies of people is, indeed, to be in a very precarious position.

A proper definition of rationality takes the focus away from whether a person is making errors, using all available information, or understanding economic theory and places the focus on the process that one employs to attempt to gain and use knowledge. To put the focus on the absence of error and so forth is to associate omniscience with rationality. In essence, the claim is that if one makes errors, does not know about or use all available information, or does not understand or use economic ideas, one is not rational. It is this confusion that leads some economists to say that ABCT does not incorporate "rational expectations."

By putting the focus on the process of using reason, or acting based on facts and logic, one can eliminate this confusion and the inappropriate distinction between various types of expectations, such as adaptive expectations and "rational expectations." One can also understand that being rational does not necessitate the absence of error and so forth. Finally, one can say that it is perfectly rational for businessmen to attempt to make money from the fluctuations that inevitably result from a fiat-money, fractional-reserve monetary and banking system.

CONCLUSION

As one can see, none of the criticisms of ABCT are valid. ABCT is not too complex. The complexity of the theory is necessary because of the complex nature of the business cycle. ABCT also accurately describes the causal relationship between interest rates, inflation, and investment. The criticisms of ABCT in connection with interest rates are based on a lack of understanding of what causes interest rates to change, the way interest rates and inflation change throughout the cycle, and how interest rates and inflation affect investment.

Further, ABCT is perfectly consistent with rational expectations, as contemporary economists use that term, and it is also consistent with a proper understanding of rationality. ABCT does not assume businessmen are ignorant in order to explain the business cycle. However, one must always keep in mind that being rational does not imply omniscience. Businessmen cannot see the future and know exactly how long an expansion will last. As long as businessmen are acting based on facts and logic they are acting rationally, even if they do make errors. More fundamentally, businessmen do not create the economic system within which they act and therefore cannot escape the incentives that such a system creates. Namely, they cannot escape the incentives created by a fiat-money, fractional-reserve monetary and banking system. Such a system is a breeding ground for periodic economic disasters. Given this, the rational thing to do would be to get rid of this system and replace it with a stable system—a 100-percent reserve gold-based monetary and banking system—within which rapid and steady rates of economic progress can occur.[49]

Part II

PRACTICE

5

The Recession of the Early 1980s

Introduction

This and the next four chapters present historical evidence for the validity of Austrian business cycle theory (ABCT). I start with an analysis of the deep recession of the early 1980s.[1] This recession provides the best illustration in recent history of the causes of the business cycle. It does so for three reasons. First, it was a fairly severe recession. This means the factors causing the cycle exerted a strong influence on the economy. Second, the recession of the early 1980s is also a great recession to study because the episode was like an economic experiment. The Federal Reserve chairman at the time, Paul Volcker, made an explicit effort to reduce inflation in the late 1970s, and he actually did end up reducing the money supply growth. He even announced his intentions in advance. So we get to see, given that he did this, what effect it had on the economic system. This is probably as close to an economic experiment as one can get in an economy. This was a situation in which the money supply and prices were rising rapidly and then the increase in the money supply was abruptly reduced. The effects this had, as I will show, were dramatic.

Third, since the recession occurred in more recent history there are more data available with which to analyze the episode. There have been more severe downturns in US history that one could analyze, such as the Great Depression. I show in chapter 8 that the Great Depression, too, had its origins in the same factors that cause all contraction phases of the business cycle. However, data are not as readily available for the Great Depression, so one cannot see what happened during the Great Depression with the depth and accuracy as one can see in the recession of the early 1980s. In addition, there was no dramatic and abrupt change in policy by the Fed prior to the Great Depression (although there was a change in policy) and no explicit announcement of a policy change prior to the commencement of such a change. Further, I also show that other factors were at work during the Great Depression and while these factors are not a part of ABCT they are perfectly consistent with the theory. These factors turned what would have been an ordinary depression of the time into the Great Depression.

I initially hesitated including an analysis of the Great Depression in this book because so much has been written on the subject and there are a number of good discussions on the causes of the Great Depression. However, I decided since there are also a number of very bad discussions on the causes of the Great

Depression, and since I have a number of new insights to share, that one more discussion is needed. I make use of many of the good discussions on the Great Depression by integrating valid points from these discussions with my own insights. Where appropriate, I also address some of the invalid claims regarding the Great Depression.

The recession of 2008–9 was also more severe than the recession of the early 1980s. I show that while this recession has the same causes as other recessions (plus, in a similar fashion to the Great Depression, a few other causes that are perfectly consistent with ABCT), it is not as good a recession to illustrate the causes of the business cycle since there was no explicit statement by the Fed about its policy to reduce inflation prior to the commencement of that policy. Furthermore, the inflation prior to the 2008–9 recession was not as severe and prolonged as the inflation prior to the early 1980s recession. So the recession of the early 1980s is a better one to start out with in this part of the book.

I analyze the recession of 2008–9 as a part of chapter 6. In that chapter I analyze episodes of the business cycle that occurred during most of the latter half of the twentieth century up through the early part of the twenty-first century (skipping over the recession of the early 1980s). While the causal factors of the business cycle are not as prominent during these episodes as they are for the recession of the early 1980s, they still help solidify one's understanding of the business cycle.

After I analyze the most recent decades of US history, in chapter 7 I go back in time to analyze another episode that provides a great illustration of the causal factors of the business cycle: John Law's financial scam in eighteenth-century France, otherwise known as the Mississippi Bubble. This, like the early 1980s in America, was like an economic experiment. It is the only case in history that I know of in which an economist was able to test his theory by implementing it in practice. It provides a great integration of the causal factors of the business cycle across time and space. It shows that it does not matter where and when in history one focuses, the same causal factors are at work. Except for the lack of data availability from such an early period, I consider John Law's scam as good an illustration of the causal factors of the business cycle as the recession of the early 1980s. As a part of the discussion in chapter 7, I also look at the South Sea Bubble, which took place in Great Britain at about the same time as John Law's financial scam.

Finally, I end with a discussion of the earlier part of the twentieth century in America. This, along with the other episodes discussed, provides readers with ample evidence of the validity of ABCT. It gives readers a chance to see the similarities across a number of episodes and understand the general causes and effects of the cycle.

The episodes of the business cycle that I could include in this part of the book are many. I have deliberately chosen to focus on the episodes that best illustrate the causal factors at work either through their severity, their proximity in time, or their illustrative power across time and space. However, the same factors are at work in all episodes of the cycle. Each episode might have slightly different, additional factors at work, such as how the government responds to the recession or depression or which industry expands and contracts the most. These factors may create slight variations in how the cycle manifests itself, but in each case the same underlying factors are at work regardless of what areas of the economy the cycle affects the most or how the government responds to the recession or depression. Let us now take a look at those factors at work during the late 1970s and early 1980s.

THE EFFECTS OF THE CYCLE DURING THE LATE 1970S AND EARLY 1980S

In this section I present data that illustrate the effects of the cycle. I restrict myself mainly to showing data from the mid-1970s to the mid-1980s. However, where necessary I show more data. To see what happened to output in the economy I provide data on gross domestic product (GDP) and gross national revenue (GNR). I also provide a comparison of these variables to show why one is better than the other at measuring the *gross* output in the economy. In addition, I show data on industrial production. This helps show how the structure of production changed during this time period. I also present data on business failures and unemployment during the period. This gives one a more complete picture of what was happening during this period.

Output

The period from the mid-1970s to the mid-1980s was a tumultuous one relative to most of the post–World War II period in America. The most significant characteristic of this period was the major recession that occurred in the early 1980s. As one can see in exhibit 5.1, real GDP remained essentially flat from 1979 to 1982. However, it did decline significantly in 1982. It also declined slightly in 1980.

On either side of this recession, real GDP increased at a rapid pace. From 1975 to 1979, after having come out of a recession in 1974–75, real GDP increased at a 4.7 percent annual rate. From 1982 to 1985, real GDP increased at a 5.3 percent annual rate. These higher rates of economic progress can be compared to the slight increase that occurred during the recession of 1980–82.

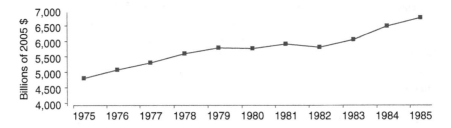

Exhibit 5.1   Real GDP, 1975–85.

Source: Federal Reserve Bank of St. Louis, FRED database, series ID GDPCA. Data obtained February 18, 2013.

Real GDP only increased a total of 0.3 percent during this period. The largest one-year decrease in real GDP during this recession occurred during 1982 and was 1.9 percent. Output as measured by GDP also declined in 1980 but by only 0.3 percent. In 1981, real GDP increased by 2.5 percent. GDP data show us that there were actually two recessions in two different years separated by a year of expansion. However, I think it is appropriate to identify the entire 1980–82 time period as one recession. We will see why below.

Real GDP is just one measure of output that can be used to characterize the period from the mid-1970s to the mid-1980s. Another, more comprehensive, measure of output can also be used to help understand the events during this period. This measure is real GNR. This measure of output provides a better estimate of total economic activity because it includes everything produced in the economy, not just a fraction of what is produced. It provides a clearer picture of what happened during this period.

GDP includes only expenditures on final goods and services in the economy, which include mainly only expenditures on consumers' goods. Such an approach fails to include spending for intermediate goods, which means a large chunk of productive expenditures is not included in GDP.[2] Intermediate goods are goods purchased by businesses to resell. Specifically, this means GDP fails to account for a huge amount of spending by businesses for inventory. The exclusion of most spending for inventory is due to the desire on the part of contemporary, mainstream economists to avoid the so-called double-counting error. This is the belief that the value of inventory used by businesses is already incorporated in the value of a good the consumer buys. For instance, the value of the raw beef, buns, lettuce, tomato, pickles, onions, and so forth that McDonald's buys to make a Big Mac is allegedly accounted for when the consumer buys the end product: the cooked burger. If we count the spending by McDonald's for all the ingredients *and* the spending for the Big Mac by the consumer, we are allegedly counting the spending for the ingredients twice: once when McDonald's purchases them and again when the consumer purchases the cooked burger.

Ironically, contemporary, mainstream economists commit an error because of their concern for avoiding the so-called double-counting error. When determining the *gross* spending in the economic system, one must count *all* the spending. It does not matter what is consumed during the course of production. The spending by producers at each stage of production counts just as much toward the total spending in the economy as the spending for goods by the end users. The spending by McDonald's for the raw ingredients is just as much a demand for goods, and thus spending, as the spending by the purchaser of the cooked Big Mac. By ignoring most of the spending by McDonald's, and all other businesses for their inventory, the GDP method of aggregate economic accounting fails to account for a huge portion of spending that actually takes place in the economy.

The GDP method of accounting only counts *net* expenditures for inventory by businesses, not gross. Net additions to inventory, its supporters claim, are the only inventory assets that businesses purchase whose value is not already accounted for in the purchase of the final product. So, for example, if McDonald's buys $1,000 worth of raw ingredients for Big Macs during a year and uses only $800 of ingredients in making Big Macs during that year, only $200 of this spending by McDonald's counts toward the gross spending in the economy (viz., GDP). This is the case because the value of $800 of raw ingredients is allegedly accounted for in the purchase of Big Macs. Hence, the claim is we should not count the value of the raw ingredients actually used to make Big Macs twice: once as raw ingredients and another time in the purchase of the Big Mac. The only raw ingredients purchased by McDonalds that should be accounted for separately as spending are the raw ingredients that are purchased during the year that did not get used to make Big Macs during the year (hence, they are not accounted for in the purchase of any Big Macs). Therefore, if the Big Macs that are produced by McDonald's are sold for, say, $1,100, gross spending in this example according to the GDP method of accounting is only $1,300 (which includes the $1,100 for Big Macs and $200 of net additions to inventory).

This creates a huge error in the measure of total spending in the economy. GDP is supposed to be a measure of *gross* spending (hence the name *gross* domestic product). However, it only includes *net* spending by businesses for inventory. The actual gross (i.e., total) spending in the example above is not $1,300 but the far larger value of $2,100 (which includes the gross expenditures for Big Macs of $1,100 and the *gross* expenditures of $1,000 for raw Big Mac ingredients by McDonald's).

Contemporary economists' concern about double counting in connection with gross spending is not necessary because no error is committed when inventory used up in production is counted as spending along with the spending for the products it helps to produce. Put another way, it is irrelevant that some assets are used up in production when measuring gross spending in the economy. The spending for assets used up in the course of production constitutes spending just as much as the spending for assets that are not used up and just as much as consumer spending. When one measures gross spending, one is supposed to measure all the spending because "gross" in this context means "total." One does not subtract out a large portion of the spending in the economy and call that the gross spending. If one subtracts out some types of spending, one is dealing with a value that is *net* of that spending.

This is a complex issue, so let me give one more example here to illustrate the error with mainstream, contemporary economic accounting. This method would be equivalent to a business calculating its sales revenue, subtracting off its costs, and calling that value the "gross" receipts of the business. Of course, the costs of a business are irrelevant and should be ignored when calculating the gross receipts of a business. The costs are only subtracted when the business calculates its profits or *net* receipts. The same is no less true for aggregate economic accounting. When one wants to know the net spending or net domestic product, that is the point at which one must subtract out the spending for those assets used up in the course of production.

An accurate measure of spending in the economy is one provided by the total amount of spending for goods and services in the economy or GNR. GNR consists of the total sales revenue of businesses plus total wage payments in the economy. This provides an accurate measure of total spending for the goods and services produced in the economy because whenever anyone buys a good or service in a modern economy, it virtually always shows up as revenue to a business or a wage to an individual. More importantly, this measure of spending includes *all* spending by businesses and thus does justice to the amount of *productive* spending (i.e., spending engaged in for the production and sale of goods and services) in the economy. When converted to real values, this measure better accounts for actual gross production in the economy (as compared to the highly netted account of production provided by real GDP).

There is much more I could say here to show why the contemporary method of aggregate economic accounting is seriously flawed and show what constitutes a good method that can be used to account for all spending in the economy. However, my primary purpose is not to explain a better method of accounting, it is to show how ABCT can be used to explain and understand the events that occurred in the 1970s and 1980s in the United States. Some discussion was needed on the contemporary method of aggregate economic accounting versus the better method that I have described here. This method will provide more insight into what occurred during this period.[3]

To give an idea of the difference between GDP and GNR, and thus enable one to see just how much spending in the economy GDP misses, here are nominal GDP and GNR data for 2010. I use 2010 data because this is the latest year for which I have GNR data. These data are not readily available and must be calculated based on data from different sources. I use gross *national* revenue instead of gross *domestic* revenue (GDR) due to data availability. As with GDP and gross national product, the differences between GDR and GNR should not be that great for the United States.

In 2010, GNR was $34,693 billion while GDP was only $14,499 billion.[4] The difference between the two is the productive expenditures by businesses that are unaccounted for by GDP. This means GDP fails to account for almost 60 percent of economic activity. This is why GDP does not provide a good basis to assess what is occurring in the economy.

In 2010, GDP accounted for 42 percent of all spending on goods and services in the economy. This is fairly high because productive spending declined much more than consumptive spending during the recession of 2008–9 and therefore GNR declined much more than GDP. By 2010, GNR had not yet recovered to its previous high but GDP had. The year 2007 provides a more typical comparison between GNR and GDP. In that year, GNR was $37,422 billion and GDP was $14,029 billion.[5] Here GDP represents only 37 percent of GNR. GDP generally only accounts for about 35 to 40 percent of all spending on goods and services in the economy. Approximately 90 percent of GDP is consumption spending (government spending, personal consumption spending, and spending on residential housing). No wonder contemporary economists, and the vast majority of people since they are just accepting the ideas of contemporary economists, believe that consumption spending is the largest form of spending in the economy. Nonetheless, this is not true. Consumptive spending is only about one-third of all spending for goods and services in the economy while productive spending accounts for about two-thirds. These have tended to be the proportions of consumptive and productive spending for goods and services in the economy since 1960. In chapter 8 on the Great Depression I calculate a value for GNR for 1919–39. Consumption tended to be much lower then: around 25 to 30 percent.

GNR can be converted to a real value, and thus a measure of the goods and services produced in the economy, in the same manner that GDP is converted to a real value: using a price index to cancel out the effects of changes in the money supply and spending on GNR. This isolates as best as possible the changes in GNR emanating only from the side of production. To convert GNR, I adjusted the consumption, production, and wage components of GNR using the consumer price index (CPI), producer price index (PPI), and a wage index I calculated using hourly wage data, respectively. I then added together these three adjusted components of real GNR to get total real GNR. Real GNR provides the best estimate of the entire physical supply of goods and services produced in a given year.[6]

Using real GNR to assess what is happening in the economy during the period in question provides us with a much better understanding of what occurred. Real GNR can be seen in exhibit 5.2 from 1975 to 1985. Real GNR tells a different story about the recession of the early 1980s. It shows that the recession was deeper than the recession shown by real GDP. Based on real GNR, output declined by about 4.8 percent from its peak in 1979 to its low point in 1982. The largest one-year decline in output was 2.8 percent in 1982. Also, while the recession occurred during the same years for GNR data, output declined for three straight years based on GNR data: 1980–82. Recall that output as measured by real GDP only declined for two of those years. The annual rates of economic progress pre- and post-recession based on GNR data were 5.5 percent from 1975 to 1979 and 2.9 percent from 1982 to 1985, respectively.

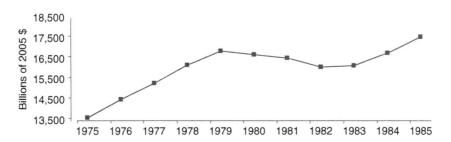

Exhibit 5.2   Real GNR, 1975–85.

Sources: A number of variables were used to calculate real GNR. Price data were obtained from the Federal Reserve Bank of St. Louis, FRED database, series IDs CPIAUCNS (CPI) and PPIACO (PPI); wage and employment data were obtained from the US Department of Labor, Bureau of Labor Statistics, historical hours, earnings, and employment data, Tables B-1 and B-2 at http://bls.gov/ces/tables.htm#ee; and gross business receipts were obtained from the US Census Bureau, *Statistical Abstract of the United States*, various editions, Washington, DC. Online data obtained January 24, 2012 (wage and employment data) and February 18, 2013 (price data). For more information related to GNR data, see the discussion in this chapter on GNR for 2007 and the references there.

Compared to real GDP, real GNR shows a much more severe recession. Over the course of the recession, output increased slightly based on real GDP but declined based on real GNR (a 0.3 percent increase vs. a 4.8 percent decline). The largest one-year decline was also greater based on real GNR (a 2.8 percent decline in 1982 vs. a 1.9 percent decline in 1982 for real GDP).

In addition, real GNR showed that the economy progressed at a 5.5 percent annual rate from 1975 to 1979, as compared to a 4.7 percent annual rate during the same period according to real GDP data. The annual rate of economic progress post-recession was lower according to real GNR: 2.9 percent from 1982 to 1985 versus 5.3 percent for the same time period based on real GDP. The much smaller rate of economic progress post-recession based on GNR was in part due to the slow recovery of this variable in 1983. In fact, one might include 1983 as a fourth year of the recession based on the very small increase in real GNR during that year of only 0.5 percent. The annual rate of economic progress post-recession based on GNR for 1983–85 is 4.2 percent. While still smaller than the comparable rate for GDP, it is much larger than the 1982–85 rate for GNR.

Based on GNR data, output dropped more over the course of the recession, the greatest one-year decline was larger, the recession lasted for three straight years, and one could even argue that the recession lasted an extra year (1983). Overall, the recession was worse based on GNR data. We will see that this tends to be the case. Furthermore, this is consistent with ABCT. As stated in chapter 3, ABCT claims that industries farther removed from final consumption should fluctuate more in response to changes in the rate of interest that occur during the business cycle. This occurs because the discounting effect makes investments farther removed from final consumption relatively more profitable relative to investments less remote from final consumption when interest rates decrease. Likewise, more remote investments become less profitable relative to less remote investments when interest rates rise. Since real GDP leaves out most producers' goods and therefore consists mainly of consumers' goods, one would expect real GNR to decline more during recessions because it accounts for all goods produced in the economy and thus contains a greater portion of producers' goods. One would also expect real GNR to rise more during expansions. With regard to the expansions, the data provide mixed support for ABCT, but we will see with industrial production data and other episodes of the cycle that the data do, in general, support ABCT.

Business Failures and Unemployment

Looking at other data can help one see the severity of the recession of the early 1980s. The business failure rate is shown in exhibit 5.3. A business failure occurs when a firm ceases to exist and some unpaid debt remains. Exhibit 5.3 shows the business failures per 10,000 enterprises falling after the recession of the mid-1970s and then rising dramatically as the economy enters the recession of the early 1980s. The failure rate in 1975 was the peak rate during the recession of the mid-1970s. Notice that the failure rate continued to climb after output

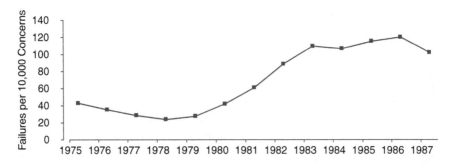

Exhibit 5.3   Business failure rate, 1975–87.

Source: US Census Bureau, *Statistical Abstract of the United States*, various editions, Washington, DC.

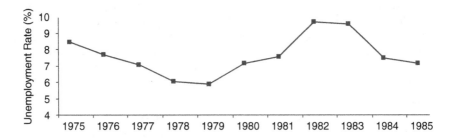

Exhibit 5.4   Unemployment rate, 1975–85.

Source: Federal Reserve Bank of St. Louis, FRED database, series ID UNRATE. Data obtained February 18, 2013.

began to recover in the early 1980s recession. The failure rate peaked in 1986 at a value almost three times greater than the maximum rate during the recession of the mid-1970s.[7] This demonstrates the severity of the early 1980s recession. The high failure rate also indicates that a greater number of firms than usual were getting into financial trouble. This typically occurs during recessions and depressions.

Another variable that helps to demonstrate the severity of the early 1980s recession is the unemployment rate. It is shown in exhibit 5.4. It shows the unemployment rate decreasing after the recession of the mid-1970s, increasing from 1980 to 1982, declining slightly in 1983 but still remaining high, and then finally declining significantly as the economy moved more decisively out of the recession in 1984. The unemployment rate actually continued to decline until the recession of the early 1990s (not shown in exhibit 5.4). These data confirm the length and severity of the recession as indicated by real GNR.

The unemployment rate in 1975 was the peak rate during the mid-1970s recession. It reached 8.5 percent during that recession, while in the early 1980s recession it peaked at 9.7 percent. This also confirms the severity of the early 1980s recession.

Industrial Production

Industrial production indices are shown in exhibits 5.5 and 5.6. Industrial production indices encompass manufacturing, mining, and gas and electric utilities.[8] The indices estimate production in these areas of the economy. Six industrial production indices are shown: consumers' goods, intermediate goods, materials, durable manufactured goods, nondurable manufactured goods, and total industrial production. Exhibit 5.5 shows data for consumers' goods, intermediate goods, and materials from 1975 to 1985. These indices represent measures of production at different stages of production. Production in these indices moves from materials to intermediate goods to consumers' goods. The idea is that materials are used to produce intermediate goods and intermediate goods are used to produce consumers' goods. They represent stages of production that move closer to final consumption.

Industrial production for consumers' goods peaked in 1978, hit a trough in 1980, and remained low through 1982, although it increased slightly in 1981. The intermediate goods and materials indices show peaks in 1979, troughs in 1982, and also rose in 1981. All three of the indices show industrial production hitting a trough in 1975 due to the recession in the mid-1970s. The recession in 1975 cannot be seen from the data presented. It will be shown and discussed in the next chapter.

The consumers' goods index increased at a 5.8 percent annual rate from 1975 to 1978 and declined at a 1.2 percent annual rate from 1978 to 1982. From 1975 to 1979, the intermediate goods index increased at a 6.1 percent average annual rate. It then decreased at a 2.2 percent annual rate from 1979 to 1982. The materials index increased at a 5.8 percent annual rate from 1975 to 1979 and then declined at a 3.7 percent annual rate from 1979 to 1982. Coming out of the recession, the consumers' goods index increased at a 3.1 percent annual

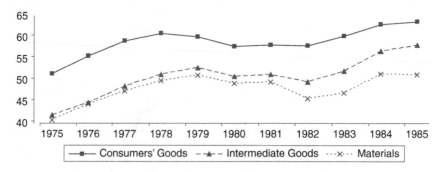

Exhibit 5.5   Industrial production (consumers' goods, intermediate goods, and materials), 1975–85.

Sources: Consumers' goods and materials industrial production data were obtained from the Federal Reserve Bank of St. Louis, FRED database, series IDs IPCONGD and IPMAT, respectively. Intermediate goods industrial production data were obtained from the *Economic Report of the President* (Washington, DC: US Government Printing Office, 2013), p. 385, Table B-52. Intermediate goods industrial production data are now referred to as non-industrial supplies in the *Economic Report*. Online data obtained February 18, 2013.

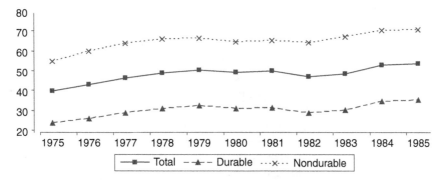

Exhibit 5.6 Industrial production (total, durable manufactured goods, and nondurable manufactured goods), 1975–85.

Sources: Total industrial production data were obtained from the Federal Reserve Bank of St. Louis, FRED database, series ID INDPRO. Durable and nondurable data were obtained from the Federal Reserve Bank of St. Louis, FRED database, series IDs IPDMAN and IPNMAN, respectively. Data obtained February 18, 2013.

rate from 1982 to 1985, the intermediate goods index increased at a 5.5 percent annual rate, and the materials index increased at a 3.9 percent annual rate. There was a slight drop in the materials index in 1985 of 0.2 percent. If we look at the annual rate of increase for the materials index in 1982–84, it was 6 percent. The largest one-year drops for the consumers' and intermediate goods indices occurred in 1980 and were 3.8 and 4 percent, respectively. The largest one-year drop for the materials index was 7.7 percent and occurred in 1982.

The consumers' goods, intermediate goods, and materials industrial production indices show that the recession was more severe in areas of the economy in which the intermediate goods and materials indices measure production. This is consistent with ABCT, since ABCT says that industries farther removed from final consumption will contract more during the recession. The three indices also show that the industries farther removed from final consumption tended to expand more during the expansions prior to and after the recession. This also confirms the validity of ABCT.

Industrial production indices for manufacturing and total industrial production are shown in exhibit 5.6. Indices are shown for durable manufactured goods, nondurable manufactured goods, and total industrial production (this latter includes all areas of the economy that are covered by the industrial production index). These indices indicate a recession from 1980 to 1982. The durable and nondurable goods indices increased from 1975 to 1979 at 8 and 5 percent annual rates, respectively, while the total industrial production index increased at a 6 percent annual rate during this same time period. The indices decreased at 4, 1.2, and 2.2 percent annual rates during the recession, respectively. They all show a small increase in the middle of the recession in 1981. From 1982 to 1985, the durable goods index increased at a 7 percent annual rate and the nondurable goods index increased at a 3.3 percent annual rate. The total industrial production index increased at a 4.2 percent annual rate during the same period.

The durable and nondurable manufactured goods industrial production indices provide more evidence in support of the predictions regarding changes in the structure of production made by ABCT. Durable goods are those goods that have a useful life much longer than nondurable goods. Durable and nondurable goods industrial production indices do not divide goods up by stages of production, as do the consumers' goods, intermediate goods, and materials indices. However, since it takes longer to consume durable goods than nondurable goods (think of how much longer it takes to completely consume an automobile vs. food), one would expect durable goods to be farther from final consumption (in this case, from being completely consumed) when they are produced and thus, based on ABCT, one would expect the production of durable goods to fluctuate more during the cycle than nondurable goods. This is exactly what occurs.

Conclusion to the Effects of the Cycle during the Late 1970s and Early 1980s

Based on output, business failure, unemployment, and industrial production data, it can be concluded that the recession of the early 1980s took place from 1980 to 1982. Data show that 1982 was the most severe year, while 1981 was less severe and may have even shown an expansion in output. They show that 1983 was a slow recovery to a flat year in terms of the change in output but that it should not be categorized as a part of the recession. It is more accurate to describe 1983 as a transition year from the recession to recovery. Business failure data best demonstrate the severity of the recession because they show a greater number of businesses failing for a while after the recession was over.

The output and industrial production data provide evidence of the changes in the structure of production that ABCT predicts. This evidence is seen in the real GDP versus real GNR data. Since GDP comprises mostly consumers' goods it is safe to say that it has far more goods closer to final consumption than GNR, which contains a much greater proportion of producers' goods. Because of this, one would expect to see real GNR expand and contract more than real GDP, and one does tend to see this. The durable and nondurable goods industrial production indices provide more definitive evidence of the changes in the structure of production that ABCT predicts. The durable goods index expands and contracts more than the nondurable goods index.

The evidence from the consumers' goods, intermediate goods, and materials industrial production indices also tends to support ABCT. A comparison of the consumers' goods index with both the intermediate goods and materials indices shows that the production of goods closer to final consumption expands and contracts less than the production of goods farther from final consumption over each phase of the cycle (at least for the total change in the variables during each phase). A comparison of the intermediate goods index to the materials index also tends to support ABCT.

It is not clear which set of indices better represents the distinction between goods closer to versus farther from final consumption: the durable/nondurable goods indices or the consumers' goods/intermediate goods/materials indices.

While the latter indices divide goods up based on which stage of production they are in, it is possible to have goods in one particular stage that are different amounts of time from final consumption. It depends on how much time passes by during the stages of production that are necessary to produce the goods and how long it takes to consume the goods. For instance, if it takes five stages of production to produce two different types of consumers' goods but one consumers' good is consumed over a period of ten years (a durable good, such as an automobile) while the other is consumed in one day (a nondurable good, such as a food item), assuming all the stages of production in both processes require the same length of time, the good that takes longer to consume will be farther from final consumption even if both are in the same stage of their respective productive processes.

As an alternative way to look at it, there could be significant overlap with the three indices (consumers/intermediate/materials) in terms of how far the goods produced in the various stages are from final consumption since, even though the goods are in different stages, the amount of time for the various goods in the different stages to be produced and ultimately consumed might be radically different. For instance, a good in the intermediate stage might be closer to final consumption than a good in the consumers' goods stage if the total time to produce and consume the latter is more than the former. This would tend to not be the case with the durable/nondurable distinction.

Moreover, durable goods (such as automobiles and home appliances) are often purchased with debt financing over significant periods of time. This can make the interest cost incurred when purchasing a product significant relative to the total cost of the product and make the production of the product sensitive to changes in interest rates. The latter occurs because as the interest cost becomes more significant, the total cost of purchasing the product is affected more by changes in interest rates. Both the amount of debt financing and the duration of the loan can affect the sensitivity of the production of a product to interest rates.

Based on the above discussion, one can say the durable and nondurable goods indices are better indicators of what is happening to the structure of production because there will tend to be less overlap between them than there is with the consumers' goods, intermediate goods, and materials indices. The durable/nondurable goods indices provide evidence that is more relevant to an assessment of the validity of ABCT. The results show that these indices more consistently support the theory than do the consumers/intermediate/materials indices.

Business failure data show that more businesses are getting into financial trouble during the recession. While one cannot say from the data presented whether they are taking on more debt in absolute terms, their debts must be rising relative to their ability to pay. Otherwise, more of them would not be failing. Taking on exorbitant debts is also consistent with ABCT, as is the failure of a greater number of businesses during the contraction.

Although some of the data do not always support ABCT, the data do tend to support ABCT overall. I am surprised the data support ABCT to such a significant extent, given the nature of economic data. As I stated in the introduction to this volume, economic data are hard to collect. That is why they are based on samples and not complete sets of data. Collecting economic data is much more difficult than collecting data in a laboratory experiment. As a result, economic data are much less accurate. There is also the problem of accounting for changes in quality in price indices and industrial production indices. Given the difficulties with economic data, the results are very good.

THE CAUSES OF THE CYCLE DURING THE LATE 1970S AND EARLY 1980S

Until now I have been showing only the effects of the business cycle. I have not shown the causal factors at work. As I discussed in chapter 3, from an economic standpoint, changes in the money supply are the fundamental causal factor. However, there are proximate causes also. These are interest rates and the rate of profit. I discuss all of these below.

Profitability and Interest Rates

Exhibit 5.7 shows the rate of profit and the interest rate. The rate of profit used is the return on equity for corporations (before taxes). I also calculated values for the return on assets to estimate the rate of profit. The return on assets shows a similar trend as the return on equity, although I do not show the return on assets data in any of the exhibits in this chapter. I decided to use the return on equity because it better captures what the owners of businesses are earning on their investments. This value better represents the rate of profit that provides individuals an incentive to open businesses.

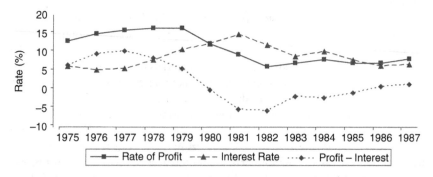

Exhibit 5.7   Rate of profit and interest rate (return on equity and commercial paper rate), 1975–87.

Sources: Active corporation net income and net worth obtained from the US Census Bureau, *Statistical Abstract of the United States*, various editions, Washington, DC. Net worth for 1976 and 1977 used to calculate the rate of profit (return on equity) were not available and were calculated through interpolation. Six-month commercial paper rate obtained from the *Economic Report of the President*, various editions, Washington, DC.

I have opted to use only rate of return data for corporations because data for partnerships are not complete for the period being analyzed. In addition, asset and net worth data for sole proprietorships are not available. While the rate of return for corporations is probably below the average rate of return in the economy, the data for corporations should still provide a fairly accurate reflection of the returns being earned. Corporations represent most of the business activity that takes place in the economy (over 80 percent in terms of business receipts and about 60 percent in terms of profits). Furthermore, for the periods when rates of return can be calculated for partnerships, if the data for partnerships and corporations are combined, they produce rates of return that are similar to corporations alone and, more importantly for my purposes here, similar trends in the rate of return over time.

The interest rate data are short-term interest rate data. The interest rate is the six-month commercial paper rate. I do not include long-term interest rate data; however, long-term interest rates tend to follow the same trend, although short-term interest rates are more volatile. Short-term rates are better to use because they tend to fluctuate more with the business cycle. They are more directly influenced by changes in the money supply, since the Fed targets short-term interest rates through its manipulation of the supply of bank reserves.

The rate of profit, interest rate, and the difference between the two behave as one would expect based on ABCT. The rate of profit starts out rising from a local minimum during the mid-1970s recession. The rising rate of profit provided businesses an incentive to expand. Starting in 1980, the rate of profit begins to fall precipitously. It falls through 1982. After 1982 the general trend of the rate of profit is upward. The falling rate of profit moving into the recession provided an incentive for businesses to contract their businesses. Coming out of the recession of the early 1980s the rising rate of profit, once again, provides an incentive for businesses to expand.

The interest rate does just the opposite. It falls coming out of the recession of the mid-1970s, rises dramatically prior to and during the early parts of the recession, and then begins to fall again during the latter part of the recession and after the recession. This is typical of interest rates. They are driven by changes in the supply of bank reserves. The changes in the money supply caused by the Fed's manipulation of bank reserves will be discussed below. The changing interest rates provide an additional incentive for businesses to expand during the expansion phase of the cycle and contract during the recession.

One can also see the changes in the rate of profit relative to the short-term interest rate in exhibit 5.7. This difference rose coming out of the recession of the mid-1970s. It also rose during the early part of the expansion in the late 1970s and began to decline during the latter part of this expansion and through the recession. In fact, this difference became negative during the recession. While this difference is not always negative during recessions, as I show in chapters 6, 8, and 9, it does tend to decline before and/or during recessions and depressions. After the recession, the general trend of the difference between the rate of profit and interest rate was up. This difference, of course, provides the same kind of incentive for businesses during each phase of the cycle as the rate of profit. That is, when the difference is high there is a stronger incentive for businesses to expand and when it is low there is a stronger incentive for businesses to contract.

The Money Supply and the Velocity of Money

While changes in profitability and interest rates are proximate causes of the business cycle, they are not the ultimate economic cause of the cycle. This role belongs to money. As I have said, it is changes in the money supply that bring about changes in spending, revenue, prices, profitability, interest rates, and production.

The time leading up to the recession of the early 1980s was one of increasing inflation. This can be seen in exhibit 5.8. In this exhibit I show changes in the money supply and prices. The exhibit shows the average annual rate of change for these variables over five consecutive, five-year periods, starting in 1960 and ending in 1985.

I use the M1 measure of the money supply plus US government, foreign official institution, and foreign commercial bank checking-account balances in my analysis. This was the best measure of the money supply during the time period under investigation. Today, as I stated in chapter 1, M1 is not a good measure of the money supply. There have been many changes in the types of bank accounts that now constitute money and M1 does not include them all. For instance, money market mutual funds (MMMFs) are now a component of the money supply. These accounts have check-writing capabilities on them but are not included in M1. MMMFs emerged in the mid-1970s but were not used very much as a form of money. As check writing on these accounts became more widespread, they have come to embody money to a greater extent. By the mid-1990s, these accounts began to constitute money to such an extent that they must be included in the measure of the money supply starting in that time period. During the mid-1970s to mid-1980s, their use as money was so limited that they need not be included.[9]

Five-year period	Rate of change of the money supply	Rate of change of prices
1960–65	3.5%	1.4%
1965–70	5.2	3.6
1970–75	5.8	8.0
1975–80	7.3	8.8
1980–85	8.1	4.0

Exhibit 5.8 Average annual rate of change of the money supply and prices during specified five-year periods, 1960–85.

Sources: Money supply data obtained from the Federal Reserve Bank of St. Louis, FRED database, series IDs M1NS, USGDCB, DDDFOINS, and DDDFCBNS for M1, US government, foreign official institution, and foreign commercial bank deposits, respectively. Data obtained February 18, 2013. For price data, see exhibit 5.2.

Exhibit 5.8 shows the money supply increasing at an accelerating rate from 1960 to 1985 (and the acceleration even started taking place in the latter 1950s, which we will see in chapter 9). The money supply increased through the late 1970s in this manner with only minor interruptions. This essentially continuous acceleration of the money supply caused prices to rise in a similar manner from 1960 to 1980. One can see prices rising in a continuously accelerating manner in exhibit 5.8 through 1980.

The measure of prices that I use is a combination of the CPI, PPI, and wages. I used these price indices in combination because it gives a comprehensive estimate of how the prices of all goods and services produced in the economy are changing. These price indices provide estimates of the price level for each of the three major components of GNR (i.e., spending on consumers' goods, spending on producers' goods, and spending on labor). Each component in my combined price index is weighted by its relative contribution to GNR.

As a part of the accelerating inflation, notice that during the first ten years of the time period shown in exhibit 5.8, 1960–70, the money supply was increasing at a faster rate than prices. However, by the second ten years, 1970–80, prices were rising at a faster rate than the money supply. This is a reflection of the fact that inflation was accelerating over a significant period of time. As the inflation increased and people came to expect it to increase further, they raised prices to a greater extent until the price increases surpassed the rate of inflation.

Inflation, in its earlier stages, appears in an economy in the form of greater spending for goods and services, greater revenues and profits for businesses, and lower interest rates (this latter due to the fractional-reserve nature of the banking system). These earlier effects of inflation tend to stimulate production and keep increases in the prices of goods, services, and commodities relatively low (compared to inflation). It is only after a prolonged period of inflation, when individuals have grown used to the rapidly rising spending, that prices and interest rates begin to rise rapidly. This, along with rising costs, tends to put downward pressure on production in the economy. This is why inflation must accelerate in order to continuously stimulate production. If inflation increases and then is merely maintained at that higher rate, costs rise, individuals become used to the inflation and make the appropriate adjustments, and the stimulating effects of inflation disappear.

The accelerating inflation is also seen in the velocity of circulation of money presented in exhibit 5.9. This exhibit presents velocity data from 1960 through 1986. The velocity in exhibit 5.9 is calculated using GNR, not GDP. This provides a better estimate of the number of times money was spent and re-spent each year (to buy goods and services) because, as I have shown, GNR is a more accurate measure of gross spending on goods and services in the economy. In this exhibit, one sees velocity increasing with no major interruptions up through the recession of the early 1980s. Why did velocity increase continuously for so long?

Accelerating inflation causes people to hold on to smaller money balances in relation to their purchases because of the ways in which accelerating inflation makes it easier to obtain money when it is needed. As I discussed in chapter 2, it

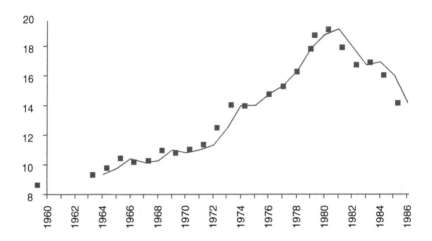

Exhibit 5.9   Velocity of money using the money supply described in exhibit 5.8 and GNR, 1960–86.

Note: No GNR data are available for 1961–63.

Sources: For money supply data, see exhibit 5.8. For GNR data, see exhibit 5.2.

does this by keeping interest rates down, especially relative to the rate of profit, and thus makes it easier to obtain loans. At the same time, it increases spending and revenues so that funds are more easily obtained by selling goods one has in inventory. Further, accelerating inflation also causes a "flight to real values."[10] As the currency begins to depreciate at a more rapid pace, and this becomes expected, people begin to decrease their money balances to hold on to goods that appreciate in terms of money. The increase in velocity exacerbates the increase in revenues, spending, profits, and prices that inflation causes.

Once the inflation slowed in the late 1970s, the dollar became more valuable (especially relative to expectations). This type of change tends to increase the demand for money. Also, slowing inflation causes revenues and profits to fall (again, especially relative to expectations), which leads to a scramble to build up money balances to prepare for the tougher-than-expected times ahead. Both of these effects manifest themselves in a fall in the velocity of circulation, which started in the early 1980s.

The slowing of inflation is not seen in exhibit 5.8. Based on that exhibit, it appears as if inflation continued to accelerate without interruption through 1985, the end of the data presented in that exhibit. However, a major interruption in inflation did occur starting in 1978 and lasting through 1981. This interruption can be seen in exhibit 5.10. This exhibit shows in more detail what the money supply was doing from 1974 until 1985. One can see that the money supply increased in an accelerating manner in 1976 and 1977. Then for four years, 1978–81, the increase in the money supply decelerated. Finally, from 1982 to 1985, the changes in the money supply became more erratic, with greater swings, but generally tended to show an increase.

By the end of the 1970s, people in America were expecting inflation to go on increasing; they were expecting a Latin American style inflation.[11] At this time, as I stated in the introduction to this chapter, the chairman of the Federal

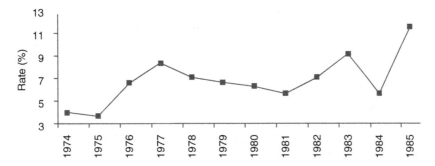

Exhibit 5.10   Rate of change of the money supply, 1974–85.
Source: See exhibit 5.8.

Reserve, Paul Volcker, made an explicit effort to reduce the rapid rise in prices that was occurring. To do this, the Fed slowed the rate of inflation by targeting the amount of nonborrowed bank reserves (reserves held by banks that are not borrowed from the Fed at the discount rate). This target allowed for greater control of the money supply relative to the Fed's typical target of the 1970s: the federal-funds rate.[12] Money supply growth started to decline and interest rates started to rise even before Paul Volcker's effort to reduce inflation. However, his effort to reduce inflation went far beyond these changes, as witnessed by even slower money supply growth and higher interest rates during the first few years of his time as chairman of the Federal Reserve.

The intentions of the Fed under Volcker were announced to the world before it started engaging in such a policy.[13] So the world got to see the effects of this intentional, abrupt change in policy. That is why I say this recession is like an experiment. Given that there was an accelerating trend in money supply growth, the world was able to witness the effects of a sudden and sustained deceleration in the rate of increase in the money supply. Those effects included, most significantly, the recession of the early 1980s.

In 1978–81, the money supply increased at only 7.4, 6.9, 6.6, and 6 percent, respectively, after having peaked after the recession of the mid-1970s at a rate of increase of 8.6 percent in 1977. Further, one must keep in mind that this significant deceleration took place in the broader context of a more or less continuously accelerating inflation since the latter 1950s. This gave a significant amount of time for an inflationary psychology to build up in the economy, where people began to expect greater inflation. When this inflation did not materialize, the result was a severe recession.

The fact inflation was accelerating more or less continuously from the latter 1950s is why I said previously that the rapid price increases during the late 1970s were characteristic of price increases late in an inflation. Given this long period of accelerating inflation, people had time to adjust to the rapid rate of increase in the supply of money and began to raise prices at greater rates. It is also likely that interest rates began to rise during the latter 1970s in part due to the rapid inflation of the money supply and consequent increase in spending. People came to expect the rise in spending and raised interest rates accordingly.

Once the recession in the early 1980s started, it did not take the Fed very long to abandon its goal of decreasing the rate of inflation. This is seen in exhibit 5.10. There one sees the rate of inflation increasing to 7.4 percent in 1982 and 9.4 percent in 1983. While the rate of inflation slowed temporarily in 1984, achieving only a 6 percent increase in the money supply during that year, it rose quickly in 1985 to 11.8 percent. After its slowing of inflation, the Fed created an overall higher inflation trend with its policies. The result can be seen in exhibit 5.8, which shows the five-year average annual increase in the money supply from 1980 to 1985 rising relative to the previous five-year period (8.1 vs. 7.3 percent) even though inflation was still being intentionally slowed at the beginning of the 1980–85 time period. In essence, the Fed used the recession as an inflationary refueling period. It justified creating much greater rates of inflation based on the fact that the country was experiencing a severe recession.

One claim made about the slowing of inflation by the Fed in the late 1970s, based on the so-called rational expectations argument, is that it should not have caused a recession because the Fed had announced in advance that it would be slowing the rate of inflation. The implication is that people should have taken this information into account and used it to adjust their plans so that a recession would not have occurred. The fact that a recession did occur has led some commentators to claim that people either do not have "rational expectations" or the Fed's statement about its commitment to reduce inflation was not credible. These conclusions, however, reveal a lack of understanding of the process of inflation.

The business cycle theory expounded in this book can shed light on this issue. Given that inflation had been building up in the US economy for over 20 years and businesses had adjusted their investments to such an environment, according to ABCT, it was inevitable that a recession occurred regardless of whether the Fed's intentions to reduce inflation were announced or whether they were perceived as credible. Once the inflation had occurred and gone on accelerating for a significant period of time, the mal-investments were already made and their profitability depended on the uninterrupted continuation of an accelerating inflation. When the accelerating inflation was interrupted in the late 1970s and early 1980s, the recession had to occur precisely because individuals had already taken actions based on the existence and expected continuation of the inflation. As we know from ABCT, recessions occur due to the buildup of mal-investment in the prior inflationary expansion.

As stated above, and as can be seen in exhibit 5.10, Fed monetary policy increased the rate of inflation toward the end of, and after, the recession of the early 1980s. One might be puzzled why such large increases in the money supply did not stimulate large increases in velocity and real output (i.e., another inflationary expansion). The reason is that the large increases in the money supply during this period took place within the context of a *deflationary* psychology caused by the slowing of inflation in the late 1970s and early 1980s. So the large increases in the money supply after the recession served only to offset a velocity that was already decreasing and did not create another expansion.

The slowing of inflation starting in the late 1970s was significant enough not only to cause velocity to eventually fall but also to decrease the rate of price increase from 1980 to 1985, as witnessed in exhibit 5.8 in the fact that the five-year average annual increase in prices during that period fell to 4 percent (from 8.8 percent in the previous five-year period). This decrease in the rate of increase of prices occurred despite the fact that the five-year average annual increase in the money supply continued to rise during the 1980–85 period. This highlights the fact that once a certain level of inflation occurs for long enough to become expected and the effects of that inflation set in (in this case, the effects being reduced profits and higher interest rates), it can take a while for expectations to change and for people to change their actions.

One might think that engaging in a policy to increase the rate of inflation during a deep recession is the appropriate thing for the Fed to do in order to prevent the recession from becoming deeper and more protracted. However, one must also look at the long-term perspective to determine if this is the appropriate thing to do. While it might be true that the Fed was able to decrease the severity of the recession that the American economy was in at the time, the Fed was also providing the reserves to fuel inflationary expansions in the future. These reserves generate more inflationary expansions because they can be used by banks to make more loans and, through the fractional-reserve checking process, increase the money supply at rapid rates. Using recessions as inflationary refueling periods simply delays the recession that an economy will have to experience once the inflation ultimately ends. The end can come sooner, by the Fed choosing to deliberately slow inflation, or later, when inflation turns into hyperinflation and leads to the breakdown of the monetary system.

Also, by using a recession as an inflationary refueling period—as a rationalization for more inflation—it makes the recessions the economy will experience in the future that much deeper, since much more mal-investment will become entrenched in the economy. From this perspective, it would have been better if the Fed simply engaged in policies to maintain a low rate of inflation and let the economy adjust on its own, so that the recession could have ended without creating the need for more and deeper recessions in the future.

It is not appropriate, both economically and morally, for the Fed to engage in policies that lead to more inflation in the midst of a recession. Economically, as I have said, the Fed merely fosters more—and more severe—recessions and depressions in the future through an inflationary policy, whether in the midst of a recession or not. One must remember that if an economy is experiencing a recession, it is prior inflation—created directly and indirectly by the government—that caused the recession. One does not cure the current bad state of the economy by offering cures that will only temporarily alleviate the negative symptoms and lead to the recurrence of the same problem—and more severe forms of the same problem—in the future. This "cure" is similar to an alcoholic choosing to fall off the wagon to eliminate the withdrawal symptoms he experiences when he tries to stop drinking. The alcoholic must suffer the pain of withdrawal symptoms in order to reach a state of better health. The withdrawal symptoms are a sign of a state of poor health the alcoholic has created for himself through his excessive drinking.

A recession is equivalent to the withdrawal symptoms of the alcoholic. The government has put the economy in a state of bad economic health through its inflationary policies. To reach a state of better economic health the economy must first suffer the pain of withdrawal symptoms. If it does this, higher rates of economic progress and greater prosperity will be the result. If it does not, and indulges in more of the exact same thing that put the economy in a state of poor health to begin with, like the alcoholic who starts to drink again, its condition will grow worse.

What the government must do to solve the problem of the recession is to completely abstain from the activity that put the economy in such a state. Further, it must refrain from intervening in other ways in the economy, which will only cause problems that will add to the recession it created. For instance, it must not provide subsidies or payments of any kind to businesses that are in financial trouble. This will only prevent adjustments from taking place that will correct the distortions created by the government's inflationary policy. Many businesses come into existence and/or expand because of the inflation. In one of the more recent expansions during the latter part of the 1990s, which I discuss in more detail in chapter 6, the dot-com industry and computer technology industries in general provided a brilliant illustration of this overexpansion.[14] Investments in businesses and the expansion of businesses due solely to inflation represent mal-investment. The recession is the process of explicitly recognizing and correcting the bad investments that were made. If the government subsidizes businesses that were created or expanded due to mal-investment, it prevents the economy from adjusting so that it can produce goods that people actually want to buy, not goods that it appeared people wanted to buy due to the distorting effects of inflation or goods that people only temporarily wanted to buy (perhaps due to overconsumption) because of the inflation.

The government must also not establish or expand any welfare programs, including so-called unemployment insurance programs. This will take away the incentive of workers who lose jobs in the transient areas of the economy created by the inflation to find new jobs in areas of the economy that are more permanent. Further, it will make it harder for businesses that are not in existence merely due to the existence of inflation to hire workers to the extent that the businesses are taxed to pay for welfare for the unemployed or to the extent they have to pay higher wages to get workers to give up their unemployment payments and take a job. (Why work when you can get paid not to!)

Also, welfare for the unemployed creates an atmosphere of dependency. It makes it so workers do not have to gain or improve their skills to earn an income. In fact, many workers will lose skills that they could have used to earn an income the more time they spend living on welfare for the unemployed. Further, many people will become psychologically dependent on welfare. Welfare can make people believe that they are unable to support themselves. Even worse, the morality of altruism that is used to justify welfare can lead people to believe that others have a duty to take care of them. Welfare and the morality that underlies it do not lead to the habits of thought and action required for individuals to support themselves.

The key to eliminating unemployment is eliminating the government controls that prevent or make it harder for wages to adjust appropriately and for workers to find jobs by offering to work for lower wages. Note that lower monetary wages do not necessarily mean lower real wages. To the extent that more people are working, that means more goods will be produced and available to purchase and prices will be lower. Further, fewer unemployed workers mean less taxes need to be taken from employers to support the unemployed. This will make it possible for businesses to hire more workers, pay higher wages, experience lower costs, and produce more goods. All this implies a higher standard of living.

It is government violations of individual rights that create recessions and depressions; specifically, it is government regulation of the banking and monetary system that leads to recessions and depressions. More government regulation will not solve the problem that regulation itself has created. Violations of individual rights, in general, are economically destructive. The recessions and depressions caused by fiat money and fractional-reserve banking are just one example of this principle.[15]

Not only is it economically destructive for the government to rationalize the expansion of welfare programs and subsidies in the face of a recession, it is economically destructive to maintain existing welfare programs and subsidies. The quickest way for the economy to recover from a recession is to abolish all government regulation—that is, government initiation of physical force. This will make it as easy as possible for people to make the appropriate adjustments and get a new job, open a new business, expand an existing business, and so forth. Any government use of force to impose the arbitrary dictates of government officials on people provides more distorted incentives and forcibly prevents people from getting on with their lives in the face of the economic chaos that has already been caused by the government in the form of the recession or depression.

More fundamentally, it is immoral for the government—or anyone else—to violate individual rights because it stands in opposition to the requirements of human life. This is why it is immoral for the Fed to inflate in the midst of a recession (as it is immoral for the Fed to inflate—or even exist—at any time). In addition, this is why it is immoral for the government to expropriate money from some to give to others in the form of welfare, subsidies, grants, et cetera. A fundamental requirement of human life is freedom (i.e., the absence of the initiation of physical force). People need the freedom to produce the goods on which their lives depend. They need the freedom to use what they have produced (or the income they earn by selling what they produce) to further their well-being. They also need the freedom to use the type of money and banks that best facilitate the production of wealth, that is, gold and 100-percent reserve banks. The government's fiat money and fractional-reserve banking system—which have been forcibly imposed on the economy—make it harder for people to further their lives and well-being. The government's violations of individual rights manifest themselves in the form of recessions, depressions, mal-investment, a lower standard of living, and many other harmful economic consequences.

The only way to fully cure the economy is to establish a laissez-faire capitalist society. This means creating a government whose sole purpose is to protect individual rights. This involves establishing a gold-based monetary system and an unregulated banking system. This will help create the highest rate of economic progress that is possible and virtually eliminate monetary-induced recessions and depressions.[16]

Unfortunately, in today's philosophically corrupt intellectual and political climate—where statism, subjectivism, and skepticism (and many other forms of the abandonment of reason) are rife—it is not possible to cure the scourge of the business cycle. The next best solution would be for the government (including the Fed) not to provide handouts to the unemployed, those who are bankrupt, or financially troubled companies. In addition, given that a gold-based monetary system cannot be established today and the banking system could not be deregulated, the second-best solution would involve the Fed making sure the supply of fiat money does not shrink. This could be done by ensuring that banks are provided all the reserves they need to meet their checking deposit obligations. Moreover, the government should ensure banks' ability to meet their savings deposit obligations, even though they are not a part of the money supply.

Let me make it clear that I am not saying that financially troubled banks should be bailed out. Accounts from bankrupt banks can be quickly transferred with the necessary reserves to existing or newly established banks as a part of the bankruptcy process. In this sense, some financial discipline can be instilled at the banks (although not as much as would be instilled if a free market in banking existed). Such a policy would, as discussed above, lead to greater inflation and more recessions and depressions once the current recession is over and the recovery begins, but that is the best one can expect from a second-best solution.

One thing the government should *not* do as a part of the second-best solution is directly spend money to keep spending in the economy from shrinking (i.e., no so-called fiscal policy). Engaging in so-called fiscal policy would create further distortions in the economy (mal-investment, keeping bankrupt companies in business, etc.). The government should achieve a budget surplus and pay down debt to free up desperately needed capital funds for economically productive pursuits as a part of the second-best solution. Of course, achieving a budget surplus (or, at a minimum, maintaining a balanced budget) would be a part of the best solution as well, but the best solution would involve, most importantly, establishing a laissez-faire capitalist society.

While shrinking spending is detrimental to the economy, government spending does not solve the problems created by shrinking spending and creates its own problems. The way to solve the problems of potential shrinkages in spending is for the government to free up markets so that wages and prices can adjust quickly and appropriately. This means deregulating markets. Further, as alluded to above, bankruptcies must be adjudicated quickly to get the assets into the hands of those who can afford to own them (and use them most efficiently and effectively in the case of business assets). Lenders and debtors must also be made aware that no government bailout is possible so they have the strongest possible incentive to renegotiate loan contracts if this is in the self-interest of both parties.

Spending often does shrink during a recession because, as discussed above, velocity declines during and even well after a recession. The demand for money increases because individuals and businesses are scrambling to prepare for the tougher-than-expected financial conditions. The way to improve financial conditions is for prices and wages to fall. This reduces costs to businesses and prices to consumers. Reducing costs to businesses is particularly important. Businesses are, in essence, holding out for favorable investment conditions to be restored in the marketplace. Since profitability is reduced during a recession due to the historical nature of costs (as discussed in chapters 2 and 3), businesses hold out for costs to fall relative to revenues. Once costs are reduced sufficiently, businesses have a strong incentive to begin investing at more normal levels. This provides what the economist George Reisman calls a "spring to profitability" and the quickest and most financially sound way out of a recession. These and other springs to profitability lift the economy out of a recession without massive amounts of borrowing (by the government and others), consumption (by the government, the unemployed, and others), and other distorting effects from so-called fiscal policy.[17]

The government engaging in or promoting greater consumption in the economy is particularly harmful since the economy suffers from a lack of savings and capital formation during a recession. This is one reason why businesses get into financial trouble during recessions. If businesses had more capital, it would be harder for them to get into financial trouble. More consumption undermines investment and capital formation and thus leads to businesses getting into greater financial trouble than they otherwise would during the recession.

The third-best solution consists of the government not deregulating, as well as trying to maintain spending using so-called monetary and fiscal policies. The third-best solution adds the distorting effects of government spending and lending to the ill-effects of the business cycle. In addition, because of the lack of deregulation, the economy is prevented from recovering in a quicker fashion.

What we have today is the fourth-best solution. In addition to the government attempting to maintain spending in the economy, the fourth-best solution involves the government imposing additional regulations on the economy (such as additional financial market regulation).

At some point, solutions transition from being "best" solutions to "worst" solutions. This transition occurs when solutions change from moving an economy closer to capitalism to moving it closer to an authoritarian government. Today, the third-best solution is the transition point, that is, it does not move the economy in either direction from where it is now. Based on this, the fourth-best solution is not a "best" solution; it is a "worst" solution. How bad of a "worst" solution it is would be an interesting topic to write about but is not one I am interested in writing about here. How bad it is depends on how onerous the additional regulations are that are being enacted by the government. The point to understand here is that the current solution employed is moving us in the direction of an authoritarian government through the more onerous and greater number of government controls being imposed.

OTHER EXPLANATIONS OF THE EVENTS
DURING THIS TIME PERIOD

One major event that had a significant impact on America during this time period was the Arab oil embargo against the West. The embargo occurred in 1973–74. The embargo has been used to explain the significant rise in prices that occurred during the 1970s and the recession that occurred in 1974–75. It is believed that the oil embargo, by reducing the total supply of goods available in the American economy, raised the general price level and caused the rapid rise in prices during the 1970s. Further, it is believed that the loss of oil, by increasing the price of oil and oil products (such as gasoline), raised costs to all other businesses and, at least in part, caused the recession of the mid-1970s.

It is true that a decrease in the supply of oil, ceteris paribus, does decrease the total supply of goods and services available in the economy and does put upward pressure on the general price level. However, the embargo would only have a *one-time* effect on prices. It does not cause prices to *continuously* rise, which was how prices rose during the 1970s. Further, the oil embargo in 1973–74 does not explain why prices were rising *before* the embargo. An accelerating increase in the money supply explains both the continuous increase in prices from 1960 to 1985 and the tendency for prices to increase at an accelerating pace during much of that period.

In addition, a decrease in the supply of oil, due to the oil embargo, does not explain a very large increase in the general price level. For example, if oil imports from the Arabs represent, say, 25 percent of total oil consumption in the United States and, perhaps, 0.1 percent of total output in the US economy (i.e., GNR), when this oil suddenly disappears from the market one will have, at most, a 0.1 percent rise in the general price level if the amount of money and spending in the economy remain constant. If the demand for oil is inelastic, then the price of oil will rise by more than 25 percent; however, this does not imply the general price level will rise by more than 0.1 percent. If the demand for oil is inelastic, this means the total spending on oil will increase with the reduction in the supply of oil but the total spending on goods other than oil will decrease. This simply means the prices of some goods, other than oil, fall.

I say the 0.1 percent increase in the general price level is the *most* one would expect because the rise in the price of oil would bring in greater supplies from foreign oil producers other than the Arab countries and cause domestic oil producers to increase their production. This would mitigate the reduction in the supply of oil and thus decrease the upward price pressure that a reduction in the supply of Arab oil would create. In essence, the upward price movement provides the incentive for more oil to be brought forward, which causes the reduction in the supply of oil and thus the total reduction in the supply of goods to be less than the portion of the supply that Arab oil represented prior to the embargo.[18]

This discussion also applies to the sharp rise in the price of oil due to the Iran hostage crisis in 1979 and the Islamic Revolution occurring in Iran at the time. These events would have only caused a one-time rise in the general price level and the rise would not have been that great.

As I indicated, some people attempt to use the oil embargo in 1973–74 to explain the recession of the mid-1970s. Some might also attempt to attribute the cause of the recession of the early 1980s to the dramatic rise in the price of oil due to the Iran hostage crisis and Islamic Revolution in Iran. Although I do not focus on the recession of the mid-1970s in this chapter, I want to briefly comment on the embargo being responsible for that recession.

While the reduction in the supply of a commodity such as oil, which is a part of virtually every productive process, is capable of reducing the rate of economic progress, it is not capable of causing all the events that were associated with the recession of the mid-1970s and is not capable of causing all the events that occur during recessions in general. Specifically, it does not cause the changes that occur on the side of money and spending. First, a decrease in the supply of goods will cause prices to rise or rise more rapidly. However, during recessions prices generally rise more slowly or fall. In addition, it does not cause the movements that occur in the rate of profit and interest rates. If a lesser supply of goods exists, less wealth exists; however, the same volume of spending will exist in the economy unless something occurs to change this. The only way to initiate a change in this is to have a change in the supply of money or a change in the velocity of circulation. The appropriate changes in these variables took place in the mid-1970s and a change in the supply of goods does not generally affect these variables.[19]

Furthermore, the reduction in the supply of one particular good cannot create economy-wide effects (at least not the pattern of effects seen in recessions and depressions). Reductions in the supply of one good would harm some industries and benefit others. In the case of the embargo, users of oil were harmed the most due to an increase in their costs. However, producers of oil other than Arab producers benefited from the restricted supply and higher price of oil. This is not the pattern one generally witnesses in recessions, including in the recession of the mid-1970s. All industries generally see downturns with industries farther removed from final consumption experiencing more severe downturns.

This discussion applies to the rise in the price of oil in connection with the Iran hostage crisis and Islamic Revolution in Iran as well. It could not have been the cause of the recession of the early 1980s because this type of price increase does not create the right pattern of events. This discussion is an application of the critique of real business cycle theory. I provide a detailed criticism of real business cycle theory elsewhere.[20]

Although a decrease in the supply of oil, or any good, does not cause recessions, including those that occurred in the mid-1970s and early 1980s, it will lower the standard of living. It will do this because if the supply of goods in the economy decreases, this means there are fewer goods available to consume and use for productive purposes. As a result, people will be poorer. Such events can certainly make recessions and depressions worse but they do not cause them.

By how much the reduction in the supply of oil made these recessions worse is a question that is hard to answer. To get an idea of the answer, as with the contribution of the reduction in the supply of oil to the rise in prices discussed above, one must look at what percentage of the total output in the United States that oil represented.[21] One must also consider the increased supply of oil coming from other sources, which would mitigate the reduction in the supply of goods. Given these two factors, it is likely that the effect of the reduction in the supply of oil was very small compared to the effect of the slowing in the growth of the money supply that caused these recessions.

However, there were other factors significantly influencing the US economy during this time period. The US government responded to the reduction in the supply of oil by imposing price controls on crude oil and oil products during the 1970s and early 1980s. Maximum price controls were placed on domestically produced oil but, fortunately, were not placed on imported oil. These price controls harmed domestic producers and had the effect of reducing the size of the domestic oil industry relative to foreign oil producers because the domestic industry was not able to benefit from the high price of oil. Price controls also cause a large number of other economic problems, such as shortages (hence, long lines at gas stations), chaos in the distribution of goods (since those who value the good more cannot bid up the price), resentment between suppliers and customers (since suppliers view customers as not willing to pay a high enough price for their product and customers view suppliers as holding back their supply to cause shortages), among other problems.

These government controls lower the standard of living and make a recession or depression worse by making it more difficult or impossible to produce. However, such interference does not cause the business cycle. One reason why is because price controls specific to one good or industry do not have an effect on money and spending. Further, they do not create the right pattern of effects in the production of goods in the economy. Performance in the controlled industries is worse than in the less regulated industries. In contrast, during recessions and depressions, the worst performing industries tend to be those farther removed from final consumption and those that expanded the most during the expansion. Hence, price controls do not create all the phenomena we see during a recession.

In addition to price controls on specific goods, universal price controls existed during the early 1970s under the Nixon administration. These types of price controls can have far-reaching effects. They do not cause recessions because they do not have an effect on the money supply and do not create the right pattern of effects in the production of goods in the economy. They tend to reduce production more in those industries in which the controls are more severe. Of course, as with price controls on individual goods, this leads to a lower productive capability and standard of living and exacerbates the effects of a recession or depression.

Another form of regulation that existed during the recession of the early 1980s and had some effect on the economy was the "windfall profits tax" that was imposed on oil companies after price controls on oil were lifted in 1981. While this tax did not cause the recession of the early 1980s, it did harm domestic oil companies by preventing them from expanding (or expanding as rapidly as they otherwise would have) and thus made the United States that much more dependent on foreign oil. Nonetheless, many of the ill effects of the price controls were eliminated (such as shortages) with the lifting of the price controls. This was a positive effect in the midst of the recession. Regulation other than that in the monetary and banking system, in general, does not cause recessions and depressions, at least not those of the recurring kind that are being analyzed in this book. While it can make a recession or depression worse, it does not create the right pattern of effects one sees during recessions and depressions.[22]

CONCLUSION

One sees in the data presented in this chapter the causes of the business cycle at work that I describe in chapter 3. The money supply was inflated in an accelerating manner from 1960 (and even starting in the latter 1950s). After the recession of the mid-1970s, as the inflation of the money supply was being taken to new levels and prices were continuing to increase at an accelerating pace, those in charge of the Fed came to realize they needed to slow the inflation to prevent so-called hyperinflation from eventually occurring. That is exactly what they did.

While the long-term trend in the 1960s and 1970s was one of accelerating inflation and rising interest rates, interest rates were temporarily pushed down in the mid-1970s as the Fed responded to the recession during that time. Interest rates eventually began to rise again, both in response to the greater rates of inflation and, later, in response to the slowing of inflation in the late 1970s. This is indicative of interest rates responding to the increased demand for loanable funds that occurs in the latter part of an inflation and then to the decrease in the supply of loanable funds (relative to the demand) in the early parts of a slowing of inflation.

The rate of profit also responded to the inflation. Following the recession of the mid-1970s the rate of profit began to rise along with the rate of inflation. Both this and the falling interest rates gave an incentive to businessmen to expand their business activities. As the inflation slowed and the rate of profit fell, this along with the rising interest rates provided an incentive to contract.

One can see these effects in real GDP, real GNR, and industrial production. One can see production expanding in the late 1970s and contracting during the recession. Changes in these data also indicate (although not always consistently) that industries farther removed from final consumption were expanding relative to industries closer to final consumption during the inflationary expansion. The data also indicate the former industries were contracting relative to the latter during the recession. Finally, one sees the respective effects on the business failure and unemployment rates that the expansion and contraction had. All of this is explained by the business cycle theory expounded in chapter 3.

6

The Business Cycle in Late Twentieth-/Early Twenty-First-Century America

Introduction

In this chapter I analyze the time period from 1965 to 2010 or 2012, depending on the variable being analyzed. For the most part I ignore the recession of the early 1980s, since that episode was analyzed in chapter 5. However, I do comment on it when it is necessary to illustrate important points relative to other recessions. I limit myself to this period in this chapter because that is the period for which I have found it easiest to obtain data for gross national revenue (GNR). This period will cover about one-and-one-half decades prior to the early 1980s recession and about three decades after that recession. During this period there were a number of episodes of the business cycle that can help one understand the causes of the cycle and see how Austrian business cycle theory (ABCT) explains the cycle. Besides the recession of the early 1980s, there were recessions in 1970, 1975, the early 1990s, the early part of the new millennium, and in 2008–9. The latter could even be classified as a depression. Let us see what the data reveal.

The Effects

In this section, as in the equivalent section of chapter 5, I analyze output, business failures, unemployment, and industrial production—the effects of the business cycle. Here we will see effects similar to what we saw during the time period investigated in chapter 5. Except for the 2008–9 recession, the effects are not quite as dramatic as they were in the years surrounding the recession of the early 1980s. The changes in the money supply—and the other causal factors—during the episodes under investigation here are also not quite as pronounced as they were during the mid-1970s and early 1980s. This is true of the 2008–9 recession as well. The latter recession involved a number of other contributory factors—various types of government interference—that made it more severe than the recession of the early 1980s.

Output

Two estimates of output are shown again: real gross domestic product (GDP) and real GNR. As I discussed in chapter 5, GNR is a better measure of spending than GDP because it includes all spending for newly produced goods and services, especially spending for all inventory produced and purchased by businesses. GDP is essentially a measure of only consumer spending. Exhibit 6.1 shows real GDP during the period 1965–2012. One sees here recessions in 1974–75, the early 1980s, 1991, and 2008–9. Even based on real GDP, the recessions of 1974–75 and 1991 were fairly mild compared to the recession of the early 1980s. The latter recession lasted three years while the other recessions lasted only one or two years. During the recession of the mid-1970s, the largest single-year decline in output was 0.6 percent in 1974. Output fell by 0.2 percent in 1975. During the recession of the early 1990s the decline in output as measured by real GDP was 0.2 percent. However, based on real GDP, the largest single-year decline in output in the recession of the early 1980s was 1.9 percent. The only recession more severe than the early 1980s recession, based on real GDP data, was the one in 2008–9. Output declined 0.3 percent in 2008 and 3.1 percent in 2009.

Real GNR provides a more comprehensive picture of what was happening during roughly the same time period. It is shown for the years 1965–2010 in exhibit 6.2. The data used to calculate real GNR are not yet available for years beyond 2010. Industrial production data will provide us with more insight into what happened during the years after 2010.

Things look a bit different with real GNR data relative to what the real GDP data show. In general, the recessions are much deeper than GDP indicates. Further, there are two additional recessions that are not shown by GDP (at least not in the form of an actual decline in output): one in 1970 and one in the early part of this millennium. GNR data show a significant recession during 2001–2 and a slight recession in 1970. GDP data in exhibit 6.1 only show a slowing of the rate of increase in output during 2001 and 1970. Hence, it only shows "recessions" in the rate of economic progress and not a recession in the level of output. GNR data show output declining by 1.9 percent in 2001 and 1 percent in 2002. This compares to only a slowing in the rate of economic progress from

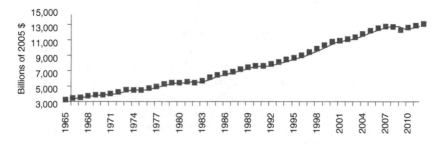

Exhibit 6.1   Real GDP, 1965–2012.
Source: See exhibit 5.1.

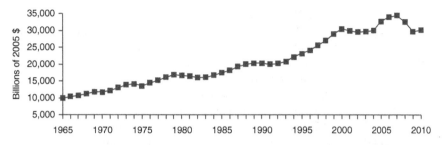

Exhibit 6.2 Real GNR, 1965–2010.

Sources: See exhibit 5.2. For gross business receipts, the source in exhibit 5.2 applies through 2008. For 2010 gross business receipts data, see the sources in chapter 2 for gross receipts data for 2010 referenced in connection with the discussion on total spending in the economy. For 2009, the gross receipts value for corporations was calculated using data from the income tax returns of active corporations. See the following source: Internal Revenue Service, *Statistics of Income—2009, Corporate Income Tax Returns* (Washington DC, 2011), p. 198. Gross business receipts for corporations include business receipts, interest, interest on government obligations (state and local), rents, and royalties for all sectors from Table 27—Balance Sheet, Income Statement, Including Investment Data, by Selected Sectors. For partnerships, 2009 data were obtained from Nina Shumofsky and Lauren Lee, "Partnership Returns, 2009," *Statistics of Income Bulletin* vol. 31, no. 2 (Fall 2011), pp. 68–157. See Table 7—All Partnerships: Total Receipts by Selected Industrial Group, 2009 on pp. 154–155. Gross business receipts for partnerships include business receipts, other income from trade or business, interest income, royalties, real estate rental net income, and other rental net income for all industries. For nonfarm sole proprietorships, 2009 data were obtained from Jason Paninos and Scott Hollenbeck, "Sole Proprietorship Returns, 2009," *Statistics of Income Bulletin* vol. 31, no. 1 (Summer 2011), pp. 5–70. See Table 1—Nonfarm Sole Proprietorships: Business Receipts, Selected Deductions, Payroll, and Net Income, by Industrial Sectors, Tax Year 2009 on pp. 18–25. Business receipts for all nonfarm industries were used. These data conform to data obtained from the *Statistical Abstract of the United States* for 2008 and prior years and are used for the purpose of including gross income from ongoing business activities.

4.1 percent in 2000 to 1.1 percent in 2001 for real GDP. The rate of increase in output rose in 2002 to 1.8 percent, which was still fairly low relative to surrounding years for real GDP. In 1970, real GNR shows a decline of 0.5 percent versus a 0.2 percent *increase* of real GDP.

GNR shows greater movement in output because it includes all spending for output. The advertising industry saw the severity of the 2001–2 recession but, unfortunately, economists did not (at least not those who assess the state of the economy using GDP).[1] GDP does not include spending by businesses on advertising because it is not considered a final good or service. One sees here one of the problems with assessing the state of the economy based on a variable that fails to account for most spending by businesses and thus is largely biased toward consumption.

Real GNR also shows recessions in 1975, 1980–82, 1991, and 2008–9. The greater severity of the recessions based on GNR data can be seen in the fact that in 1975 real GNR declined by 4 percent while in 1974–75 real GDP declined a total of 0.8 percent. Also, it can be seen in the fact that from 1980 to 1982 real GNR declined a total of 4.8 percent and only increased by 0.5 percent in 1983, while real GDP *increased* 0.3 percent during the 1980–82 time period and rose by 4.5 percent in 1983. In addition, real GNR fell 1.6 percent in 1991while real GDP fell only 0.2 percent in that year and real GNR fell a very large 13.8 percent in 2008–9 while real GDP fell only a total of 3.4 percent during that period. In 2010, real GNR rose by 1.2 percent. Real GDP has risen every year since 2009 (at a 2.1 percent annual rate). One gets a much better idea of the severity of the 2008–9 recession based on GNR data. In fact, in every recession real GNR declined by a greater percentage than real GDP, as expected.

Real GNR also tends to expand more during the expansion phases of the cycle than does real GDP. For example, real GNR increases at a 4.6 percent annual rate from 1965 (the start of data in this chapter) to the recession in 1970 while real GDP increases at only a 4.2 percent pace. The annual rate of increase from 1970 to the recession in the mid-1970s is 4.8 percent for both real GNR and GDP. Real GNR shows a 5.5 percent annual rate of increase during the latter 1970s expansion, a 4.8 percent annual rate of expansion during the 1990s, and a 3.1 percent annual rate of expansion during the 2000s. This compares to real GDP's annual rates of expansion during similar periods of 4.7, 3.8, and 2.6 percent, respectively. The only time real GDP shows a greater annual rate of expansion relative to real GNR is in the 1980s, when GDP expands at a 4 percent annual rate and GNR expands at a 3 percent annual rate.[2] In expansion as in contraction, real GNR tends to show greater reaction to the causal factors at work that are creating the business cycle.

This is consistent with our knowledge of ABCT. Since real GDP is mainly only an estimate of the production of consumers' goods, it more closely reflects the changes in output in industries closer to final consumption than real GNR, which is an estimate of all output in the economy, both capital and consumers' goods. So, one would expect real GNR to show greater fluctuations than real GDP.

Business Failures and Unemployment

The business failure rate is shown from 1965 to 1998 in exhibit 6.3. Unfortunately, collection of these data was discontinued after 1998, so data are not available after that time. Nonetheless, in conjunction with the recessions, this exhibit shows that the business failure rate peaked in 1970, 1975, 1986, and 1992. This variable peaked during or after the recessions. The business failure rate peaked much later relative to the recession of the early 1980s than it did relative to other

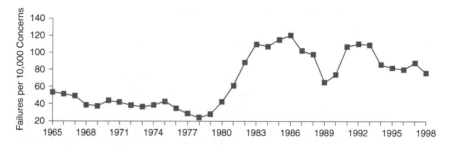

Exhibit 6.3 Business failure rate, 1965–98.

Source: See exhibit 5.3.

recessions because of the severity of that recession. During the recessions of the early and mid-1970s, the business failure rate peaked during the recession years. During the early 1990s, the business failure rate peaked more or less from 1991 to 1993. The peak lasted for a duration of two years after the recession, which occurred in 1991. In contrast, the business failure rate remained at a high point for more or less six years (1983–88) after the early 1980s recession. The peak occurred four years after the last year of the recession. Because of the severity of this recession (both its depth and duration), it had a much more long-lasting effect than did other recessions for which business failure data exist.

In addition, notice that the business failure rate remains higher in general after the recession of the early 1980s than it was prior to this recession. This is due to the fact that the failure rate was extraordinarily low in the 1960s and 1970s. In chapter 9 we will see that the failure rate was low starting just after the trough of the Great Depression. The easy money policies of the government after the trough of the Great Depression, during World War II, and during the accelerating inflation that started in the latter 1950s and lasted through most of the 1970s had something to do with that. Such policies make it easier for businesses to obtain credit and stay in business even when they are no longer viable. This creates mal-investment.

In order to improve the rate of economic progress and the ability of businesses to produce goods that buyers want to purchase, it is important that businesses that are no longer viable are not kept in business through government policies. It is the sign of a healthy economy when businesses that produce products inefficiently or that are no longer demanded are driven out of business. Of course, it would be better if such failures did not occur, but given that humans are not omniscient and thus do not know automatically what is demanded or how to produce efficiently, business failures are inevitable and must not be prevented.

The unemployment rate is shown for the years 1965 to 2012 in exhibit 6.4. It shows peaks in 1971, 1975, 1982–83, 1992, 2003, and 2010. In general, these peaks are after the recessions or toward the latter part of the recessions. This is typical of the unemployment rate. It tends to lag behind other changes in the

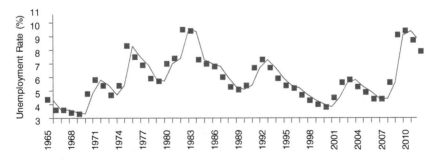

Exhibit 6.4 Unemployment rate, 1965–2012.

Source: See exhibit 5.4.

economy. This is due to the fact that businesses tend to hold on to employees as long as they possibly can, both to maintain employee morale and because it is expensive to find and hire good workers.

Industrial Production

Industrial production indices for consumers' goods, intermediate goods, and materials are shown in exhibit 6.5 from 1965 to 2012. The three indices together provide evidence for changes in the structure of production that ABCT says should occur during the cycle. In general the materials index is more volatile than the intermediate goods index, which is more volatile than the consumers' goods index, although this is not always the case.

The indices generally show recessions in 1970, 1974–75, 1980–82, 1991, 2001, and 2008–9. However, the materials index shows two additional, minor contractions in 1967 and 1985–86. The years in which the indices show expansions and contractions and the annual rate of change of output during each expansion and contraction are shown in exhibits 6.6–6.8 for the consumers' goods index, the intermediate goods index, and the materials index, respectively. These tables start with the expansion that was occurring in 1965 (in mid-expansion) and end with the current expansion that is still ongoing. One sees here that the intermediate goods index expands or contracts more than the consumers' goods index in 13 out of 13 episodes, and the materials index expands or contracts more than the intermediate goods index in 6 out of the 11 episodes they have in common (6 contractions and 5 expansions) and has the same rate of contraction in a seventh case. The materials index expands or contracts more than the consumers' goods index in 10 out of 11 of the episodes they have in common and has the same expansion rate in the eleventh case. While this support for ABCT is somewhat mixed, it does significantly lean in favor of ABCT, since the production of goods farther removed from final consumption tends to fluctuate

Exhibit 6.5 Industrial production (consumers' goods, intermediate goods, and materials), 1965–2012.

Source: See exhibit 5.5.

Expansion		Contraction	
Dates (years)	Annual rate of change of output (%)	Dates (years)	Annual rate of change of output (%)
1965–69	4.3	1970	−1.1
1971–73	6.1	1974–75	−3.4
1976–78	5.8	1979–82	−1.2
1983–90	2.7	1991	0.0
1992–2000	2.9	2001	−1.1
2002–7	1.3	2008–9	−5.9
2010–12	1.7		

Exhibit 6.6 Expansions and contractions based on consumers' goods industrial production index (years and annual rate of change of output), 1965–2012.

Source: See exhibit 6.5.

Expansion		Contraction	
Dates (years)	Annual rate of change of output (%)	Dates (years)	Annual rate of change of output (%)
1965–69	5.3	1970	−1.5
1971–73	7.2	1974–75	−5.8
1976–79	6.1	1980–82	−2.2
1983–90	3.9	1991	−2.5
1992–2000	4.2	2001	−4.0
2002–7	1.4	2008–9	−10.3
2010–12	2.6		

Exhibit 6.7 Expansions and contractions based on intermediate goods industrial production index (years and annual rate of change of output), 1965–2012.

Source: See exhibit 6.5.

Expansion		Contraction	
Dates (years)	Annual rate of change of output (%)	Dates (years)	Annual rate of change of output (%)
1965–66	9.0	1967	−1.0
1968–69	6.3	1970	−3.5
1971–73	6.8	1974–75	−5.8
1976–79	5.8	1980–82	−3.7
1983–84	6.0	1985–86	−0.1
1987–90	3.0	1991	−1.5
1992–2000	5.5	2001	−4.5
2002–7	2.2	2008–9	−7.2
2010–12	5.7		

Exhibit 6.8 Expansions and contractions based on materials industrial production index (years and annual rate of change of output), 1965–2012.

Source: See exhibit 6.5.

more than the production of goods closer to final consumption. We will see that movements in the durable and nondurable manufacturing indices support ABCT more consistently.

The fact that the intermediate goods index expands or contracts at greater rates than the materials index in four cases—when ABCT predicts the materials index should move more than the intermediate goods index—is not of great concern. This behavior was seen with the same variables in chapter 5. One component of the intermediate goods index is construction supplies. This component provides inputs for the construction of new homes and commercial buildings (among other things). New homes and commercial buildings are far removed from final consumption at the time of their construction because new buildings take such a long time to be completely consumed. This implies that construction supplies are even farther removed from final consumption. Hence, as I discussed in chapter 5, there is probably a great deal of overlap in the distance from final consumption between many of the goods in the intermediate goods index and many of the goods in the materials index. In addition, as I also discussed in chapter 5, because the purchase of some products is financed with significant amounts of debt and it takes such a long time to pay off the loans in some cases, the sensitivity to interest rates can be a factor in making the output in industries later in the production chain move more than the output in industries earlier in the production chain. This is especially true for the construction industry, and this will affect the production of construction supplies. So it is not surprising that the intermediate goods index sometimes expands or contracts at a greater rate than the materials index, and this should not necessarily be seen as contradicting ABCT.

Industrial production indices for manufacturing and total industrial production are shown in exhibit 6.9. For manufacturing, as in chapter 5, indices are shown for durable and nondurable manufactured goods. The indices are shown in this exhibit from 1965 to 2012.

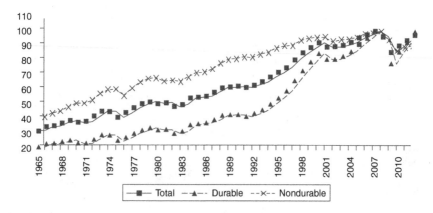

Exhibit 6.9 Industrial production (total, durable manufactured goods, and nondurable manufactured goods), 1965–2012.

Sources: See exhibit 5.6 for all years for the total industrial production index and for 1972 and later years for the manufactured goods indices. For 1971 and prior years, manufactured goods data were obtained from the *Economic Report of the President*, various editions, Washington, DC.

Expansion		Contraction	
Dates (years)	Annual rate of change of output (%)	Dates (years)	Annual rate of change of output (%)
1965–69	5.2	1970–71	–4.1
1972–73	12.1	1974–75	–7.1
1976–79	8.0	1980–82	–4.0
1983–90	4.6	1991	–3.1
1992–2000	8.3	2001–2	–2.4
2003–7	4.3	2008–9	–11.7
2010–12	8.6		

Exhibit 6.10 Expansions and contractions based on durable manufactured goods industrial production index (years and annual rate of change of output), 1965–2012.
Source: See exhibit 6.9.

Expansion		Contraction	
Dates (years)	Annual rate of change of output (%)	Dates (years)	Annual rate of change of output (%)
1965–69	5.2	1970	0.0
1971–74	4.5	1975	–7.3
1976–79	5.0	1980–82	–1.2
1983–90	2.9	1991	–0.4
1992–2000	1.8	2001	–3.0
2002–7	1.2	2008–9	–6.8
2010–12	1.6		

Exhibit 6.11 Expansions and contractions based on nondurable manufactured goods industrial production index (years and annual rate of change of output), 1965–2012.
Source: See exhibit 6.9.

Exhibits 6.10 and 6.11 summarize the annual rates of expansion and contraction for the durable and nondurable goods indices, respectively, during this time period. They provide greater evidence in support of ABCT given that the durable goods index expands or contracts more in 10 out of 13 of the episodes. In one of the cases, the two indices move at the same rate (the expansion from 1965 to 1969). In the two cases in which the nondurable goods index moves at a greater rate (the recession in the mid-1970s and the first recession of the new millennium), the durable goods index actually falls more over the entire recession and has a larger one-year decline. In the mid-1970s recession, the durable goods index declines a total of 13.7 percent over two years, with the largest one-year decline being 13.1 percent (1975). The nondurable goods index falls only 7.3 percent over the entire recession (one year according to this index).

Likewise, during the first recession of the new millennium, the durable goods index falls just over 4.7 percent during the entire recession (two years according to this index) and the largest one-year drop was just under 4.7 percent (2001).

Expansion		Contraction	
Dates (years)	Annual rate of change of output (%)	Dates (years)	Annual rate of change of output (%)
1965–69	5.3	1970	−3.3
1971–73	6.3	1974–75	−4.7
1976–79	6.0	1980–82	−2.2
1983–90	3.2	1991	−1.5
1992–2000	4.6	2001	−3.4
2002–7	1.9	2008–9	−7.6
2010–12	4.4		

Exhibit 6.12 Expansions and contractions based on total industrial production index (years and annual rate of change of output), 1965–2012.

Source: See exhibit 6.9.

This compares to the nondurable goods index falling only 3 percent over the entire recession (one year according to this index). So while at first glance the changes in these variables during these two recessions appear not to be consistent with ABCT, they really are. The lengthier recessions, as shown by the durable goods index relative to the nondurable goods index, mask this fact.

The rates of expansion and contraction for the total industrial production index are shown in exhibit 6.12. They confirm the other results in terms of the timing of the expansions and contractions, the duration, and the rate of change in industrial production. This is to be expected given that total industrial production is merely made up of the consumers' goods, intermediate goods, and materials indices.

Conclusion to the Effects of These Episodes of the Business Cycle

Overall, the evidence supports the changes in the structure of production as predicted by ABCT. Based on changes in the consumers' goods/intermediate goods/materials industrial production indices, the support is not completely consistent. However, comparisons of real GNR with real GDP and the durable goods industrial production index with the nondurable goods index show more consistent support. The empirical evidence so far and the logic backing ABCT provide sufficient evidence for the validity of the theory. More empirical evidence will be presented below as we investigate the causes of the business cycle.

THE CAUSES

As in chapter 5, I start with an analysis of the proximate causes of the business cycle (viz., interest rates and the rate of profit). I end with an investigation of the fundamental causal factors at work: changes in the money supply. Changes in the velocity of money are particularly important to make sense of what was happening during the latter decades of this time period.

Profitability and Interest Rates

Exhibit 6.13 shows interest rate data from 1965 to 2012, as well as rate of profit data and the difference between the two from 1965 to 2010. As in chapter 5, the rate of profit in exhibit 6.13 is the return on equity for active corporations. These data are only shown through 2010 due to a lack of data availability for corporate profits and net worth. The interest rate is a combination of two short-term rates: the six-month commercial paper rate through 1996 and the three-month AA nonfinancial commercial paper rate starting in 1997. I had to use two different rates due to a lack of data availability. The six-month rate is not available after 1996 and the three-month rate is not available before 1997. However, given the fact that these are similar types of debt and that the difference in maturity between them is only three months, I do not think there would be too much difference between these rates. In fact, no discontinuities appear in the data during the transition years (1996–97).

The rate of profit, interest rate, and the difference between them generally behave as one would expect. The interest rate rises prior to the recession of the early 1970s, while the rate of profit and the rate of profit minus the interest rate generally fall during this same time. These variables then reverse course during the brief expansion of the early 1970s.

The interest rate reverses course a year earlier than the other two variables. The interest rate then turns up in 1973–74, while the rate of profit minus the interest rate shows a downward trend during this time, leading into the recession of 1975. The rate of profit heads up through 1974 and then declines.

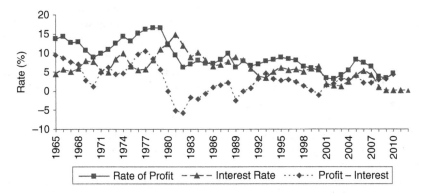

Exhibit 6.13 Rate of profit and interest rate (return on equity and commercial paper rate), 1965–2012.

Sources: See exhibit 5.7. For the rate of profit, the source in exhibit 5.7 applies for 2008 and prior years. For 2009, the net worth used to calculate the return on equity was obtained from the Internal Revenue Service, *Statistics of Income—2009, Corporate Income Tax Returns* (Washington DC, 2011), p. 27. See Table 1—Number of Returns, Selected Receipts, Cost of Goods Sold, Net Income, Deficit, Income Subject to Tax, Total Income Tax before Credits, Selected Credits, Total Income Tax after Credits, Total Assets, Net Worth, Depreciable Assets, Depreciation Deduction, and Coefficients of Variation, by Minor Industry. For 2010, net worth was obtained from the Internal Revenue Service, "2010 Corporation Source Book, Publication 1053, Section 2," http://www.irs.gov/uac/SOI-Tax-Stats-Corporation-Source-Book:-U.S.-Total-and-Sectors-Listing. Online data obtained February 18, 2013.

The interest rate falls and the difference between the rate of profit and interest rate rises in 1975, leading into the expansion of the latter 1970s. The difference continues to rise through 1977 while the interest rate falls or, at least, shows a downward trend during this time. Both show a definite reversal by 1978, leading into the recession of the early 1980s, and continue this trend into this recession. The rate of profit rises until 1979 (although at a declining rate) and then falls dramatically at the start of the recession of the early 1980s, until 1982.

One can see the severity of the recession of the early 1980s, based on these variables, in comparison with the other recessions during this almost five-decade time period. The rate of profit and the difference between the rate of profit and interest rate fall much more during this recession than during any other in this time period. The interest rate also rises much more in connection with this recession than with any other in the time period under investigation.

As is often the case, the interest rate begins to fall prior to the end of the recession, as the Fed began to engage in inflationary policies (once again) while the economy was in the recession. It generally falls through much of the expansion of the 1980s, starting an increasing trend in 1987. The rate of profit and the difference between the rate of profit and interest rate reach bottoms in 1982 and show rising trends until 1988. The differential variable shows one year of significant decline, in 1989, prior to the recession of the early 1990s. The rate of profit begins declining in 1989, prior to the recession of the early 1990s, and remains low through the recession. It starts an upward trend in 1992. The interest rate rises prior to the recession of the early 1990s, peaking in 1989. It begins to fall in 1990 and falls through this recession, reaching a bottom in 1993.

The interest rate rises briefly in 1994 and 1995, before showing a slight downward trend through 1998. The stock market declined slightly in 1994 in response to the higher interest rates. However, the higher rates were not enough to cause a recession. This might have been because the rise was not significant enough and because the rate of profit was rising at the same time. The rate of profit rose until 1995 and started a downward trend in 1996. The downward trend was slight in 1996 and 1997 and became more significant in 1998. It continued to fall through the first recession of the new millennium and stopped declining in 2002.

The interest rate rose a bit in 1999 and 2000, just prior to the first recession of the new millennium. Once in the midst of the recession of 2001–2, the Fed took action to push interest rates down again, so the three-month commercial paper rate declined and continued to do so through 2003. In 2004 through 2006, the Fed took action to push rates up and so the three-month commercial paper rate rose during this period.

The difference between the rate of profit and interest rate reached a peak in 1993, declined a bit until 1995, rose slightly in 1996, and then started a more significant downward trend in 1997 that lasted through 2000, when it reached bottom just before the recession of 2001–2. This variable then showed an upward trend through 2005. The dramatic actions by the Fed to push interest rates down, during and after the 2001–2 recession and after the 2001 terrorist attacks, caused interest rates to fall at a faster rate than the rate of profit through 2002. This caused the difference between the rate of profit and interest rate to rise. The difference continued to rise as the rate of profit rose through 2005. The rise in the rate of profit was a response to the "easy" monetary policy the Fed engaged in due to the 2001–2 recession and the terrorist attacks of 2001.

The variables also behaved as expected prior to the start of the 2008–9 recession. The Fed started pushing interest rates higher in 2004 and continued this policy until 2006. It then began to push interest rates lower and has kept them low through the end of the data presented in 2012. The rate of profit fell starting in 2006 and continued to fall through 2009. It rose in 2010. The difference between the rate of profit and interest rate fell in 2006–7 and rose through 2010, the last year of data for this variable.

One might wonder whether different measures of the rate of profit and interest rate provide different results than what I have presented here. They do not. Exhibit 6.14 shows the rate of profit as measured by the return on assets of active corporations and the short-term interest rate as measured by the federal funds rate. In general they show similar movements and timing as the data in exhibit 6.13. In fact, the two interest rates are often very close to having the exact same value. Of course, the return on assets is lower than the return on equity because companies usually finance the purchase of assets with both debt and equity. This leads to a lower difference between the rate of profit and the interest rate in exhibit 6.14 as well.

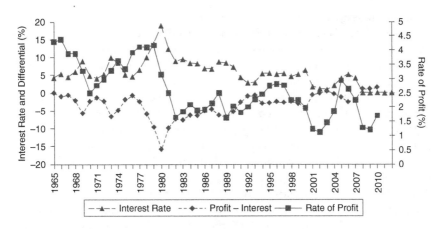

Exhibit 6.14 Rate of profit and interest rate (return on assets and federal funds rate), 1965–2012.

Sources: Through 2008, active corporation net income and assets were obtained from the US Census Bureau, *Statistical Abstract of the United States*, various editions, Washington, DC. For 2009, assets and net income were obtained from the Internal Revenue Service, *Statistics of Income—2009, Corporate Income Tax Returns* (Washington DC, 2011), p. 2. See Figure A—Returns of Active Corporations: Number of Returns, Total Assets, Total Receipts, Net Income (Less Deficit), Income Subject to Tax, Total Income Tax before Credits, Total Income Tax after Credits, by Size of Total Assets, Tax Years 2008 and 2009. For 2010, see source of net worth for 2010 in exhibit 6.13. Federal funds rate obtained from the Federal Reserve Bank of St. Louis, FRED database, series ID FEDFUNDS. Online data obtained February 18, 2013.

There are a few general patterns that emerge from these data. Using real GNR, we first see that interest rates rise before recessions and fall before expansions (although the converse is not true). This happened in every case for both the expansions and contractions in exhibits 6.13 and 6.14. It is indicative of the Fed's alternating "tight" monetary policy prior to contractions and "loose" policy during the contractions and leading into the expansions. For example, in exhibit 6.13, one can see the interest rate rising from 1965 to 1969, prior to the recession of 1970, and falling slightly during the recession year, prior to the next expansion that started in 1971, at which time the interest rate continues to fall.

Second, the rate of profit tends to reach a minimum after the interest rate reaches a peak and reaches a peak after the interest rate reaches a minimum. This occurred for every expansion and all but one recession in both exhibits 6.13 and 6.14. For example, in exhibit 6.14 the interest rate reaches a peak in 1973, two years prior to the recession of 1975 when the rate of profit reaches a minimum. Likewise, the interest rate reaches a minimum in 1976 while the rate of profit reaches a maximum in 1979, both of which occur during the expansion of the late 1970s. The only exception is the peak the interest rate reaches prior to the early 1990s recession in exhibit 6.13. It occurs in the same year (1989) in which the rate of profit reaches a minimum. However, the rate of profit does tend to stay low through the recession of the early 1990s. So, at least in one sense this is not an exception to this pattern.

The above is true when looking at the peaks and minimums at the frequency of the business cycle. As indicated above, there are some interest rate peaks that do not coincide with recessions. However, when the interest rate reaches a maximum and then a recession occurs, the minimum rate of profit comes after the maximum interest rate. The same is true for minimum interest rates and maximum rates of profit in connection with expansions.

Third, the rate of profit is near its minimum (and in many cases actually at the minimum value) during each recession and reaches a maximum during each expansion in both exhibits (although the converse is not true). For example, in exhibit 6.14 the rate of profit reaches a minimum point in 1982 during the recession of the early 1980s and reaches a maximum in 1988 during the expansion of the 1980s.

Finally, the difference between the rate of profit and the interest rate tends to rise prior to expansions and fall prior to contractions (although the converse is not true). For example, in exhibit 6.13, the difference between these two parameters falls and reaches a minimum in 1989, two years prior to the recession of 1991. It then rises prior to the expansion of the 1990s, reaching a peak in 1993. Finally, it has a downward trend from 1994 to 2000, falling most rapidly from 1997 to 2000, prior to the recession of 2001–2.

All of these patterns are consistent with ABCT. Rising interest rates prior to recessions, low rates of profit during recessions, and the opposite in connection with expansions are causing the recessions and expansions. However, these variables themselves have causes. As we know, they are moved by manipulations of the money supply. That is the next subject.

The Money Supply and the Velocity of Money

The analysis of the money supply and velocity of money for this period is a little more complicated than the analysis for the other variables. This is because, due to various regulations and changes in technology, the most accurate measure of the money supply changes during this period. For much of the period under consideration, M1 is an accurate measure of the money supply. However, as I discuss in chapter 1, during the expansion of the 1980s it begins to lose its accuracy. This is because a number of monetary categories become more significant in their use as money. These include money market mutual funds (MMMFs), money market deposit accounts (MMDAs), and sweep accounts. By the end of the recession of the early 1990s, these categories have become so significant that the measure of money must change. Therefore, I present M1 monetary data from 1965 to 1992 and M1 plus an estimate of the portion of MMMFs that are used for checking purposes plus retail sweep accounts starting in 1990. I also add in US government, foreign official institution, and foreign commercial bank checking deposits for both periods. The value I use starting in 1990 is close to what I call M1.5 in chapter 1. I do not include commercial sweep accounts and MMDAs because of a lack of data availability. Although I included an estimate for these categories in my estimate of the money supply in chapter 1, since here I am concerned with changes in the money supply, I do not include them because the estimates are not accurate enough.

It is probably the case that there is no clean cutoff between when M1 represents an accurate measure of the money supply and when it is no longer accurate. The breakdown probably occurs slowly as the new types of accounts are used more and more as money. Unfortunately, there is no way to accurately measure the exact growth in the use of the new accounts as a medium of exchange. Therefore, at some point it is necessary to switch over completely to the new measure. The early 1990s is a good point since it is right after a mild recession and at the start of a long expansion.

As I discussed in chapter 5, the money supply rose at an accelerating rate from 1960 to 1985 (and as I also said in chapter 5, we will see in chapter 9 that the acceleration actually started in the latter 1950s). In exhibit 6.15, the rate of change of the money supply that is close to M1 is shown from 1965 to 1992. One can see in this exhibit the details of the acceleration discussed in chapter 5. One can even see that the acceleration continued beyond the recession of the early 1980s, after the four-year interruption in 1978–81. The last year of the acceleration was 1986. It ended abruptly in 1987. Unfortunately, this did not mean a permanent end to the US government's policy of inflation. The government continues up to the present day to inflate the money supply at a rapid rate, although at least for now it is not causing an accelerating increase in the money supply like it did starting in the latter 1950s. There will be more discussion about this when the 1990s and the money supply that is closer to M1.5 are discussed. For now, let us focus on the years in which M1 is the accurate measure of the money supply.

In exhibit 6.15 one can see that the money supply accelerated briefly in 1967–68 and then slowed in 1969, prior to the recession of 1970. This slowing of inflation led to the recession of 1970. It also led to the higher interest rates just prior to and during that recession.

The Fed engaged in a more inflationary policy during and after the 1970 recession. This led to lower interest rates during the same time period. The slowing of inflation in 1973–75 caused the recession of 1975 and the higher interest rates just prior to this recession.

After the recession of 1975, the Fed once again began engaging in a more inflationary policy to prevent the recession from going deeper than it otherwise would have. As I discussed in chapter 5, this might appear to be a proper solution to a recession, however, as I also discussed in chapter 5, it is not. Inflation, for any reason, is harmful. Recessions and depressions are just one harmful effect of inflation.[3] Instead of creating more inflation, once a recession begins, the proper solution is for the government to stay out of the way so individuals in the economy can adjust and recover as quickly as possible.

Nonetheless, the Fed engaged in a more inflationary policy in the mid-1970s. At this point, as I stated in chapter 5, people came to expect a Latin American style inflation. However, as I also discussed in chapter 5, in the latter 1970s (through 1981) the Fed decided to reverse course on its policy of greater inflation. This, along with the fact that inflation had been showing a secular upward trend, led to record-high interest rates in the late 1970s/early 1980s and a severe recession starting in 1980.

After the reduction of inflation in the late 1970s/early 1980s, the Fed's policies led to more erratic inflation. The Fed's polices led to greater inflation toward the end of the recession of the early 1980s and eventually to a dramatic inflation in the mid-1980s in an attempt to ameliorate the harmful effects of the recession. This inflation merely offset a significant deflationary psychology that existed due to the recession of the early 1980s. This deflationary psychology is witnessed by the large decline in velocity that occurred starting in the early 1980s (shown in subsequent exhibits).

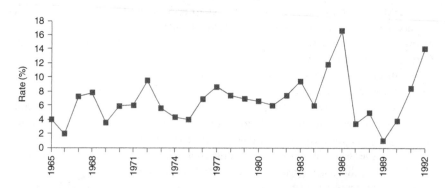

Exhibit 6.15   The rate of change of the money supply, 1965–92.

Note: The money supply is the same as that used in chapter 5.

Source: See exhibit 5.8.

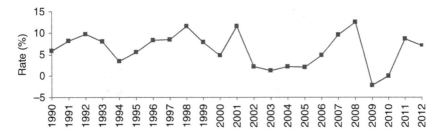

Exhibit 6.16   Rate of change of the money supply that is close to M1.5, 1990–2012.

Sources: Retail sweeps data obtained from the St. Louis Federal Reserve monthly data on sweeps of transactions deposits into MMDAs. The St. Louis Fed stopped reporting retail sweeps data in May of 2012. The 2012 figure for this variable was extrapolated based on its trend. Other money data obtained from the Federal Reserve Bank of St. Louis, FRED database are as follows (with series IDs in parentheses): M1 (M1NS), retail money funds (RMFNS), institutional money funds (IMFNS), US government demand deposits at commercial banks (USGDCB), demand deposits due to foreign commercial banks (DDDFCBNS), and demand deposits due to foreign official institutions (DDDFOINS). Data obtained February 18, 2013.

After the massive inflation of the mid-1980s the Fed's policies led to dramatically lower inflation in 1987–89. This pushed interest rates up. It also pushed the rate of profit down and led to the mild recession of the early 1990s.

As I said previously, due to various regulations and technological changes, M1 became an inaccurate measure of the money supply in the 1990s. Exhibit 6.16 shows the rate of change of the larger estimate of the money supply used in this chapter from 1990 to 2012. While the money supply increased at a more rapid rate just prior to and during the recession of the early 1990s, as shown in the last few years of exhibit 6.15 and the first few years of exhibit 6.16, the rate of change in the money supply began to slow after this, reaching a minimum point in 1994 (seen in exhibit 6.16). This did not cause a recession; however, it did slow the rate of economic progress and cause the stock market to fall. Both the NASDAQ and New York Stock Exchange (NYSE) indices were down about 4 percent in 1994. This slowing of inflation also caused interest rates to rise in 1994 and 1995.

In 1995 through 1998, the Fed engaged in an inflationary policy and during this episode inflation reached a maximum value of 11.5 percent (in 1998). This created a slight downward trend in interest rates from 1995 to 1998. The Fed then slowed the rate of inflation in 1999 and 2000. This caused a spike in interest rates in 1999 and 2000, as well as the recession of 2001–2. In the midst of this recession and immediately after the terrorist attacks of September 11, 2001, the Fed inflated massively once again as a part of its policy of using recessions as inflationary refueling periods. This inflation drove interest rates lower in 2001–3. The inflation and low interest rates are what drove real estate prices to extremely high levels. The crash was eventually brought about when, to offset the effects of this accelerating inflation, the Fed slowed inflation in 2002–5. This had the effect of causing interest rates to rise starting in 2004 and continuing through 2006. In 2006, as interest rates were rising, the Fed engaged in an inflationary policy. However, the stage had already been set and the economy moved into a severe recession, worse than the recession of the early 1980s. After a brief stint of actual deflation in 2009–10, the Fed resumed its inflationary policies during the latest year of data (2012) and as a result has kept interest rates dramatically low in the face of the slow recovery.

One point needs to be made about the first recession of the early part of the new millennium. Some people think it was caused by the terrorist attacks in 2001. However, this is not true. The recession started in early 2001 *before* the attacks. Such an event would not be expected to create a recession—a general decline or slowing in spending and a decline in profitability—except maybe in the few days immediately after the attack when no air travel was allowed. It would be expected to (and did) create a shift in spending. People spent less on such things as air travel and hotel accommodations and more on things such as recreational vehicles, Cipro, and airport security. Eventually, spending increased coming out of the recession in response to the increased money supply.

In addition, many people thought inflation was low during the expansion period of the 1990s because prices did not rise at that fast a rate. Prices, as measured by the consumer price index (CPI), rose at only a 2.6 percent annual rate during the expansion from 1991 to 2000. One problem with the CPI is that it does not provide a very comprehensive measure of price changes. A more comprehensive index (one that includes the CPI, the producer price index, and the prices of stocks on the NYSE and NASDAQ stock exchanges) shows that prices rose at the much higher rate of 8.5 percent annually during the 1990s.[4] An even more comprehensive index would include not only changes in the prices of producers' goods and stocks, but changes in wages, the prices of used goods (such as cars, although an estimate of the prices of existing homes is already in the CPI), bonds, and foreign currency.

Inflation was high despite the fact that the CPI did not rise very quickly. One must remember that rising prices are merely one symptom of inflation and are not inflation itself. Inflation, as discussed in chapter 1, is high when the money supply rises at a rapid rate. Based on this standard, inflation was high and rising for much of the 1990s. Of course, one must also remember that it is changes in the money supply, not prices, that drive the rate of profit, interest rates, the velocity of money, and the business cycle. I now turn to velocity to see just how changes in the money supply were driving this variable during the roughly five decades under investigation.

Velocity during the period 1965–92, calculated using the money supply figure that is close to M1, can be seen in exhibit 6.17. One can see the rising trend prior to the recession of the early 1980s and the generally declining trend after this recession. This was due to the accelerating tendency of inflation prior to the recession of the early 1980s and the deceleration of inflation that led to the recession of the early 1980s. The recession of the early 1980s itself and the absence of a long-term accelerating trend in the money supply after the recession also contributed to the declining velocity after the recession. Notice also that velocity generally declines during recessions, as it does during the recessions of 1970, 1975, 1980–82 (and afterwards), and 1991. Velocity also typically rises during expansions. This is indicative of the easy availability of money and credit caused by inflation during expansions and the scramble to build up money balances (relative to one's spending) to prepare for the tougher-than-expected times during recessions.

The recession of the early 1980s had a particularly long-lasting effect on velocity because of the concerted effort by the Fed to reduce inflation that led to the recession and because of the severity of the recession itself. Velocity began an upward trend, again, only in 1987. However, it began to decline again in 1991 as the effects of slowing inflation in the late 1980s, and the recession it caused, began to influence it.

The major characteristic of velocity from exhibit 6.17 is the general upward trend prior to the early 1980s recession and the general downward trend afterward. Exhibit 6.18 shows velocity from 1990 to 2010 using the money supply that is close to M1.5. The downward trend in velocity, based on exhibit 6.18, continued through the recession of the early 1990s, flattening out afterward and until the present (with a downward trend toward the end). The effort by the Fed to slow inflation starting in the late 1970s, with some help from the recession in the early 1990s, led people to build up liquidity through the early 1990s. Once the memory of the hard financial times in the early 1980s faded, greater inflation began to cause higher velocity in the 1990s.

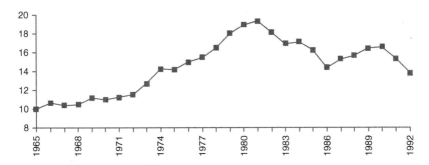

Exhibit 6.17 Velocity of money using GNR and the same money supply used in exhibit 5.9, 1965–92.

Source: See exhibit 5.9.

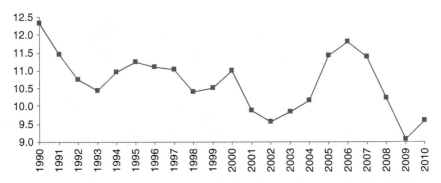

Exhibit 6.18 Velocity of money using GNR and money supply variable that is close to M1.5, 1990–2010.

Sources: For the money supply data, see exhibit 6.16. For GNR, see exhibit 6.2.

Based on exhibit 6.18, it appears that the increase in velocity after the recession of the early 1990s was short-lived, lasting only through 1995. This is because exhibit 6.18 does not provide a complete picture of the velocity of money. For the complete picture, in exhibit 6.19, I show velocity from 1990 to 2010 for the money supply that is close to M1.5 relative to spending that constitutes GNR plus spending on stocks as measured by an estimate of the dollar volume of spending on US stock exchanges. I also reproduce for comparison in this exhibit the velocity in exhibit 6.18. In exhibit 6.20, I do the same for the money supply that is close to M1 from 1965 to 1992. Prior to 1985, spending on stocks includes spending on all stock exchanges in the United States. After 1984, spending on stocks includes only spending on the NYSE and NASDAQ.

Including spending for stocks becomes important because spending for stocks increased dramatically relative to spending as measured by GNR starting in the 1980s. In 1980, spending for stocks represented only about 6 percent of GNR. In 1990 it represented about 13 percent of GNR. In 2000, spending on stocks represented 120 percent of GNR. This was the high watermark. By 2010 the number was around 70 percent, but that is still dramatically higher than the 1980 and 1990 numbers. Exhibit 6.21 shows the history of spending on stocks from 1965 to 2010 relative to spending that constitutes GNR.

Exhibit 6.20 shows that velocity both with and without spending on stocks looks very similar. The fact that the velocity with spending on stocks is only

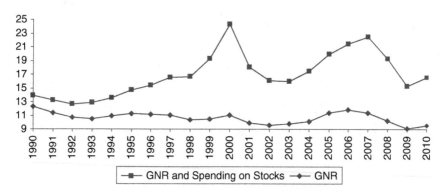

Exhibit 6.19 Velocity of money using GNR, spending on shares of stock on US stock exchanges, and the money supply variable that is close to M1.5, 1990–2010.

Note: Data from different sources for the same exchange do not match exactly during overlapping years but are close.

Sources: For money supply and GNR, see exhibits 6.16 and 6.2, respectively. Spending on stocks has various sources. NYSE data from 1990 to 2004 obtained from the "Historical" chapter at http://www.nyxdata.com/Data-Products/Facts-and-Figures under the "Total volume in round & odd lots—average prices" item. NYSE data from 2005 to 2010 obtained from the "NYSE Group Share and Dollar Volume in NYSE Listed" item under the "Market Activity" chapter at the same webpage. Data last obtained on February 19, 2012. NASDAQ data from 1990 to 1996 obtained from the National Association of Securities Dealers, Inc. website http://www.marketdata.nasdaq.com/mr4b.html. Data last obtained on February 19, 2000 (sic). NASDAQ data from 1997 to 2010 obtained from http://www.nasdaqtrader.com/Trader.aspx?id=MonthlyMarketSummary on the NASDAQ OMX website. Data last obtained on February 19, 2012.

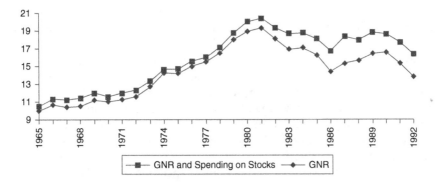

Exhibit 6.20 Velocity of money using GNR, spending on shares of stock on US stock exchanges, and the money supply variable that is close to M1, 1965–92.

Note: Data from different sources for the same exchange do not match exactly during overlapping years but are close.

Sources: For money supply and GNR, see exhibits 5.8 and 6.2, respectively. Spending on stocks has various sources. From 1965 to 1984, data obtained from the "market value of shares sold on registered exchanges" item under the "Historical" chapter at http://www.nyxdata.com/Data-Products/Facts-and-Figures. Data last obtained on February 19, 2012. NYSE data from 1985 to 1992 obtained from the same source as the NYSE data from 1990 to 2004 in exhibit 6.19. NASDAQ data from 1985 to 1992 obtained from the same source as the NASDAQ data from 1990 to 1996 in exhibit 6.19.

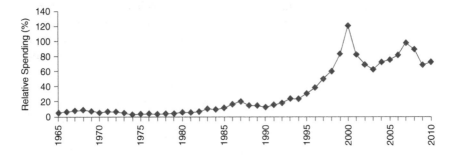

Exhibit 6.21   Spending on stocks relative to GNR, 1965–2010.
Sources: For GNR, see exhibit 6.2. For spending on stocks, see exhibits 6.19 and 6.20.

slightly higher than velocity without it shows that spending on stocks is not that much relative to GNR. However, in the 1980s the two velocities begin to separate more because spending on stocks becomes larger relative to GNR. By 1992, the difference is significant. One can explicitly see the growing significance of spending on stocks relative to GNR in exhibit 6.21.

Exhibit 6.19 shows that the gap continues to grow and becomes largest in 2000, when the velocity inclusive of spending on stocks reaches a peak. This is the same year that spending on stocks relative to GNR reaches a peak in exhibit 6.21. So, showing velocity declining through the early 1990s recession and fluctuating around a flat trend after that, as in exhibit 6.18, is not an accurate picture. As exhibit 6.19 shows, velocity inclusive of spending on stocks rises continuously after the early 1990s recession and does not decline until the recession in 2001. Then it begins to rise after this recession and does not decline until the recession of 2008. It is fair to say that the early 1980s recession (and the slowing of inflation that caused it) had a significant effect, influencing velocity until the early 1990s recession; however, at that point the memory of the early 1980s recession faded and velocity began to rise. It did so in connection with the rise in inflation during the mid- to latter 1990s. The difference between earlier rises in spending and those in the 1990s is that much more of the spending was concentrated in stocks in the 1990s.

When calculating velocity, one can ignore spending for stocks up until the early 1990s because measures of velocity both with and without spending for stocks show the same trend. This is not true through the mid- and latter 1990s and is not true through 2010 because of the significant role played by spending for stocks. The greater fluctuation in spending for stocks makes the fluctuations in velocity inclusive of spending on stocks much greater. It makes sense that spending for stocks is more volatile than GNR given that stocks are extremely liquid assets with well-developed secondary markets and very sensitive to interest rates. One could show an even more comprehensive measure of velocity with an even more comprehensive measure of spending. This would include spending not only on stocks but bonds, currencies, used goods (such as used cars), and more.[5] This may provide a different picture of velocity, especially given that spending in currency markets dwarfs spending elsewhere. However, for purposes here, velocity calculated using GNR and spending on stocks provides us with adequate knowledge of what is happening in the economy to make sense of it.

On the basis of the rise in spending for stocks and the consequent rise in stock prices during the latter part of the 1990s, as well as due to the length of the expansion during the 1990s (from 1991 to 2000), many commentators thought we had reached a "new era of prosperity" and that the business cycle was dead. This view was similar to the view many had just prior to the stock market crash of 1929. Consider the following description of the atmosphere during the late 1920s:

> The "Boom," it seemed, would last indefinitely....As trading closed that day [September 3, 1929], brokers, bankers, corporation executives and individual stockholders all had a sense of optimism. More stocks were owned by more people than ever before. What they were seeing was not a boom but a "new era of prosperity." Thousands had made fortunes in the stock market and everyone assumed that the future would be as bright as the past.[6] (Emphasis added.)

It is very similar to the atmosphere in the late 1990s. Eventually, however, the slowing inflation and rising interest rates in 1999 and 2000 led to a dramatic decline in spending on stocks and the recession of 2001. The same occurred in connection with the real estate crash that started in 2007 and the recession that started in 2008. People become caught up in the euphoria of the boom and forget (or, probably in most cases, have never understood) the nature of our monetary and banking system, which guarantees that we will have booms *and* busts until the system is fundamentally changed.[7]

Before I end my discussion of the data, I have a couple of final points to make. The rate of profit throughout the more than 45-year time period under investigation generally follows the pattern of rising and/or being higher during expansions and falling and/or being lower during recessions. One significant pattern in the rate of profit, as can be seen in exhibits 6.13 and 6.14, is the significant decrease that occurs after the recession of the early 1980s relative to the values for the rate of profit prior to that recession. In exhibit 6.13, the rate of profit, as measured by the return on equity for active corporations, averages 13.2 percent from 1965 to 1979. However, from 1982 to 2010, the rate of profit averages only 6.6 percent. Exhibit 6.14 shows the same trend. These results might be due to the change in velocity with regard to the purchase of goods and services (i.e., GNR). During the period prior to the early 1980s recession, the rate of inflation was generally increasing, as was the velocity of circulation. The trend in inflation during this period can be seen in exhibits 6.15 and 5.8. Velocity for the period 1965 to 1992 is shown in exhibit 6.17. After the early 1980s recession, the trend in velocity (based on GNR) and inflation was down and then flat (see exhibits 6.15–6.18). These changes in velocity are significant with regard to the rate of profit.

Just as a change in the rate of change of the money supply changes the rate of profit in the same direction, changes in the velocity of circulation cause changes to the rate of profit in the same direction as well. Both of these effects were discussed in chapter 3. Anything that operates to change the amount of spending in the economy also operates to change the average rate of profit prevailing in the economy. This is due to the historical nature of costs. While the increasing velocity and the rising inflation prior to the early 1980s recession operated to cause a higher rate of profit during that time, the falling and then flat velocity (based on GNR) and rate of inflation pushed the rate of profit lower after the recession of the early 1980s.

In addition, I was somewhat surprised to see that the rate of profit did not follow changes in the money supply more closely (as does the interest rate). This may be due to the fact that more factors affect the rate of profit (besides changes in the supply of money) than interest rates and some of these factors can have a significantly longer effect. For instance, as I mentioned, changing velocity affects the rate of profit. Any changes in the average useful life of business assets will change the rate of profit as well. What is significant about the rate of profit, however, is that it does change in connection with the boom and bust of the business cycle, which I have shown both in theory and practice is caused by changes in the money supply.

Other Causal Factors at Work

There are often other causal factors at work influencing the economy during the business cycle. These include other forms of government interference or the lack of such interference. Nonetheless, the main driver is the government's manipulation of the supply of money and credit through the Fed and the banking system.[8] Throughout the episodes of the cycle investigated here and in chapter 5, it is the case that sometimes the only cause (or, at least, the only cause that had a significant effect) is the manipulation of the supply of money and credit by the government. This was true of the recession during the early 1980s. The early 1980s recession was caused by the Fed explicitly shifting to a policy of lower inflation. This was also true of the recession of 1970. However, other forms of government interference played a more prominent role during the recession of the mid-1970s. Government interference also played a significant role in the recession of 2008–9. It made the recession much more severe than it otherwise would have been.

I discussed some of the factors affecting the economy in the 1970s in chapter 5. Here are some examples that influenced the economy during the recession that started in 2008. The existence of Fannie Mae and Freddie Mac significantly contributed to this crisis. This is just one form of government interference that helps to explain why the housing market in the United States was affected so severely during this crisis. Canada does not have the equivalent of these institutions and its housing market was not affected as severely. Canada also has stricter bankruptcy laws, including a greater ability to enforce the garnishment of wages should borrowers default on home loans, which serves to discipline borrowers and provides them with an incentive to not borrow so much.

Fannie Mae (the Federal National Mortgage Association) was created by the US government, as a government agency, in the 1930s to increase lending to low-income individuals. In the late 1960s, Fannie was converted by the government into a publicly traded company whose shares are listed on a public stock exchange. Freddie Mac (the Federal Home Loan Mortgage Corporation) was created by the government in 1970 as a publically traded company to create competition for Fannie. During their time as publicly traded companies they had an implicit government guarantee that they would not be allowed to fail. That implicit guarantee became explicit in 2008 when they were on the verge of collapse and the government took them over.

In 2008, Fannie and Freddie owned or guaranteed around half of all US mortgages. They were able to become so large and influential because of their government backing. The government guarantee they possessed enabled them to raise far more capital at far lower interest rates than they otherwise would have been able to. These two financial organizations have fostered unsound borrowing and lending practices, including lending to home buyers who are not credit worthy, through their creation of mortgage-backed securities and purchase of mortgage loans from lenders. To the extent that lenders can easily sell mortgages in the secondary mortgage markets that Fannie and Freddie created, a strong incentive is created for lenders to be less careful in their lending practices and provide risky products such as low-down-payment loans and no-income-verification loans. In fact, due to pressure from politicians to increase home ownership among the poor, Fannie and Freddie invented a number of high-risk mortgage loans. Because of their influence, housing prices rose far more than they otherwise would have.

The US government also engaged in extortion to force lenders to lend to borrowers who were not credit worthy, which drove housing prices higher than they otherwise would have gone. It did this through the Community Reinvestment Act of 1977 (CRA). The CRA was created to increase lending to low-income individuals in inner cities by forcing banks to make a certain percentage of their loans to individuals in these areas as a condition of doing business in other, more lucrative areas. In essence, if the banks wanted to remain in business they were forced by the government to lend to people who could not afford to borrow. It is no accident that the "subprime" market (which is made up of these low-income borrowers) rose and fell dramatically starting in the 1990s. The CRA was enforced much more strictly starting in the 1990s under the Clinton administration.[9]

The government has also limited the number of rating agencies for evaluating risk and has forced financial organizations (including pension funds) to use them to determine what investments they can make. These rating agencies have been notorious for performing poorly. For example, Enron and the government of Orange County, California were both AAA rated weeks before they declared bankruptcy.[10]

The government has also engaged in massive bailouts and increases in government spending. These keep inefficient and bankrupt companies in business that do not produce what buyers want to purchase. As I discussed in chapter 5, they also create further distortions in the economy. The key with regard to bankrupt companies and home foreclosures is to adjudicate them quickly to get creditors paid off as much as possible and the assets into the hands of individuals who can afford to own them (and use them efficiently and effectively in the case of business assets). Taking a long time to wipe bad debts off individual and business balance sheets causes economic stagnation. Lenders will not lend if there is a lot of bad debt on potential borrowers' books because they cannot tell who owns what assets and whether someone is a good credit risk. Businesses in general will limit with whom they do business if they cannot tell who is in good shape financially. This was one of the major factors causing more than a decade of slow rates of economic progress and stagnation in Japan throughout the 1990s and into the 2000s after its recession that started in the early-1990s. Bankruptcies were not adjudicated quickly in Japan.[11]

The experience of Japan in the 1990s and 2000s also shows that government "stimulus packages" do not help an economy recover. After its own real estate bubble burst in the early 1990s, the Japanese government passed 10 different fiscal "stimulus packages" totaling over 100 trillion yen. Nonetheless, its rate of economic progress is still very low compared to other industrialized nations and its debt-to-GDP ratio is one of the highest of all industrialized nations.[12] Recovery requires getting the government out of the way so people are free to produce and further their lives. This means protecting individual rights, which includes protecting property rights and enforcing contracts in a timely and objective manner.

I also discussed the harmful nature of welfare for the unemployed in chapter 5. This has been particularly harmful since the beginning of the recession that occurred in 2008–9 because such welfare has been routinely extended. The duration of welfare for the unemployed has been extended from six months to almost two years in some cases. This is one reason why the unemployment rate has been slow to fall. There were other forms of government interference influencing the economy as well, but this gives one an idea how the government made the recession worse and drove the economy to a much more extreme high during the boom that preceded it.[13]

A few other points must be stressed in connection with the housing crisis, recession, and the inflationary expansion that led up to them. They were not caused by bankers, mortgage lenders, and Wall Street brokers. They were caused, as all such events are, by government interference in the economy. The bankers and the rest are largely victims, like borrowers and homeowners. The bankers and the like are guilty only to the extent they advocated for government interference. However, borrowers and homeowners are guilty on this point as well. The real guilt lies with the politicians and government bureaucrats who create and implement the regulations and, more fundamentally, with the intellectuals who provide ideological justification for government interference.

In addition, deregulation in the banking and financial industry did not cause the crisis either. There was no such deregulation. The few instances of deregulation that have taken place in recent decades have been offset by far more new regulations.[14]

Finally, the massive increase in government interference that took place in response to the recession under the Bush administration in the form of increases in government borrowing and bailouts of companies, and the even more massive increases in government interference under the Obama administration in the form of more bailouts, even more massive borrowing, the Affordable Care Act (a.k.a., Obamacare), the Dodd-Frank Financial "Reform" Act, and more have created significant uncertainty in the business climate and are causing the recovery to take far longer than necessary. Obamacare alone has already significantly raised costs to many businesses in the form of higher health insurance premiums and will continue to do so by forcing them to insure their workers or pay large penalties if they do not. Bailouts and more borrowing imply potentially higher taxes to pay off the debt (and thus higher costs for businesses) in the future as well. The increases in welfare for the unemployed mentioned above have also contributed to higher costs for businesses by causing the unemployed to hold out for higher wages, which they can afford to do thanks to the welfare. All of these forms of government interference lead to reduced investment because of the added uncertainty and reduced profitability they create. When times are uncertain due to massive increases in regulation and the costs they create, businesses would rather hold on to large amounts of money, instead of investing it, because it is the safer option. This is exactly what many businesses have been doing. Hence, the recovery is slow because recovery requires greater investment on the part of businesses.

Conclusion

This chapter provides further empirical support for ABCT. It shows that there is no break between theory and practice with regard to the business cycle. ABCT is valid because it is a logically consistent theory and is grounded in the facts of reality. This chapter shows that changes in the rate of inflation (ultimately caused by the Fed) drive interest rates, the velocity of money, the rate of profit, and the business cycle.

In addition, the expansion starting in the 1990s provided the opportunity to see how new money can move into different areas of the economy, as spending on stocks, and eventually housing, rose dramatically. We also had a chance to see how other forms of government interference make the business cycle worse. We will see even more numerous and devastating examples of this in connection with the Great Depression, which is discussed in chapter 8.

7

John Law's Financial Scam and the South Sea Bubble

Introduction

I showed in the previous two chapters how Austrian business cycle theory (ABCT) can explain the episodes of the business cycle that occurred during recent history in America. This period is the best period to investigate to understand the business cycle because of the great availability of data and other information relevant to the cycle. The occurrence of the recession of the early 1980s during this period provides a great opportunity to understand the cycle because there is an abundance of data available during this cycle and because this is about as close as one can get to an economic experiment, where one variable is changed (the inflation of the money supply) and we get to see the effects this had. However, the Fed's actions in connection with the recession of the early 1980s are not the only example of an episode that has occurred in economic history and is almost like an economic experiment. What has come to be known as the Mississippi Bubble in France in the early eighteenth century is another example. This episode is more appropriately titled "John Law's Financial Scam" and is the main subject of this chapter.[1] Why it was a scam will become apparent as the discussion progresses.

In some ways this episode is even more like an experiment than the actions of the Fed during the 1980s recession because of the control John Law was able to exert over the French economy. However, data are harder to acquire in connection with Law's scam. Nonetheless, the data that economists and other historians have been able to obtain during this event provide an excellent illustration of the causes of the business cycle. Most importantly, they show that these causes are universal, since this episode takes place about 300 years ago and on another continent, within a very different cultural and economic context. This episode provides great evidence of the universal validity of ABCT, especially when integrated with the present-day examples of the business cycle.

I also say a few words about the South Sea Bubble, which occurred in England on the heels of the Mississippi Bubble. This is not as good an episode as the Mississippi Bubble for a few reasons: inflation did not play as dominant a role, no one in England had the power over the English economy that John Law had over the French economy, and data are not as readily available as they are for the Mississippi Bubble. Ultimately, however, inflation did drive the economy during the South Sea Bubble as well.

THE MISSISSIPPI BUBBLE

Background on John Law

John Law was born in Edinburgh, Scotland in 1671 and was the son of a goldsmith—a banker during this time. Law worked for three years in his father's business and learned about banking from this experience. Law was also a gambler and quite good at it. He won a substantial amount of money as a gambler and was barred from a London gambling club because of his success. He made a living during various portions of his life by gambling throughout Europe. He became an expert at calculating odds. Law was described by one biographer as "nicely expert in all manner of debaucheries."[2]

Law was also a "ladies man." He was tall and considered handsome. The ladies called him "Beau Law." Law fought a sword duel with another man, one Edward Wilson, over a woman on April 9, 1694. Law mortally wounded Wilson in one pass and was sentenced to hang as a result.

Law escaped to Holland in 1695 while awaiting execution. He moved around Europe and did not return to London until after he was given a royal pardon 25 years later. While in Holland he studied the workings of the Bank of Amsterdam, a bank established by the city of Amsterdam. This bank was a quasi-central bank that had some, but not all (or even most), of the powers of today's central banks. The Bank of Amsterdam was founded in 1609. It was believed that this bank was needed to "guarantee the value of the currency." Even though it did not have all the powers of today's central banks, it was a precursor to those banks. It was an early attempt by a government to use a bank to "manage the currency," which is the ostensible purpose of central banks. The Bank of Amsterdam prevented the clipping of coins. This occurred when local governments engaged in "competitive debasements" of coins by shaving metal off coins to make new coins. The bank also made it possible for depositors to hand in their coins for promissory notes that traded as currency.[3] Law saw this bank as a way to issue credit with which to trade.[4]

John Law was a mercantilist and therefore is ideologically linked with Keynesian economists. He published a book titled *Money and Trade Considered, with a Proposal for Supplying the Nation with Money* in Scotland in 1705. He lived toward the end of the era of the mercantilists, and their pseudo-economics, but prior to the rise of the Classical economists. He believed—as did mercantilists in general—that trade and the production of wealth depended on the quantity of money. For instance, he believed that the more money there was in an economy the more people that could be employed because wages could be paid to a greater number of people. This meant that, allegedly, more goods could be produced and traded. If less money existed in the economy, this would lead to less employment, production, and trade. In his own words:

> The quantity of money in a state must be adjusted to the number of its inhabitants.... One million can create employment for only a limited number of persons,... a larger amount of money can create employment for more people than a smaller amount, and each reduction in the money supply lowers the employment level to the same extent.[5]

Law did show great insight in identifying the benefits of trading with money (instead of barter) and how the use of money developed through barter. However, he did not just believe that money was necessary to facilitate trade by lowering the cost of trading. He believed that an increase in the supply of money meant that people in the economy would be wealthier because more people would be employed and there would be more economic activity as a result. He erroneously concluded that if increases in the production of wealth and trade could be derived from the use of money, further increases could be achieved from the continuous increase in the money supply (and likewise that production and trade would decrease as the money supply decreases).[6]

Keynesian "fiscal" and "monetary" policies are mercantilist policies as well and are essentially equivalent to Law's prescription for greater employment and wealth. They are based on the premise that demand needs to be "managed." As I have shown in chapter 2, they are really just policies of inflation and are no different, in terms of essentials, than the schemes by mercantilists to increase the money supply in countries during and prior to the eighteenth century.

There is one crucial difference between Law and the Keynesians: Law had a better excuse for believing what he did than Keynes and his followers because Law did not have the benefit of knowledge from such great economists as Adam Smith, Jean-Baptiste Say, James Mill, Carl Menger, and Ludwig von Mises to help him understand sound economics. Nonetheless, Law's ideas are still invalid. The production of wealth requires freedom and the protection of individual rights, as I discuss at length in my book *Markets Don't Fail!* and briefly elsewhere in this book (such as in chapter 5). Money creation schemes by the government undermine the protection of individual rights.

Although he did not explicitly state it, Law's ideas are equivalent to the belief that if unemployment exists, wages will not move downward so that more people who want to find work can. This is equivalent to what Keynesians believe today, that is, that wages are "sticky" and are therefore prevented from adjusting or would adjust too slowly.[7] Hence, the claim is that demand has to be "stimulated" by increasing spending in the economy, and I have shown that such "stimulation" comes from the inflation of the money supply.

This book is a demonstration of the fact that inflation does not eliminate unemployment, but in fact is a cause of unemployment. Inflation—and the government interference that creates it—leads to recessions and depressions and the high unemployment that accompanies these episodes. Government interference in the labor markets in the form of minimum wage laws, pro-labor union legislation, and welfare for the unemployed, among other forms of interference, also causes unemployment.[8]

Because of Law's "Keynesian" nature and because Keynesian economics is still popular today, many contemporary economists consider Law's financial scam a great innovation.[9] They admire it because contemporary, mainstream economists believe a central bank is necessary to stabilize an economy and the bank that Law created was like a central bank in many ways. Contemporary economists also often believe it is good to find ways to finance government budget deficits and increase government spending, and Law's scam certainly did this. Contemporary economists often speak of "innovations" created by Law that are in use today, such as the use of a central bank to finance government spending by buying government debt. I will show below that his so-called innovations were a type of pyramid scheme and if anyone—anyone, that is, but government officials—was caught engaging in such a scheme today he would be thrown in jail for fraud, as he should be. This should give one an indication of the nature of Keynesian economics and the moral status of financial institutions such as the Federal Reserve.

John Law's Scam

John Law first proposed his scam in Scotland, where it was rejected by the Scottish Parliament in 1705.[10] He also proposed it to monarchs and ministers in Turin, Vienna, and The Hague, all to no avail. Finally, he turned to France and Louis XIV (the Sun King), who also turned him down. However, Louis XIV died in 1715 and left France in financial ruins due to his unbridled extravagance and exhaustive wars. France repudiated part of its internal debt, forced a reduction of the interest rate on the rest, and was still in arrears.[11] Further, the coinage had been debased and was almost worthless. This gave Law a great opportunity. Many assets sat idle in France due to widespread bankruptcies. Power passed from Louis XIV to the Duke of Orleans, who as Regent held the throne on behalf of the child-king Louis XV.

In May of 1716, Law gained approval to open a bank to test his scam. This bank was known as the General Bank and opened for business in June of 1716. Law sought to increase the money in circulation and redeem French government debt. He had an opportunity that few economists have ever had: an attempt to put his theory into practice. As I will show, the control he had over the French economy was so extensive that it makes this episode, as I have said previously, like an economic experiment.

Three-quarters of the payments to provide the initial capital to Law's bank were provided in the form of bills of credit (i.e., government debt). The other quarter was provided in specie. Law accepted the bills of credit at face value even though they were trading at a steep discount.

The first ten months for Law's bank were uneventful. However, in April of 1717 a decree was issued requiring the tax collectors to accept Law's banknotes in payment for taxes. This edict also required that tax collectors and officials at the royal treasury redeem in specie any of Law's banknotes that were presented and make remittances to Paris exclusively in Law's notes.[12] This widened the sphere of activity for Law's bank by increasing the demand for Law's notes and making them easily exchangeable for gold.

In August of 1717, Law gained approval from the French government to organize the Company of the West, which exploited commercial opportunities in Louisiana and was given a monopoly trade with Canada in beaver skins. To finance this venture, Law traded 200,000 shares at 500 livres per share for bills of credit. Law's company published exaggerated accounts of the commercial opportunities in Louisiana, and in the first year of operations only feeble attempts were made to trade with the New World and develop Louisiana. The association with the Mississippi region is why this episode has come to be known as the Mississippi Bubble.

In September of 1718, Law obtained the tobacco monopoly and in November of 1718 he obtained the property of the Senegalese Company, which, respectively, gave him the exclusive privilege of trading tobacco between France and the outside world and engaging in the slave trade in Africa. He also took over the East India and China Companies in May of 1719. He then formed the Company of the Indies with the Company of the West and his other acquisitions. He monopolized all French trade outside Europe.

Meanwhile, in December of 1718, the General Bank was converted to the Royal Bank. At this point, issues of banknotes were sanctioned by the Council of State and guaranteed by the Crown. Law's bank became a government bank. By January of 1720, he was collecting all taxes and minting coins for France. He paid the government to be able to do this.

During Law's financial scam, prices and money wages rose from mid-1718 to the end of 1720 and then fell dramatically through early- to mid-1721. For 30 months as a private institution it is doubtful if Law's bank (the General Bank) increased the currency much. The bank issued 148 million livres in notes and retired 101 million livres in bills of credit, also used as money, and had specie on reserve. The quantity of specie in circulation at the time of the chartering of the General Bank is believed to have been between 714 million and 1.2 billion livres. One guess puts it at one billion livres. Add to this the quantity of bills of credit in circulation and the money in circulation at the time of the chartering of the General Bank is estimated to have been about 1.25 billion livres.[13]

Once the General Bank was converted to the Royal Bank, the money supply began to rise. Banknote issue rose about 75 percent in the first six months after the conversion.[14] My estimates put the increase in the money supply due to this note issue at perhaps 1 to 2 percent per month.[15] The increase in the money supply was lower than the note issue because some notes of both the General Bank and the Royal Bank were taken out of circulation. Some gold was taken out of circulation as well.[16] Prices during this time had not yet begun to rise (or, at least, rise very much).

From June to September of 1719, the Royal Bank issued 410 million livres worth of notes. This was a little over twice the quantity previously outstanding. My estimate puts the increase in the money supply during this time at about 5 percent per month. During this time some General Bank notes were taken out of circulation, as well as some gold. From late October of 1719 to early February of 1720, the Royal Bank's notes in circulation increased by 680 million livres.[17] This represented perhaps a 6 percent monthly rise in the money supply. From May to December of 1719, prices rose approximately 2 to 3 percent per month. At this point, the increase in prices still lagged behind the rise in the money supply.[18]

The boom started with the conversion of the General Bank to the Royal Bank and the massive note issues engaged in by the Royal Bank. The Royal Bank also granted loans on company stock at extremely low interest rates.[19] Maintaining low interest rates, as I have discussed in chapter 3 and elsewhere, is a part of the expansion phase of the cycle.

The stock price of Law's company began to rise in July of 1719.[20] Economic activity began to increase dramatically in September of 1719. France saw the employment of once idle factors of production and a greater demand for goods.

Evidence of the inflationary boom exists in a number of forms. For example, the production of goods increased dramatically during the increase in note circulation. There is evidence of this from the French plate glass industry. French plate glass was a luxury good at the time and was used for mirrors and windows. Sales volume at the Royal Plate Glass Company increased by 2 to 2.5 times in 1720 relative to the volume in previous years.[21]

Speculators were attracted from the entire kingdom and foreign states to Paris. Fortunes were made overnight: coachmen, cooks, and servants became millionaires. There was a real estate boom. Shares of stock that originally had a par value of 500 livres were selling for 9,500 livres in January of 1720. This represents an approximately 7 percent appreciation *per month* or roughly *125 percent* annually. Share prices rose on the prospect for profits on the government debt held by Law's company and the expanding commercial activities for his company. They also rose based on Law's widening control of the economy. The new money being created was used to pay the rapidly rising prices (and, of course, was the source of the rising prices). This is how individuals were also able to buy more plate glass, bid up the price of real estate, and how menial workers became millionaires. More money led to greater profitability and lower interest rates during the boom as well.[22]

Share prices peaked in February of 1720. In March of 1720, Law began to purchase shares at 9,000 livres to stem the decline. To do this, he resorted to a massive inflation. During essentially the month of April, the Royal Bank issued 1.5 billion livres of notes. This note issue is estimated to have represented approximately a 100 percent or so increase in the total notes outstanding.[23] The use of gold ceased at this point. Based on this information, as well as the previously estimated monthly increases in the money supply above and the fact that by May or June the money supply is believed to have been at its maximum of around 2.7 billion livres (all notes issued by the Royal Bank), my estimate of the increase in the money supply in February through May or June is 5.5 to 7 percent per month (although the increase came essentially in April). Since the use of gold had disappeared, and given that all of the General Bank's notes were retired, in approximately four years (from the start of the General Bank) the money supply slightly more than doubled. Prices increased by a little less than double.[24]

The stock price of Law's company began to decrease dramatically in June of 1720. Law tried to save his "system" between June and September of 1720 by reducing the notes in circulation. This failed and in December Law fled to Belgium. His company and bank were liquidated.

Prices peaked in October of 1720. The money supply at that point is believed to have been around 2.4 billion livres, half of which was in the form of specie that had reappeared.[25] The depression in Paris was quite severe but lasted less than a year.[26] There were runs on banks, which closed for a period of 10 days. Merchants would often not accept paper money or would only accept it at a steep discount.

In accordance with ABCT, interest rates remained low during the inflationary expansion as the supply of credit increased. Law lowered the rates at which he loaned money from 6 percent to 1.25 percent during the four years of his scam.[27] Keeping interest rates low during the inflationary expansion makes it easier for people to borrow and purchase goods. It also makes it easier for businesses to expand their activities.

What are the key features of Law's financial scam? Essentially, Law created a bank that would issue banknotes (i.e., make loans) and convert government debt to lower interest rates and longer terms. Peter Garber states it most clearly of all the writers on the scam. He says Law's scam was "a large-scale money printing operation and a government debt-for-equity swap."[28] Investors in Law's ventures traded in government debt for an ownership position in Law's companies and Law gave the government better terms on its debt.[29] Since shares in Law's companies were paid for in part with government debt, the market for such debt expanded and the price rose. The market value of government debt had been quite depressed due to the poor financial state the French government had gotten itself into during the reign of Louis XIV. Law also initially accepted some of the payment for shares in his ventures in gold to raise funds to make purchases. However, the largest portion of the payments was in government debt.

Eventually, Law would accept only his banknotes and/or government debt. Further, taxes had to be paid in Law's notes. This boosted the confidence in and use of his notes and got the government out of bankruptcy. He also helped to keep interest rates low by issuing loans in his notes at low rates in large part to buy his stock. As a result of the increased money supply, spending and profitability rose, there was a real estate boom, once idle assets began to be employed, unemployment decreased, and the economy in general expanded.

One can see Law's pyramid scheme at work here: open a company, issue stock, accept government debt for the stock, print money, get taxes collected in your money, make loans to people with your money to buy your stock, all to drive the value of your money and the price of your stock up. This also drives up the price of government debt and gets it out of debt. This is clearly a financial scam backed by the government, and it is clearly a mercantilist scam: create more money to allegedly bring economic prosperity to all. What Law and the rest of his contemporaries did not know or care about (at least the ones who did not oppose his scam) is that all they were doing was creating the business cycle. They were not creating any form of real or permanent prosperity. They were creating just a fleeting moment of what feels like prosperity, equivalent to the high a drug addict feels when he is on drugs.

While Law did make some attempts to develop commercial trade in Louisiana, it is doubtful whether he was serious about doing so given that he provided false accounts of riches in the New World to get people to move there. When that did not work, he forced people—including prisoners, prostitutes, and hospitalized boys and girls—to move there. "In the end," as Peter Garber states, "the commercial scheme chosen was to print money."[30]

The scam broke down because it required larger increases in the money supply to keep it going. This leads to hyperinflation and dramatically rising prices. It becomes impossible to use money as a medium of exchange because the value of money declines so rapidly. It creates much uncertainty and risk in using the rapidly depreciating money. Eventually, Law had to reduce the money supply in a desperate attempt to restore the value of his notes and try and keep the scam going.

Notice how Law's scam required the support of the government to get it started and expand its scope. He peddled his scam from government to government until he finally found one that was willing to allow him to try it—because it was financially strapped and willing to try anything except, apparently, acting in a financially responsible manner to get itself out of debt! Once he found a government willing to allow him to try his scam, that government had to grant him a charter to open a bank. This government-granted monopoly made it appear as if it was a respectable venture. After all, why would the government support the venture if it was not sound? This is not to say that individuals do not perpetrate financial scams without the approval of the government; however, it is much easier to do so if one has a legal sanction from the government.

Then, the government granted him a monopoly in all foreign trade outside of Europe. It also granted him a monopoly in the issuing of banknotes and the minting of coins. Next it made him the tax collector. The government granted wider and wider powers to Law.

The scam highlights the destructive and corrupt nature of government regulation and control of the economy; it highlights the destructiveness of the government violating individual rights by forcibly preventing competition in banking and in foreign trade, as well as through Law's money-creation scheme. Law could not have pulled off his scam without the backing of the government.

It is important to highlight the extent of Law's power. At the height of his power he controlled all government finances and spending and was the head of a private firm that controlled all of France's overseas trade. He collected France's taxes, minted its coins, and held the bulk of France's national debt. In America today this would be equivalent to being Secretary of the Treasury and the CEO, president, and chairman of the board of a publicly traded corporation that controls all foreign trade in the United States outside the continent of North America. It would also include being the chairman of the Federal Reserve and head of the IRS, as well as holding most of the US government's debt. These massive powers allowed Law to work his scam and wreak far more havoc on the French economy than he otherwise would have been able to.

I also want to highlight the rise in stock prices and general price level with the increase in the money supply. Money was created and eventually moved into the stock market and the goods markets. It is also important to note how interest rates fell through the process of credit expansion. As in the episodes of the business cycle in late twentieth- and early twenty-first-century America, changes in the money supply were driving spending, interest rates, prices, profits, and the boom-bust.

Law issued a number of edicts toward the beginning of 1720 in an attempt to maintain the value of his money during his scam.[31] For instance, laws were passed banning individuals from wearing jewelry with precious stones and giving authorities the ability to confiscate such jewelry. Furthermore, laws were passed requiring individuals to hand the gold and silver they possessed above a certain value over to the mint, and if they did not comply the law gave authorities the power to confiscate it. These laws were so vicious that they even gave authorities the power to enter people's homes to search for and confiscate money that had not been brought to the mint and punish those who possessed it.

Law was able to pass his scam off on people and work it to his advantage for a while because of the acceptance of the false belief that money is wealth and that more money means a wealthier economic system. However, more money only leads to an inflationary expansion and the boom-bust business cycle based on all of the distorted incentives that are created. In the end, inflation leads to a net decrease in wealth because it undermines the productive capability of the economic system by causing capital decumulation.[32]

The way to generate economic progress and permanent increases in wealth is not through inflation, but by establishing and maintaining a capitalist society. France's problems could have been solved if it did this. The idle assets would have eventually been employed in their most profitable uses, not based on the artificial stimulation of inflation but based on individuals' demand for goods and services to sustain their lives and happiness. Unemployment would have eventually been permanently reduced, as workers competed for jobs to support themselves. One needs freedom for these things to happen and for the swift transfer of ownership from debtors to creditors due to the massive bankruptcies in France at the death of Louis XIV.

The bankruptcy of the government also needed to be recognized and a bankruptcy proceeding needed to take place. Such a proceeding would be different from the bankruptcy proceeding for a private institution because the government would not be broken up, sold off piecemeal, and dissolved. The government would have still existed after the bankruptcy but in a reduced form. Ideally, it would have been reduced to its proper functions of protecting individual rights. To reduce the size of the government, the assets it should not have owned or did not need could have been sold. Payments to creditors could have been reduced, so creditors would have received their money over a longer period of time than stated in the loan contract. In fact, some creditors might not have been paid at all. This is a part of the risk of making financially irresponsible loans to an irresponsible borrower. From a financial standpoint, the most important thing that could have been done would have been to instill financial responsibility in the government. This might have involved setting limits on how much the government could borrow. Most importantly, limits should have been set on the power of the French government.

Unfortunately, none of this happened and given the ideas prevalent in France at the time I would not have expected it to happen. Such a movement requires the acceptance of reason as man's only means to knowledge, the morality of rational egoism, and a political philosophy based on individualism. It requires the rejection of the opposite ideas, that is, a rejection of mysticism, altruism, and collectivism.[33] These latter ideas were the ones accepted in France (and, unfortunately, still are).

Conclusion to John Law's Scam

The real tragedy of Law's scam is that it is typically seen as a failure of markets. It is often believed that asset prices being driven up to unsustainable levels is a normal part of the operation of the market. However, it should be clear that Law's scam was no failure of markets. It was a government-created failure. It was a failure on the part of the government to protect the existence of a free market (or even establish the existence of one). The government-granted monopolies in trade, banking, note issue, and minting coins violated individual rights and prevented a free market from existing in these areas. The government protection made it possible for Law to work his scam and drive the price of his stock to astronomical levels. So the market takes the blame while government violations of individual rights avoid it.

The South Sea Bubble

One cannot properly discuss the Mississippi Bubble without saying a few words about the South Sea Bubble, the British version of Law's scam. As I stated in the introduction, this is not as good as the Mississippi Bubble for illustrating the causes and consequences of the business cycle (for a few reasons), but nonetheless it is an example of the cycle. As with Law's scam, the collapse of this scam came in late 1720. However, the South Sea scam started much later, in early 1720, with the initiation of a plan by a company known as the South Sea Company (SSC) to acquire all the British government debt for the purpose of refinancing that debt.[34] Also, as with Law's scam, the South Sea scam arose in an environment in which the government was overloaded with debt. The British government had taken on massive debts during the War of the Spanish Succession (1702–13). In addition, as with Law's scam, violations of individual rights by the government played a role in the South Sea financial scam in the form of granting monopoly privileges to businesses. Government corruption also played a role through bribes to government officials that were necessary to gain the privilege of being the company to refinance the government debt and do business in general. However, the South Sea financial scam was not the money-printing operation that was the essence of Law's scam (although money printing was involved). So it does not provide as good an example of what causes the business cycle. It was essentially a government-supported pyramid scheme to refinance its debt on better terms. Some words on this scam are necessary in order to understand the essence of its nature and its relation to the business cycle.

The SSC was formally created on September 10, 1711.[35] The SSC was proposed in 1710 by George Caswell (a London merchant, financier, and stockbroker) and John Blunt (a London scrivener turned stockbroker) to refinance the immense debts the British government had been accumulating during the War of the Spanish Succession. They proposed the SSC to the English government and remained the primary forces behind the company until the collapse of the bubble in October of 1720. The SSC was given a monopoly by the government to trade in the South Seas (Mexico and South America). The SSC also purchased short-term government war debt not funded by a specific tax. In essence, this was a debt-for-equity swap. They converted short-term government debt into an equity stake in a joint-stock company. The government debt the SSC acquired was converted to a longer term at a lower interest rate. The Bank of England (BOE) and the East India Company were created in a similar manner in 1694 and 1698, respectively.[36]

The rapid expansion of the SSC's balance sheet through the acquisition of large amounts of government debt was similar to what Law's company had engaged in. Also as with Law's company, the SSC's activities had spectacular payoffs to the government. However, there were differences between the SSC and Law's companies. The SSC did not involve itself in large-scale takeovers of commercial companies or the minting of coins, the collection of taxes, and the creation of legal tender. These were all controlled by the government at the time in Great Britain. Therefore, the activities of the SSC and the bubble that resulted from those activities were much more limited in scope.[37]

The SSC did attempt to engage in commercial activities in Spanish America. However, trade was restricted by the Spanish government and eventually the SSC's ships were seized by the Spanish and the company gave up on trade and focused solely on government debt conversion. Based on the much more limited nature of the scheme, and especially since the SSC did not have a government-granted monopoly in the printing of money, it does not appear that there was as large an expansion and contraction of the money supply and as great a general boom and bust as in France under Law's scam. This is seen, in one sense, in the relative price appreciation of Law's stock versus the stock of the SSC. SSC stock increased about 8 times at its peak.[38] However, as was shown in the previous section, Law's stock increased 19 times.

While the SSC was created in 1711, the rise of the bubble did not start until 1720. With the apparent success of John Law in France, the British government decided it needed a similar scheme to reduce its debt burden. The British government thought Law would make France more powerful than Britain.[39] The SSC's proposal in 1720 was the scheme it chose.

What did the financial scam known as the South Sea Bubble involve? The SSC outbid the BOE for the privilege of converting government debt to longer terms and lower interest rates. It paid £7.5 million for the privilege of doing this. The SSC issued stock to do this. It accepted partial payment for the stock up front, accepting as little as only 10 percent down and allowing the rest to be paid in over as much as 4.5 years. This obviously made the investment much more attractive to investors because they could buy into the scheme with little money down and therefore leverage their returns. The SSC also accepted government debt for stock.[40]

Stock in the company was not actually delivered when it was purchased.[41] It was delivered at a much later date. This decreased the number of shares of stock in the market and correspondingly drove up the price. The SSC had multiple stock offerings in which it did this. The SSC also loaned out some of the money it received in the stock issues (as well as other funds) to investors to buy outstanding shares of stock in the company, which, of course, drove the price up further. The SSC also had the Sword Blade Bank make loans for the same purpose.[42] The Sword Blade Company started out producing—as one might guess—sword blades, but eventually abandoned this business and became a bank. The Sword Blade Bank was closely tied to the SSC since some of the directors and officers of the SSC were directors and officers of the Sword Blade Bank as well. This lending helped to attract new funds to the market to purchase more shares, which further drove up the price. The SSC also made maximum use of dividend announcements— announcing increasing and sometimes extremely unrealistic dividends—to drive up the price of the stock.[43] One can clearly see the pyramid scheme at work: issue stock, delay the delivery of the stock to drive up its price, announce exorbitant dividends to push the stock price up more, and make loans with some of the proceeds of the stock issues to drive the price up even further. The main thing they lacked to make their scam appear even more attractive, which John Law had, was a government-granted monopoly in the printing of money.

The share price of SSC stock rose and fell quickly as the corrupt nature of the scam was quickly seen. It started at about £120 per share at the beginning of 1720. The price jumped to around £310 per share in March of 1720 with the passage of the act authorizing the refunding of debt by the SSC. The price rose on the projected revenues that it was believed would be generated from the ownership of government debt. The price peaked in July of 1720 at about £950. It declined precipitously, to around £300, in September as the scam unraveled. By the end of the year the stock was trading between £150 and £200 per share. In the end, the BOE bailed out the SSC and became its biggest shareholder.[44]

Money supply data are not available for Great Britain at this time to the extent that they are for France during Law's scam, but there is reason to believe the money supply rose dramatically as foreign investors bought stock in the SSC and other companies, including many that were started around this time (known as "bubble companies") to take advantage of the investment frenzy. The inflow of foreign capital occurred, in part, due to the search by foreign investors for a place to put their money because of the unraveling of Law's scam.[45] This would create an influx of gold and silver and increase the money supply. In addition, the Sword Blade Bank was making loans to the SSC and its shareholders out of newly created banknotes, much of which the evidence indicates were unbacked by specie.[46] The BOE appears to have been doing the same thing.[47] Interest rates also appear to have been lower during the inflationary expansion than prior to it or afterward.

Furthermore, there are descriptions of a general boom in England at the time. Lavish parties were thrown by royalty (lavish even by the standards of royalty). New mansions were built and bought by SSC directors and stockholders. There was a great deal of speculation in land. Even investors of more modest means bought shares of SSC stock that made them fairly large sums of money. The prices of shares of stock in other companies (such as the BOE, the East India Company, and the "bubble companies") also rose, although not by quite as much as the stock of the SSC.[48]

The boom quickly turned to bust. Exchange Alley (the area in which much stock trading took place in London) was far more quiet than it had been during the height of the scam. Many servants were laid off and banks shut their doors and went bankrupt. Houses were left half-built and orders for new ships were suddenly cancelled. The markets for coaches, jewelry, and fine clothing declined dramatically. Credit markets were tight. The downturn even reached the entire continent of Europe; however, it affected mainly France and Holland. The unraveling of the SSC scam added to the downturn being created by the collapse of Law's scam, which was still in the process of unraveling.[49]

The contraction in Britain that occurred in connection with the collapse of the SSC scam appears to have been much more limited than the collapse in France in the wake of Law's scam. This makes sense since, as I have said, the SSC did not have the power to print money that John Law had. The evidence indicates that the money supply was increasing in England due to capital inflows and credit expansion, especially by the Sword Blade Bank. However, because the creation of money was not as closely tied to the SSC scam and because of the lack of data availability, this does not represent as good an example of the business cycle as Law's scam. Do not think that the causal factors of the business cycle were not at work. They were. From what the evidence shows, though, they were not as strong and pronounced as in Law's scam.

The government's role in the South Sea scam was far more minimal than in John Law's scam. John Law was a government official with enormous powers. At the same time, he was the head of a number of private commercial enterprises. The main characters in charge of the SSC were not government officials. However, as I have stated, the government was involved in the form of being paid for the privilege of the SSC to be able to refinance the government's debt. Further, a number of politicians were on the board of directors of the SSC. This was not only legal at the time, it was necessary given the government interference of the day that allowed the government to grant charters that bestowed monopoly privileges for commercial ventures on private enterprises. Because political officials had the ability to make or break a venture through their political power, companies needed to ensure they had political officials on their side. The SSC also bribed particular government officials to ensure the passage of laws in its favor. This was considered inappropriate even in the eighteenth century, but necessary given the government interference that existed.

The government's main responsibility for the existence of the South Sea Bubble was through the violation of individual rights in the provision of monopoly powers to private enterprises (including the SSC). Moreover, the government is responsible because of the bribes the government officials took instead of performing the only proper duty of the government: protecting individual rights and freedom. While it is possible for corrupt officials to exist in any government (even the government of a free society), when the government has the ability to violate individual rights through such means as granting monopoly privileges, it creates a stronger motivation for corrupt individuals to go into government because of the prospect of ruling over others and enriching themselves through the exercise of this inappropriate political power. It also provides far greater opportunities for corrupt individuals to engage in corrupt acts.[50] In addition, while it is true that fraudulent acts by private individuals can occur even when governments consistently protect individual rights, it is much easier to engage in them—and the scope of the fraud can extend much further—when private enterprises are aligned with a government or particular government officials that have the power to violate individual rights. So even in the case of the South Sea Bubble, government violations of rights were responsible for the existence of the scam.

A few words must be said on what makes the South Sea scheme a scam. Many of the activities the SSC engaged in were not fraudulent. A debt-for-equity swap with government debt is a legitimate business activity (although not necessarily sound). During the time period, it was legitimate to pay the government for the privilege to refinance its debt and it was also legitimate to have government officials on one's board of directors.

Furthermore, it is legitimate to use dividend announcements to boost the stock price, it is legitimate for companies to buy back shares of their stock to boost the price, and it is legitimate for investors to buy stocks on margin (i.e., with debt). However, it is fraudulent for a company to issue stock and use some of the proceeds to loan money to shareholders to buy more stock (as it is fraudulent, in general, for a company to loan money to people to buy its stock). This is a pyramid scheme. It is also fraudulent to use dividend announcements, buy back shares, and only require partial down payment on the purchase of shares if one is merely doing these things to boost the company's stock price for the short term to make a quick profit. In addition, it is fraudulent to delay delivery of shares to boost the price. These are the activities that make it a scam.

What about providing bribes to individual politicians? I do not place the ultimate responsibility for the existence of such bribes on private businessmen. The ultimate responsibility falls on government officials and the system of government that makes possible violations of individual rights and thus necessitates such bribes to engage in business activities that people should not have to obtain the government's permission to engage in in the first place. When government officials wield power over who can engage in honest means of earning a living, honest men may have to engage in bribery and other corrupt acts to do so.

One writer on the South Sea Bubble has insinuated that providing bribes to government officials is essentially akin to paying stock options to corporate executives because both "secure the support of those who were in a position to help the South Sea Company."[51] However, paying stock options to corporate executives and bribes to government officials are fundamentally different and should not be lumped together as if they are the same. The government officials are, in essence, engaging in extortion and the company executives are engaging in mutually advantageous, voluntary trade. The government officials are initiating physical force and thus violating individual rights. The corporate executives are respecting rights. The bribes by the SSC were not necessary to get government officials to *help* the SSC. The bribes were necessary to stop government officials from initiating force to *harm* the company. Corporations do not pay stock options to prevent corporate executives from violating the rights of the corporations' owners. They pay such options to give executives the strongest possible motivation to maximize shareholder value.

CONCLUSION

Law's scam is a brilliant illustration of how economy-wide financial scams are a product of government interference, that is, government violations of individual rights. The South Sea scam does not go as far only because the interference was not as great. However, neither episode could have occurred on such a wide scale—and probably at all for that matter—without government interference. Certainly Law could not have engaged in his scam without help from the government and the South Sea scam may never have been tried without "inspiration" from Law's scam. If the scams had been attempted solely through private means they would have been limited to how many people the individuals behind the scams could have duped into giving them their money to engage in the fraudulent activity. If the governments had acted properly, once the fraudulent nature of the scams was recognized, the operations would have been shut down and the perpetrators thrown in jail or fined.

Besides helping to illustrate what causes the business cycle—and making it possible to provide an indication of how to cure it—these episodes help to illustrate how to limit the amount of fraud that exists in the economy. The solution in both cases is to ban government interference in the economy and limit the government's actions to protecting individual rights, that is, to protecting people from the initiation of physical force and fraud. When the one entity that has a legal monopoly on the use of force in a country—the government—begins wielding that force in the manner of a criminal, it should come as no surprise that criminal activities, such as fraud, multiply. The way to reduce the amount of fraud and other criminal activities in a country is to bring the government fully on the side of stopping crime and get it completely off the side of aiding and abetting criminals and actually committing crimes itself.

8

THE GREAT DEPRESSION

INTRODUCTION

This chapter analyzes the Great Depression in detail. The Great Depression has been analyzed many times, even a few times based on Austrian business cycle theory (ABCT).[1] Most writers on the Great Depression do not analyze that episode using ABCT and therefore are led to commit a number of errors. These errors include, but are not limited to, believing that the constraints of the gold standard caused or made the Great Depression worse and that recovery was only possible by abandoning the gold standard. They also include the belief that the Great Depression was caused by a reduction in consumption and that the solution to recovery was expansionary "fiscal policy."[2] These claims will not be addressed in this chapter. I address them elsewhere.[3]

An error is even committed in probably the most well-known analysis of the Great Depression by an Austrian economist. While Murray Rothbard, in his *America's Great Depression*, does a good job identifying the government controls imposed on the economy by President Herbert Hoover in response to the depression that started in 1929 and how those controls made the Great Depression far worse than it otherwise would have been, he commits an error in his measure of the money supply by including time deposits and the cash surrender value of life insurance policies as a part of the money supply.[4] Fortunately, this error does not change any of the main conclusions made in connection with changes in the money supply during the period Rothbard investigated.

My analysis of the Great Depression uniquely contributes to understanding that episode. My originality consists of my detailed analysis of the rate of profit and interest rates and their relationship to output, changes in the money supply, and changes in the velocity of circulation. To have a complete understanding of the Great Depression, and the business cycle in general, one must understand the relationship between these variables.

While the Great Depression is another episode of the business cycle, it is no ordinary episode. I show that the same things that cause business cycles in general caused the Great Depression. However, I also show there were other factors at work, besides the standard factors identified by ABCT, which made the Great Depression much more severe. As I discussed in chapter 6 in connection with the financial crisis and recession of 2008–9, other factors can influence the business cycle and dampen its effects or make it worse. One will see that the other factors at work during the Great Depression do not deny the validity of ABCT but merely show that other forms of government control of the economy, in addition to those identified by ABCT, are capable of wreaking havoc on the economic system.

It is often believed that the Great Depression is an example of the failure of capitalism. However, this could not be further from the truth. The Great Depression is a painful example of the failure of government control of the free market. The Great Depression is a product of that statist institution known as the Federal Reserve. It is no accident that the Great Depression occurred only 15 years after that institution began manipulating the money supply and regulating the banking system. I show that the Great Depression was started through the Fed's inflation of the money supply during the early 1920s and its slowing of inflation during the latter 1920s. This is something that has been recognized by a number of economists.[5] The ripple in the pond the Fed created was turned into a tidal wave by Hoover. The drowning of America in a wave of government controls was continued, and intensified, by President Franklin Delano Roosevelt (FDR). I will describe in detail below the statist controls imposed by Hoover and FDR on the American economy and the effects they had.

The Great Depression began in 1929. The economy peaked in July of that year. The stock market peaked on September 7, 1929, and plunged in October. The money supply fell by 26 percent from 1928 to 1933. Unemployment rose to over 25 percent in 1933, business investment (as measured by spending on plant and equipment and the net change in inventories) fell by over *90 percent* in real terms from 1929 to 1932, and industrial production fell by 46 percent from 1929 to 1933. Real output fell by almost 40 percent from 1929 to 1932. During the four years of the downturn, 40 percent of all banks went bankrupt or closed their doors. American businesses had an aggregate loss of almost $6 billion in 1932. They had never experienced an aggregate loss before the Great Depression. Let's make sense of this economic carnage caused by statist controls on the economy.

THE EFFECTS OF THE GREAT DEPRESSION

Most of the same variables included in this section were included in the equivalent section of chapters 5 and 6. Gross national revenue (GNR) is measured in a different way than in chapters 5 and 6, as I discuss below, since the data that I use in chapters 5 and 6 to estimate GNR do not exist prior to 1960. I also use gross national product (GNP) instead of gross domestic product (GDP). GNP is similar to GDP in that it is a measure of spending only on final goods and services. However, GNP includes final goods and services based on the nationality of the person or company that produced them instead of the geographical location in which they were produced, which is the basis for GDP. GDP has been the preferred measure of spending on final goods and services only for the last few decades. Before that, GNP was regularly used. For a country such as the United States, which is large and has many subsidiaries of foreign firms located within its borders and many subsidiaries of US firms located abroad, GNP and GDP are very close in value.

Output

Real GNP is shown in exhibit 8.1 for the period 1921 to 1940. The year 1921 was a depression year (based on real GNP data) and represented a local minimum for real GNP. This recession is analyzed in the next chapter. Real GNP increased at a 6 percent annual rate from 1921 to 1929. Real GNP then began a four-year decline in 1930. This was the Great Depression. By the time it was over, real GNP declined from a high of $203.5 billion to a low of $141.5 billion in 1958 dollars, which translates to a 9 percent annual rate of decline. To see the severity of the Great Depression, one need merely compare it with the recession of the early 1980s. Real GNP declined for four straight years during the Great Depression, 1930 through 1933, while real GDP declined in only two of the three years during the recession of the early 1980s (see exhibit 5.1). Furthermore, the very large 30.5 percent overall decline in real GNP during the Great Depression can be compared to the overall *increase* in real GDP of 0.3 percent during the recession of the early 1980s. In addition, the maximum one-year decline in output during the Great Depression was 15 percent in 1932, while it was only 2 percent in 1982 during the recession of the early 1980s.

From 1933 to 1937 output expanded at a 9.5 percent annual pace. This expansion was interrupted by a depression in 1938, after which output continued to expand. I discuss the depression in 1938 in the next chapter. It was not until 1939 that real GNP surpassed the peak reached in 1929. In terms of real GNP alone, one can see the severity of the Great Depression. However, as summarized in the introduction, this severity was not limited to output. The Great Depression was severe based on every economic measure.

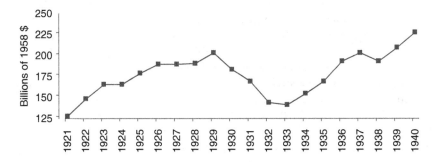

Exhibit 8.1   Real GNP, 1921–40.

Source: US Bureau of the Census, *Historical Statistics of the United States, Colonial Times to 1970*, part 1 (Washington, DC: US Government Printing Office, 1975), series F4, p. 224.

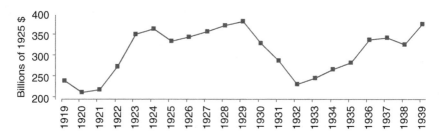

Exhibit 8.2   Real GNR, 1919–39.

Sources: Consumption and production spending components were obtained from Jay Cochran III, "Of Contracts and the Katallaxy: Measuring the Extent of the Market, 1919–1939," *The Review of Austrian Economics* vol. 17, no. 4 (2004), pp. 407–466. See the appendix of this reference and the note pertaining to GNR in this chapter for the methods used to calculate real GNR. Wage data used to calculate GNR came from various sources. Private wage data were obtained from Chapter 8 on income and employment of the National Bureau of Economic Research online *NBER Macrohistory Database*, series A08181 titled "U.S. Wages and Salaries, Total 1919–1939." Government wage data from 1919 to 1937 were obtained from Robert F. Martin, *National Income of the United States, 1799–1938* (New York: National Industrial Conference Board, Inc., 1939), p. 90. Government wage data for 1938 and 1939 were calculated with data from the US Bureau of the Census, *Historical Statistics of the United States, Colonial Times to 1970*, part 1 (Washington, DC: US Government Printing Office, 1975), series D764 and D762, p. 167 and part 2 series Y308, p. 1102 and Y332, p. 1104 using the method described in the note pertaining to GNR in this chapter. For the source of the consumer price index and producer price index data, see exhibit 5.2. Online data obtained February 18, 2013.

As one would expect, real GNR shows more dramatic declines than real GNP. Real GNR is shown from 1919 to 1939 in exhibit 8.2.[6] Real GNR reached a local minimum in 1920, as compared to 1921 for real GNP. These differences are discussed in the next chapter. Real GNR also shows greater fluctuations up through the peak reached just before the start of the Great Depression in 1929. These fluctuations and the differences between real GNR and real GNP are also discussed in the next chapter.

After the peak was reached in 1929, real GNR declined until 1932. It declined a total of almost 40 percent for an average annual decline of 15 percent. While the Great Depression was one year shorter based on GNR data (relative to GNP data), it was a much more severe depression based on the overall and annual drops in output. This is as expected based on our knowledge of how industries farther from final consumption move more in response to changes in rates of interest. In addition, as with real GNP, the changes in real GNR during the Great Depression are much larger than the changes in real GNR during the recession of the early 1980s. This again indicates the severity of the Great Depression.

Real GNR then expanded through 1937, although the rate of expansion slowed in 1937. It showed a depression in 1938. This is the same type of movement as shown by real GNP. Real GNR expanded at an 8 percent annual rate from 1932 to 1937. This is slower than the rate at which real GNP expanded from 1933 to 1937. This is not consistent with what ABCT predicts, although the total increase during the expansion is more for GNR. The depression of 1938 is discussed in the next chapter. One can see the severity of the Great Depression in both GNR and GNP data and that the fluctuations in output (at least in a total sense) are consistent with ABCT.

Business Failures and Unemployment

The business failure rate is shown in exhibit 8.3 for the period 1923–37. One can see that the failure rate remained fairly low through 1929 and then rose dramatically through 1932 before declining precipitously through 1934 and continuing to decline, but at a slower pace, until 1937. The business failure rate reached a peak value of 154 failed businesses per 10,000 existing businesses. This is compared to a failure rate of 120 per 10,000 in 1986, after the recession of the early 1980s. However, the failure rate remained at a much higher level after the recession of the early 1980s compared to the post–Great Depression period. As I stated in chapter 6, the government's inflationary policies starting after the trough of the Great Depression and lasting through most of the 1970s had something to do with that.

The unemployment rate is shown in exhibit 8.4 from 1923 to 1937 as well. The rate remains fairly low throughout the 1920s and then rises dramatically from 1929 to 1933, reaching a peak of 25.2 percent. For comparison, the unemployment rate reached a peak of only 9.7 percent in 1982 during that recession. Given the unemployment rate, it is not surprising that output declined by almost 40 percent during the Great Depression.

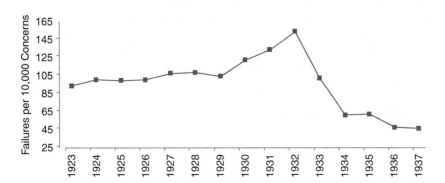

Exhibit 8.3 Business failure rate, 1923–37.

Source: See exhibit 5.3.

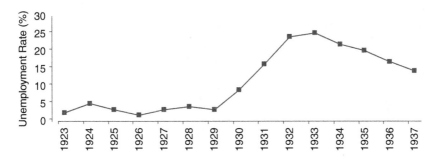

Exhibit 8.4 Unemployment rate, 1923–37.

Source: US Bureau of the Census, *Historical Statistics of the United States, Colonial Times to 1970*, part 1 (Washington, DC: US Government Printing Office, 1975), series D86, p. 135.

Industrial Production

All industrial production indices are shown for the period 1929–37 in exhibits 8.5 and 8.6, except for total industrial production, which is shown from 1921. Data are available for the earlier years for total industrial production but not for the others. Exhibit 8.5 shows industrial production indices for the production of manufactured goods and minerals. They provide an estimate of production at different stages, with minerals being further removed from final consumption than manufactured goods. Some of the industrial production indices used in this chapter are a little different than the industrial production indices used in chapters 5 and 6 because the indices used in this chapter do not include separate measures for intermediate and consumers' goods, since the data for these indices are not available during the time period being considered. Furthermore, industrial production data for this period include a minerals index as an estimate for production in the earliest stages. In chapters 5 and 6, a materials index is used. Based on the broad nature of the materials index, it is probably broader than the minerals index.[7] Values for the total manufacturing and minerals indices in exhibit 8.5 decline continuously from 1929 to 1932 and then rise through 1937.

Prior to the Great Depression, the manufacturing and minerals indices probably peaked in 1929. Although data for the manufacturing and minerals indices are not available to verify this, data on total industrial production are available prior to 1929 and do verify this, since this index peaked in 1929, as shown in exhibit 8.6. It is safe to say that the manufacturing and minerals indices follow the same trend as the total industrial production index since they follow the same trend after 1929.

The 1929 peak is also confirmed by data from Lionel Robbins's book *The Great Depression*. He shows industrial production from 1925 to 1932 for producers' and consumers' goods indices. Both indices peaked in 1929. The producers' goods index rose 22 percent from 1925 to 1929, while the consumers'

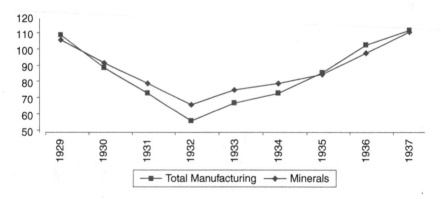

Exhibit 8.5   Industrial production (total manufacturing and minerals), 1929–37.

Source: The Economic Report of the President (Washington, DC: US Government Printing Office, 1953), p. 182, Table B-17.

goods index rose only 7 percent during this same time. The indices fell 74 and 21 percent, respectively, from 1929 to 1932.[8]

From 1929 to 1932 total manufacturing industrial production in exhibit 8.5 declined at a 20 percent average annual rate. The minerals index declined at a 14 percent average annual rate during the same period. Then, from 1932 to 1937, the total manufacturing index rose at a 15 percent annual rate while the minerals index increased at an 11 percent annual rate. A depression ensued in 1938, so 1937 was a local maximum. The 1938 depression is discussed in the next chapter.

The trends in the total manufacturing and minerals industrial production data are not as one would expect based on ABCT. The manufacturing index changes more rapidly than the minerals index in both the contraction and expansion. However, the minerals index represents production farther back in the production process and thus the goods produced in these industries are farther from final consumption. One would expect production in these industries to respond more to changes in interest rates that occur during the business cycle. In contrast to this, the producers' and consumers' goods industrial production indices from Lionel Robbins are consistent with ABCT.

In chapters 5 and 6 we saw that the consumers' goods, intermediate goods, and materials industrial production indices are not always consistent with ABCT. We also saw that this might be due to differences in the length of periods of production, the time to consume products, and the debt financing used to pay for products. Because of these factors, products produced in later stages might respond more to interest rates. This applies to the total manufacturing and minerals indices as well.

The above does not apply to the indices used by Robbins. He does not include durable manufactured goods in his consumers' goods index. His producers' goods index includes the iron and steel, tin, and cement industries while his consumers' goods index includes the textiles, leather, and food industries. Moreover, his producers' goods index includes goods that are more durable than his consumers' goods index. As a result, one would expect his data to be more consistent with ABCT, which they are.

We also saw in chapters 5 and 6 that the durable and nondurable industrial production indices are more consistent with ABCT because they do not have the problems of the indices presented in this book that represent production at different stages. Durable and nondurable industrial production data, along with total industrial production data, are shown in exhibit 8.6. Total industrial production, like real GNP, had a local minimum in 1921. It also showed recessions in 1924 and 1927, like real GNP. These are discussed in the next chapter.

The total industrial production index declined at a 19 percent average annual rate from 1929 to 1932. This means that total industrial production in the economy was almost cut in half during the Great Depression! The durable manufactured goods industrial production index declined at a 32 percent annual rate during this same period, while the nondurable goods index declined at a 9 percent annual rate. From 1932 to 1937, the indices rose by 14, 24, and 9 percent annual rates, respectively. It took five years after the deepest point of the Great

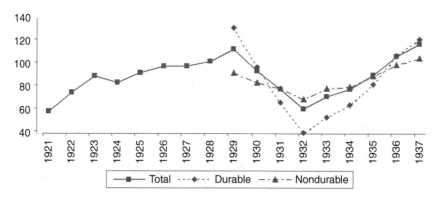

Exhibit 8.6 Industrial production (total, durable manufactured goods, and nondurable manufactured goods), 1921–37.

Sources: For durable and nondurable manufactured goods, see exhibit 8.5. For total industrial production, see exhibit 5.6. Online data obtained February 18, 2013.

Depression for total industrial production to regain its pre-depression high, although this high was only temporary due to the depression in 1938 (which will be discussed in the next chapter).

The severity of the Great Depression can be seen if one compares the changes in industrial production during the Great Depression to changes in industrial production during the recession of the early 1980s. The recession of the early 1980s occurred from 1980 to 1982 based on total industrial production and durable and nondurable goods industrial production. These variables declined at 2.2, 4, and 1.2 percent average annual rates, respectively. Even the rates of decline during the recession of 2008–9 are small compared to the Great Depression. In that recession, the corresponding annual rates of decline were 7.6, 11.7, and 6.8 percent, respectively.

A comparison of the total industrial production index relative to real GNP shows that the depression was more severe than indicated by real GNP but of shorter duration. Real GNP declined by only 30.5 percent in total or at a 9 per-cent average annual rate from 1929 to 1933, compared to a 46 percent overall decline or a 19 percent annual rate of decline of industrial production from 1929 to 1932. Total industrial production also increased more than real GNP coming out of the Great Depression until 1937: 92 percent versus 44 percent or, as stated above, 14 and 9.5 percent annual rates, respectively.

The larger changes in total industrial production are similar to what can be seen based on the data in chapter 6. In that chapter one can see that total indus-trial production declined at a greater average annual rate relative to real GDP in all the contractions and expanded at a greater annual rate relative to real GDP in all but two expansions. The relative movements of these variables are consistent with the fact that the industrial production index includes a greater proportion of goods that are farther removed from final consumption than do GNP and GDP, since GNP and GDP comprise mainly spending on consumers' goods. This provides evidence in support of ABCT. The fact that the durable manufactured goods index rose and fell by greater annual rates than the nondurable manufactured goods index (and more in total terms as well) also provides evidence for ABCT.

The difference in the duration of the depression, as indicated by industrial production and real GNP, could be due to the fact that production in the capital goods industries might have begun to recover sooner than production in the consumers' goods industries. Evidence for this exists in the fact that real GNR shows an increase, like industrial production, in 1933. In addition, evidence from real GNP suggests that the worst part of the depression was over by 1932, since the decline in that variable from 1932 to 1933 was small compared to the rate of decline in the previous three years. The average annual rate of decline of real GNP from 1929 to 1932 was 10.8 percent, while in 1933 real GNP declined by only 1.9 percent. Based on all the variables, one can say the worst rate of decline was over in 1932 and recovery began in 1933 (at least in industries earlier on in the production chain).

Overall, the industrial production data here, as with the same data in chapters 5 and 6, tend to support ABCT. While movement in the total manufacturing index, when compared to the minerals index, does not support ABCT, movement in the durable manufactured goods index relative to the nondurable manufactured goods index does. Robbins's producers' and consumers' goods data support ABCT as well. So does a comparison of total industrial production to real GNP. Moreover, the lack of support from the comparison of the total manufacturing and minerals indices is understandable given that the manufacturing index includes the production of durable goods.

THE CAUSES OF THE GREAT DEPRESSION

In this section I include the standard causes of the business cycle that I have been discussing throughout this book, namely, changes in the rate of profit and interest rates, which are themselves ultimately caused by changes in the money supply. However, since the Great Depression was no ordinary depression, I must include the factors that made it a devastating example of the business cycle. These are not the traditional factors included in ABCT but are perfectly consistent with the theory. They are the government controls imposed on the economy by Hoover and FDR. Since there were so many government controls imposed by these presidents, my discussion of them will take up the bulk of this section.

Profitability and Interest Rates

Profit and interest rate data can be seen in exhibit 8.7. The interest rate is the 2-to-6-month commercial paper rate and is shown from 1920 to 1937. The rate of profit is the return on assets for active corporations (after interest expenses but before tax expenses, as in chapter 6). The return on assets was used due to a lack of business net worth data. The return on assets is only shown from 1926 to 1937 due to a lack of data prior to 1926.

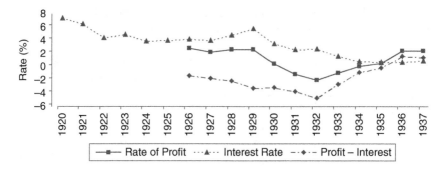

Exhibit 8.7   Rate of profit and interest rate (return on assets and commercial paper rate), 1920–37.

Sources: Active corporation net income and asset data obtained from the US Census Bureau, *Statistical Abstract of the United States*, various editions, Washington, DC. Interest rate obtained from Chapter 13 on interest rates of the National Bureau of Economic Research online *NBER Macrohistory Database*, series 13002 titled "Commercial Paper Rates, New York City." Online data obtained February 18, 2013.

One can see that the interest rate declined in the early 1920s and remained low for most of the decade of the 1920s. This was due to policies of the Federal Reserve. The fact that interest rates remained low for such a significant period of time helped to create the dramatic expansion during the period. It helped to, in part, make the 1920s "roaring." The low interest rates made it easier for businesses to expand their activities. It was not until 1928, just prior to the start of the Great Depression, that interest rates rose. This was also due to Fed policy as well. After rising briefly, they began a precipitous decline in 1930. This decline continued until 1935, when the commercial paper rate fell to 0.75 percent.

One sees here the typical pattern of interest rates: low during the expansion, rising just prior to the contraction, and falling during and/or after the contraction. With the Great Depression, things are a little different because interest rates fell so dramatically and stayed low for so long after the depression started. I will show what caused this, below, in the subsection on money.

The rate of profit also followed the typical pattern we have come to expect. It remained high during the expansion of the 1920s (at least we know it did during the years for which data exist), then it fell moving into the depression. It continued to decline until the deepest point of the depression, in 1932, and then began to rise as the American economy slowly lifted itself out of the depression. The difference between the rate of profit and the interest rate did the same.

One significant point to notice in exhibit 8.7 is the fact that the return on assets was negative in 1931–33. If one looks back at the rate of profit data presented in chapter 6, one will notice that nowhere from 1965 on was the return on assets negative. This is something that has not happened since the Great Depression and, as I noted in the introduction to this chapter, did not happen before the Great Depression. This is just one more fact that illustrates the severity of the Great Depression.

The Money Supply and the Velocity of Money

Of course, changes in the rate of profit and interest rates are driven by changes in the money supply. Data on the annual rate of change of the money supply can be seen in exhibit 8.8 from 1921 to 1935. The best money supply data available during the period in question are data on currency in the hands of the public and demand deposits, which is essentially the same as M1.

Interest rates were driven higher during World War I (WWI) due to the attendant uncertainty of war and the massive inflation in the United States at the time. Normally inflation pushes interest rates down (and it did do this initially), but large changes in the money supply can make the long-run effects of changes in the rate of inflation occur sooner than they otherwise would. After the war, interest rates began to fall along with inflation. In fact, Fed policy deflated the money supply in 1920 and 1921. See the next chapter for interest rate data during WWI and the 1920 value for the change in the money supply.

In 1922, the recently formed Fed began its first peacetime inflationary policy. There was a sharp increase in the purchases of government securities by the Fed in 1922. There were also massive purchases in 1924 by the Fed to expand the credit available to banks. Fed policy continued to be inflationary through the mid-1920s and this resulted in the money supply increasing at a generally accelerating pace through 1925. This inflation helped to continue to drive interest rates lower after they had begun to fall due to the slowing inflation experienced after WWI.

In 1926 Fed policy became contractionary and actually caused the money supply to deflate a little. This led to slightly higher interest rates in 1926. In 1927 Fed policy was once more inflationary. At this point it caused the money supply to increase with the last round of large purchases of government securities before the Great Depression. Nevertheless, the inflation trend remained downward from 1925 on.[9]

In 1928 and 1929, the Fed made a concerted effort to raise interests.[10] It did this by selling government securities (i.e., engaging in a policy to lower the rate of inflation of the money supply, and in 1929 the Fed's policy caused an outright deflation of the money supply). As the Fed allowed the money supply to shrink

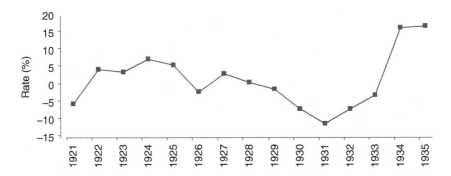

Exhibit 8.8 Rate of change of currency and demand deposits, 1921–35.

Source: Banking and Monetary Statistics: 1914–1941 (Washington, DC: Board of Governors of the Federal Reserve System, 1943), p. 34.

even further in the early 1930s, and spending in the economy began to fall (in 1930), interest rates began to fall. The short-run effect of slowing inflation (and deflation)—higher interest rates—disappeared in 1930 and the long-run effect—lower interest rates—began to appear.

The rate of profit also began to fall in 1930. The rate of profit became negative in 1931 and remained so until 1933, which was also the last year of the continuous decreases in the money supply that started in 1929. The rate of profit became positive as the money supply, spending, and revenues began to increase.

Interest rates remained low even as the rate of profit recovered in 1936 and 1937. This was in large part due to the lingering effects of the poor financial state businesses and banks were in. As I stated in the introduction, 40 percent of all banks had gone bankrupt by 1932 and as exhibit 8.3 shows the rate of business failure increased by almost 50 percent. Borrowers were generally unwilling (and unable) to take on the risk of borrowing money. To get them to borrow at all, creditors had to charge very low interest rates.

One might wonder how the Fed manipulated the money supply during this period since the United States was on a gold standard. The money supply was manipulated by taking the United States off gold gradually. A part of this process involved, in 1917, amendments to the Federal Reserve Act, the act that created the Federal Reserve in 1913. The 1917 amendments lowered the reserve requirements for banks below the ones that were established when the Federal Reserve was created. In addition, the 1917 amendments legally prevented banks from holding gold as reserves; the government forced the banks to hand the gold over to the Fed.[11] This lowering of reserve requirements and the confiscation of gold reserves by the Fed made it possible for the Fed to create a larger number of dollars not backed by gold. Many of these newly created dollars were then deposited at banks and the banks could then use them to create more money through the fractional-reserve banking process. This action by the Fed is known as the pyramiding of reserves: a larger supply of standard money reserves confiscated by the Fed was used as the basis to create more claims to the standard money, which were then used to create even more money through the fractional-reserve checking process.

The velocity of circulation of money, as calculated using GNR, can be seen in exhibit 8.9 from 1921 to 1936. Velocity rose dramatically after the depression of the early 1920s and tended to remain high (with only a slight downward trend) until the Great Depression. The generally high velocity during much of the 1920s was due to the inflationary policies of the Fed during WWI and the generally accelerating inflation of the early and mid-1920s.

While the velocity based on GNR does not increase with the increased inflation of the early and mid-1920s, velocity based on a more comprehensive measure of spending (which includes spending on financial assets) shows the more traditional increase with the greater inflation of this period. In *Contracts, Collapse, and Coercion: A Katallactic Reappraisal of the Great Depression*, Jay Cochran III presents velocity data that are calculated using currency and demand deposits for the money supply and a different measure of what is essentially GNR

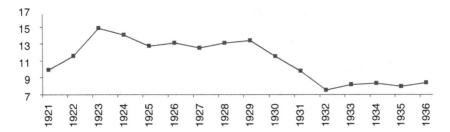

Exhibit 8.9 Velocity of money based on GNR, 1921–36.

Sources: For money supply, see exhibit 8.8. For GNR, see exhibit 8.2.

plus spending for financial assets as the spending in the economy. He shows that from the depression at the beginning of the 1920s until the start of the Great Depression, velocity rose by about 85 percent. He also shows velocity falling about 60 percent during the Great Depression, compared to a fall of velocity in exhibit 8.9 of 43 percent.[12] This indicates a significant shift in spending to financial markets during the expansion of the 1920s and out of financial markets during the Great Depression.

The declining velocity in 1924–25 and 1927 is attributable to the slowing inflation (or deflation) in 1923 and 1926. Once the money supply began to increase at a slower pace for a couple of years toward the end of the 1920s—and the massive deflation during the Great Depression actually started—velocity began a precipitous decline. It generally remained at these low levels until well past the point when the depression was over. It remained low for a long period of time because of the deflation psychology the Great Depression created—due directly to the massive amount of unemployment and number of bankruptcies during the Great Depression. This caused people to act in a much more financially conservative manner for many years. In addition, as discussed in chapter 1, the universal maximum price controls and consequent rationing imposed by the US government during World War II led to lower velocity during the years that they were enforced.

Was Reinflation the Cure for the Great Depression?

Given that the money supply shrank dramatically from 1929 to 1933, as shown in exhibit 8.8, some might think the Federal Reserve should have engaged in a massive policy of inflation to prevent the money supply and spending in the economy from declining and therefore preventing production from declining as much as it did during the depression. This issue was addressed in chapter 5 in connection with the recession of the early 1980s. However, it is worth applying the general discussion on this topic in chapter 5 to the Great Depression to come to a better understanding of what the government should do in the midst of a recession or depression.

First, it must be understood that letting the money supply shrink was not the main problem during the Great Depression. Recall from chapter 1 that the problem is fractional-reserve banking, which makes possible dramatic increases and decreases in the money supply. If the United States had been on a 100-percent reserve gold standard, instead of the fractional-reserve gold standard it was on at the time, it would have been virtually impossible for the money supply to shrink.[13]

The proximate causes of the decreasing money supply were President Hoover's policy of using coercion and intimidation against business owners to keep wages arbitrarily high in response to the start of the depression, as well as the uncertainty in the business climate that was created due to the large number of regulations that were imposed on the US economy under his administration. I discuss Hoover's interventionist policies in the next subsection. Here I merely state that his policies made it more risky and unprofitable for businesses to invest. As a result, and as I stated in the introduction to this chapter, one measure of business investment declined by over 90 percent from 1929 to 1932. This reduced spending and profits and made it harder for debtors to pay off debts, as revenues and incomes that businesses and individuals used to pay off loans declined dramatically. Once this occurred, individuals and businesses began to default on loans, and banks began to get into financial trouble as they became insolvent. At this point, people began to engage in runs on banks because of the risk of not being able to get all of their money out of the bank. The money supply then started to shrink down to the level of standard money, and although the money supply did not shrink completely down to the level of standard money it did shrink significantly. This further decreased spending, made it harder to pay off debts, led to more runs, more bank failures, and a lower money supply. The process was self-reinforcing.

The deep and drawn-out economic disaster created by the government interference of Hoover stands in stark contrast to the hands-off policy the government engaged in during the depression of the early 1920s. The result of the government leaving the economy alone in the early 1920s was that a rapid recovery took place. The early 1920s depression is discussed in the next chapter.

The violations of individual rights by Hoover were not the ultimate cause of the Great Depression. As I have said, Hoover was reacting to a depression that had already begun. So he did not cause the Great Depression but turned what probably would have been a typical depression of the time into the Great Depression.

The inflationary policies of the Federal Reserve during the 1920s were the ultimate economic cause. The more rapid inflation of the early 1920s and the slowing inflation of the late 1920s started the depression. To eliminate this cause, the government controls in money and banking that are its source must be eliminated.

Government controls in money and banking lead to the ability of the government to manipulate the money supply and thus manipulate the rate of inflation. By creating the fractional-reserve checking system, government controls also open the door to possible massive deflations.[14] The government controls imposed by Hoover in response to the depression that had already begun turned the possibility of massive deflation into a reality.

Any attempt by the government to reinflate during the Great Depression, and prevent the money supply from shrinking (or shrinking further), would have been just another government control used in an attempt to ameliorate the problems caused by previous rounds of government controls. The problem is that, besides violating individual rights (which is bad enough on its own), each round of government controls has negative economic consequences. As discussed in chapter 5, inflating in the midst of a recession or depression is, at best, only a temporary solution. If the government uses a recession or depression as an inflationary refueling period, this might lessen the harmful effects of the current episode but it merely paves the way for future recessions and depressions. Further, it leads to all the long-term negative effects of inflation, which ultimately mean a lower productive capability and standard of living.[15]

The analogy used in chapter 5 of the alcoholic falling off the wagon is applicable here as well. It only leads to a short-term cover up of the problems and leads to greater problems in the future. To eliminate the problems, we need to get the economy off the government-supplied alcohol (i.e., the inflation) and all other government controls. If the controls of Hoover had not existed, then investment, spending, revenues, and incomes would not have shrunk and therefore the money supply would not have shrunk (at least not to the extent it did). If these controls had not existed, a situation in which people thought inflation was needed never would have been created. Taking it back one step further, if the government controls in money and banking had not existed there would have been no government manipulation of the money supply and no fractional-reserve banking. This would have prevented a situation from arising (viz., the start of a depression) in which Hoover thought he needed to act to keep wages high and use various forms of other controls. So here we see that inflation is not the solution, it is a part of the problem. This is true whether it comes in the middle of a depression or not.

Some might think that, even though government controls in money and banking and the changing rates of inflation they create are the ultimate cause of recessions and depressions, once Hoover had imposed his controls, caused the money supply to shrink, and turned an ordinary depression into the Great Depression, the solution was to reinflate to bring the economy out of the depression. This is not true. Given that Hoover wreaked havoc upon the economy through the controls he imposed, the solution is not more government control of the economy. As I have stated, more controls to solve the problems of previous rounds of controls might mask or temporarily eliminate the harmful effects of the previous rounds of controls, but the additional controls bring further problems. The solution to the problems caused by government controls is to get rid of the controls causing the problem. The solution to the problems caused by Hoover's controls would have been for Hoover to admit his mistake, reverse course, and eliminate the controls he imposed on the economy. This would have restored investment, spending, revenues, profits, and incomes more generally and prevented further declines in the money supply all without sowing the seeds for future recessions and depressions. It would have created an environment that is conducive to high rates of economic progress in a more stable monetary and regulatory environment.

Of course, as stated in chapter 5, in a philosophically corrupt intellectual and political environment—an environment in which government interference is desired—the best solution is not possible. In fact, in such an environment the second- and third-best solutions discussed in chapter 5 are probably not viable options either. This leaves the fourth-"best" solution and, in fact, the Great Depression was a case of being at least the fifth-"best" solution. If government officials are unwilling to admit their mistakes and reverse course, these are the best "solutions" for which one can hope.

The Statist Controls Imposed by Hoover

ABCT, by itself, does not explain the depth and duration of the Great Depression. As I mentioned above, other factors were at work during the depression making it worse than it otherwise would have been. These other factors are the massive violations of individual rights of Presidents Hoover and Roosevelt. The factors ABCT identifies as the cause of recessions and depressions were at work: the inflation during the early 1920s and the slowing inflation during the latter 1920s initiated the depression. The government controls imposed by Hoover turned what probably would have been a normal depression for the time into the Great Depression. The controls imposed by FDR were a continuation of the creation of controls by Hoover, albeit in a far more massive way. The controls imposed by FDR caused the Great Depression to last far longer than it otherwise would have.[16]

The fact that other factors were at work does not deny the validity of ABCT. It merely shows that other factors can work with the factors that ABCT identifies and make a recession or depression worse. Likewise, factors can also work to ameliorate the effects of a recession or depression, make it easier for recovery to occur, and thus make the recession or depression shallower in amplitude and/or shorter in duration. However, the primary driver of the routine financial crises, recessions, and depressions the world has been experiencing throughout the history of mankind is what ABCT identifies. The other factors, while they may in some cases be able to create economic crises on their own, have played only a secondary role. This is true even during the Great Depression, when the secondary factors had larger detrimental effects than the primary causes of the depression.

Since a depression to a great extent is an adjustment that is made necessary due to the mal-investment during the inflationary expansion, people need the freedom to be able to adjust. This means prices need to be able to fluctuate appropriately, some workers will need to be laid off and find new jobs, some businesses will need to be closed, and so on. If the government passes laws making any of these things harder or impossible, it will make the recession or depression longer and/or deeper. This is what the government controls imposed by Hoover and FDR did. Even though these controls are not a necessary part of a recession or a depression, since the controls were so numerous and had such a large effect during the Great Depression, it will help to discuss what some of these controls were and analyze how they made this economic crisis much worse than it needed to be.

Prior to the depression of 1929, a policy of laissez faire was, roughly, the rule the government followed during depressions.[17] However, this was not the case under President Hoover. Hoover was an altruist and collectivist and as a result believed in greater government control of the economy, especially during depressions.[18] Hoover wanted to temper nineteenth-century "rugged individualism." He thought that capitalists were "too greedy." He wanted a "better...individualism," one that called for "increasing responsibility and service to our fellows." He preached about the need to serve others: those to whom we come into contact, the nation, and even the world.[19] In other words, he wanted to destroy individualism and replace it with collectivism. It was not surprising that after WWI, FDR, Herbert Croly of the left-leaning magazine *The New Republic*, and other Democrats supported Hoover for the democratic ticket for the presidency.[20] Hoover clearly was not an advocate of capitalism. The belief that he was during his presidency was based on the fact that he was a Republican and that he was opposed to direct relief to people, specifically, government handouts to the unemployed. But Republicans are not advocates of capitalism—they are advocates of the mixed economy at best—and Hoover was a left-wing Republican.[21]

In response to the depression that began in mid-1929, Hoover started out by using the presidency as a bully pulpit. He held a series of White House Conferences to impose his will on the economy. In one of these, he invited prominent industrialists of the day, such as Henry Ford, Pierre DuPont, and Alfred P. Sloan, to the White House and urged them to keep wages high.[22] Hoover wanted to sacrifice employers to workers. He wanted the effects of the depression to fall on businessmen and not workers. He also believed that for the goods produced by businesses to be purchased, wages had to remain high so workers would have the money to buy them. Apparently Hoover did not understand that businesses also buy goods produced by businesses (and buy far more than wage earners, as the discussion on GDP versus GNR in chapter 5 makes clear). Apparently he also did not understand that if wages fall and more workers are employed as a result, total wage payments in the economy do not have to fall and therefore the total demand for goods by workers need not fall either.

For instance, whether 10 workers are hired at $10 per hour or 20 workers are hired at $5 dollars per hour, if the hours worked per worker remain the same, the same total wage payments are made. Even if total wage payments fall, if it is the case of businesses spending less money on labor as the result of spending more money on capital goods, total demand in the economy still does not fall. This is a case of a shift in demand from labor to capital goods. The fundamental change that causes a decrease in demand in the economy is a decrease in the money supply (or a sufficient slowing of its increase), but apparently this fact escaped Hoover.[23]

Hoover denounced those who said wages needed to fall and businesses needed to go bankrupt to weed out the mal-investments made during the inflationary expansion as "bitter-end liquidationists."[24] However, these were the very things that, had they occurred, would have minimized the depth and duration of the depression. Thanks to Hoover, the depression reached a depth and duration greater than any depression or recession has ever reached before or since.

Hoover's bullying of businessmen over wages had a long-lasting and widespread effect. As a result of his actions, nominal manufacturing wages did not fall until after June of 1930 and fell by less than 10 percent by December of 1931 (more than two years into the depression). Real wages actually rose from the beginning to the end of the contraction phase of the depression, if one could get a job.[25] Hoover's push to keep wages high was the most destructive of his policies. It kept costs to businesses high and was responsible for reducing investment spending on plant and equipment and the net change in business inventories (in real terms) by 30 percent in 1930, 61 percent in 1931, and 93 percent in 1932![26] This downward spiral occurred because Hoover's wage policy made it so unprofitable for businesses to invest. Twisting the arms of industrialists to keep wages high—which the industrialists did, and they also urged businesses in general to keep wages high—drove unemployment up to unprecedented levels as the money available for spending declined, including the money businesses had available for spending on labor. The lower investment and higher unemployment drove production in the economy down dramatically.

Falling production—not falling money wages—is what lowers the standard of living in the economy. Falling money wages do not have to result in a lower standard of living because they lower costs to businesses and, as a result, the prices businesses charge for their products. They also help to maintain investment and employment.[27] All of these help to maintain the same level of real wages. But apparently Hoover did not understand any of this and as a result far more people in the economy suffered than needed to, including many of the very workers Hoover was attempting to help. Such is the nature of altruism and the statist policies to which it leads.

Hoover also engaged in a massive program to subsidize businesses and consumers. He held a farm subsidy conference to call for large increases in subsidies to farmers. He also signed into law the Agricultural Marketing Act of 1929, which provided loans to farmers and purchased farm surpluses. He created the Reconstruction Finance Corporation (RFC) in January of 1932 to provide low-interest loans to businesses (mostly banks). He pushed for the Home Loan Bank System to make low-interest government mortgage loans. He also instigated spread-the-work schemes through, among other means, the Davis-Bacon Act, which instituted an eight-hour maximum workday.

All government subsidies, whether in the form of low-interest loans or outright payments to businesses, keep inefficient and less productive businesses in business. Many businesses may have been in financial trouble only because of Hoover's destructive policy to keep wages high; however, subsidies to prop up businesses in trouble due to this policy do not solve the problem. They merely create further problems. They make it harder for the economy to adjust appropriately. They prevent some businesses from being driven out of business and thus prevent capital and labor from being freed up to move into industries and geographic regions where they are more highly demanded. The subsidies therefore prevent businesses from producing goods that are the most highly demanded given the new economic circumstances that have arisen as a result of the depression.

Furthermore, the government does not know which areas of the economy need to contract and which need to expand because it does not respond to profits and losses. Reacting to profits and losses is how businesses know what to produce and what not to produce. Ceteris paribus, those goods people have the greatest demand for are the most profitable to produce; those which they have the least demand for are the least profitable to produce. By subsidizing businesses and instigating spread-the-work schemes, the government keeps businesses and workers producing in areas of the economy without regard to what goods people actually want to purchase.

To fully understand the effect of government subsidies, whether to businesses or consumers, there is a key question to ask: Who pays for the subsidies? Government subsidies always come at someone else's expense, regardless of how they are financed. If they are financed out of taxes, the recipient benefits at the expense of taxpayers. If they are financed by government borrowing, they come at the expense of future taxpayers who will have to pay off the loan and at the expense of those who are now unable to borrow because of the reduced supply of credit available in the loan market due to the government's borrowing. If they are financed through inflation, they come at the expense of those who are unable to purchase goods because they have been purchased by those who have received the newly created money, not to mention all of the other harmful effects of inflation.[28] In all these cases, the subsidies do not reduce the negative effects of a policy to keep wages artificially high. They merely transfer the negative effects of such a policy from some people to others and, at the same time, encourage greater consumption if they are provided to consumers or keep inefficient businesses in business if they are provided to businesses. Both of these latter two effects further reduce the productive capability of the economic system and thus further decrease the standard of living. That is, the subsidies add to the economic destruction brought down upon the economy.

Hoover also urged state governments to expand their make-work projects, as he expanded federal make-work projects through the Employment Stabilization Act of 1931. Through various government make-work projects during the Great Depression, such things as the Hoover Dam, roads and lodges in national parks, and buildings on university campuses were constructed. While these might seem like worthy projects to undertake and many people benefited from them and still benefit from them today, they come at the expense of what is not so easy to see. They come at the expense of all the goods that could not be produced. Resources—capital goods and labor—exist in limited supply and if some resources are used to produce some goods then they cannot at the same time be used to produce other goods. What people needed during the Great Depression was not lodges and roads in national parks (i.e., buildings and roads in the middle of nowhere used for recreation purposes that few people could afford at the time) or electrical power plants in the west (which had relatively little population compared to the east at the time). They needed the basics—such as food and shelter—in places easily accessible to them, which in the 1930s meant in the east. By engaging in such make-work schemes the government benefited some people at the expense of others; it benefitted small numbers of people at the expense of much larger numbers. Like the subsidy programs discussed above, it engaged in another horrendous policy of sacrifice.

Make-work projects wreak havoc on an economy because they have as their primary goal not the production of wealth but putting people to work for its own sake. The end is job creation without regard to whether the jobs are productive or goods are being produced that people actually want or need and for which they are willing to pay voluntarily. This is destructive because the purpose of economic activity is not to create jobs but to produce wealth with which people can sustain their lives and raise their standard of living. If the purpose of economic activity was merely to create jobs, it would be easy to do this. One could put everyone to work 40, 60, 80 hours a week—even 24/7—by having them dig holes and fill them all day. Everyone would have a job but everyone would also be miserably poor.

The way to create productive jobs is to protect people's freedom to respond to the profit motive. The profit motive, through the price system, provides the incentive to produce things that people actually want to buy. But the government does not act on the profit motive, so it has little or no idea what people want to buy. It ends up producing goods for which there is less demand at the expense of goods for which there is more demand. It thus reduces the level of satisfaction and well-being in the economy and, in this way, reduces the standard of living.

It must be noted here that make-work projects are worse for those who already have jobs than having to provide handouts to the unemployed. The wages that are paid to the workers in these jobs are typically higher than any unemployment handouts they would receive. In addition, not only do taxpayers have to pay for the higher wages, they have to pay for the capital goods used by the workers.[29] My point here is not that the unemployed workers should receive handouts (they should not; the policies causing them to be unemployed should be abolished). My point is that the violations of rights in the form of make-work projects are worse economically than the violations of rights in the form of handouts to the unemployed.

Hoover also dramatically increased government spending during the depression. The federal government went from surpluses to deficits from 1930 to 1931. Since the government is a consumer, as I discussed in chapter 2, any increase in consumption beyond its appropriate bounds—beyond the protection of individual rights—detracts from the ability to produce wealth.

In addition, taxes were raised in 1932 to help pay for the additional spending.[30] The tax increase was more onerous for high-income earners. The tax rate on the highest income earners was raised from 25 to 63 percent. Higher taxes on the wealthiest income earners are particularly destructive. First, they are immoral because they sacrifice the rich to the poor by redistributing income from the former to the latter. Second, higher taxes on the wealthy take money away from the most productive individuals in the economy and redistribute it to the least productive individuals. As discussed in chapter 2, this reduces the productive capability and standard of living.[31]

Hoover also raised tariffs dramatically and effectively banned immigration. The Smoot-Hawley Tariff that was passed in June of 1930 effectively imposed a tax rate of 60 percent on more than 3,200 products and materials imported into the United States.[32] The tariff did not cause the depression, as is sometimes believed, but it did make the depression worse. The Smoot-Hawley Tariff did not cause the Great Depression because it was imposed about a year after the depression had already begun.

Even so, tariffs in general do not cause recessions and depressions. They do not reduce the amount of spending in the economy (or reduce the rate of increase in spending) and they do not cause economy-wide decreases in profits, both of which are necessary for recessions and depressions. Tariffs do not reduce the money supply—which is what drives the spending down—if a country has a floating exchange rate and might actually increase the money supply and spending if the country has a fixed exchange rate.

International trade in the context of a floating exchange rate, whether with tariffs or not, affects only the exchange rate between two currencies; it does not change the amount of either currency in existence. Traders buy and sell currencies in the foreign exchange market but no new money is created by the government in response to activities in the foreign exchange market; the government just lets the exchange rate move up and down in response to the changing factors that affect this market.

Even money from one country that ends up in accounts overseas typically does not reduce the money supply of a country. Typically, the money finds its way back to the country of origin through loans made by foreigners to individuals in the originating country or through the purchases of goods from the originating country by foreigners. The fiat money of one country generally cannot be used to purchase goods and services in another country, so as long as the exchange rate is floating the money eventually finds its way back to the country of origin (if it leaves the country of origin at all) and does not affect the supply of money in either country involved in the trade.[33]

For example, if British goods are sold in America the British seller will either spend the dollars in the United States, place the funds in an American bank (or its foreign subsidiary), which will then loan them out in the United States, or purchase pounds with his dollars to spend the money in Britain, in which case the funds are spent or leant in America by the purchaser of the dollars in the foreign currency market. Either way, since the dollars cannot be used in Britain to buy goods, they generally end up back in America. So the money supply and spending in America (and Britain) are not changed.[34]

What does change in connection with international trade is the supply of goods in each country. In this case, a greater supply of goods is available in America since it is the importing country and a lesser supply is available in Britain since it is the exporting country. Changes in the supply of goods can affect the level of prices and the standard of living even though the supply of money and spending remain unchanged.

In the case of fixed exchange rates, international trade can affect the supply of money in a country if there are differences in the value of goods imported and exported to and from a country. This occurs because any differences between the supply of and demand for currencies in the foreign exchange market are made up for by purchases or sales of the appropriate currency by the government. Here the government does not allow exchange rates to float but keeps the exchange rates fixed by making up any differences between demand and supply.

For example, if an American sells goods in Britain and uses his newly obtained pounds to purchase dollars and no seller of dollars can be found in the foreign exchange market, he would purchase newly created dollars from the US government. This would increase the supply of dollars in America. In the case of fixed exchange rates, exports tend to increase the money supply in a country (since foreigners are, in essence, buying more of the domestic currency to purchase goods from the exporting country) and imports tend to reduce the money supply (since domestic citizens are, in essence, selling the domestic currency to buy foreign currency that can be used to buy the foreign goods).

If tariffs are imposed in the context of a fixed exchange rate, the effect will likely be to increase the money supply in the country imposing the tariffs. This occurs because tariffs reduce imports. This means when a tariff is put into place, ceteris paribus, imports will be reduced relative to exports and thus the sale of the domestic currency will be reduced relative to its purchase and use. This result is the exact opposite of that which occurs during a recession or depression, where the money supply is reduced or increases at a slower-than-expected pace.

Based on this, one might conclude that a tariff might actually cause an expansion, since the money supply is now increasing. Further, it might be believed that the tariff will increase domestic production since domestic firms are now protected from foreign competition. However, the imposition of tariffs will probably not increase the money supply (at least not much), since imports and exports tend to move in the same direction. What a country exports is ultimately used to pay for what it imports. Moreover, tariffs in one country are often responded to by retaliatory tariffs in other countries, since reducing imports into the country that imposed the tariffs simultaneously reduces exports from other countries. This occurred in response to the Smoot-Hawley Tariff. Thirty countries almost immediately responded with their own tariffs on US exports.[35] This brings about in a quicker fashion the reduction in exports from the country that originally imposed the tariffs.

In addition, tariffs do not increase the overall supply of goods in the country that imposes them. The overall supply of goods will decrease because the tariff is keeping goods out. Any replacement goods produced by domestic manufacturers will be more expensive and/or of lower quality than the imports. That is why individuals buy the imported goods. If they could have gotten the less expensive and/or higher quality goods domestically, they would not have bought the imports in the first place. Since the domestically produced goods will be more expensive and/or of lower quality, the effect will be a reduction in supply (and/or decrease in quality), which will lower the average standard of living in the economy imposing the tariff. This is how a tariff makes a recession or depression worse than it otherwise would have been. It deprives citizens of another source of goods (or makes the other source of goods less accessible) and further lowers their standard of living.

In terms of causing recessions and depressions, tariffs also do not reduce overall profitability in the economy, which is required to have a recession or depression. Tariffs will make some companies profitable at the expense of others. Importers and businesses that use the imported goods as inputs will be less profitable but domestic firms that compete with the imported goods will be more profitable. However, do not believe that it is a mere transfer that tariffs cause. They actually decrease the average standard of living by reducing the supply (and quality) of goods in a country, as previously discussed.

Tariffs do not even increase the production of domestic firms overall. Those domestic firms protected by the tariffs will engage in greater production. However, those domestic firms that used the imports as inputs will produce less because their costs will be higher. Further, sales at some firms will be reduced because individuals and businesses will need more money to buy the expensive goods produced by the firms protected by the tariffs. Moreover, to the extent that exports fall with imports, exporting industries will experience reduced sales as well. In essence, factors of production are pulled from other areas of the economy to increase production in the areas that are protected by the tariffs. So, tariffs lead to some domestic firms producing more at the expense of other domestic firms.

The above discussion on exchange rates not only pertains to countries on fiat-money monetary systems, it applies to countries on commodity systems of money as well. For example, if two countries are both on a gold standard and therefore have a fixed exchange rate, the money supplies can change based on international trade if there are differences in exports and imports between the countries and thus net transfers of gold occur. The discussion on fixed exchange rates above is applicable to two countries on a gold standard because both currencies are defined in terms of gold and thus fixed relative to each other.

If one country is on a gold standard and another is on a fiat-money system and the country with the fiat-money system has a fixed exchange rate, then trade between the two countries can change the money supply in both countries for the reasons discussed in the section on fixed exchange rates above. Likewise, if the country with fiat money allows the exchange rate to float, the effect is essentially no different in either country than that discussed in the section on floating exchange rates above as long as there are no net transfers of gold. If there are net transfers of gold then the country on the gold standard would have a change in its money supply (although, at least in connection with international trade, gold would probably only flow toward the country on the gold standard). So the same results obtain in these situations as in the cases of fiat money discussed above. That is, either the money supply is not affected by tariffs or, if it is affected at all, it might change in the opposite direction of the change that occurs during a recession or depression.

So the Smoot-Hawley Tariff made Americans worse off than they already were during the Great Depression. Hoover's policy on immigration had the same effect. Hoover's immigration restrictions reduced immigration by 90 percent from Europe, which is where most of the immigration came from.[36] Although it is likely that immigration would have decreased dramatically without the restrictions, since America was not a land of prosperity during the Great Depression capable of attracting the throngs of immigrants it did prior to the depression, to the extent peaceful, productive immigrants who wanted to come here were kept out, the amount of productive talent in the country was reduced. This lowers the productive capability and standard of living because fewer goods are then produced.[37]

Hoover also weakened bankruptcy laws during the depression. Weakening such laws makes it possible for financially unsound businesses to stay in business and thus prevents assets from being acquired by more productive individuals. In addition, he signed pro-labor union legislation into law that led to greater inefficiency and made it harder or impossible for businesses to *not* deal with unions. Specifically, the Norris-La Guardia Act, which became law in 1932, forbade yellow-dog contracts and curtailed the use of injunctions against mass picketing and other forms of union coercion. Yellow-dog contracts are employment contracts in which workers agree to not join or form unions. They make it easier for employers to avoid having to deal with unions. This law gave greater power to unions, such as the power to demand higher wages for their members (driving unemployment even higher), engage in strikes (reducing production in the economy), and engage in unproductive workplace practices (such as featherbedding: the practice of requiring employers to keep employees in obsolete positions).

Finally, Hoover used coercive tactics against the New York Stock Exchange to get it to stop short-selling, which he blamed for the stock market decline.[38] However, the falling stock market was merely an effect of the decline in money, spending, revenues, and profits that was taking place. It was also an effect of the large number of regulations being imposed by Hoover. Preventing short-selling merely adds to the problems. It reduces the efficiency of markets by preventing them from reacting in a quicker fashion to the economic forces at work. It prevents the market from declining as quickly as it could when the economy heads into a recession and prevents the market from rising as quickly as it could when the economy recovers (and short-sellers have to buy back shares they previously sold to pay them back).

The above does not include all the policies Hoover implemented. However, it gives one a good idea of the destructive nature of the government interference he imposed on the US economy. There are many good sources on this subject for further reading. See the sources I have been citing for more on Hoover's destructive policies.

Based on the altruist and collectivist ideas he accepted, Hoover wanted to sacrifice capitalists and businessmen—the most productive people in the economy—to wage earners. It is worth quoting Hoover at length to see this. In a fall 1932 campaign speech, during the deepest point of the worst economic disaster in US history—a disaster created largely by Hoover himself—he stated:

> We might have done nothing. That would have been utter ruin. Instead we met the situation with proposals to private business and to Congress of the most gigantic program of economic defense and counterattack ever evolved in the history of the Republic....No government in Washington has hitherto considered that it held so broad a responsibility for leadership in such times....For the first time in the history of depression, dividends, profits, and the cost of living, have

been reduced before wages have suffered.... They were maintained until the cost of living had decreased and the profits had practically vanished.

Creating new jobs and giving to the whole system a new breath of life; nothing has ever been devised in our history which has done more for... "the common run of men and women." Some of the reactionary economists urged that we should allow the liquidation to take its course until we had found bottom.... We determined that we would not follow the advice of the bitter-end liquidationists and see the whole body of debtors of the United States brought to bankruptcy and the savings of our people brought to destruction.[39]

Hoover actually thought that what he was doing was good, both morally and economically. He did not care how many capitalists, businessmen, and unemployed workers were sacrificed. His desire to sacrifice businessmen and capitalists is seen particularly in his statement of approval about dividends and profits being reduced before wages fell. Of course, Hoover's actions not only sacrificed businessmen and capitalists, but many workers as well. This is the nature of altruism. Putting altruism into practice leads to economically destructive policies that ultimately harm everyone. In this case, even workers who remained employed suffered to the extent that goods were harder to obtain due to the fact that the businesses that produced them went out of business or reduced their productive capacity. Altruist and collectivist policies go against what production and human life require. Human life requires the pursuit and production of values, not their abnegation and destruction.[40]

The Statist Controls of Roosevelt

Although FDR started out his campaign for the presidency in 1932 in a pragmatic fashion, changing his position depending on who he was speaking to, he was an altruist and collectivist like Hoover. His altruist and collectivist nature ultimately showed through in the large number of statist policies for which he was responsible. His altruism and collectivism can also be seen in the following statement about his policies, which include telling quotes from FDR himself:

Roosevelt... pushed on with his summons to a New Deal. He promised that the federal government should assume responsibility for relief where local aid had broken down. He called for public works and for unemployment insurance.... [H]e proposed measures of "regularization and planning for balance among industries and for envisaging production as a national activity." Business "must think less of its own profit and more of the national function it performs. Each unit of it must think of itself as a part of a greater whole."[41]

Roosevelt went far beyond Hoover. He continued and massively expanded what Hoover had started. While Hoover was responsible for creating the worst depression in the history of America by signing into law unprecedented legislative acts that violated individual rights, FDR was responsible for making it impossible for the economy to recover during his first few years through his own violations of rights. Because of FDR, it took until 1939 for real GNP and the total industrial production index to permanently recover their pre-depression levels. Based on GNR, the recovery took even longer.[42] Let us take a look at what FDR did to make the recovery much harder than it needed to be.

FDR's first act was the so-called banking holiday forced on the banking system only two days after he took office. As a result of this legislation, banks were forced to close for ten days (March 6–15, 1933). This prevented depositors from obtaining funds which banks, in many cases, had a legal obligation to pay on demand. It allowed financially unsound banks to regroup and stay in business. Requiring the banks to fulfill their contractual obligations to pay depositors on demand would have driven these unsound banks out of business and put the financial system in a much stronger position by increasing the fraction of reserves at the base of the monetary system, requiring banks to be much more financially conservative to survive, and thus making it much more difficult for financial contractions to occur. The banking holiday provided banks with a signal that they could count on the government to help them cover up the bad decisions they made. It gave them a license to engage in greater financial irresponsibility in the future.

The Glass-Steagall Act of 1933 forcibly imposed further instabilities on the banking system. Among other things, it created the Federal Deposit Insurance Corporation (FDIC) and separated commercial and investment banking. The FDIC made it possible for banks to be even more financially irresponsible by providing government deposit insurance on bank deposits. Although banks had to pay a small premium for the insurance, it is well known that the premiums are not large enough to cover the potential claims that could be made under the insurance scheme. If the system cannot fund itself, taxpayers will be responsible for bailing the system out and paying off depositors. To the extent taxpayers are at least partially, potentially responsible for paying off depositors, this lifts some of the financial responsibility for making sound decisions off bankers and gives them an incentive to be more irresponsible. This means they will make worse business decisions, including making more risky loans and operating with a lower fraction of reserves relative to their checking deposits. This leads to a more unstable banking and financial system.[43]

Forcibly preventing commercial and investment banking from being undertaken in the same business creates further instabilities. It prevents banks from diversifying into different types of businesses and thus makes the activities in which they engage more risky. Some might believe that separating commercial and investment banking is beneficial because it prevents a bank's commercial banking division from promoting products to its customers that are offered by its investment banking division for the sole purpose of increasing the bank's sales, not because the products are in the customers' interests. While it is possible for banks to do this, banks, and businesses in general, that do not provide products and services in their customers' interests do not last very long. To the extent no fraud exists (i.e., that banks are not withholding any information they should be providing to their customers so their customers can make well-informed decisions), the types of services banks offer their customers should be determined in the marketplace. If customers do not want banks to offer both commercial and investment banking services, it will pay banks not to offer both. If customers do want both services in one bank, it will pay banks to offer both. There are certainly benefits to customers being able to obtain multiple products and services from the same provider, such as not having to incur the costs of searching for more than one bank and any economies of scope gained by the bank and thus reduced costs and prices for bank customers.

To the extent banks engage in fraud in connection with the provision of both commercial and investment banking services, it would be proper for the government to punish those banks. But the Glass-Steagall Act does not do this. It, like all regulation of its kind, assumes people are guilty until proven innocent by preventing banks from engaging in many legitimate business activities. Assuming people are guilty until proven innocent is very dangerous. Acting on this principle will lead a nation down the road to a police state. The way to protect people from fraud while at the same time respecting individual rights is to have fraud units in local, state, and federal law enforcement agencies investigate cases and apprehend suspects in which actual evidence exists that a crime is being committed.

The Securities Act of 1933 was harmful as well. It was designed to compel truth in information about securities. However, one does not do this by, in essence, holding a gun at the heads of innocent businessmen. One does this by protecting property rights and making it possible for the full incentive of the profit motive to work. If this is done, to make large profits businesses will have to provide appropriate information about their products and services. If they do not, they will likely drive potential customers to other firms or turn people off altogether from the products the industry provides.

The profit motive provides the incentive for businesses to provide the information that customers need to make well-informed decisions. If customers are able to make good decisions based on the information a business provides, they will benefit, come back to do more business, and recommend that others do business there as well. If customers are not provided the right information, they will make bad decisions, not come back to do business (and probably not be able to afford to do more business anyway), and recommend that others *not* do business with that particular company.

By forcibly requiring securities firms to provide certain information in connection with the promotion and sale of securities, the government not only violates the rights of the owners of the securities firms but punishes innocent securities firms and provides firms with an incentive to provide only the minimum level of information wanted by the government, not the information that customers care about getting and actually consider worth paying for. Such regulation raises the costs of providing services in the securities business by forcing businesses to provide information that customers might not want. The best way to ensure that customers get the information they want is to leave the provision of information in the hands of profit-seeking businesses that stand to make money by providing customers the information they need to maximize returns on their investments. Those businesses that do not provide the proper information will tend to lose customers and go out of business. A company does not make large profits and remain in business very long by providing poor information to its customers and causing them to lose money. Further, as stated above, in the case of fraud, the government must punish the perpetrators, not regulate and stifle the innocent.[44]

The Securities Act of 1933 was incorporated into the Securities and Exchange Act of 1934, which created further regulations (including creating the Securities and Exchange Commission and extending financial regulation into the secondary financial markets). The same analysis above that applies to the Securities Act of 1933 applies to the new provisions in the Securities and Exchange Act of 1934.

The National Industrial Recovery Act (NIRA) of 1933 imposed minimum wages and restricted imports, among other things. These further lower the standard of living by decreasing the supply of goods available. Minimum-wage laws make low-skilled labor more expensive to hire and thus cause unemployment. This reduces the productive capability because fewer people are working to produce wealth. When considered in light of the fact that unemployment had already reached previously unheard of levels during the Great Depression, imposing a minimum wage was asinine.

Those low-skilled workers who are forced to join the unemployed bear the brunt of the loss, since their incomes are forcibly reduced to zero. Those low-skilled workers who remain employed receive higher income. These people receive the higher income at the sacrifice of the unemployed low-skilled workers. All non-minimum-wage workers who purchase products produced by low-skilled workers have a slightly reduced real income, since the products of the low-skilled workers will be more expensive due to the higher minimum wage. Overall, the higher minimum wage is a net loss for the economy because costs have been raised, and therefore production reduced, by the artificially high wage.

As discussed above on tariffs in the section on the statist controls of Hoover, restricting imports closes off a potential supply of goods from foreign producers. This simply makes it that much harder to purchase goods because the supply is reduced by the imports kept out.

Contrary to popular beliefs, import restrictions do not increase employment. They merely protect inefficient producers and thus decrease the productive capability and standard of living in the country with the restrictions. They prevent a country from benefitting from the law of comparative advantage, which shows that free international trade maximizes the standard of living in all countries and is thus to the advantage of all people and countries. Imports do not decrease employment and exports do not increase employment. Free international trade in general does not change the amount of employment; it merely changes the pattern of employment. With free international trade, businesses and workers are employed at more productive tasks and thus the average standard of living is higher.[45]

The Supreme Court struck down the NIRA in 1935. However, in response Congress passed the National Labor Relations Act (NLRA), also known as the Wagner Act, in 1935, which reintroduced some of the legislation declared unconstitutional in the NIRA and introduced new legislation forcing employers to recognize and bargain with labor unions. The pro-labor union portion of the NLRA added to the ability given to unions by Hoover to forcibly impose higher wages on employers and engage in strikes and unproductive workplace practices. This gave unions the ability to cause further unemployment and reduce production in the economy even more.[46]

Through the Gold Reserve Act of 1934, the government raised the price of gold from $20.67 per ounce to $35 per ounce, confiscated private gold holdings, and allowed for the repudiation of gold clauses in debt contracts. Those who refused to hand over their gold faced fines up to $10,000 and three-year jail terms. The confiscation of private gold holdings made possible, as did the confiscation of gold held on reserve at banks in 1917, further inflation of the money supply through the pyramiding of reserves. The raising of the price of gold had the same effect. Now the government could create $35 for every ounce of gold it possessed and banks could create further dollars through the fractional-reserve checking process. The repudiation of gold clauses prevented individuals from protecting themselves from the government's irrational monetary policies.

It should be clear from the above that the gold standard was not abandoned in the United States due to any deficiency of gold. A gold standard is necessary to prevent inflation and deflation and thus recessions and depressions. The United States was forced off the gold standard by the government. These violations of individual rights have had the effect of causing massive amounts of inflation and the attendant recessions, slower rate of capital accumulation, and slower rate of economic progress that these bring about.[47]

As a part of the inflation, the government massively increased spending beginning in November of 1933. Spending averaged about $400 million per month for the first ten months of 1933. However, spending increased to $505 million in November of 1933, $703 million in December, and $956 million in January of 1934. Spending rose by 139 percent in just three months!

FDR promised to raise the federal deficit to $7 billion by July of 1934 (the end of the fiscal year). He was only able to hit $4 billion by that time. He just could not spend money fast enough, although he certainly did try. As discussed in chapter 2, increased government spending means increased consumption at the expense of production in the economy. This occurred at a time when the economy desperately needed to increase production to restore the productive capability and standard of living. Contrast these policies with the government's policies of reducing spending and taxes, achieving budget surpluses, and paying down debt during the rapid recovery from the depression of the early 1920s.[48]

With regard to taxes, FDR raised taxes on the highest income earners to the highest rates in the world. On incomes of $5 million and over, the tax rate was raised to 69.9 percent. The estate tax was raised to 60.5 percent.[49] These more onerous violations of individual rights take more money away from the most productive individuals in the economy. They either funnel more money to government consumption or redistribute funds to less productive individuals in the economy. This decreases the standard of living in the economy by decreasing the productive capability, as discussed in chapter 2.

An undistributed profits tax was also imposed by FDR in 1936. This was a tax on corporate *savings and reinvestment*. If they retained their profits to reinvest into the company, they were taxed. If they paid dividends, they were not taxed. This created a massive increase in dividend payments.[50]

This was one of the more destructive pieces of legislation signed into law by FDR, and that is saying a lot because there were many pieces of destructive legislation signed into law by FDR. This legislation harmed the productive capability—and even the ability of businesses to survive—for a number of reasons. First, reinvestment of corporate profits is a way companies increase their productive capability and therefore it is a source of economic progress. Forcing businesses to pay dividends to avoid a tax undermines the ability of a company to expand and thus undermines economic progress.

Second, this is particularly harmful for small but quickly expanding companies. These companies typically earn high rates of return on capital invested and plow most or all of the profits back into the business instead of paying dividends to their investors. This is done because taking advantage of the fast expansion rate of the company provides the best means for the company to maximize the rate of return for investors. This tax prevents these companies from expanding as rapidly and might prevent them from expanding at all. This reduces competition in the economic system by preventing new but innovative companies from becoming dominant. It gives monopoly power to older and larger companies. Even if the older and larger companies have become stagnant, it may be impossible for innovative, young companies to displace them.

In addition, savings in good periods can be used by companies to offset losses in bad periods. However, if companies are forced to reduce their savings in good periods they might not be able to survive the bad periods. Moreover, to the extent that businesses might still have some (low) profits during bad periods, it makes it harder for them to save, accumulate capital, and improve their chances of surviving the bad periods. Finally, many businesses were under contract by creditors to retain profits. This meant that they had no way of avoiding the tax.

The undistributed profits tax was a "progressive" tax; the top rate was 27 percent. This meant that the more that was saved, that is, the more a business tried to expand its productive capability, the more it was taxed. This greater violation of individual rights of the most profitable companies is particularly harmful to the productive capability and standard of living—even more so than a flat undistributed profits tax. Fortunately, it was repealed in 1938 but the damage had already been done.

FDR also signed into law the Agricultural Adjustment Act of 1933, which was a continuation of Hoover's Agricultural Marketing Act. These made possible the provision of loans and subsidies to farmers, the purchase of surplus agricultural products, and a mechanism for devaluing the currency. FDR's version was shot down by the Supreme Court in 1935; however, Congress quickly passed the Soil Conservation and Domestic Allotment Act of 1936 that did many of the same things. It also passed the Agricultural Adjustment Act of 1938.[51] In addition, FDR provided handouts to the unemployed for the first time with federal funds through the Federal Emergency Relief Act of 1933. Moreover, he signed into law the Communications Act of 1934, which created the Federal Communications Commission, and he signed into law the Social Security Act of 1935, which (among other things) raised the cost of hiring workers to businesses and thus decreased the productive capability.

FDR issued almost 3,500 executive orders, almost six a week on average and more than the total number issued by all US presidents who came after FDR up through George H. W. Bush, almost 50 years after FDR died in office.[52] The legislation he signed into law was based on the destructive philosophical ideas of altruism and collectivism. All of it undermined the productive capability, standard of living, and made it harder for the United States to recover from the depression.

The first 100 days of FDR's administration are notorious for the massive number of legislative acts he signed into law—all acts that violated individual rights. He signed into law the Emergency Banking Relief Act on March 9, 1933. This act shut down banks, gave the Reconstruction Finance Corporation and Federal Reserve the power to bail out banks, and gave the government broad powers over transactions in gold, silver, and foreign exchange.

The Civilian Conservation Corps Reforestation Relief Act became law on March 31. This created make-work projects to create and improve national parks and forests. The Federal Emergency Relief Act and the Agricultural Adjustment Act became law on May 12. The Tennessee Valley Authority was created on May 18. This was a massive make-work project to build dams and provide electricity in Tennessee. The Securities Act became law on May 27. The National Employment System Act became law on June 6. This act created the US Employment Service, an information exchange on employment opportunities (mainly those created by the government through make-work schemes). The Homeowners Refinancing Act, which provided subsidies to homeowners through loans, became law on June 13. The Glass-Steagall Banking Act and National Industrial Recovery Act became law on June 16. The Farm Credit Act (FCA) and Emergency Railroad Transportation Act (ERTA) also became law on June 16. The FCA provided subsidies to farmers through loans and the ERTA regulated railroads with the Interstate Commerce Commission.[53]

FDR signed into law more New Deal legislation in his first 100 days than Hoover passed during his entire four years in office.[54] While the New Deal is not typically associated with Hoover, as I have shown, the legislation he signed into law in response to the 1929 depression is certainly consistent with the New Deal legislation of FDR. Hoover's New Deal was merely FDR light.

Apart from the long-term effect of directly undermining the productive capability through such things as make-work schemes, loans to inefficient businesses, handouts to the unemployed, and so forth, the main short-term effect this massive increase in regulation created was a stifling environment of uncertainty within which businessmen had to act. Such a climate does not inspire businessmen to be innovative and expand their productive activities, but causes them to remain in areas they can be reasonably sure are safe. This hinders, not aids, the recovery from a depression.

Not knowing what law the government will pass next is a very risky climate in which to operate. When, at any moment, the government could pass a law that violates the rights of businessmen and reduces the value of their investments, individuals and businesses have less incentive to invest and engage in economically productive activity. This is one reason investment declined to such a great extent under Hoover and remained below its peak value in 1929 for many years under FDR.

CONCLUSION

The greatest lesson to be learned from the Great Depression is what happens when a massive deflation occurs and the government passes massive numbers of regulations. These two had a self-reinforcing effect. The laws passed created a climate of uncertainty and made it too risky to invest. This led to huge decreases in investment, less spending in the economy, lower revenues, declining profits (and incomes more generally), and more bankruptcies. The lower spending and massive layoffs made it harder for debtors to pay off debts. This caused banks to become insolvent and decreased the money supply because of the fractional-reserve nature of the banking system.

When banks become insolvent and cannot make good on their outstanding claims—including checks written on the accounts of their depositors—their checks are no longer accepted and the funds in checking accounts at the banks lose their character as money. As the money supply shrinks, this further decreases spending, revenues, and profits and makes it even harder to pay off debts. This fuels the closing of more banks. Meanwhile, the continuous onslaught of regulations—imposed largely in an attempt to solve the problem of declining spending—maintains a climate of uncertainty, reduces investment, and makes it harder to produce. This merely hampers the recovery (or, in fact, causes further decline).

I have used a lot of space to discuss the problems caused by the government interference of Hoover and FDR. What should the government have done, instead, in response to the depression of 1929? The implication is clear from my discussion in this chapter on why government interference makes depressions worse and how the government's more-or-less hands-off approach in the depression of the early 1920s led to a quick recovery during that episode. Further, my discussions of what the appropriate response of the government would have been during the recessions discussed in chapters 5 and 6 can be applied to the Great Depression.[55]

One point that critics of ABCT make in connection with the Great Depression is that ABCT does not explain the international fluctuations that took place.[56] That is, not only was America experiencing a depression at the time but many other countries were as well. This is not a valid criticism of ABCT. First, to the extent that countries trade with each other the economic events that occur in one country can affect other countries and thus as problems arise in a country they can be transmitted to other countries through trade with those countries. Furthermore, during the Great Depression, despite the fact that world trade was declining, a substantial amount of trade still existed. One estimate shows that world trade declined by almost 70 percent during the depression.[57] This means that over 30 percent of the pre-depression trade still existed and therefore substantial ability for economies to influence each other still existed as well.

In addition, economies around the world had fractional-reserve banking systems just like the United States. If one investigates world economies one will probably find that the various supplies of money and credit were manipulated by the respective governments (or by private banks due to regulations created by the respective governments) in a manner similar to how the supply of money and credit was manipulated in the United States. All of these events are perfectly consistent with ABCT. ABCT does not say or imply that events in one country cannot influence other economies or that monetary manipulations cannot exist simultaneously in multiple economies.

Lastly, I have not discussed all the regulations imposed on the economy by Hoover and FDR. This book is not primarily about the Great Depression. I discuss the Great Depression only as a vehicle for illustrating the causes of the business cycle. However, I have discussed enough to show there were massive numbers of regulations imposed on the economy and to show the destructive effects they had. For more detailed discussions of the regulations imposed on the US economy during the Great Depression, see the references cited in the notes to this chapter. In particular, see the works by Murray Rothbard, Jay Cochran III, Benjamin M. Anderson, Richard M. Salsman, and Arthur M. Schlesinger Jr.

9

The Business Cycle in America
from 1900 to 1965

Introduction

In this chapter I discuss the period in America from 1900 to 1965. Data for a number of variables can be found as far back as 1900 and some data go back even farther. Other data, industrial production indices and the rate of profit, do not go back so far. However, the data that do exist will help solidify one's understanding of the business cycle. This chapter completes my historical analysis of the business cycle and provides further empirical evidence of the validity of Austrian Business Cycle Theory (ABCT). During this period, according to real gross national product (GNP), recessions or depressions occurred in 1904, 1908, 1914–15, during the post–World War I (WWI) period, 1924, 1927, 1930–33, 1938, toward the end of and immediately after World War II (WWII), 1954, and 1958.

The Effects

In this section, for the most part, I discuss the same variables I discussed in the equivalent section in chapter 8. The only gross national revenue (GNR) data that exist are the 21 years used in chapter 8 and a couple of years at the end of the period under consideration in this chapter. I do not present in this chapter the GNR data from the end of the period being considered here. For the majority of years I rely on GNP. However, I do present statistics on the rate of change of real GNR for the years it is available, along with the rates of change for other variables.

Output

Real GNP is shown in exhibit 9.1 from 1900 to 1965 in 1958 dollars. Real GNP is used instead of real gross domestic product (GDP) to measure output because GDP data do not exist for most of the time period under consideration. However, as discussed in chapter 8, both GDP and GNP are primarily measures of spending on consumers' goods, and for the United States the two tend to be fairly similar. These data show 11 recessions and depressions during this

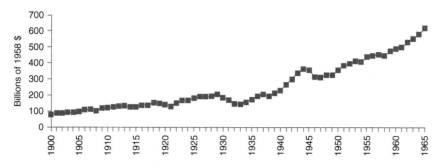

Exhibit 9.1   Real GNP, 1900–65.

Source: See exhibit 8.1.

period. The first recession was in 1904, when real GNP declined by 1.2 percent. The next contraction was the depression of 1908, when real GNP declined by 8.2 percent. The latter contraction was a part of the financial crisis of 1906–7. The next recession occurred during the years 1914–15, prior to America's entry into WWI. Real GNP declined by a total of 5.3 percent during this recession.

The depression that began in 1919, according to real GNP, was the first post–WWI contraction. According to these data, it lasted through 1921. Real GNP declined by almost 16 percent during the contraction. This was followed by two mild recessions in 1924 and 1927, according to real GNP. Here real GNP declined by 0.2 and 0.1 percent, respectively.

Looking at exhibit 8.2, one can see real GNR data for the period 1919–39. These data show the depression after WWI ending in 1920. Based on real GNR, 1921 was a mild expansion year. One cannot tell whether 1919 was a depression year according to real GNR, since the data start in 1919. In the one year of depression shown by real GNR for the post–WWI depression, it declined by almost 11 percent. This is greater than the maximum one-year decline of real GNP during the depression years (according to that variable), which is almost 9 percent in 1921.

After the early 1920s depression, real GNR shows only one recession prior to the Great Depression. This occurred in 1925. Real GNR declined by almost 8 percent, a much larger decline compared to real GNP during the nearest recessions according to that variable. The decline in real GNR is indicative of a depression rather than a recession. However, below we will see that other variables indicate two mild recessions like real GNP, although total industrial production shows a more significant decline in 1924.

Next is the Great Depression. As discussed in the previous chapter, this contraction lasted from 1930–33 according to real GNP and 1930–32 according to real GNR. Real GNP declined by over 30 percent while real GNR declined by almost 40 percent during this episode. The greater decline of real GNR is consistent with what ABCT predicts about the structure of production.

During the midst of recovery from the Great Depression, America experienced another depression, in 1938, according to real GNP. Here real GNP declined by 5.1 percent. Real GNR shows the depression occurring in 1938 as well but shows a decline of only 4.8 percent. The greater decline of real GNP relative to real GNR is not consistent with what ABCT predicts.

The next depression was the post–WWII depression which, according to real GNP, lasted from 1945–47. Here real GNP declined by over 14 percent, with the largest one-year decline of 12 percent occurring during the first full year after the war in 1946. Finally, there were mild recessions in 1954 and 1958 when real GNP declined by 1.4 and 1.1 percent, respectively.

Business Failures and Unemployment

The business failure and unemployment rates are shown in exhibits 9.2 and 9.3, respectively, for the years 1900–65. They confirm the real GNP data, showing spikes on or around the years of contractions and troughs during or near the years of expansions. Here one gets a better idea of the severity of the Great Depression, as the values of these variables were much worse during that episode than during any other recession or depression (especially with respect to the unemployment rate).

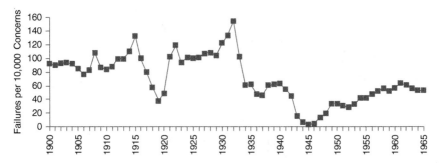

Exhibit 9.2   Business failure rate, 1900–65.

Source: See exhibit 5.3.

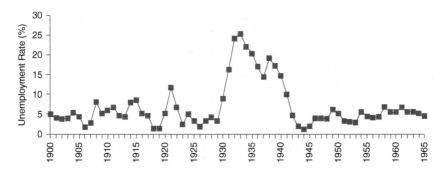

Exhibit 9.3   Unemployment rate, 1900–65.

Sources: For 1900–47, see exhibit 8.4. For 1948–65, see exhibit 5.4.

Industrial Production

Industrial production data are shown in exhibits 9.4–9.11. Some of these exhibits provide comparisons between output variables and show real GNP and GNR as well. Total industrial production is shown in exhibit 9.4. Industrial production for durable and nondurable manufactured goods is shown in exhibit 9.5. Total industrial production is shown from 1900 through 1965, while durable and nondurable manufacturing industrial production data are shown from only 1929 through 1965. Data for the latter two variables do not exist prior to the earliest years shown.

The total industrial production index shows 14 total recessions and depressions during the time period under consideration in this chapter. They occurred in 1904, 1908, 1910–11, 1914, 1918, 1921, 1924, 1927, 1930–32, 1938,

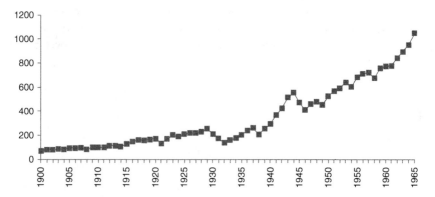

Exhibit 9.4   Total industrial production, 1900–65.

Sources: For 1919 and later years, see exhibit 5.6. For 1918 and prior years, see Table 2 of Jeffrey A. Miron and Christina D. Romer, "A New Monthly Index of Industrial Production, 1884–1940," *The Journal of Economic History* vol. 50, no. 2 (June 1990), pp. 321–337.

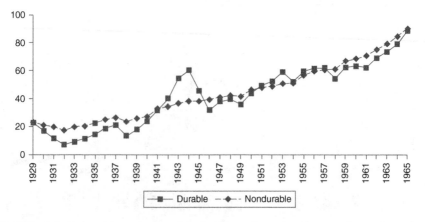

Exhibit 9.5   Industrial production for durable and nondurable manufactured goods, 1929–65.

Source: The Economic Report of the President (Washington, DC: US Government Printing Office, 1972), p. 235, Table B-35.

1945–46, 1949, 1954, and 1958. Of significance, besides the Great Depression, were the depressions in 1908, 1921, 1938, and the post–WWII depression in 1945–46. These depressions showed the largest declines in industrial production (not including the Great Depression), with the post–WWII depression having the largest decline and the 1921 depression the second largest decline. A comparison of the percent declines in output during the contractions as shown by real GNP, real GNR, total industrial production, and industrial production for durable and nondurable manufactured goods can be seen in exhibit 9.6.

The first depression during this time period was in 1908. GNP and total industrial production data exist for this year. Total industrial production declined by far more than real GNP (13.9 vs. 8.2 percent).

Jumping to the depression of the early 1920s, total industrial production declined by 23.1 percent (in 1921) while real GNP declined by 15.8 percent. However, the depression according to real GNP occurred over three years (1919–21), as indicated by note (b) in exhibit 9.6. Real GNR, as seen in chapter 8, showed a decline in 1920 of 10.9 percent and a rise in 1921 of 2.9 percent.

What the total industrial production and real GNR data indicate is that the depression was concentrated in a shorter time frame than shown by real GNP. The decline in real GNP occurred at an average annual rate of 5.6 percent over three years. The largest one-year decline for real GNP was 8.7 percent in 1921, the same year as the decline shown by the total industrial production index. The annual decreases for real GNP during 1919–20 were smaller—3.6 percent

Contraction years	Real GNP	Real GNR	Total IP	Durable goods IP	Nondurable goods IP
1904	1.2	DNA	1.4	DNA	DNA
1908	8.2	DNA	13.9	DNA	DNA
1910–11	N/A	DNA	2.7	DNA	DNA
1914	5.3[a]	DNA	6.6	DNA	DNA
1918	N/A	DNA	2.2	DNA	DNA
1921	15.8[b]	10.9[c]	23.1	DNA	DNA
1924	0.2	7.8[d]	6.3	DNA	DNA
1927	0.1	N/A	0.1	DNA	DNA
1930–32	30.5[e]	38.9	46.3	69	24.8
1938	5.1	4.8	20.9	35.9	11
1945–46	14.2[f]	DNA	26	47.2	0.3[g]
1949	N/A	DNA	5.6	9.1	1.7
1954	1.4	DNA	5.7	11.9	N/A
1958	1.1	DNA	6.5	12.4	N/A
1961	N/A	DNA	N/A	1.9	N/A

Exhibit 9.6 Percent total decrease in output during contractions as measured by real GNP, real GNR, and total, durable manufactured goods and nondurable manufactured goods industrial production.

Notes: [a]1914–15, [b]1919–21, [c]1920 (however, since 1919 was the first year of data for real GNR it is not known whether real GNR increased or decreased in 1919 and thus how long this contraction lasted according to real GNR), [d]1925, [e]1930–33, [f]1945–47, [g]1945, DNA ≡ Data Not Available, IP ≡ Industrial Production, and N/A ≡ Not applicable (value increased).

Sources: See exhibits 9.1, 9.4, and 9.5 for real GNP, total industrial production, and durable and nondurable goods industrial production, respectively. See exhibit 8.2 for real GNR.

in 1919 and 4.4 percent in 1920—and were accompanied by increases in total industrial production of 4.2 percent in 1919 and 4.7 percent in 1920.

For the economy as a whole—as opposed to just the small portion of the economy that GNP focuses on—the indication is that the first post–WWI depression lasted from 1920–21, based on all the output data, with a decline in the consumers' goods sectors occurring in 1919 but no overall decline in the economy during that year. Unfortunately, it is not known whether real GNR increased or decreased in 1919. The unemployment rate and business failure rate indicate that 1919 was not a year of contraction. In addition, as I have mentioned, the early 1920s depression was the last one in which the US government followed a more-or-less laissez-faire policy, which included *reducing* spending *and* taxes, maintaining a budget *surplus*, and *paying down* debt.[1] The economy was able to recover quickly as a result.

One can also see in exhibit 9.6 that in 1924 total industrial production and real GNR declined much more than real GNP (although the decline in real GNR was for 1925), 6.3 and 7.8 percent versus 0.2 percent, respectively, and that in 1927 total industrial production and real GNP declined by the same small amount (0.1 percent) and real GNR showed no decline during this year or adjacent years.

The side-by-side comparison in exhibit 9.6 helps to show more clearly the severity of the Great Depression according to total industrial production and real GNR relative to real GNP. This severity is even more pronounced given that the decline in real GNP took place over four years while the decline in real GNR and total industrial production took place over three years. We also see here the large decline in durable manufactured goods industrial production versus nondurable manufactured goods industrial production. These declines were, of course, discussed in chapter 8. We also see the large decline in total industrial production relative to real GNP and real GNR for the depression of 1938. The production of durable goods declined even more dramatically during this depression relative to the other variables when compared to its relative decline to these variables during the Great Depression.

We see the same pattern throughout the rest of the data available: total industrial production declines by more than real GNP and the decline is greatest in the production of durable goods, while nondurable goods production declines the least (in fact, nondurable goods production increased in the last three episodes shown in exhibit 9.6). For the depression at the end of WWII, the difference between total industrial production and real GNP is even more pronounced than is indicated in the exhibit since the decline of real GNP occurred over three instead of two years.

One sees in the data presented in exhibit 9.6 that total industrial production almost always declines by a greater percentage than real GNP during the contractions. Further, durable manufactured goods production declines more than nondurable goods production in every case. The same is seen during the expansions. That is, total industrial production almost always increases by a greater percentage than real GNP and durable manufactured goods production increases more than nondurable goods production in every case (at least based on the average annual rate of increase). Exhibit 9.7 shows a comparison of the percentage increases in output for the expansions of the same variables shown in exhibit 9.6.

The only expansion during which total industrial production does not increase more than real GNP is the first expansion shown in exhibit 9.7, during the years 1905–7. Total industrial production expands by 14.5 percent and real GNP expands by 21.7 percent. The next expansion value for real GNP is for the period 1909–13. It expands 31.1 percent or at a 5.6 percent annual rate. Total industrial production does not show a continuous expansion during this five-year period. It shows two expansions that lasted for a total of three years with a two-year contraction in the middle. The annual rate of expansion for real GNP compares to the 23.4 percent rate of expansion of total industrial production in 1909 and the 7.2 percent annual rate of expansion during the period 1912–13. So during 1909–13, total industrial production expands at a more rapid rate than real GNP on an annual basis in the years it shows an

Expansion years	Real GNP	Real GNR	Total IP	Durable goods IP	Nondurable goods IP
1905–7	21.7	DNA	14.5	DNA	DNA
1909	N/A	DNA	23.4	DNA	DNA
1912–13	31.1[a]	DNA	14.8	DNA	DNA
1915–17	21.9[b]	DNA	54.2	DNA	DNA
1919–20	N/A	DNA	9.1	DNA	DNA
1922–23	29.8	69.8[c]	51.7	DNA	DNA
1925–26	14.8	N/A	16.5	DNA	DNA
1928–29	7.2	13.7[d]	15.6	DNA	DNA
1933–37	43.6[e]	47.3	92.2	198.6	52.6
1939–44	87.3	DNA	168.2	349.3	62.6
1947–48	N/A	DNA	17.3	24.2	10.8[f]
1950–53	33.2[g]	DNA	41.4	64.3	N/A
1955–57	11.2	DNA	19.3	19	N/A
1959–69[h]	62.2	48.9[i]	91	16.8,[j] 77.1[k]	167.7[l]

Exhibit 9.7 Percent total increase in output during expansions as measured by real GNP, real GNR, and total, durable manufactured goods and nondurable manufactured goods industrial production.

Notes: [a]1909–13, [b]1916–18, [c]1921–24, [d]1926–29, [e]1934–37, [f]1946–48, [g]1948–53, [h]Data for 1966–69 are incorporated into these values to show the entire expansion, [i]1961–69 (However, since data start in 1960 for GNR it is not known exactly how long the expansion of this variable lasted. In addition, data are not available for 1961–63 so it is not known whether there was a continuous expansion during this period for this variable.), [j]1959–60, [k]1962–69, [l]1950–69, DNA ≡ Data Not Available, IP ≡ Industrial Production, and N/A ≡ Not Applicable (the period did not coincide with a complete expansion phase).

Sources: See exhibits 9.1, 9.4, and 9.5 for real GNP, total industrial production, and durable and nondurable goods industrial production, respectively. Data for the years 1966–69 are not shown in these exhibits but have the same sources as the data in these exhibits. Data for 1966–69 are shown in exhibit 6.9, except for real GNP. Real GNP is not shown anywhere for these years but real GDP is shown in exhibit 6.1. The data and sources for real GNR for 1919–39 and 1965–69 can be seen in exhibits 8.2 and 6.2, respectively. Data for real GNR for the years 1960 and 1964 are also used but are not shown in any exhibit. They have the same source as the data shown for real GNR in exhibit 6.2 (see note (i) above for more on this issue).

expansion. Total industrial production also expands more in total during this period—37.8 percent—even with the contraction in the middle.

Jumping to the expansion of 1922–23, total industrial production increases by over 50 percent while real GNP increases by only about 30 percent for annual rates of 23.2 and 13.9 percent, respectively. Real GNR expanded by 69.8 percent but during the years 1921–24, for a 14.2 percent annual rate, which is slightly greater than the annual rate of expansion of real GNP during the 1922–23 expansion. During 1925 and 1926, industrial production increased by 16.5 percent while real GNP increased by 14.8 percent.

During the expansion of 1928–29, industrial production increased by 15.6 percent while real GNP increased by only 7.2 percent for average annual increases of 7.5 and 3.5 percent, respectively. Real GNR increased by 13.7 percent but over the period 1926–29 for an average annual increase of 3.3 percent, which is slightly less than the average annual increase of real GNP during the 1928–29 expansion.

During the period from 1933 to 1937 industrial production increased by 92.2 percent, while during the period 1934–37 real GNP increased by only 43.6 percent from its previous low point. This implies average annual increases of 14 and 9.5 percent, respectively. Real GNR increased 47.3 percent from 1933–37 for an average annual increase of 8 percent, which is lower than the average annual increase for real GNP. During the wartime, inflation-fueled expansion industrial production increased by 168.2 percent, while real GNP increased by 87.3 percent.

Total industrial production also shows greater increases than real GNP, on a total and average annual basis, for all the remaining expansions in the time period being considered in this chapter. In addition, based on data for real GNR from the 1960s (shown in chapter 6 from 1965), real GNP increased by a greater amount than real GNR during the last expansion shown in exhibit 9.7. However, as stated in the note to that particular real GNR value, data for real GNR could be obtained only back until 1960 and data could not be obtained for 1961–63, so it is not known with certainty how long the expansion lasted for real GNR or whether it was a continuous expansion.

Shifting the focus to durable manufactured goods industrial production, this index almost always shows greater increases on a total and average annual basis when compared to real GNP, the total and nondurable industrial production indices, and real GNR (for the expansions for which data exist for both real GNR and durable goods industrial production). The total industrial production index increases slightly more than the durable goods index during only one expansion: 1955–57.

During the last period shown in exhibit 9.7, 1959–69, the durable goods index shows two expansions (with a contraction in 1961) while the other variables show only one, although not all show an expansion for the same years. Real GNP and total industrial production expand from 1959 to 1969, real GNR expands from 1961 to 1969 (although see the qualifications above), and the nondurable manufactured goods industrial production index shows a continuous expansion from 1950 to 1969. On an average annual basis, however, the durable goods index increased more in each of its expansions than the other variables did during their respective expansions.

One interesting point to highlight from above is the slightly greater increase of total industrial production relative to durable goods industrial production from 1955 to 1957. One might think based on this that the nondurable goods industrial production index increased more than the durable goods index during this period. While this is a possibility, it did not occur. The nondurable index increased 18.6 percent from 1955 to 1957. The reason the total industrial production index increased by more than the durable goods index is because the materials industrial production index increased by 21.3 percent during this period, which is a greater increase than both the total and durable goods industrial production indices. It pulled total industrial production above the production of durable manufactured goods (and above the consumers' and intermediate goods industrial production indices as well [see exhibit 9.11]). The materials index is not shown in any exhibit. I opted to show a minerals/mining index instead (see exhibits 9.9–9.11) because it covers more years. The minerals/mining index and materials index do not cover the same industries. As discussed in chapter 8, the materials index is a broader index. The materials index has the same source as the durable and nondurable goods industrial production indices (see exhibit 9.5).

What do all the data mean? Since real GNP measures mainly only the production of consumers' goods and total industrial production has a greater relative focus on the production of capital goods, the goods whose production is measured by industrial production will, on average, be farther removed from final consumption than the goods whose production is measured by real GNP. This means, according to ABCT and as discussed in previous chapters, the industrial production index will fluctuate more than real GNP. This occurs in most cases. On a total basis it occurs in 10 out of 11 and 9 out of 11 cases for which valid comparisons can be made during the contractions and expansions, respectively. On an annualized basis, it occurs in 10 out of 11 cases during both the contractions and expansions.

The statistic of 9 out of 11 expansions in which total industrial production shows greater increases than real GNP on a total basis includes a comparison of the expansion of real GNP from 1909 to 1913 with the expansion of total industrial production from 1912 to 1913. If one considers the entire time period during 1909–13 for total industrial production, one could increase this ratio to 10 out of 11 expansions. I use the lower ratio because the period from 1909 to 1913 includes multiple expansions for total industrial production. Regardless of how the comparisons are made, these variables behave as ABCT predicts.

The durable manufactured goods and nondurable manufactured goods indices also behave as ABCT predicts. The durable manufactured goods industrial production index increases at a greater average annual rate than the nondurable manufactured goods industrial production index in every case (four out of four for the contractions and four out of four for the expansions). This includes separate comparisons of the last four expansions of the durable goods index during the period from 1950 to 1969 with the last expansion of the nondurable goods index, which lasted from 1950 to 1969 as well. I only count this as one comparison.

In addition, in seven out of eight of the cases, the durable goods index expands more in total than the nondurable goods index. The only case in which it does not is the last expansion for the nondurable goods index, which occurs over the above-mentioned 20-year period. In contrast, there are three contraction phases interspersed during this period for the durable goods index. The comparison expansion period up to 1969 for the durable goods index goes for only eight years, spanning the period 1962–69. Nonetheless, the durable goods index shows a total expansion from 1950 to 1969—even with the three contractions during this period—of 206.4 percent, which is much more than the nondurable goods index. Based on this, one could say the durable goods index expands more in total than the nondurable goods index in eight out of eight cases. But as with total industrial production and real GNP, I use the lower ratio because the 1950–69 period of time covers multiple expansion phases for the durable goods index. In any case, no matter how the comparisons of these two indices are made they provide even stronger support for ABCT. One can visually confirm this support for ABCT by looking at exhibit 9.5. There one can see the greater fluctuations of the durable goods industrial production index relative to the nondurable goods index.

Real GNR versus real GNP shows mixed support for ABCT. Real GNR moves more on an average annualized basis in two of three contractions and in one of three expansions for which valid comparisons can be made. I do not include the contraction in the late 1910s and early 1920s or the expansion from 1959/61 to 1969 due to a lack of data availability for real GNR. Despite the mixed results in comparing real GNR to real GNP, the overall results provide significant support for the validity of ABCT.

Consumers' goods and intermediate goods industrial production indices are shown in exhibit 9.8 for the years 1947–65. Data for these indices are not available before 1947. Even though this provides a very limited look into the movement of these variables, it does help one understand the nature of the business cycle. These variables are fairly similar to the industrial production variables discussed previously in this chapter in terms of the timing of the fluctuations. The main exceptions are that the consumers' goods index decreases in 1951 and the intermediate goods index decreases in 1952. Since the industrial production variables presented above in this chapter do not decrease at these times, these declines are not indicative of a recession in the economy but decreases in production in only some portion of the economy during these years.

Total manufacturing and minerals/mining industrial production data are shown in exhibit 9.9 from 1919–65. I use industrial production data on minerals from 1919 to 1928 and industrial production data on mining starting in 1929, hence the name "minerals/mining" index. It appears that at some point the name for essentially the same data changed. Movements in the minerals and mining data are very similar, so it is not problematic to combine these data to provide a longer series of data. Total manufacturing data are available back to 1919 even though the components of durable and nondurable manufactured goods industrial production data, shown in exhibit 9.5, are only available back to

1929. These variables show good agreement with the fluctuations in the industrial production variables discussed above in this chapter. The only anomaly I will highlight here is that, like the intermediate goods index, the minerals/mining index shows a contraction in 1952.

Summaries of the percent changes in the variables presented in exhibits 9.8 and 9.9 during the contractions and expansions are provided in exhibits 9.10 and 9.11. These exhibits show a greater number of expansions and contractions of the consumers' goods, intermediate goods, and minerals/mining indices relative to the total manufacturing index during the years that data for all of the variables exist. The former indices show four contractions and five expansions during this period while the latter index shows only three contractions and four

Exhibit 9.8 Industrial production for consumers' and intermediate goods, 1947–65.

Source: The Economic Report of the President (Washington, DC: US Government Printing Office, 1972), p. 235, Table B-35.

Exhibit 9.9 Industrial production for all manufactured goods and minerals/mining, 1919–65.

Sources: For 1929–65, see *The Economic Report of the President* (Washington, DC: US Government Printing Office, 1972), p. 235, Table B-35. For 1919–28, see the *Annual Report of the Board of Governors of the Federal Reserve System* (Washington, DC: US Government Printing Office, 1937), p. 173, Table No. 81.

Contraction years	Consumers' goods	Intermediate goods	Total manufacturing	Minerals/ mining
1921	DNA	DNA	23.4	21.5
1924	DNA	DNA	7.2	8.4
1927	DNA	DNA	1.9	1.9[a]
1930–32	DNA	DNA	48.2	37.8
1938	DNA	DNA	23.1	13.4
1945–46	DNA	DNA	30.6	3.6
1949	0.5	5.1	5.4	11.3
1951	1	N/A	N/A	N/A
1952	N/A	0.6	N/A	0.8
1954	0.7	0.4	6.5	2
1958	0.9	2.1	7	8.3

Exhibit 9.10 Percent total decrease in output during contractions as measured by consumers' goods, intermediate goods, total manufactured goods, and minerals/mining industrial production.

Notes: [a]1927–28, DNA ≡ Data Not Available, and N/A ≡ Not Applicable (value increased).

Sources: See exhibit 9.8 (for consumers' and intermediate goods) and exhibit 9.9 (for total manufacturing and minerals/mining).

Expansion years	Consumers' goods	Intermediate goods	Total manufacturing	Minerals/ mining
1922–23	DNA	DNA	51.6	50
1925–26	DNA	DNA	15	12.4
1928–29	DNA	DNA	12.3	8.6[a]
1933–37	DNA	DNA	98.3	68.1
1939–44	DNA	DNA	182.8	44
1947–48	3[b]	5.6[b]	15.9	18.8
1950–53	14.2,[c] 8.5[d]	22.1,[e] 7[f]	42.4	22.6,[e] 2.7[f]
1955–57	18.6	18.5	18.8	17.5
1959–69[g]	77.5	75.3	94.2	41.5[h]

Exhibit 9.11 Percent total increase in output during expansions as measured by consumers' goods, intermediate goods, total manufactured goods, and minerals/mining industrial production.

Notes: [a]1929, [b]1948 (however, since data start in 1947 for these variables it is not known exactly how long the expansion of these variables lasted), [c]1950, [d]1952–53, [e]1950–51, [f]1953, [g]Data for 1966–69 are incorporated into these values to show the entire expansion, [h]1959–70, and DNA ≡ Data Not Available.

Sources: See exhibit 9.8 (for consumers' and intermediate goods) and exhibit 9.9 (for total manufacturing and minerals/mining). Data for the years 1966–69 are not shown in these exhibits but have the same sources as the data in these exhibits. Data for 1966–69 are shown in exhibit 6.5, except for the total manufacturing and minerals/mining data, which are not shown anywhere (although a materials industrial production index is shown in exhibit 6.5 and the durable and nondurable manufactured goods industrial production indices are shown in exhibit 6.9).

expansions. The greater number of fluctuations is due to the contractions discussed above in the former indices in 1951 and 1952.

Comparisons can be made between the total manufacturing and minerals/mining indices to determine if the results are consistent with ABCT. The same is true of the consumers' goods, intermediate goods, and minerals/mining indices. The indices in these two sets represent measures of output at different stages of production.

Let us first focus on the manufacturing and minerals/mining indices. During the contractions, in only three out of nine cases for which contractions occur for both indices does the minerals/mining index fall more than the manufacturing index based on the average annual rate of change. The average annual rate of change is not provided but can be calculated for each variable from the data in exhibit 9.10.

For the expansions, the change in the minerals/mining index is greater based on the average annual rate of change in only two out of eight cases. For the period 1950–53, the minerals/mining index shows two expansions and the manufacturing index shows one. One of the minerals/mining expansions has a greater average annual rate of expansion than the manufacturing index and one has a smaller rate of change. Therefore, the results from this period are not included in the statistics. If all the comparisons had favored one index, it would have been included as one case in the statistics, as was done for comparisons of indices above. Of course, if this time period was included using the average annual rate of expansion for each index during the entire period—despite the fact this period encompasses a complete contraction for the minerals/mining index—it would change the statistics to two out of nine cases in which the minerals/mining index expands more than the manufacturing index. However, this is not consistent with the method followed in the comparison of annual rates of change for other indices.

For the consumers' goods, intermediate goods, and minerals/mining indices, I compare the contractions in 1949, 1951 and 1952, 1954, and 1958. For the expansions, I compare the last four expansions shown for these variables during the last three time periods in exhibit 9.11. This includes the two expansions for each variable in the period from 1950 to 1953. We are looking for the minerals/mining index to move more than the intermediate goods index and the intermediate goods index to move more than the consumers' goods index. This should occur due to the different stages of production that these indices represent.

This relative movement occurs in two of the four cases for the contractions (1949 and 1958). For the expansions, the variables do not behave as ABCT predicts in any of the cases on an annualized basis. One point that can be made in favor of ABCT based on the expansions is that the first expansion shown for these indices during the period 1950–53 behaves as ABCT predicts in terms of the total change for each index. Another point that shows potential support for ABCT is that the expansion of 1947–48 appears to be as ABCT predicts (on a total and annualized basis). However, since the data start in 1947 for the intermediate and consumers' goods indices, one cannot be sure exactly how much they change. Overall, there is little support for ABCT based on the relative changes of the consumers' goods, intermediate goods, and minerals/mining indices.

This lack of support is not a major concern. In previous chapters, especially chapter 6, the comparisons of these or similar indices showed less support for

ABCT than comparisons of other indices in those chapters, although the results are worse in this chapter. As discussed in chapters 5 and 6, the reason why this is not a major concern is due to the existence of durable goods in these indices. The existence of durable goods in the consumers' goods index, for example, can cause the consumers' goods index to move more in some cases than the intermediate goods and minerals/mining indices. This occurs in part due to the sensitivity of the production of durable goods to interest rates. The same is true of the total manufacturing goods and minerals/mining indices that are compared in this chapter. The existence of durable goods in the manufacturing index can cause it to move more than the minerals/mining index. The better comparison to make is between durable and nondurable manufactured goods. The indices for these goods show greater agreement with ABCT in this chapter and all chapters in which such data are presented.

One final comparison to make is between the durable manufactured goods index and the consumers' goods index. I make this comparison because while data only exist from 1947 for the consumers' goods index presented here, industrial production data are provided by C. A. Phillips, T. F. McManus, and R. W. Nelson in their book *Banking and the Business Cycle* for what they call consumption goods and durable goods from 1899 to 1933.[2] The data for durable goods in the graph they present fluctuate much more than the data for consumption goods. It shows that durable goods industrial production moves more in both the contractions and expansions. The same is true for the durable manufactured goods and consumers' goods industrial production indices presented here. That is, the durable manufactured goods index moves more in both the contractions and expansions (where comparisons can be made). This provides further support for ABCT.

Comparing the durable and consumers' goods indices is valid even though there is some overlap. For example, clothes washing and drying machines and automobiles are both durable goods and consumers' goods (when used for consumption purposes). Nonetheless, durable goods will tend to be farther from final consumption and therefore the durable goods index should fluctuate more. Durable goods tend to be farther from final consumption because consumers' goods include many nondurable goods. The durable goods index also includes more goods that are in stages farther removed from final consumption, since the consumers' goods index includes only goods that are headed to their final user.

While the output data are mixed in this chapter in support of ABCT, overall they do support the theory. The comparisons between real GNP and GNR; consumers' goods, intermediate goods and minerals/mining industrial production indices; and total manufactured goods and minerals/mining indices do not provide consistent support for ABCT. However, in the cases of the industrial production indices that do not provide consistent support, the lack of support can be explained by the effect of durable goods in the indices. In contrast, comparisons of durable and nondurable manufactured goods industrial production, total industrial production and real GNP, and durable and consumption goods industrial production all provide substantial support for the theory.

THE CAUSES

In this section, as in the similar sections from previous chapters, I look at the rate of profit, interest rates, the money supply, and the velocity of circulation of money. Data for the rate of profit are limited. However, interest rate and money supply data are more abundant. Let's see if these variables support ABCT.

Profitability and Interest Rates

A short-term interest rate, the rate of profit, and the rate of profit minus the interest rate are presented in exhibit 9.12. The short-term rate comprises two different commercial paper rates (the same as those in chapter 8) and the rate of profit is the return on assets after interest expense and before taxes. The interest rate is available for the entire time period under investigation. The rate of profit is only available starting in 1926.

One sees that the interest rate generally rises just prior to recessions and depressions and falls just prior to expansions, while the rate of profit tends to be at or near a minimum during recessions and depressions and at or near a maximum during expansions. The difference between the two tends to fall just prior to or during recessions and depressions and rise just prior to or during expansions. These patterns are consistent with those seen in chapter 6, although they are not all exactly the same as in chapter 6 and the patterns in this chapter are not adhered to as consistently. The Great Depression and WWII play a role in disrupting the patterns.

The interest rate peaks in 1903 and 1907, just prior to the recession and depression, respectively, of 1904 and 1908. Likewise, it reaches a local minimum in 1904 and 1909, just prior to and during the expansions taking place at those times. The interest rate then rises in 1910, at the beginning of the decline in total industrial production that started in that year. It falls in 1911 and rises through 1913, just prior to the recession in 1914–15. It then bottoms in 1915–16, just

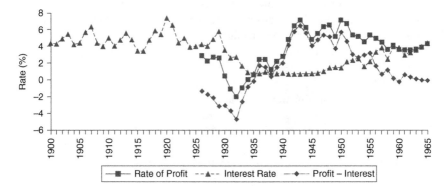

Exhibit 9.12   Rate of profit and interest rate (return on assets and commercial paper rate), 1900–65.

Source: See exhibit 8.7.

prior to and during the first year of the expansion during WWI. Next, it rises dramatically from 1917 to 1920 (prior to and during the post–WWI depression), it falls in 1921–22 (prior to and during the early part of the expansion of the early 1920s), and rises in 1923 (prior to the recession of 1924).

The interest rate then falls in 1924 and remains low in 1925, during the expansion of the mid-1920s. It then has a small peak in 1926, just prior to the very mild recession of 1927. At this point one can also see the rate of profit reaching a local minimum during the recession of 1927. The interest rate then falls slightly in 1927, just prior to the expansion of the latter 1920s, while the rate of profit rises in 1928, during the expansion. The difference between the rate of profit and the interest rate generally declines from the mid-1920s through the depths of the Great Depression. The interest rate rises and then peaks in 1929, prior to the Great Depression, while the rate of profit falls only slightly in 1929 and then precipitously from 1930 to 1932. Both the rate of profit and interest rate fall and remain low during the early 1930s in response to the dramatic decrease in the money supply and spending during the early 1930s. I will discuss the money supply below. One estimate of the decline in spending on consumers' and producers' goods during the Great Depression shows that spending decreased by over 60 percent during the period 1930–32.[3]

The interest rate rises slightly in 1937, prior to the depression of 1938. The rate of profit and rate of profit/interest rate differential rise through 1936, remain fairly flat in 1937, and fall during the depression of 1938. After this depression, the rate of profit and the rate of profit/interest rate differential rise and the interest rate falls slightly and remains flat during the WWII inflationary expansion. The interest rate rises prior to and during the post-war depression (which began during the last year of the war in 1945). The rate of profit and rate of profit/interest rate differential fall prior to and during the post-war depression. The post-war depression occurred due to the reduction in the massive wartime inflation of the money supply, which will be discussed below.

After the first post-war depression the interest rate continues to rise. This trend continues through the first post-war expansion. This was probably due to the quick adjustment of the economy to the post-war reduction of the massive wartime inflation. Individuals and businesses were flush with cash during the war due to the massive inflation and the inability to spend money due to restrictions on the production of civilian goods, as well as the maximum price controls imposed during the war and subsequent rationing. The rate of profit and differential both rise until 1948 and 1947, respectively, during the first post-war expansion, and fall during the one-year decline in total industrial production in 1949.

During the middle of its post-war upward trend, in 1949–50, the interest rate flattens out. The upward trend is resumed in 1951–53. This presages the recession of 1954. The rate of profit and differential rise in 1950 and fall during the early 1950s, reaching local minimums in 1954 and 1953, respectively.

The interest rate falls in 1954, prior to the expansion from 1955 to 1957. It then rises during the expansion, which precipitated the contraction of 1958. The rate of profit and differential initially rise during the expansion and then fall, reaching local minimums in 1958 and 1957, respectively.

At this point, the interest rate falls during the recession of 1958, rises in 1959, falls in 1960–61, and then rises continuously throughout the rest of the period under investigation. The rate of profit rises a small amount in 1959, falls in 1960, and remains fairly flat until 1963, when it rises through the end of the period being investigated here. The rate of profit minus the interest rate rises in 1958, falls in 1959–60, rises in 1961, and then falls continuously (but at a slowing pace) through 1965.

Although the interest rate rises toward the end of the period under consideration, no recession was experienced for the rest of the period. In fact, a recession did not occur until 1970. The US economy was beginning to see the effects of rapidly growing spending taking place, and therefore the rise in interest rates did not necessarily reflect a policy on the part of the Federal Reserve to slow the increase in the money supply. In fact, just the opposite was occurring: the rising interest rates, more and more, reflected an accelerating increase in the money supply. The increase in spending was initially fueled by demand that was unleashed after the war due to the buildup of unspendable money during WWII and then by accelerating inflation until the late 1970s. As a result of this increased money and spending, interest rates had an upward trend from the end of WWII to the early 1980s.

The Money Supply and the Velocity of Money

The rate of change in the money supply during the period 1897 to 1965 is shown in exhibit 9.13. The measure of the money supply used in this chapter, as in the last chapter, is the amount of currency in circulation plus demand deposits. One sees the same types of changes in the money supply driving the fluctuations of the business cycle as has been seen in previous chapters.

One sees in exhibit 9.13 that the rate of change of the money supply reached a local maximum in 1898 (this is also true based on money supply data prior to 1897, although they are not shown in the exhibit). It then began to decline in

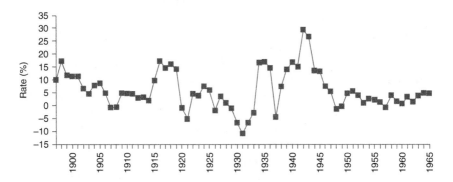

Exhibit 9.13   Rate of change of currency and demand deposits, 1897–1965.
Source: See exhibit 8.8.

1899 and reached a local minimum in 1903. This drove short-term interest rates to a local peak in 1903 and caused the recession of 1904. The money supply then began to increase at more rapid rates, driving the expansion from 1905 to 1907 and pushing interest rates lower. The rate of change of the money supply reached a local peak in 1905 and then a local minimum in 1907. This fall in the rate of change of the money supply drove interest rates to their peak in 1907 and precipitated the depression of 1908. The money supply actually declined during this contraction.

Inflation then picked up through 1909 (it was actually a lessening of deflation in 1908) and more or less plateaued through 1911. This kept short-term interest rates relatively low. Then the rate of change of the money supply had a downward trend through 1914. This caused interest rates to reach a local peak in 1913 and caused the recession at the start of WWI.

Prior to the creation of the Federal Reserve System, the government had indirect control of the money supply (for the most part), but it still had control of the money supply. It exercised its control through various regulations on the monetary and banking system. For example, prior to the Fed the government would sometimes allow banks to suspend payment of specie when the banks were obligated to pay specie on demand. This blatant disregard for the sanctity of contract made it possible for banks to issue more notes (when banks were still allowed to do this) and lend more reserves than they would have otherwise been able to. As banks loaned reserves, interest rates would be temporarily low, spending, revenues and profits would increase, and an inflationary expansion would ensue if the inflation was taken far enough. Once the banks could no longer maintain the low level of reserves, they would have to reduce their lending. At this point, interests rates would rise, spending, revenues and profits would fall (or not rise quickly enough), and a contraction or financial crisis would often occur. This is one way the government, through regulation, created the business cycle before the Fed existed.

Prior to the Fed, the government also restricted competition through the chartering of banks. This prevented the more financially sound banks from expanding and driving out the less sound banks. It led to less geographical diversification of banks as well. Both of these led to less stability in the monetary and banking system.

Sometimes the government directly affected the money supply through regulation prior to the Fed. For example, starting during the Civil War the US government issued the first fiat money: greenbacks. The creation of national bank notes and taxing state bank notes out of existence through the National Bank Act of 1863 and subsequent legislation are other ways the government exercised control over the money supply. There are many ways in which the government controlled the monetary and banking system prior to the Fed. So even though the Fed did not exist during the first 14 years of the period under investigation in this chapter, the government was still responsible for creating the business cycle.[4]

Since the Fed was created by Congress in 1913 and started engaging in operations in 1914, at that point it became the primary driver of the business cycle. The Fed created much higher rates of inflation of the money supply almost immediately. Its newly expropriated gold reserves that it confiscated from banks in 1917 enabled it to continue its inflationary policy beyond WWI. Then, in 1920 and 1921, there was an actual deflation of the money supply. This induced the first post–WWI depression and drove interest rates, which had already been driven up by the massive inflation during WWI, to their peak in 1920.

In 1922 there was a mild inflation and then a slight reduction in inflation in 1923, which caused a small spike in interest rates and produced the recession of 1924. During this recession, the money supply was inflated at a more rapid rate. However, the slowing of inflation in 1925 and deflation in 1926 precipitated a slight rise in interest rates during a time when interest rates were generally lower (at least relative to the peaks of 1920 and 1929). The slowing of inflation and outright deflation also precipitated the recession and lower rate of profit in 1927. The money supply was then inflated more rapidly in 1927, the inflation slowed in 1928, and then deflation occurred from 1929 to 1933.

The dramatic slowing of inflation in the latter 1920s and outright deflation in the late 1920s/early 1930s started the depression of that period and helped drive the United States deeper and deeper into depression during the early 1930s. The slowing inflation and outright deflation initially drove interest rates up in the late 1920s but then drove them down to levels that would not be seen again until the 2008–9 recession. The deflation of the money supply also reduced the rate of profit and, as we have seen previously, induced economy-wide losses in 1931–33.

The money supply was then inflated dramatically from 1934 to 1936, which created the expansionary period and higher rate of profit in the mid-1930s. In 1937 the money supply was deflated, which induced a depression in the middle of the slow recovery from the Great Depression, caused interest rates to rise slightly, and the rate of profit to decline.

The money supply was then inflated at dramatically higher rates just prior to and during WWII. This was obviously a part of how the government financed the war. As the rate of inflation slowed toward the end of the war, a post-war depression was induced along with slightly higher interest rates and lower rates of profit. After the depression at the end of the war, the US economy experienced an expansion. The expansion during the latter 1940s occurred despite the fact that the rate of increase in the money supply fell from 1943 to 1948. The economy was able to expand as government wartime restrictions on production and consumption were lifted and due to the unleashing of pent-up demand from unspendable money balances individuals and businesses had been building up during the war (discussed in detail below). Once the restrictions were lifted, it became possible to produce goods on which people could spend their money. This greater spending by individuals manifested itself in one way through a rising velocity of circulation of money after the war. The velocity of circulation is discussed below as well.

Interest rates climbed from the end of the war to 1948 as the rate of increase in the money supply was reduced (and even turned negative in 1948 and 1949). At this time, interest rates essentially plateaued through 1950. Due to these changes, a decline in total industrial production was induced in 1949, along with a reduced rate of profit in that year.

The money supply was then increased in an accelerating manner from 1950 to 1951 and then decelerated in 1952 and 1953, causing interest rates to reach a local maximum in 1953 and creating a recession and causing the rate of profit to reach a local minimum in 1954. The rate of inflation increased in 1954 and decreased gradually through 1957, when a slight deflation of the money supply occurred. This precipitated a recession, caused the rate of profit to reach a local minimum in 1958, and drove interest rates up from a local minimum in 1954 to a local maximum in 1957.

From this point to the end of the period under investigation in this chapter, no more recessions or depressions occurred. This was the result of a general upward trend in the rate of increase in the money supply and a velocity of circulation that rose dramatically with few interruptions. These two factors created an upward trend in interest rates and drove them up to levels they had not seen since prior to the Great Depression. Let us now look in detail at just how velocity changed.

Velocity data for the period 1900 to 1965 are shown in exhibit 9.14. Velocity is calculated with GNP in this chapter, since data for GNP exist during the entire time period. One will see here similar changes in velocity in relation to the business cycle as have been seen throughout the last few chapters of this book.

One sees the velocity of circulation reaching a local minimum point during the recession of 1904. As has been shown throughout this book, this is typical of velocity during recessions and depressions. It tends to decrease during these episodes as people and businesses increase their money balances relative to their spending because of the tough financial times. Individuals and businesses tend to become artificially illiquid during the inflationary expansion and then restore their liquidity when the inflation stops or slows sufficiently (or does not increase sufficiently).

This process can be seen in the inflationary expansion of 1905–7, when velocity increases, and then during the depression of 1908, when velocity decreases again. This process is also seen during the last pre–WWI expansion, as velocity generally rises, and again during the contraction at the start of the war, when velocity falls dramatically (in 1914).

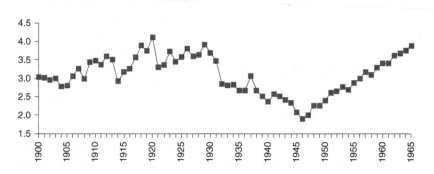

Exhibit 9.14   Velocity based on GNP, 1900–65.

Sources: For GNP, see exhibit 9.1. For the money supply, see exhibit 9.13.

Velocity then rises dramatically from 1915 to 1920, as the money supply is inflated at a radically accelerated rate during the war. Velocity then falls dramatically during the first post–WWI depression. It then rises during the expansion of the early 1920s, falls during the small recession of 1924, rises during the expansion of the mid-1920s, falls during the small recession of 1927, and rises again during the expansion of the late 1920s. Velocity then drops dramatically moving into and beyond the Great Depression. It then rises briefly in 1937, after the rapid inflation of the mid-1930s. However, it then falls during the contraction of 1938 and continues to fall until 1940.

After rising briefly during 1941, velocity falls continuously throughout WWII and after the war through 1946, despite the rapid rates of inflation during the war. The continuous decline of velocity during this time is due to a number of factors. These include the lasting effects of the Great Depression and the depression of 1938, the effects of various wartime policies of the US government that violated individual rights (beyond its policy with regard to inflation), and the effects of the first post-war depression (that started during the last year of the war). Given the severe nature of the depressions of the 1930s, they had a strong effect on people for a significant period of time. Many people and businesses went bankrupt and many people were unemployed. The financial hardship imposed on individuals because of these episodes would naturally provide people with a strong motivation to act in a much more financially conservative manner for a long period of time. This would include people increasing, and then maintaining, their liquidity.

In addition, a number of government wartime policies made it much more difficult to spend money during WWII. First, there were restrictions on the production of some goods. The government also imposed maximum price controls on virtually all goods. This led to universal shortages and, because of the shortages, a general lack of goods to purchase. Next, the government imposed rationing (made necessary by the maximum price controls and shortages they create) and thus made it harder to purchase goods. One could not simply buy a good if one was willing and able to pay the price being asked. One also needed rationing coupons, which were distributed by the government, to be able to purchase a good. All of these contributed to the inability of people to spend money, which reduces velocity. Finally, increased downward pressure must have also been placed on velocity as the economy entered a depression in 1945.

Three factors then pushed velocity upward: the economy exited the first post-war depression, wartime controls were abolished after the war, and the painful memories of the financially hard times during the depressions of the 1930s began to fade. Velocity continued to rise until just prior to the decline in total industrial production in 1949. It remained constant during 1949. It then resumed its upward movement until the recession of 1954 and again until the recession of 1958. At this point velocity increased until 1965, except in 1961 when it remained flat. The general rising trend of velocity from the end of WWII until the end of the period is due to the end of the wartime controls, the fading of the bad memories of the financial and economic disasters of the 1930s, and the generally accelerating inflation trend from the latter 1950s on. This rising trend in velocity helped to prevent any contractions until 1970.

World War II, the End of the Great Depression, and Prosperity

A popular explanation for the end of the Great Depression is that wartime spending upon entry into WWII put people back to work and lifted the United States out of the Great Depression. It is believed that this created greater prosperity because of the increase in output to which it led. There are a number of problems and issues to untangle with this view.

War is sometimes necessary to defend one's rights and freedom, and in the case of WWII the United States most certainly needed to enter the war, especially against the Japanese, to defend its rights. However, war always comes at great cost in terms of people wounded or killed and wealth destroyed both in terms of military equipment on the battlefield and factories, homes, and so forth that are bombed. So war does not create prosperity. It leads to a lower standard of living for the average person.

Furthermore, wartime spending is not necessary to lift a country out of a depression and is not a long-term solution to end recessions and depressions. It is true that the massive inflation and spending by the government to fight WWII led to a wartime inflationary boom and did increase output dramatically. In addition, *maximum* wage controls and forcing millions of men, through conscription, to join the military reduced unemployment to extremely low levels (and even created labor shortages, as maximum price controls do). However, this is not the path to prosperity and recovery from a recession or depression. As I discussed in chapters 5 and 6, the government engaging in massive spending through inflation only leads to a temporary recovery (at best) because it sows the seeds for further booms and busts. Such spending also prevents individuals in the economy from making appropriate adjustments (in terms of how much debt they have taken on, what products they are producing, etc.) and adds its owns distortions to the mix. See the details in chapters 5 and 6.

In terms of the standard of living during WWII, it was actually lower for the average person during WWII than it was during the Great Depression. As previously stated, the universal maximum price controls, shortages such controls create, and consequent rationing led to many goods that were available during the Great Depression being unavailable during WWII. Further, the outright restrictions by the government on the production of some goods made the situation even worse. The government did not allow new cars, new houses, and new major appliances to be produced. Also, basic goods such as chocolate bars, nylon stockings, gasoline, sugar, and meat were unobtainable or very difficult to obtain due to the government-imposed price controls and rationing. Moreover, the quality of the greatly diminished supply of goods was much lower than prior to the war due to the maximum price controls. Such controls lead to lower quality because businesses (justifiably) cut corners in an attempt to restore profitability due to the artificially low prices they are forced to accept.

Making the standard of living even lower is the fact that the focus of production during wartime is not consumers' goods that individuals can directly benefit from or capital goods that eventually lead to the production of more consumers' goods, but the production of wartime goods from which individuals derive no direct economic benefit. Additionally, those who were employed prior to the start of the war are forced to pay for the employment of people producing the wartime goods. Those employed prior to the war pay because they have to produce the goods those now employed in the war-goods industries purchase with their salaries. Those employed prior to the war also have to produce the equipment and materials used by those who are now producing the war goods. Finally, those employed prior to the war pay in the form of additional taxes (both directly and through inflation) necessary to pay for the war goods the government purchases. So any gain by those now employed due to the war is not an overall rise in the average standard of living. It comes at the expense of those who were employed prior to the war.

The reduction in the standard of living during WWII can also be seen in the fact that many people who did not have a need to work before the war had to during the war. This included housewives, those in high school who had to quit school, and retirees. Note that their work did not mean more goods being produced to raise the average standard of living. It largely just made up for the reduced amount of work engaged in to produce wealth by those now forced into the military. So more people worked and fewer goods were available for the average person.

During the war, people might have thought they were better off because they were amassing large sums of unspendable money and government war bonds. In addition, people were motivated by patriotism to work harder and suffer privation. While the wartime controls on the economy did not last long enough to completely destroy the economy, the standard of living was much lower. Prosperity did not return until after the war when military personnel returned to production for civilians, wartime controls were abolished, and government spending and inflation were dramatically reduced.[5]

Wartime prosperity is an illusion. As the Austrian economist Ludwig von Mises stated, "War prosperity is like the prosperity that an earthquake or plague brings."[6] It lowers the standard of living for the average person.

CONCLUSION

This chapter, like the other empirical chapters, provides evidence in support of ABCT. The support is not always consistent, as is seen in the comparisons of real GNP to real GNR, consumers' goods, intermediate goods and minerals/mining industrial production, and manufactured goods versus minerals/mining industrial production. However, many of the discrepancies here are understandable. Moreover, the comparisons of total industrial production and real GNP, durable and nondurable manufactured goods industrial production, and durable and consumption goods industrial production provide substantial support for ABCT.

In addition, it can be clearly seen that variables such as the rate of profit, interest rates, and the velocity of money move relative to the rate of change of the money supply as ABCT predicts and thus provide strong support for the theory. The readily observable fashion in which these variables move relative to each other may be due to the fact that the components of the money supply during this period remained constant. That is, money consisted of currency in circulation plus demand deposits throughout the entire period. Even though the country moved from a gold standard to an essentially fiat-money standard during this period, new types of accounts were not yet being created at banks that had characteristics of both savings and checking accounts and which make it more difficult to measure the money supply. The rise of such assets as money market mutual funds during the 1970s, 1980s, and 1990s makes it more difficult to measure the money supply during that period because it is hard to tell exactly to what extent people use such assets as money versus a form of savings. The constancy in the types of bank accounts that constituted money until the 1970s makes it much easier to measure the money supply during this period. Inaccuracy in the measure of a variable makes it harder to witness the effects it produces.

This is the last chapter on the empirical support of ABCT. I have shown both the theoretical and empirical evidence for ABCT. It is clear that ABCT is a valid theory of the business cycle. It explains all aspects of the cycle and is consistent with the existence of other factors that can affect the cycle.

Epilogue

One sees from the preceding chapters the causes of the business cycle and those causal factors at work in history. Austrian business cycle theory (ABCT) is a powerful tool. It makes sense of a complex subject.

There is a question many readers might ask themselves after reading my discussion of ABCT. If what I say is correct, why is it that I have not been able to become wealthy by investing based on this theory? This is a legitimate question that needs to be addressed—because it is true.

Making good investments requires extensive study of specific markets and businesses to know how they respond during the cycle and what factors in general affect the value of investments. This requires the knowledge of a broker or investment analyst. This is knowledge that I have not pursued.

Also, knowing what causes the business cycle is important to being a better investor but it does not guarantee that one will do well in one's investments. The same is true of investment knowledge in general. Possessing such knowledge does not guarantee one will make money investing. Just as knowing a lot about the game of basketball does not guarantee that one will be a good basketball player. One must be able to successfully apply one's knowledge.

Additionally, an investor does not need explicit knowledge of what causes the business cycle to use the cycle to his advantage. He might merely base his decisions on the changes, created by the cycle, in profits, interest rates, unemployment, and so forth without knowing the details about the causal relationships involved. In fact, one does not need knowledge of the business cycle at all to be a successful investor. One could ride out the downturns of the cycle and still make money in the long term by investing in undervalued companies. So having knowledge of the business cycle is neither necessary nor sufficient to be a good investor. Of course, no matter how much money one makes, one could make still more by incorporating valid business cycle theory into one's investment strategy.

It is important to understand that it is very difficult to predict the timing of the cycle even if one has knowledge of what causes it. No one can predict when the next phase of the cycle will occur. The changes in the phases of the cycle are largely dependent on those in charge at the Federal Reserve (at least for the United States). One would need to get inside their heads to see what is going to happen next and when it is going to happen. However, even if one could do this, those in charge at the Fed probably do not know when they will make the necessary changes to bring about the next phase of the cycle.

Moreover, even if those in charge of the Fed knew exactly what moves they were going to make and when, there is no particular set of actions that guarantee the exact timing of the phases of the cycle. One time the Fed might raise interest rates a little without causing a recession and another time the same actions might create a recession. Other factors come into play, such as the memory of past experience of individuals in the economy. Likewise, a massive inflation in the midst of a deflationary psychology might produce little or no increase in spending. However, a more moderate inflation in the midst of an inflationary expansion might produce dramatic results. A proper understanding of economics tells us *that* inflation-induced expansions and recessions will occur given the nature of our monetary and banking system today but not *when* they will occur.

While the discussion in this volume tells us what causes the business cycle and shows how this theory can be applied to understand the cycle in history, it does not provide a complete discussion of the business cycle. One needs to show why alternative theories of the cycle are not valid. One also needs to show how fiat money and fractional-reserve banking came into existence. In addition, one needs to understand what government policies must be implemented to cure us of monetary-induced cycles. That is the task of volume two of my work on the business cycle.

NOTES

INTRODUCTION

1. Murray N. Rothbard, *The Panic of 1819: Reactions and Policies* (New York: Columbia University Press, 1962).

1 MONEY, BANKING, AND INFLATION

1. Brian Simpson, "Money, Banking, and the Business Cycle," audio recording (Irvine, CA: Second Renaissance, Inc., 2005) and Brian P. Simpson, *Trade Cycle Theory: A Market Process Perspective* (Ann Arbor, MI: Bell & Howell Information and Learning Company, 2000), pp. 78–79.
2. George Reisman, *Capitalism: A Treatise on Economics* (Ottawa, IL: Jameson Books, 1996), pp. 512–513.
3. See Chapter 4 of Brian P. Simpson, *Money, Banking, and the Business Cycle, Volume 2: Remedies and Alternative Theories* (New York: Palgrave Macmillan, 2014) for a discussion of this topic.
4. Lawrence H. White, "A Subjectivist Perspective on the Definition and Identification of Money," in Israel M. Kirzner, ed., *Subjectivism, Intelligibility and Economic Understanding* (Washington Square: New York University Press, 1986), pp. 301–314. See in particular pp. 310–311.
5. I ignore the existence of fractional-reserve banking here. The creation of money through credit-card loans under fractional-reserve banking (to the extent that it occurs) is not particular to credit-card loans. It is true of all loans made through the fractional-reserve process and thus is not a phenomenon of credit-card loans but of fractional-reserve banking. Fractional-reserve banking is discussed below in this chapter and in Chapter 4 of Simpson, *Money, Banking, and the Business Cycle, Volume 2.*
6. See Steven J. Pilloff, "Money Market Mutual Funds: Are They a Close Substitute for Accounts at Insured Depository Institutions?" *The Antitrust Bulletin* vol. 44, no. 2 (Summer 1999), pp. 365–385 for the estimates of MMMFs that have check-writing capabilities on them. See especially p. 373.
7. White, "A Subjectivist Perspective," p. 313.
8. Joseph T. Salerno, "The 'True' Money Supply: A Measure of the Supply of the Medium of Exchange in the U.S. Economy," *Austrian Economics Newsletter* (Spring 1987), pp. 1–6. In particular, see p. 4.
9. All data except for sweep data were obtained from the St. Louis Federal Reserve's FRED database under the monetary aggregates and their components (values that are not seasonally adjusted). As stated in the main text for M1.5 and M1.6, only the portions of retail and commercial MMMF data on which checks can be written were used as estimates of these funds' contribution to the money supply. The percentages

used were 74.2 percent and 21.8 percent for retail and commercial MMMFs, respectively, based on Pilloff, "Money Market Mutual Funds," p. 373. Also as stated in the main text, MMDA data have not been separated from savings account data since 1990. Hence, MMDA data are based on an estimate of the proportion of MMDAs relative to total savings deposits inclusive of MMDAs. The estimated proportion used is 55 percent and is based on the actual proportion during the years the data were reported in a disaggregated manner. Retail sweep data were obtained from the St. Louis Federal Reserve, "Federal Reserve Board Data on OCD Sweep Account Programs," Monthly Sweeps Data. Commercial sweep data were obtained from Treasury Strategies, Inc., "2011 Deposit & Sweep Study Findings Deck." Since 2004, I have not been able to obtain the proportion of commercial sweep funds swept into MMMFs. This figure was estimated based on trends of these data established for periods during which data could be obtained. The proportion used for 2010 was 29.5 percent. In addition, commercial sweep funds swept into MMMFs are assumed to be uniformly swept into MMMFs that do and do not have check-writing capabilities. Online data obtained October 14, 2013.

10. I ignore the effects of fractional-reserve checking here. In the context of fractional-reserve checking, turning checking-deposit money into cash can reduce the money supply since there are fewer reserves available for banks to "multiply" through the lending of checking-deposit reserves. However, the reduction of money in this situation is not a function of the withdrawal of checking-account money but of fractional reserves, so my point is still valid. Moreover, during the Y2K event the Federal Reserve offset the withdrawals from banks with additional reserves so banks were not adversely affected and did not have to temporarily reduce their lending.

11. The quote is from Murray Rothbard, *America's Great Depression*, 5th ed. (Auburn, AL: The Ludwig von Mises Institute, 2000), p. 87. See pp. 87–91 for Rothbard's full discussion on what should be included in the money supply. Also see Murray Rothbard, *The Mystery of Banking*, 2nd ed. (Auburn, AL: The Ludwig von Mises Institute, 2008), pp. 252–261 for further discussion. See Salerno, "The 'True' Money Supply" for a similar view.

12. Rothbard, *America's Great Depression*, p. 87.

13. Harry Binswanger, ed., *The Ayn Rand Lexicon: Objectivism from A to Z* (New York: Penguin Books, 1986), pp. 104–105.

14. Rothbard, *America's Great Depression*, p. 91 and Rothbard, *The Mystery of Banking*, pp. 254–255.

15. White, "A Subjectivist Perspective," pp. 310–311.

16. Discussed below in this chapter and in Chapter 4 of Simpson, *Money, Banking, and the Business Cycle, Volume 2*.

17. See Dale K. Osborne, "What Is Money Today?" *Economic Review* (January 1985), pp. 1–15. See in particular pp. 1–6.

18. If one does not understand why, see the discussion on fractional reserves in the section on banking below.

19. I am ignoring the fact that the Fed cannot directly create money for the government to spend. The Treasury must first borrow from the public and the Fed must then buy the Treasury bonds from the public. See chapter 2 for more on this process.

20. Reisman, *Capitalism*, p. 512.

21. *Merriam-Webster's Collegiate Dictionary*, 10th ed. (Springfield, MA: Merriam-Webster, Inc., 1993).

22. For some specific false conclusions to which a bad definition of inflation leads, see David Laidler, "The Price Level, Relative Prices and Economic Stability: Aspects of the Interwar Debate," *BIS Working Papers* no. 136 (September 2003), pp. 1–23. See

especially pp. 1, 6, 8, 15, and 20. In addition, for a discussion on a topic related to that of defining concepts appropriately, see Brian P. Simpson, *Markets Don't Fail!* (Lanham, MD: Lexington Books, 2005), pp. 35–37.

23. See also Chapter 7 of Simpson, *Money, Banking, and the Business Cycle, Volume 2.*
24. Reisman, *Capitalism*, pp. 539 and 895.
25. For the price level in America and Great Britain during these periods, see Roy W. Jastram, *The Golden Constant* (New York: John Wiley & Sons, 1977), pp. 36–37 and 148–149.
26. Reisman, *Capitalism*, p. 895.
27. Ibid., pp. 907–920 for a thorough refutation of these and many similar attempts to explain "inflation."
28. Ludwig von Mises, *The Theory of Money and Credit* (Indianapolis, IN: Liberty Fund, 1981 [1934]), p. 272 and Richard Salsman, "The Myth of Market Bubbles," audio recording (Gaylordsville, CT: Second Renaissance Books, 2000).
29. For further explanation of what the demand for money is, including why I use the qualifier "attempt" when describing an increase in the demand for money, see the discussion of the velocity of circulation of money in chapter 2.
30. Reisman, *Capitalism*, p. 524.
31. Ibid.
32. See Chapter 4 of Simpson, *Money, Banking, and the Business Cycle, Volume 2.*

2   How Does the Government Cause Inflation?

1. Richard M. Salsman, *Breaking the Banks: Central Banking Problems and Free Banking Solutions* (Great Barrington, MA: American Institute for Economic Research, 1990), pp. 17–78.
2. Charles Goodhart, *The Evolution of Central Banks* (Cambridge: The MIT Press, 1988), pp. 4 and 19–20 and Richard M. Salsman, "The End of Central Banking, Part I," *The Objective Standard* vol. 8, no. 1 (Spring 2013), pp. 13–29. See especially pp. 13–14, 16, 18–19, 23, and 26–27 in the latter reference.
3. See George Reisman, *Capitalism: A Treatise on Economics* (Ottawa, IL: Jameson Books, 1996), pp. 229, 654, and 762–774 for more on this. Note that this is not changed if the assets are paid off over time, since their purchase price was determined at the time of purchase.
4. The rate of profit in this example increases to 15.5 percent because the increase in money and spending increases the original 5 percent rate of profit by a factor of 1.1 (i.e., $15.5 = [(1.05 \times 1.1) - 1] \times 100$). If prices rise by 10 percent, the real rate of profit stays at 5 percent (i.e., $5 = [(1.155 / 1.1) - 1] \times 100$). If prices rise by less than 10 percent, the apparent real rate of profit is between 5 percent and 15.5 percent (i.e., Real Rate of Profit $= [(1.155 / (1 + (\text{Percent Change in Prices} / 100))) - 1] \times 100$).
5. There are obviously multiple rates of profit and interest in the economy. When I refer to *the* rate of profit or interest, think of it, as I mention in the text, as an average rate of profit or interest. Furthermore, one can think of the average rate of interest as an average of interest rates for all loan maturities.
6. While the same 2 percent gap between the rate of profit and the interest rate might not be maintained, some gap would remain. Interest rates are generally lower than the rate of profit because of the greater risk associated with equity investments relative to lending. Equity provides protection to lenders by reducing the risk of lenders losing money on loans due to borrowers defaulting on loans.

7. While the US dollar circulates as the currency of choice in some countries and is held as a foreign-exchange reserve in many countries, these do not deny the validity of my claim. The former does not cause fluctuations in the money supply and spending in connection with US government borrowing from foreigners, since those outside the United States who use the dollar as a currency of choice are generally not involved in US government bond markets. With regard to the latter, such reserves are generally loaned back in the United States.

8. The exception to changes in spending being caused by changes in the money supply is changes in spending due to changes in the demand for money. However, as I discussed in chapter 1, changes in the demand for money are largely driven by changes in the supply of money, especially under a fiat-money, fractional-reserve monetary and banking system, which is the system prone to significant fluctuations of the money supply. I provide additional discussion on the demand for money below in this chapter.

9. The claim that the Fed is supposed to be independent of the government does not deny my claim that the Fed is a government entity. The Fed was created by Congress and the president and can be abolished by them. Ultimately, an entity cannot be independent of that from which it derives its powers and to which it answers. The claim that the Fed is owned by banks does not deny my claim either. Ownership by the banks is in name only. They do not get to keep any income "earned" by the Fed and they do not have the power to set Fed policy or shut the Fed down if they want to, all of which actual owners of organizations are able to do.

10. See Reisman, *Capitalism*, pp. 829–830 and 888–889 for further discussion of how changes in government spending affect spending in the economy.

11. I demonstrate the truth of this statement in Chapter 4 of Brian P. Simpson, *Money, Banking, and the Business Cycle, Volume 2: Remedies and Alternative Theories* (New York: Palgrave Macmillan, 2014).

12. See Brian P. Simpson, *Markets Don't Fail!* (Lanham, MD: Lexington Books, 2005), pp. 5–26 for a discussion of the appropriate functions of the government.

13. See chapter 3 for a discussion of the business cycle. See Chapter 7 of Simpson, *Money, Banking, and the Business Cycle, Volume 2* for a discussion of other effects of inflation.

14. This and the following discussion on economically productive versus consumptive activity are based on Reisman, *Capitalism*, pp. 441–456.

15. On the benefits of the division of labor, see Simpson, *Markets Don't Fail!*, pp. 10–11 and 196–198.

16. I say more than offset the benefits of the tax cuts because borrowing or inflating undermines the productive capability more than financing government spending through taxes. On this point, see Reisman, *Capitalism*, pp. 830–831 and 928–937.

17. I provide a thorough refutation of Keynes's theory of chronic unemployment in Chapter 1 of Simpson, *Money, Banking, and the Business Cycle, Volume 2*.

18. For a typical exposition of the "Keynesian multiplier," see Paul A. Samuelson and William D. Nordhaus, *Economics*, 13th ed. (New York: McGraw-Hill Book Co., 1989), pp. 167–168.

19. Individuals might not save directly out of the proceeds of a loan but a loan can enable them to save more. For example, if an individual cannot afford to purchase a car with his current income and he does not obtain a loan to purchase the car, he would have to use his savings to purchase the car. So the loan makes it possible for him to maintain a higher level of savings.

20. My definition is based on Reisman, *Capitalism*, p. 691; however, my definition is slightly different. I add the "to be consumed in the present" at the end. I do this because consumers' goods that are consumed over a long time are a form of savings. The purchase of a home provides a good example. It is a consumers' good because, if it is purchased for personal use, it is not purchased for the purpose of making money (i.e., renting it out, fixing it up and reselling it, etc.). However, because it lasts for many years, the portion of the useful life that has yet to be consumed at any point in time constitutes a part of one's savings.

21. Total spending on goods and services in the United States consists of gross receipts of corporations, partnerships, and nonfarm proprietorships, as well as annual wages for labor (for gross spending on labor). In determining wages, I assumed the wage rates for government workers were the same as wage rates for workers in the private sector. This makes my estimate of total spending less accurate than it could be but it is still a much better estimate of total spending in the economy than GDP, and doing it this way simplifies the collection of the appropriate data, especially for earlier years, which I use starting in chapter 5. Government spending is the government spending component of GDP plus the payment of wages by the government. Spending by individual consumers is the personal consumption component of GDP plus fixed residential investment. Fixed residential investment is consumption and not investment because it is spending not engaged in for the purpose of making subsequent sales (to the extent it is for homes people live in themselves and do not rent out or fix up and resell). All categories of GDP—government spending, private consumption spending, and business investment—were adjusted on a pro-rata basis by net exports. GDP data and its components were obtained from the Federal Reserve Bank of St. Louis, FRED database, series IDs GDPA (Gross Domestic Product), GCEA (Government Consumption Expenditures and Gross Investment), PCECA (Personal Consumption Expenditures), GPDIA (Gross Private Domestic Investment), PRFIA (Private Residential Fixed Investment), and NETEXP (Net Exports of Goods and Services). Data were obtained February 18, 2013. Wage data were obtained from the US Department of Labor, Bureau of Labor Statistics, historical hours, earnings, and employment data, Tables B-1 and B-2 at http://bls.gov/ces/tables.htm#ee. Wage data were obtained January 24, 2012. The gross business receipts value for corporations was calculated using data from the following source: Internal Revenue Service, "2010 Corporation Source Book, Publication 1053, Section 2," http://www.irs.gov/uac/SOI-Tax-Stats-Corporation-Source-Book:-U.S.-Total-and-Sectors-Listing. Data for corporations were obtained February 18, 2013. Gross business receipts for corporations include business receipts, interest, interest on government obligations (total), rents, and royalties. For partnerships, the value was calculated using data from the following source: Nina Shumofsky, Lauren Lee, and Ron DeCarlo, "Partnership Returns, 2010," *Statistics of Income Bulletin* vol. 32, no. 2 (Fall 2012), pp. 79–168. See Table 7—All Partnerships: Total Receipts by Selected Industrial Group, Tax Year 2010 on pp. 165–166. Gross business receipts for partnerships include business receipts, other income from trade or business, interest income, royalties, real estate rental net income, and other rental net income for all industries. For nonfarm sole proprietorships, the value was obtained from Adrian Dungan, "Sole Proprietorship Returns, 2010," *Statistics of Income Bulletin* vol. 32, no. 1 (Summer 2012), pp. 5–70. See Table 1 – Nonfarm Sole Proprietorships: Business Receipts, Selected Deductions, Payroll, and Net Income, by Industrial Sectors, Tax Year 2010 on pp. 18–27. The value for business receipts for all nonfarm industries was used. See the notes to the

discussion on the calculation of gross national revenue for 2010 in chapter 5 for why gross receipts were calculated in the manner described above.

22. Gross receipts for 2008 were obtained from the US Census Bureau, *Statistical Abstract of the United States: 2012*, 131st ed. (Washington, DC, 2011), p. 491. Wages, GDP, and the GDP components were obtained from the same sources cited above.

23. See Reisman, *Capitalism*, pp. 694–699 for a more detailed discussion on how savings are the source of greater consumption and virtually all spending in the economy.

24. See Roger A. Arnold, *Economics*, 5th ed. (Cincinnati, OH: South-Western College Publishing, 2001), pp. 208–209 for more on this.

25. In Chapter 1 of Simpson, *Money, Banking, and the Business Cycle, Volume 2*, I address a number of other problems with claims Keynesian economists make about the adjustment of interest rates.

26. For more on saving, spending, hoarding, liquidity, and the rate of profit, see Reisman, *Capitalism*, pp. 519–522, 692–696, 778–784, and 837–838.

3 WHAT CAUSES THE BUSINESS CYCLE?

1. This introduction and entire chapter are based to some extent on sections of Chapter 2 in Brian P. Simpson, *Trade Cycle Theory: A Market Process Perspective* (Ann Arbor, MI: Bell & Howell Information and Learning Company, 2000) and Brian P. Simpson, "Money, Banking, and the Business Cycle," audio recording (Irvine, CA: Second Renaissance, Inc., 2005).

2. For references to writings on ABCT by the economists mentioned, see Ludwig von Mises, *Human Action*, 3rd rev. ed. (Chicago: Contemporary Books, Inc., 1966), pp. 550–571; Friedrich A. Hayek, *Prices and Production*, 2nd ed. (New York: Augustus M. Kelly, 1935); and Murray Rothbard, *Man, Economy, and State*, Volume 2 (Los Angeles: Nash Publishing, 1962), pp. 850–879. Also see George Reisman, *Capitalism: A Treatise on Economics* (Ottawa, IL: Jameson Books, 1996), pp. 938–940; "When Will the Bubble Burst" (August 7, 1999), http://capitalism. net/articles/stockmkt.htm; "The Stock Market, Profits, and Credit Expansion" (2002), http://capitalism.net/articles/Stock%20Market,%20Profits,%20Credit%20 Expansion.htm; "The Housing Bubble and the Credit Crunch" (August 10, 2007), http://capitalism.net/articles/A_Blog_08_07.html; "The Myth That Laissez Faire Is Responsible for Our Financial Crisis" (October 21, 2008), http://capitalism.net /articles/A_Blog_10_08.html; "Economic Recovery Requires Capital Accumulation Not Government 'Stimulus Packages'" (February 21 and 22, 2009), http://capital ism.net/articles/A_Blog_02_09.html#02_21_09; and "Credit Expansion, Crisis, and the Myth of the Saving Glut" (July 4, 2009), http://capitalism.net/articles/A _Blog_07_09.html. The articles by George Reisman were accessed December 10, 2011, and provide excellent explanations and applications of ABCT.

3. See Chapters 1–3 of Brian P. Simpson, *Money, Banking, and the Business Cycle, Volume 2: Remedies and Alternative Theories* (New York: Palgrave Macmillan, 2014).

4. See Reisman, *Capitalism*, pp. 762–774 for how increases in the quantity of money add to the rate of profit.

5. Of course, if there are increases in the productive capability and supply of goods each year due to economic progress, prices would increase by less than 2 percent and may even decline, depending on how large the increase in the supply of goods is. However, this increase in the supply of goods is not due to the increase in money and spending. It is due to factors that cause economic progress, such as freedom and

respect for individual rights, capital accumulation, technological progress, and the acquisition of knowledge. The influence of these factors on the ability to produce wealth is separate from changes in the money supply and spending. Their influence would exist even if the money supply and spending stayed the same from year to year. They will be discussed more below in the chapter.

6. One can see this if we use the general price level equation introduced in chapter 1, $P = D / S$, but in a slightly altered form. That is, for the different levels of spending and profits in these cases, the supply of goods ($S = D / P$) is the same in both cases. So $1,020 / $1.02 = $1,000 / $1 or $51 / $1.02 = $50 / $1.

7. I say the appearance of a real increase because real increases in revenues and profits are determined by increases in production, not money and spending. So far in the example there has been no increase in production. Furthermore, increases in production are ultimately based on the factors that cause economic progress. The increases in production that stem from the expansion phase of the business cycle, as I will show, are temporary. On net, production in the economy decreases due to the factors that cause the business cycle.

8. Again, this can be shown with the variation on the price level equation, $S = D / P$. So $S_2 = $1,040 / $1.02 = 1,019.61$; $S_1 = $1,000 / $1 = 1,000$; and $S_2 \approx 1.02 \times S_1$. The same is true if one uses the profits.

9. For those familiar with the terminology of modern economics, this type of expectation is based on so-called rational expectations theory. I discuss rational expectations theory in chapter 4.

10. For a similar but more detailed example and explanation of the factors involved, see Reisman, *Capitalism*, pp. 762–774.

11. This might be a bit exaggerated but it is merely for purposes of illustration. The same essential results obtain with less pronounced changes in velocity.

12. See Reisman, *Capitalism*, pp. 519–522 for more on this.

13. For a discussion on the business cycle and the structure of production, see Hayek, *Prices and Production*, pp. 32–68.

14. For those who are unfamiliar with PV analysis, such analysis helps one determine the value of future cash flows and thus how much an investment that produces future profit streams is worth today. The higher the PV, the more the profit streams are worth today. For an explanation of PV analysis, see any basic finance textbook, such as Eugene F. Brigham and Louis C. Gapenski, *Financial Management: Theory and Practice*, 6th ed. (Orlando, FL: The Dryden Press, 1991), pp. 171–205. Even some economics textbooks have a discussion on PV analysis.

15. For those who do not know, the equation for the PV used here is $FV / (1 + i)^n$ where FV is the future value (i.e., the future cash flow), i is the interest or discount rate, and n is the number of periods in the future that FV will be realized.

16. For a typical discussion of the WACC, see Brigham and Gapenski, *Financial Management*, pp. 271–303.

17. For more discussion on what makes the production of wealth and economic progress possible, see Brian P. Simpson, *Markets Don't Fail!* (Lanham, MD: Lexington Books, 2005), pp. 10–13, 22–26, 45, and 115.

18. I discuss this topic in Chapter 4 of Simpson, *Money, Banking, and the Business Cycle, Volume 2*.

19. I discuss the effects of inflation on economic progress in detail in Chapter 7 of ibid.

20. See ibid. for further discussion of mal-investment.

21. For those who are not familiar with time preference, see Reisman, *Capitalism*, pp. 55–58.

22. See chapter 8 of this book and Chapter 3 of Simpson, *Money, Banking, and the Business Cycle, Volume 2* for treatment of the issue of whether changes in the amount of imports and exports due to changes in trade restrictions cause the cycle. I demonstrate that they do not.
23. See Chapters 4 and 5 of Simpson, *Money, Banking, and the Business Cycle, Volume 2*.
24. Again, see Chapter 7 of ibid. for the details on the harmful effects of inflation on economic progress.
25. Ibid.
26. See chapter 2 on why the rate of profit tends to be higher than the interest rate.
27. See Reisman, *Capitalism*, pp. 762–774 for how changes in the quantity of money affect the rate of profit. The effect on interest rates in the long run would be similar, although it would ultimately occur through the rate of profit. See ibid., pp. 186–187 for a discussion on the relationship between interest rates and the rate of profit.
28. For a discussion of these subjects, see Chapters 4, 5, and 7 of Simpson, *Money, Banking, and the Business Cycle, Volume 2*.

4   In Defense of Austrian Business Cycle Theory

1. For references to writings on ABCT by the economists mentioned, see chapter 3.
2. I show that ABCT is based in reality by showing that it is both logically coherent (chapter 3) and consistent with the facts of reality (chapters 5–9). For an example of an economist who claims ABCT does not explain the contraction, see Maurice W. Lee, *Macroeconomic Fluctuations, Growth, and Stability*, 5th ed. (Homewood, IL: Richard D. Irwin, Inc., 1971), pp. 223–227. For an example of an economist who claims the theory is not based in reality, see Robert A. Gordon, *Business Fluctuations*, 2nd ed. (New York: Harper and Row, 1961), pp. 358–363.
3. For an example of a criticism that has no intellectual content, see Leland B. Yeager, "The Significance of Monetary Disequilibrium," *Cato Journal* vol. 6, no. 2 (Fall 1986), pp. 369–420. See p. 378. For examples of incoherent arguments, see Gordon Tullock, "Why the Austrians Are Wrong about Depressions," *The Review of Austrian Economics* vol. 2, no. 1 (1988), pp. 73–78 and Gordon Tullock, "Reply to Comment by Joseph T. Salerno," *The Review of Austrian Economics* vol. 3, no. 1 (1989), pp. 147–149.
4. See Harry Binswanger, ed., *The Ayn Rand Lexicon: Objectivism from A to Z* (New York: Penguin Books, 1986), pp. 404–405 and 407–410 for a discussion of this topic.
5. Also on this point, see Roger W. Garrison, "Hayekian Trade Cycle Theory: A Reappraisal," *Cato Journal* vol. 6, no. 2 (Fall 1986), pp. 437–459. See in particular p. 448.
6. See Chapters 1–3 of Brian P. Simpson, *Money, Banking, and the Business Cycle, Volume 2: Remedies and Alternative Theories* (New York: Palgrave Macmillan, 2014).
7. See Gordon, *Business Fluctuations*, p. 360; Tyler Cowen, *Risk and Business Cycles: New and Old Austrian Perspectives* (New York: Routledge, 1997), pp. 81–86 and 88–94; and Richard Salsman, "The Myth of Market Bubbles," audio recording (Gaylordsville, CT: Second Renaissance Books, 2000). For critiques of Cowen, see William Barnett II and Walter Block, "Tyler Cowen and Austrian Business Cycle Theory: A Critique," *New Perspectives on Political Economy* vol. 2, no. 2 (2006), pp. 26–85 and Lawrence J. Sechrest, "Book Review of *Risk and Business Cycles: New and Old Austrian Perspectives*," *The Quarterly Journal of Austrian Economics* vol. 1, no. 3 (Fall 1998), pp. 73–79.

8. For an example of those who place too much emphasis on interest rates, see Walter Block and William Barnett II, "Contra Eichengreen and Mitchener on ABCT," *Studies in Economics and Finance* vol. 28, no. 2 (2011), pp. 111–117. See in particular p. 112. For an example of someone who does not place too much emphasis on interest rates, see the references to George Reisman's works at the beginning of chapter 3.

9. Cowen, *Risk and Business Cycles*, pp. 88–90.

10. Ibid., pp. 81–83.

11. For an example in the banking industry of this type of incentive, see John A. Allison, *The Financial Crisis and the Free Market Cure* (New York: McGraw-Hill, 2013), p. 28.

12. Cowen, *Risk and Business Cycles*, p. 83.

13. Ibid., pp. 84–85.

14. Ibid., pp. 92–94.

15. Jeffrey Rogers Hummel, "Problems with Austrian Business Cycle Theory," *Reason Papers* no. 5 (Winter 1979), pp. 41–53. See in particular pp. 41–42.

16. Cowen, *Risk and Business Cycles*, pp. 85–86.

17. On productive spending and costs, see chapter 2. On the rate of profit and time preference, see George Reisman, *Capitalism: A Treatise on Economics* (Ottawa, IL: Jameson Books, 1996), pp. 743–744.

18. Salsman, "The Myth of Market Bubbles."

19. Cowen, *Risk and Business Cycles*, pp. 90–91.

20. For an example, see John Hicks, *Critical Essays in Monetary Theory* (Oxford: Oxford University Press, 1967), pp. 207–209.

21. Hummel, "Problems with Austrian Business Cycle Theory," pp. 46–47. There are many other criticisms of ABCT that Hummel makes in this paper. Many are addressed (at least implicitly) throughout this book. Responses to Hummel's claims are also provided in William Barnett II and Walter Block, "On Hummel on Austrian Business Cycle Theory," *Reason Papers* no. 30 (Fall 2008), pp. 59–90.

22. For examples, see Hicks, *Critical Essays*, pp. 207–208 and David Laidler, "The Price Level, Relative Prices and Economic Stability: Aspects of the Interwar Debate," *BIS Working Papers* no. 136 (September 2003), pp. 1–23. See especially pp. 12–13.

23. For examples, see Jesús Huerta de Soto, *Money, Bank Credit, and Economic Cycles*, translated by Melinda A. Stroup (Auburn, AL: Ludwig von Mises Institute, 2006), pp. 440–441 and Walter Block and William Barnett II, "On Laidler Regarding the Austrian Business Cycle Theory," *The Review of Austrian Economics* vol. 20, no. 1 (2007), pp. 43–61. See especially pp. 53 and 55.

24. As one can see I am not using the term full employment in the traditional economic sense, to denote the level of employment in which there is some positive level of frictional and structural unemployment and no cyclical unemployment. I use the term full employment here to denote 100 percent employment. This is a harder standard for ABCT to meet. If mal-investment only occurs at full employment and full employment only exists at 100 percent employment—a level never attained—malinvestment should never occur based on this criticism. I will show that it does.

25. I discuss this briefly below in this chapter in the section on "rational expectations" and in chapter 5. I also discuss this topic in more detail in Chapters 5 and 7 of Simpson, *Money, Banking, and the Business Cycle, Volume 2*.

26. See Ludwig von Mises, *Human Action*, 3rd rev. ed. (Chicago: Contemporary Books, Inc., 1966), p. 548 for a discussion of the nature of "forced savings."

27. Laidler, "The Price Level," pp. 13–15 and 17.

28. Reisman, *Capitalism*, p. 937.

29. See Chapter 7 of Simpson, *Money, Banking, and the Business Cycle, Volume 2* for a discussion of the effects of inflation. On mal-investment, also see chapter 3 above.

30. See Laidler, "The Price Level," pp. 11, 12, 14, 16, 18, and 20 for this criticism.

31. Ibid., pp. 14 and 18.

32. For discussion of why these claims are true, both factually and logically, see Brian P. Simpson, *Markets Don't Fail!* (Lanham, MD: Lexington Books, 2005). See especially Chapter 1.

33. See ibid. for more evidence.

34. Reisman, *Capitalism*, p. 36.

35. For examples, see Cowen, *Risk and Business Cycles*, p. 77 and Tullock, "Why the Austrians Are Wrong," p. 73. Also see Richard E. Wagner, "Austrian Cycle Theory: Saving the Wheat while Discarding the Chaff," *The Review of Austrian Economics* vol. 12, no. 1 (1999), pp. 65–80. See especially p. 71.

36. This section is based on Brian P. Simpson, "Austrian Trade Cycle Theory and Rationality," *New Perspectives on Political Economy* vol. 4, no. 2 (2008), pp. 113–129.

37. See John F. Muth, "Rational Expectations and the Theory of Price Movements," *Econometrica* vol. 29, no. 3 (1961), pp. 315–335, especially pp. 330 and 333. Also see Thomas J. Sargent and Neil Wallace, "'Rational' Expectations, the Optimal Monetary Instrument, and the Optimal Money Supply Rule," *Journal of Political Economy* vol. 83, no. 21 (1975), pp. 241–254, especially pp. 246–247.

38. A similar point is made in Garrison, "Hayekian Trade Cycle Theory," p. 442 and Walter Block, "Yes, We Have No Chaff: A Reply to Wagner's 'Austrian Cycle Theory: Saving the Wheat While Discarding the Chaff,'" *The Quarterly Journal of Austrian Economics* vol. 4, no. 1 (2001), pp. 63–73. See especially p. 65 in the latter reference.

39. See Block, "Yes, We Have No Chaff," p. 67 on this point also.

40. See Allison, *The Financial Crisis*, pp. 23, 28, 30, 32, and 102.

41. See Huerta de Soto, *Money*, pp. 422–423 on this point also.

42. For more on this, see Reisman, *Capitalism*, pp. 588 and 938–940.

43. See Chapter 4 of Simpson, *Money, Banking, and the Business Cycle, Volume 2* for a demonstration of how fiat money and fractional-reserve banking exist due to violations of freedom.

44. On a 100-percent reserve gold standard, see Chapters 7 and 8 of ibid. Also see Reisman, *Capitalism*, pp. 951–963 and Ludwig von Mises, *The Theory of Money and Credit* (Indianapolis, IN: Liberty Fund, 1981 [1934]), pp. 456–459 and 480.

45. To see Aristotle's statements regarding definitions, see Richard McKeon, ed., *Introduction to Aristotle* (New York: Random House, 1947), pp. 76–77.

46. On Aristotle's definition of man, see W. D. Ross, *The Works of Aristotle Translated into English* (London: Oxford University Press, 1928), pp. 130, 980, and 1095.

47. On this definition of reason, see Ayn Rand, *The Virtue of Selfishness* (New York: Signet, 1964), p. 22. For more on the Aristotelian method of definition and this view of rationality, see Binswanger, *The Ayn Rand Lexicon*, pp. 117–121, 404–405, and 407–410 and the references provided there.

48. For more on the cognitive function of definitions, see Leonard Peikoff, *Objectivism: The Philosophy of Ayn Rand* (New York: Meridian, 1991), pp. 96–105. See Reisman, *Capitalism*, pp. 920–922 for a discussion of more economic examples that illustrate the importance of having good definitions.

49. See Chapters 4, 7, and 8 of Simpson, *Money, Banking, and the Business Cycle, Volume 2* on these topics.

5   The Recession of the Early 1980s

1. A significant portion of this chapter is based on Chapter 3 of Brian P. Simpson, *Trade Cycle Theory: A Market Process Perspective* (Ann Arbor, MI: Bell & Howell Information and Learning Company, 2000) and Brian Simpson, "Money, Banking, and the Business Cycle," audio recording (Irvine, CA: Second Renaissance, Inc., 2005).

2. On productive versus consumptive expenditures, see the section in chapter 2 on the effects of "fiscal policy."

3. For a detailed critique of the contemporary method of aggregate economic accounting and a detailed description of the better method described here, see George Reisman, *Capitalism: A Treatise on Economics* (Ottawa, IL: Jameson Books, 1996), pp. 673–715. This material is used as the basis for my discussion.

4. The value for GDP was obtained from the Federal Reserve Bank of St. Louis, FRED database, series ID GDPA. The value was obtained February 18, 2013. Data for GNR are based on the total wage payments in the economy and the gross receipts for corporations, partnerships, and nonfarm proprietorships. For the sources of the gross receipts data, see the same sources for the 2010 gross receipts data given in chapter 2 in the discussion of total spending in the economy. The data used from these sources conform to data obtained for earlier years for gross business receipts from the *Statistical Abstract of the United States* and are used for the purpose of including gross income from ongoing business activities. Operating revenue would be a better figure to use to estimate the revenues of businesses because gross receipts include revenues from sources that are not the principal economic activities of the business, such as interest. Operating revenues include only revenues earned from the principal activities of the business. Gross receipts were used based on data availability and should not change any of the conclusions drawn from the data. For more on this topic, see Jay Cochran III, "Of Contracts and the Katallaxy: Measuring the Extent of the Market, 1919–1939," *The Review of Austrian Economics* vol. 17, no. 4 (2004), pp. 407–466. See especially p. 442, note 44. For the source of the wage data, see the source of the wage data in chapter 2 in connection with the discussion of total spending in the economy in 2010. As I said in chapter 2, to calculate total wage payments the wage rates of government workers are assumed to be the same as the wage rates of workers in the private sector. Although this is not true, it should not change any conclusions drawn from the GNR data.

5. Gross receipts for 2007 for corporations, partnerships, and nonfarm proprietorships were obtained from the US Census Bureau, *Statistical Abstract of the United States: 2012*, 131st ed. (Washington, DC, 2011), p. 491. GDP and wage data for 2007 were obtained from the same sources as the 2010 data.

6. To be completely accurate, GNR should include a component for agricultural activity. I excluded agricultural activity to simplify the data collection process. An even more comprehensive measure of economic activity would include financial transactions (the purchase price of stocks, bonds, and other financial instruments) and spending for used goods, such as used cars. However, this latter measure would go beyond a measure of spending on newly produced goods and services. Although using the sales revenue of businesses to measure gross spending for the goods produced by businesses ends up including some spending for used goods, such as purchases of used cars from car dealerships, the great majority of sales revenue is generated from the purchase of newly produced goods. So the inclusion of the purchase of some used items in sales revenue should not create any major inaccuracies.

7. The method of calculating the business failure rate changed in 1984 and values on either side are said by some to not be comparable. However, there is reason to believe that the peak failure rate of the early 1980s recession was dramatically greater than the peak rate of the mid-1970s recession. See Michele I. Naples, "Business Failure and the Expenditure Multiplier, or How Recessions Become Depressions," *Journal of Post-Keynesian Economics* vol. 19, no. 4 (Summer 1997), pp. 511–523. She creates an index post-1983 that is consistent with pre-1984 values and shows that values in the early 1980s recession are still much higher than values in the mid-1970s recession.

8. Carol Corrado, "Industrial Production and Capacity Utilization: The 2002 Historical and Annual Revision," *Federal Reserve Bulletin* vol. 89 (April 2003), pp. 151–176. See p. 155.

9. See David E. Lindsey, "Recent Monetary Developments and Controversies," *Brookings Papers on Economic Activity* vol. 1 (1982), pp. 245–271 for more on this topic.

10. Ludwig von Mises, *Human Action*, 3rd rev. ed. (Chicago: Contemporary Books, Inc., 1966), pp. 426–428 and 469.

11. Reisman, *Capitalism*, p. 525.

12. On this point, see Cheryl L. Edwards, "Open Market Operations in the 1990s," *Federal Reserve Bulletin* vol. 83 (November 1997), pp. 859–874. While this article mainly focuses on Fed policy in the 1990s, the author does make brief comments regarding the late 1970s/early 1980s.

13. For one account, see Marcia Stigum, *The Money Market*, rev. ed. (Homewood, IL: Dow Jones-Irwin, 1983), pp. 257–258.

14. For one example, see Scott Thurm, "After the Boom: A Go-Go Giant of Internet Age, Cisco Is Learning to Go Slow," *Wall Street Journal* (May 7, 2003), p. A1.

15. For a number of other examples of the economically destructive nature of violating individual rights, see Brian P. Simpson, *Markets Don't Fail!* (Lanham, MD: Lexington Books, 2005). In that book I show the economically destructive nature of violating individual rights in connection with socialism and the mixed economy, monopolies, the antitrust laws, "externalities," "public goods," asymmetric information, economic inequality, the environment, and the regulation of the quality of goods, services, and working conditions.

16. See Chapters 4–8 of Brian P. Simpson, *Money, Banking, and the Business Cycle, Volume 2: Remedies and Alternative Theories* (New York: Palgrave Macmillan, 2014) for a discussion on how laissez-faire capitalism virtually eliminates monetary induced recessions and depressions. See Chapter 1 of Simpson, *Markets Don't Fail!* for how laissez-faire capitalism leads to the highest rate of economic progress that is possible

17. See Reisman, *Capitalism*, pp. 778–787.

18. In this discussion I focus on the reduction in the supply of oil alone. If one also takes into account the oil products and other products and services (such as transportation services) that Arab oil helps to produce or provide, the portion of total output and the rise in the general price level caused by the disappearance of the Arab oil would be greater than 0.1 percent. However, the value should still be small.

19. I discuss changes in the money supply and velocity that are related to changes in the supply of goods in Chapters 3 and 4 of Simpson, *Money, Banking, and the Business Cycle, Volume 2*. However, these changes have nothing to do with the business cycle.

20. See Chapter 3 of ibid. There I demonstrate why changes in real factors, such as changes in technology, are not the cause of the business cycle.

21. In addition, one must take into account the supply of oil products and other products and services that oil helps to produce or provide.

22. See Chapter 3 of Simpson, *Money, Banking, and the Business Cycle, Volume 2* for a discussion on why regulation other than in the monetary and banking system does not cause recessions and depressions.

6 THE BUSINESS CYCLE IN LATE TWENTIETH-/ EARLY TWENTY-FIRST-CENTURY AMERICA

1. For an article that shows what the advertising industry witnessed but economists did not, see Rance Crain, "Why '01's 'Mild' Recession Wasn't: GDP Doesn't Include Advertising," *Advertising Age* (March 6, 2006), http://adage.com/article/rance -crain/01-s-mild-recession-gdp-include-advertising/107007/. Article accessed June 23, 2012.

2. The expansion data show the annual rate of expansion from trough to peak; however, in some cases for real GDP there were no troughs. This is true in 1970 and 2001. In these cases, the slowing in the increase in real GDP at the end of the previous expansion was used as the beginning of the expansion.

3. See Chapter 7 of Brian P. Simpson, *Money, Banking, and the Business Cycle, Volume 2: Remedies and Alternative Theories* (New York: Palgrave Macmillan, 2014) for a detailed discussion of the harmful effects of inflation.

4. Brian P. Simpson, *Trade Cycle Theory: A Market Process Perspective* (Ann Arbor, MI: Bell & Howell Information and Learning Company, 2000), p. 168.

5. For an example of a more comprehensive measure of spending used to analyze the Great Depression, see Jay Cochran III, "Of Contracts and the Katallaxy: Measuring the Extent of the Market, 1919–1939," *The Review of Austrian Economics* vol. 17, no. 4 (2004), pp. 407–466.

6. John W. English and Gray E. Cardiff, *The Coming Real Estate Crash* (New Rochelle, NY: Arlington House Publishers, 1979), p. 36.

7. Just how the system needs to be changed to cure our economy of the ills of the business cycle is discussed in Chapters 4, 5, 7, and 8 of Simpson, *Money, Banking, and the Business Cycle, Volume 2*.

8. I show in Chapter 4 of ibid. how the government, not the banking system itself, is ultimately responsible for the changes in the supply of money and credit through the banking system.

9. Yaron Brook and Don Watkins, *Free Market Revolution: How Ayn Rand's Ideas Can End Big Government* (New York: Palgrave Macmillan, 2012), p. 51.

10. Yaron Brook, "The Financial Crisis: What Happened and Why," video recording (August 4, 2009), http://arc-tv.com/the-financial-crisis-what-happened-and-why/, accessed February 22, 2013. In particular, hear part one of lecture three.

11. See Benjamin Powell, "Explaining Japan's Recession," *The Quarterly Journal of Austrian Economics* vol. 5, no. 2 (Summer 2002), pp. 35–50 on the Japanese recession. See especially pp. 42 and 44–47.

12. Steven Horwitz and Peter Boettke, "The House That Uncle Sam Built: The Untold Story of the Great Recession of 2008" (October 8, 2010), http://c457332.r32.cf2. rackcdn.com/wp-content/uploads/2009/12/HouseUncleSamBuiltBooklet.pdf, pp. 13–15, accessed February 22, 2013

13. See Horwitz and Boettke, "The House That Uncle Sam Built" for more discussion on these and other forms of interference. Also, hear Brook, "The Financial Crisis";

see Brook and Watkins, *Free Market Revolution*, pp. 47–59; and see John A. Allison, *The Financial Crisis and the Free Market Cure* (New York: McGraw-Hill, 2013).

14. See Horwitz and Boettke, "The House That Uncle Sam Built," pp. 11–14, 17, and 18 and Brook and Watkins, *Free Market Revolution*, pp. 52–56.

7 John Law's Financial Scam and the South Sea Bubble

1. My discussion of the Mississippi Bubble is based in part on Brian Simpson, "Money, Banking, and the Business Cycle," audio recording (Irvine, CA: Second Renaissance, Inc., 2005).

2. As quoted in Sir John Clapham, *The Bank of England: A History*, vol. 1 (Cambridge: Cambridge University Press, 1970), p. 106.

3. See Stephen Quinn and William Roberds, "The Big Problem of Large Bills: The Bank of Amsterdam and the Origins of Central Banking," *Federal Reserve Bank of Atlanta, Working Paper Series*, working paper 2005–16 (August 2005) for a discussion of the Bank of Amsterdam. See in particular pp. 1–11 and 35–36.

4. For more background information on Law, see Charles Mackay, *Extraordinary Popular Delusions and the Madness of Crowds* (New York: Farrar, Straus, and Giroux, 1932 [1841]), pp. 1–5.

5. As quoted by Friedrich Hayek in Chapter 10 of *The Trend of Economic Thinking*. See W. W. Bartley III and Stephen Kresge, eds., *The Collected Works of F. A. Hayek*, vol. 3 (Chicago: The University of Chicago Press, 1991), p. 158.

6. Bartley and Kresge, *Collected Works*, pp. 157–158 and John Law, *Money and Trade Considered, with a Proposal for Supplying the Nation with Money* (New York: Augustus M. Kelley, 1966 [1705]), pp. 5–13.

7. See Chapter 2 of Brian P. Simpson, *Money, Banking, and the Business Cycle, Volume 2: Remedies and Alternative Theories* (New York: Palgrave Macmillan, 2014) for a discussion of Keynesian "sticky price and wage theory."

8. See ibid. for how these cause unemployment.

9. For one sympathetic assessment of Law's "system," see Antoin E. Murphy, "John Law: Innovating Theorist and Policymaker" in William N. Goetzmann and K. Geert Rouwenhorst, eds., *The Origins of Value* (Oxford: Oxford University Press, 2005), pp. 225–238.

10. This section is based mainly on the following references: Antoin E. Murphy, *John Law: Economic Theorist and Policy-Maker* (Oxford: Clarendon Press, 1997); Earl J. Hamilton, "Prices and Wages at Paris under John Law's System," *The Quarterly Journal of Economics* vol. 51, no. 1 (November 1936), pp. 42–70; Peter M. Garber, *Famous First Bubbles: The Fundamentals of Early Manias* (Cambridge: The MIT Press, 2000), pp. 91–107; and Andrew McFarland Davis, "An Historical Study of Law's System," *The Quarterly Journal of Economics* vol. 1, no. 3 (April 1887), pp. 289–318. Hamilton provides the most detailed description of the relevant economic events occurring during Law's scam and I primarily use his article. Garber also does a good job and I refer to his book often as well.

11. Garber, *Famous First Bubbles*, p. 92.

12. John Carswell, *The South Sea Bubble* (Stroud, UK: Sutton Publishing Limited, 2001), p. 70.

13. Hamilton, "Prices and Wages at Paris," pp. 55 and 59–60.

14. Ibid., p. 56.

15. Based on data in ibid. and Murphy, *John Law: Economic Theorist*, p. 185.

16. Hamilton, "Prices and Wages at Paris," p. 60

17. Ibid., p. 56.

18. Ibid. and Garber, *Famous First Bubbles*, p. 102.

19. Hamilton, "Prices and Wages at Paris," p. 57.

20. Garber, *Famous First Bubbles*, p. 98.

21. Warren C. Scoville, "Large-Scale Production in the French Plate-Glass Industry, 1665–1789," *The Journal of Political Economy* vol. 50, no. 5 (October 1942), pp. 669–698. See Table 1 on p. 677.

22. Hamilton, "Prices and Wages at Paris," pp. 57–58; Garber, *Famous First Bubbles*, p. 98; and Mackay, *Extraordinary Popular Delusions*, pp. 24 and 27. Some report share prices much higher (as high as 18,000 livres). See Hamilton, "Prices and Wages at Paris," p. 58 and Garber, *Famous First Bubbles*, pp. 97 and 99. I use the more conservative, lower value.

23. Hamilton, "Prices and Wages at Paris," p. 58 and Garber, *Famous First Bubbles*, pp. 101–102. Garber actually claims that the increase in notes represented a 100 percent increase in the money supply, but this does not make sense given that the note issue doubled and specie was disappearing from use. It is also not consistent with note issues prior to April of 1720 discussed by Garber and others. Hamilton claims the note issue (not the money supply) increased by nearly 125 percent during (essentially) April. My estimate of the increase in the money supply through the May/June time frame of 1720 is much less based on the probable dramatic decrease in the use of specie, given that its use was outlawed in late January of 1720. See Hamilton, "Prices and Wages at Paris," p. 60 on the use of specie being outlawed.

24. Hamilton, "Prices and Wages at Paris," p. 60.

25. Garber, *Famous First Bubbles*, p. 102.

26. Hamilton, "Prices and Wages at Paris," p. 62.

27. Ibid., p. 63.

28. Garber, *Famous First Bubbles*, p. x.

29. Ibid., p. 92.

30. Ibid., p. 98. On Law's attempts to develop commercial ventures in the New World, see Hamilton, "Prices and Wages at Paris," pp. 47–48 and 57; Cynthia Crossen, *The Rich and How They Got That Way* (New York: Crown Publishers, 2000), pp. 136–137; Carswell, *The South Sea Bubble*, pp. 71–72; and Malcolm Balen, *The Secret History of the South Sea Bubble* (New York: Fourth Estate, HarperCollins Publishers Inc., 2003), pp. 54–57.

31. Murphy, *John Law: Economic Theorist*, pp. 219–223 and Thomas E. Kaiser, "Money, Despotism, and Public Opinion in Early Eighteenth-Century France: John Law and the Debate on Royal Credit," *Journal of Modern History* vol. 63 (March 1991), pp. 1–28. See pp. 16–17 of Kaiser.

32. See Chapter 7 of Simpson, *Money, Banking, and the Business Cycle, Volume 2* for a detailed discussion of the effects of inflation, including how it causes capital decumulation.

33. On the relation of these ideas to government power, see Brian P. Simpson, *Markets Don't Fail!* (Lanham, MD: Lexington Books, 2005), pp. 3, 5–26, 43, 79, 116, 118, 202, and 209.

34. Garber, *Famous First Bubbles*, pp. 109–110.

35. Balen, *The Secret History*, pp. 30 and 32.

36. Larry D. Neal "How the South Sea Bubble Was Blown Up and Burst" in Eugene N. White, ed., *Stock Market Crashes and Speculative Manias* (Cheltenham, UK: Edward Elgar Publishing Limited, 1996), pp. 154–177. See pp. 156–157.

37. Garber, *Famous First Bubbles*, p. 109 and Carswell, *The South Sea Bubble*, p. 120.

38. Garber, *Famous First Bubbles*, p. 116.

39. Carswell, *The South Sea Bubble*, pp. 74 and 79; Neal, "How the South Sea Bubble Was Blown Up," p. 156; and Balen, *The Secret History*, pp. 50–52 and 64–67.

40. Garber, *Famous First Bubbles*, pp. 111–118 and Balen, *The Secret History*, p. 80.

41. Neal, "How the South Sea Bubble Was Blown Up," pp. 162 and 168 and Richard Dale, *The First Crash: Lessons from the South Sea Bubble* (Princeton, NJ: Princeton University Press, 2004), p. 101.

42. On loans for the purpose of purchasing stock, see Dale, *The First Crash*, p. 100; Carswell, *The South Sea Bubble*, pp. 111, 125, 129, and 145; Balen, *The Secret History*, pp. 102, 116, and 132–133; Garber, *Famous First Bubbles*, pp. 115 and 117; and Neal, "How the South Sea Bubble Was Blown Up," pp. 167–169.

43. Dale, *The First Crash*, p. 101; Carswell, *The South Sea Bubble*, p. 111; and Balen, *The Secret History*, p. 135.

44. Garber, *Famous First Bubbles*, pp. 115–120.

45. On capital inflows, see Balen, *The Secret History*, p. 118; Carswell, *The South Sea Bubble*, pp. 118 and 121–122; and Neal, "How the South Sea Bubble Was Blown Up," p. 164.

46. For the evidence of inflation, see Neal, "How the South Sea Bubble Was Blown Up," p. 168 and Carswell, *The South Sea Bubble*, pp. 125, 145, 152, and 159–160.

47. See Jesús Huerta de Soto, *Money, Bank Credit, and Economic Cycles*, translated by Melinda A. Stroup (Auburn, AL: Ludwig von Mises Institute, 2006), p. 108 and Clapham, *The Bank of England*, p. 230 on the claim that the BOE was engaging in inflationary policies.

48. On the boom, see Balen, *The Secret History*, pp. 103–104 and Carswell, *The South Sea Bubble*, pp. 121–122.

49. On the bust, see Balen, *The Secret History*, pp. 143–146; Carswell, *The South Sea Bubble*, pp. 164–166; Dale, *The First Crash*, pp. 134–135; and Garber, *Famous First Bubbles*, pp. 119–120.

50. For greater discussion on this topic, see Simpson *Markets Don't Fail!*, pp. 105–106.

51. Dale, *The First Crash*, pp. 92–93.

8   THE GREAT DEPRESSION

1. For examples of analyses of the Great Depression from an Austrian perspective, see Murray N. Rothbard, *America's Great Depression*, 5th ed. (Auburn, AL: Mises Institute, 2000); Jay Cochran III, "Of Contracts and the Katallaxy: Measuring the Extent of the Market, 1919–1939," *The Review of Austrian Economics* vol. 17, no. 4 (2004), pp. 407–466; and Lionel Robbins, *The Great Depression* (London: Macmillan and Co., 1934).

2. For an example of a book in which the former error is committed, see Barry Eichengreen, *Golden Fetters* (New York: Oxford University Press, 1992). For an example of a book in which the latter error is committed, see Peter Temin, *Did Monetary Forces Cause the Great Depression?* (New York: W. W. Norton & Co., 1976).

3. Regarding the role of gold in causing the Great Depression, I have not addressed these claims in a discussion specifically pertaining to the Great Depression but have

addressed them in discussions on the benefits of the gold standard and refutations of criticisms of the gold standard in Chapter 7 of Brian P. Simpson, *Money, Banking, and the Business Cycle, Volume 2: Remedies and Alternative Theories* (New York: Palgrave Macmillan, 2014). Regarding the claims concerning consumption and the Great Depression, I have not addressed them specifically as they pertain to that event but address them in chapter 2 in this book on the discussion of so-called fiscal policy and the alleged Keynesian multiplier and in chapters 5 and 6 on the discussion of proposed Keynesian solutions to recessions in the latter part of the twentieth century and the beginning of the new millennium. My refutation of the underconsumption theory of the business cycle, including the Keynesian version of this theory, in Chapter 1 of Simpson, *Money, Banking, and the Business Cycle, Volume 2* also addresses the claims regarding consumption and the Great Depression. Chapter 3 of ibid. (specifically, the refutation of real business cycle theory) can be used to address other attempted explanations of the Great Depression.

4. Rothbard, *America's Great Depression*, pp. 89–90. See the section on money in chapter 1 above for my discussion of Rothbard's and others' theories of money.

5. For an example, see Rothbard, *America's Great Depression*, pp. 85–135.

6. GNR was calculated by adding gross operating revenue of corporations, partnerships, and sole proprietorships to total wage payments and total rents paid by consumers and businesses. All but the wage data were obtained from Cochran, "Of Contracts and the Katallaxy," pp. 426–429. See exhibit 8.2 for the sources of the wage data. Nominal values were then converted to real values by using the consumer price index and producer price index. These indices were used, respectively, to convert nominal values of total consumption and production spending to real values. These components were then added together to get real GNR. Nominal consumption was calculated by adding total consumption katallactics, autarkic household production, government wages, and government purchases of goods and services. Of these consumption components, all but government wages were obtained from ibid. See exhibit 8.2 for the sources of government wage data. Government wages were calculated based on the note to government purchases of goods and services in ibid. Nominal production was then calculated by subtracting consumption from GNR.

7. Carol Corrado, "Industrial Production and Capacity Utilization: The 2002 Historical and Annual Revision," *Federal Reserve Bulletin* vol. 89 (April 2003), pp. 151–176. See p. 165 for a statement of the broad nature of the materials index.

8. Robbins, *The Great Depression*, pp. 46 and 211.

9. See Benjamin M. Anderson, *Economics and the Public Welfare: A Financial and Economic History of the United States, 1914–46* (Indianapolis, IN: Liberty Press, 1979 [1949]), pp. 156 and 190 for the details of purchases of government securities by the Fed during this period.

10. Jeremy Atack and Peter Passell, *A New Economic View of American History*, 2nd ed. (New York: W. W. Norton & Company, 1994), p. 588.

11. Anderson, *Economics and the Public Welfare*, pp. 56–57.

12. Jay Cochran III, *Contracts, Collapse, and Coercion: A Katallactic Reappraisal of the Great Depression* (Ann Arbor, MI: Bell & Howell Information and Learning Company, 2000), p. 43.

13. See Chapter 4 of Simpson, *Money, Banking, and the Business Cycle, Volume 2* for a detailed discussion of the destructive nature of fractional-reserve banking and Chapter 7 of ibid. for a discussion of the beneficial aspects of gold and 100-percent reserves.

14. For a discussion of the government controls that create a fractional-reserve checking system and, in general, make it possible for the government to manipulate the money supply, see Chapter 4 of ibid. and chapter 2 above.

15. See Chapter 7 of Simpson, *Money, Banking, and the Business Cycle, Volume 2* for a detailed discussion of the negative effects of inflation.

16. On the point of government controls making the Great Depression far worse than it needed to be, see Cochran, *Contracts, Collapse, and Coercion*, pp. 6–10 and 59–124; George Reisman, *Capitalism: A Treatise on Economics* (Ottawa, IL: Jameson Books, 1996), pp. 589–591; Robert Higgs, "Regime Uncertainty," *The Independent Review* vol. 1, no. 4 (Spring 1997), pp. 561–590; and Richard M. Salsman, "Roosevelt's Raw Deal," *The Intellectual Activist* vol. 18, no. 8 (August 2004), pp. 9–20.

17. Rothbard, *America's Great Depression*, pp. 185–186.

18. See Brian P. Simpson *Markets Don't Fail!* (Lanham, MD: Lexington Books, 2005) for why altruism and collectivism lead to government controls. See Chapters 1, 4, 6, and 7.

19. Richard M. Salsman, "Hoover's Progressive Assault on Business," *The Intellectual Activist* vol. 18, no. 7 (July 2004), pp. 10–20. See in particular pp. 13–15.

20. Arthur M. Schlesinger Jr., *The Age of Roosevelt: The Crisis of the Old Order, 1919–1933*, vol. 1 (Boston: Houghton Mifflin Co., 1956), pp. 81–82.

21. On Hoover's leftist nature, see Rothbard, *America's Great Depression*, pp. 185–207.

22. Ibid., pp. 210–212.

23. See Chapter 1 of Simpson, *Money, Banking, and the Business Cycle, Volume 2* for a discussion on the role of changes in wage rates, changes in employment, and shifts in demand between capital goods and labor in causing changes in spending in the economy.

24. Rothbard, *America's Great Depression*, p. 187.

25. Ibid., p. 332.

26. See US Bureau of the Census, *Historical Statistics of the United States, Colonial Times to 1970*, part 1 (Washington, DC: US Government Printing Office, 1975), series F54 and F60, pp. 229–230 for the data used to calculate these numbers.

27. This topic is addressed in detail in the underconsumption section of Chapter 1 in Simpson, *Money, Banking, and the Business Cycle, Volume 2.*

28. See Chapter 7 of ibid.

29. Reisman, *Capitalism*, p. 591.

30. Rothbard, *America's Great Depression*, pp. 286–288.

31. On this topic, also see Simpson, *Markets Don't Fail!*, pp. 171–179.

32. Salsman, "Hoover's Progressive Assault on Business," p. 15.

33. Reisman, *Capitalism*, pp. 528–531.

34. Although the US dollar does circulate as the currency of choice in some countries and many countries hold significant amounts of dollars as a foreign-exchange reserve, these do not deny the claims I am making here. The former does not create meaningful fluctuations in the money supply due to changes in international trade. With regard to the latter, such reserves are generally loaned back in the United States. Nonetheless, as I discuss below, any factors creating international flows of money would not create the correct change in the money supply in connection with the imposition of a tariff.

35. Salsman, "Hoover's Progressive Assault on Business," p. 15.

36. Rothbard, *America's Great Depression*, pp. 243–244.

37. For a detailed discussion on the benefits of free immigration, see Reisman, *Capitalism*, pp. 362–367.

38. Rothbard, *America's Great Depression*, pp. 246–247.

39. As quoted in ibid., p. 187.

40. See Simpson, *Markets Don't Fail!*, Chapters 1, 6, and 7 for the destructive nature of altruism and collectivism when put into practice.

41. Schlesinger, *The Crisis of the Old Order*, p. 433.

42. The total industrial production index in exhibit 8.6 shows the index surpassing its 1929 peak in 1937. However, this index declined in 1938 and did not surpass the 1929 peak permanently until 1939. This will be shown and discussed in the next chapter. Real GNP did not reach its 1929 peak at all until 1939. Real GNR does not show a recovery beyond the 1929 peak through the end of the available data in 1939.

43. I discuss issues related to banking stability in detail in Chapters 4, 5, and 7 of Simpson, *Money, Banking, and the Business Cycle, Volume 2*.

44. For a detailed discussion of how best to improve the quality of products and services and provide appropriate information, see Simpson, *Markets Don't Fail!*, pp. 101–134 and 193–194 on the regulation of the safety and quality of products and working conditions and on asymmetric information.

45. For more on these topics, see Reisman, *Capitalism*, pp. 350–354 and Henry Hazlitt, *Economics in One Lesson* (New York: Arlington House Publishers, 1979), pp. 74–89.

46. On the economically destructive nature of pro-labor union legislation, see Hazlitt, *Economics in One Lesson*, pp. 140–151 and Reisman, *Capitalism*, pp. 655–659.

47. See Chapter 7 of Simpson, *Money, Banking, and the Business Cycle, Volume 2* for a detailed discussion of gold and inflation.

48. Anderson, *Economics and the Public Welfare*, pp. 92–93 and 349–352.

49. Ibid., pp. 365–367.

50. Ibid., pp. 372–375 and 380–381.

51. On these three agricultural acts, see Cochran, *Contracts, Collapse, and Coercion*, pp. 70–71 and Gary M. Walton and Hugh Rockoff, *History of the American Economy*, 9th ed. (Toronto: Thomson Learning, Inc., 2002), pp. 529–531.

52. Wikipedia, "List of United States Federal Executive Orders," http://en.wikipedia. org/wiki/List_of_United_States_federal_executive_orders#cite_note-0, accessed April 12, 2012.

53. See Atack and Passell, *A New Economic View*, pp. 668–669 for a list of FDR's legislative initiatives during his first 100 days in office.

54. Cochran, *Contracts, Collapse, and Coercion*, pp. 149–150. Cochran's list of legislation signed into law during the first 100 days of FDR's first term is slightly different than Atack and Passell's. For yet another slightly different list, see Arthur M. Schlesinger Jr., *The Age of Roosevelt: The Coming of the New Deal*, vol. 2 (Boston: Houghton Mifflin Co., 1958), pp. 20–21.

55. In addition, see Chapter 7 of Simpson, *Money, Banking, and the Business Cycle, Volume 2* for what the appropriate government policies are to prevent recessions and depressions from occurring in the first place. This knowledge can also be applied to what governments can do during the middle of a recession or depression to limit the damage and help the economy recover.

56. Jeffrey Rogers Hummel, "Problems with Austrian Business Cycle Theory," *Reason Papers* no. 5 (Winter 1979), pp. 41–53. See especially pp. 50–51. Hummel does not specifically focus on the Great Depression but on international aspects of ABCT in general. In addition, his argument focuses on the claim that ABCT needs more work in this area.

57. Atack and Passell, *A New Economic View*, p. 602.

9 THE BUSINESS CYCLE IN AMERICA FROM 1900 TO 1965

1. Benjamin M. Anderson, *Economics and the Public Welfare: A Financial and Economic History of the United States, 1914–46* (Indianapolis, IN: Liberty Press 1979 [1949]), pp. 92–93 and 349–352.
2. C. A. Phillips, T. F. McManus, and R. W. Nelson, *Banking and the Business Cycle* (New York: The Macmillan Co., 1937), p. 127.
3. Jay Cochran III, "Of Contracts and the Katallaxy: Measuring the Extent of the Market, 1919–1939," *The Review of Austrian Economics* vol. 17, no. 4 (2004), pp. 407–466. See in particular pp. 427–429 for the data on which this value is based.
4. I discuss in great detail many of the regulations used by the government—pre- and post-Fed creation—to exert influence over the monetary and banking system and the effects these controls had (and still have today) in Chapters 4 and 7 of Brian P. Simpson, *Money, Banking, and the Business Cycle, Volume 2: Remedies and Alternative Theories* (New York: Palgrave Macmillan, 2014).
5. My discussion on WWII, the Great Depression, and prosperity is based on George Reisman, *Capitalism: A Treatise on Economics* (Ottawa, IL: Jameson Books, 1996), pp. 262 and 592–594. Also see Ludwig von Mises, *Nation, State, and Economy*, translated by Leland B. Yeager (Menlo Park, CA: Institute for Humane Studies, 1983), pp. 183–197 and Robert Higgs, "Wartime Prosperity? A Reassessment of the U.S. Economy in the 1940s," *The Journal of Economic History* vol. 52, no. 1 (March 1992), pp. 41–60.
6. Mises, *Nation, State, and Economy*, p. 186.

Selected Bibliography

Allison, John A., *The Financial Crisis and the Free Market Cure* (New York: McGraw-Hill, 2013).

Anderson, Benjamin M., *Economics and the Public Welfare: A Financial and Economic History of the United States, 1914–46* (Indianapolis, IN: Liberty Press 1979 [1949]).

Arnold, Roger A., *Economics*, 5th ed. (Cincinnati, OH: South-Western College Publishing, 2001).

Atack, Jeremy, and Peter Passell, *A New Economic View of American History*, 2nd ed. (New York: W. W. Norton & Company, 1994).

Balen, Malcolm, *The Secret History of the South Sea Bubble* (New York: Fourth Estate, HarperCollins Publishers Inc., 2003).

Barnett II, William, and Walter Block, "On Hummel on Austrian Business Cycle Theory," *Reason Papers* no. 30 (Fall 2008), pp. 59–90.

———, "Tyler Cowen and Austrian Business Cycle Theory: A Critique," *New Perspectives on Political Economy* vol. 2, no. 2 (2006), pp. 26–85.

Bartley III, W. W., and Stephen Kresge, eds., *The Collected Works of F. A. Hayek*, vol. 3 (Chicago: The University of Chicago Press, 1991).

Binswanger, Harry, ed., *The Ayn Rand Lexicon: Objectivism from A to Z* (New York: Penguin Books, 1986).

Block, Walter, "Yes, We Have No Chaff: A Reply to Wagner's 'Austrian Cycle Theory: Saving the Wheat While Discarding the Chaff,'" *The Quarterly Journal of Austrian Economics* vol. 4, no. 1 (2001), pp. 63–73.

Block, Walter, and William Barnett II, "Contra Eichengreen and Mitchener on ABCT," *Studies in Economics and Finance* vol. 28, no. 2 (2011), pp. 111–117.

———, "On Laidler Regarding the Austrian Business Cycle Theory," *The Review of Austrian Economics* vol. 20, no. 1 (2007), pp. 43–61.

Brigham, Eugene F., and Louis C. Gapenski, *Financial Management: Theory and Practice*, 6th ed. (Orlando, FL: The Dryden Press, 1991).

Brook, Yaron, "The Financial Crisis: What Happened and Why," video recording (August 4, 2009), http://arc-tv.com/the-financial-crisis-what-happened-and-why/, accessed February 22, 2013.

Brook, Yaron, and Don Watkins, *Free Market Revolution: How Ayn Rand's Ideas Can End Big Government* (New York: Palgrave Macmillan, 2012).

Carswell, John, *The South Sea Bubble* (Stroud, UK: Sutton Publishing Limited, 2001).

Clapham, Sir John, *The Bank of England: A History*, vol. 1 (Cambridge: Cambridge University Press, 1970).

Cochran III, Jay, "Of Contracts and the Katallaxy: Measuring the Extent of the Market, 1919–1939," *The Review of Austrian Economics* vol. 17, no. 4 (2004), pp. 407–466.

———, *Contracts, Collapse, and Coercion: A Katallactic Reappraisal of the Great Depression* (Ann Arbor, MI: Bell & Howell Information and Learning Company, 2000).

Corrado, Carol, "Industrial Production and Capacity Utilization: The 2002 Historical and Annual Revision," *Federal Reserve Bulletin* vol. 89 (April 2003), pp. 151–176.

Cowen, Tyler, *Risk and Business Cycles: New and Old Austrian Perspectives* (New York: Routledge, 1997).

Crain, Rance, "Why '01's 'Mild' Recession Wasn't: GDP Doesn't Include Advertising," *Advertising Age* (March 6, 2006), http://adage.com/article/rance-crain/01-s-mild-recession-gdp-include-advertising/107007/, accessed June 23, 2012.

Crossen, Cynthia, *The Rich and How They Got That Way* (New York: Crown Publishers, 2000).

Dale, Richard, *The First Crash: Lessons from the South Sea Bubble* (Princeton, NJ: Princeton University Press, 2004).

Davis, Andrew McFarland, "An Historical Study of Law's System," *The Quarterly Journal of Economics* vol. 1, no. 3 (April 1887), pp. 289–318.

Edwards, Cheryl L., "Open Market Operations in the 1990s," *Federal Reserve Bulletin* vol. 83 (November 1997), pp. 859–874.

Eichengreen, Barry, *Golden Fetters* (New York: Oxford University Press, 1992).

English, John W., and Gray E. Cardiff, *The Coming Real Estate Crash* (New Rochelle, NY: Arlington House Publishers, 1979).

Garber, Peter M., *Famous First Bubbles: The Fundamentals of Early Manias* (Cambridge: The MIT Press, 2000).

Garrison, Roger W., "Hayekian Trade Cycle Theory: A Reappraisal," *Cato Journal* vol. 6, no. 2 (Fall 1986), pp. 437–459.

Goodhart, Charles, *The Evolution of Central Banks* (Cambridge: The MIT Press, 1988).

Gordon, Robert A., *Business Fluctuations*, 2nd ed. (New York: Harper and Row, 1961).

Hamilton, Earl J., "Prices and Wages at Paris Under John Law's System," *The Quarterly Journal of Economics* vol. 51, no. 1 (November 1936), pp. 42–70.

Hayek, F. A., *Prices and Production*, 2nd ed. (New York: Augustus M. Kelly, 1935).

Hazlitt, Henry, *Economics in One Lesson* (New York: Arlington House Publishers, 1979).

Hicks, John, *Critical Essays in Monetary Theory* (Oxford: Oxford University Press, 1967).

Higgs, Robert, "Regime Uncertainty," *The Independent Review* vol. 1, no. 4 (Spring 1997), pp. 561–590.

———, "Wartime Prosperity? A Reassessment of the U.S. Economy in the 1940s," *The Journal of Economic History* vol. 52, no. 1 (March 1992), pp. 41–60.

Horwitz, Steven, and Peter Boettke, "The House That Uncle Sam Built: The Untold Story of the Great Recession of 2008" (October 8, 2010), http://c457332.r32.cf2.rackcdn.com/wp-content/uploads/2009/12/HouseUncleSamBuiltBooklet.pdf, accessed February 22, 2013.

Huerta de Soto, Jesús, *Money, Bank Credit, and Economic Cycles*, translated by Melinda A. Stroup (Auburn, AL: Ludwig von Mises Institute, 2006).

Hummel, Jeffrey Rogers, "Problems with Austrian Business Cycle Theory," *Reason Papers* no. 5 (Winter 1979), pp. 41–53.

Jastram, Roy W., *The Golden Constant* (New York: John Wiley & Sons, 1977).

Kaiser, Thomas E., "Money, Despotism, and Public Opinion in Early Eighteenth-Century France: John Law and the Debate on Royal Credit," *Journal of Modern History* vol. 63 (March 1991), pp. 1–28.

Laidler, David, "The Price Level, Relative Prices and Economic Stability: Aspects of the Interwar Debate," *BIS Working Papers* no. 136 (September 2003).

Law, John, *Money and Trade Considered, with a Proposal for Supplying the Nation with Money* (New York: Augustus M. Kelley, 1966 [1705]).

Lee, Maurice W., *Macroeconomic Fluctuations, Growth, and Stability*, 5th ed. (Homewood, IL: Richard D. Irwin, Inc., 1971).

Lindsey, David E., "Recent Monetary Developments and Controversies," *Brookings Papers on Economic Activity* vol. 1 (1982), pp. 245–271.

Mackay, Charles, *Extraordinary Popular Delusions and the Madness of Crowds* (New York: Farrar, Straus, and Giroux, 1932 [1841]).

McKeon, Richard, ed., *Introduction to Aristotle* (New York: Random House, 1947).

Miron, Jeffrey A., and Christina D. Romer, "A New Monthly Index of Industrial Production, 1884–1940," *The Journal of Economic History* vol. 50, no. 2 (June 1990), pp. 321–337.

Mises, Ludwig von, *Nation, State, and Economy*, translated by Leland B. Yeager (Menlo Park, CA: Institute for Humane Studies, 1983).

———, *The Theory of Money and Credit* (Indianapolis, IN: Liberty Fund, 1981 [1934]).

———, *Human Action*, 3rd rev. ed. (Chicago: Contemporary Books, Inc., 1966).

Murphy, Antoin E., "John Law: Innovating Theorist and Policymaker" in William N. Goetzmann and K. Geert Rouwenhorst, eds., *The Origins of Value* (Oxford: Oxford University Press, 2005), pp. 225–238.

———, *John Law: Economic Theorist and Policy-Maker* (Oxford: Clarendon Press, 1997).

Muth, John F., "Rational Expectations and the Theory of Price Movements," *Econometrica* vol. 29, no. 3 (1961), pp. 315–335.

Naples, Michele I., "Business Failure and the Expenditure Multiplier, or How Recessions Become Depressions," *Journal of Post-Keynesian Economics* vol. 19, no. 4 (Summer 1997), pp. 511–523.

Neal, Larry D., "How the South Sea Bubble was Blown Up and Burst" in Eugene N. White, ed., *Stock Market Crashes and Speculative Manias* (Cheltenham, UK: Edward Elgar Publishing Limited, 1996), pp. 154–177.

Osborne, Dale K. "What Is Money Today?" *Economic Review* (January 1985), pp. 1–15.

Peikoff, Leonard, *Objectivism: The Philosophy of Ayn Rand* (New York: Meridian, 1991).

Phillips, C. A., T. F. McManus, and R. W. Nelson, *Banking and the Business Cycle* (New York: The Macmillan Co., 1937).

Pilloff, Steven J., "Money Market Mutual Funds: Are They a Close Substitute for Accounts at Insured Depository Institutions?" *The Antitrust Bulletin* vol. 44, no. 2 (Summer 1999), pp. 365–385.

Powell, Benjamin, "Explaining Japan's Recession," *The Quarterly Journal of Austrian Economics* vol. 5, no. 2 (Summer 2002), pp. 35–50.

Quinn, Stephen, and William Roberds, "The Big Problem of Large Bills: The Bank of Amsterdam and the Origins of Central Banking," *Federal Reserve Bank of Atlanta, Working Paper Series*, working paper 2005–16 (August 2005).

Rand, Ayn, *The Virtue of Selfishness* (New York: Signet, 1964).

Reisman, George, "Credit Expansion, Crisis, and the Myth of the Saving Glut" (July 4, 2009), http://capitalism.net/articles/A_Blog_07_09.html, accessed December 10, 2011.

———, "Economic Recovery Requires Capital Accumulation Not Government 'Stimulus Packages'" (February 21 and 22, 2009), http://capitalism.net/articles/A_Blog_02_09.html#02_21_09, accessed December 10, 2011.

———, "The Myth That Laissez Faire Is Responsible for Our Financial Crisis" (October 21, 2008), http://capitalism.net/articles/A_Blog_10_08.html, accessed December 10, 2011.

———, "The Housing Bubble and the Credit Crunch" (August 10, 2007), http://capitalism.net/articles/A_Blog_08_07.html, accessed December 10, 2011.

Reisman, George, "The Stock Market, Profits, and Credit Expansion" (2002), http://capitalism.net/articles/Stock%20Market,%20Profits,%20Credit%20Expansion.htm, accessed December 10, 2011.

——, "When Will the Bubble Burst" (August 7, 1999), http://capitalism.net/articles/stockmkt.htm, accessed December 10, 2011.

——, *Capitalism: A Treatise on Economics* (Ottawa, IL: Jameson Books, 1996).

Robbins, Lionel, *The Great Depression* (London: Macmillan and Co., 1934).

Ross, W. D., *The Works of Aristotle Translated into English* (London: Oxford University Press, 1928).

Rothbard, Murray, *The Mystery of Banking*, 2nd ed. (Auburn, AL: The Ludwig von Mises Institute, 2008).

——, *America's Great Depression*, 5th ed. (Auburn, AL: The Ludwig von Mises Institute, 2000).

——, *Man, Economy, and State*, vol. 2 (Los Angeles: Nash Publishing, 1962).

——, *The Panic of 1819: Reactions and Policies* (New York: Columbia University Press, 1962).

Salerno, Joseph T., "The 'True' Money Supply: A Measure of the Supply of the Medium of Exchange in the U.S. Economy," *Austrian Economics Newsletter* (Spring 1987), pp. 1–6.

Salsman, Richard M., "The End of Central Banking, Part I," *The Objective Standard* vol. 8, no. 1 (Spring 2013), pp. 13–29.

——, "Roosevelt's Raw Deal," *The Intellectual Activist* vol. 18, no. 8 (August 2004), pp. 9–20.

——, "Hoover's Progressive Assault on Business," *The Intellectual Activist* vol. 18, no. 7 (July 2004), pp. 10–20.

——, "The Myth of Market Bubbles," audio recording (Gaylordsville, CT: Second Renaissance Books, 2000).

——, *Breaking the Banks: Central Banking Problems and Free Banking Solutions* (Great Barrington, MA: American Institute for Economic Research, 1990).

Samuelson, Paul A., and William D. Nordhaus, *Economics*, 13th ed. (New York: McGraw-Hill Book Co., 1989).

Sargent, Thomas J., and Neil Wallace, "'Rational' Expectations, the Optimal Monetary Instrument, and the Optimal Money Supply Rule," *Journal of Political Economy* vol. 83, no. 21 (1975), pp. 241–254.

Schlesinger Jr., Arthur M., *The Age of Roosevelt: The Coming of the New Deal*, vol. 2 (Boston: Houghton Mifflin Co., 1958).

——, *The Age of Roosevelt: The Crisis of the Old Order, 1919–1933*, vol. 1 (Boston: Houghton Mifflin Co., 1956).

Scoville, Warren C., "Large-Scale Production in the French Plate-Glass Industry, 1665–1789," *The Journal of Political Economy* vol. 50, no. 5 (October 1942), pp. 669–698.

Sechrest, Lawrence J., "Book Review of *Risk and Business Cycles: New and Old Austrian Perspectives*," *The Quarterly Journal of Austrian Economics* vol. 1, no. 3 (Fall 1998), pp. 73–79.

Simpson, Brian P., *Money, Banking, and the Business Cycle, Volume 2: Remedies and Alternative Theories* (New York: Palgrave Macmillan, 2014).

——, "Austrian Trade Cycle Theory and Rationality," *New Perspectives on Political Economy* vol. 4, no. 2 (2008), pp. 113–129.

——, "Money, Banking, and the Business Cycle," audio recording (Irvine, CA: Second Renaissance, Inc., 2005).

——, *Markets Don't Fail!* (Lanham, MD: Lexington Books, 2005).

————, *Trade Cycle Theory: A Market Process Perspective* (Ann Arbor, MI: Bell & Howell Information and Learning Company, 2000).

Stigum, Marcia, *The Money Market*, rev. ed. (Homewood, IL: Dow Jones-Irwin, 1983).

Temin, Peter, *Did Monetary Forces Cause the Great Depression?* (New York: W. W. Norton & Co., 1976).

Thurm, Scott, "After the Boom: A Go-Go Giant of Internet Age, Cisco Is Learning to Go Slow," *Wall Street Journal* (May 7, 2003), p. A1.

Tullock, Gordon, "Reply to Comment by Joseph T. Salerno," *The Review of Austrian Economics* vol. 3, no. 1 (1989), pp. 147–149.

————, "Why the Austrians Are Wrong about Depressions," *The Review of Austrian Economics* vol. 2, no. 1 (1988), pp. 73–78.

Wagner, Richard E., "Austrian Cycle Theory: Saving the Wheat while Discarding the Chaff," *The Review of Austrian Economics* vol. 12, no. 1 (1999), pp. 65–80.

Walton, Gary M., and Hugh Rockoff, *History of the American Economy*, 9th ed. (Toronto: Thomson Learning, Inc., 2002).

White, Lawrence H., "A Subjectivist Perspective on the Definition and Identification of Money" in Israel M. Kirzner, ed., *Subjectivism, Intelligibility and Economic Understanding* (Washington Square: New York University Press, 1986), pp. 301–314.

Yeager, Leland B., "The Significance of Monetary Disequilibrium," *Cato Journal* vol. 6, no. 2 (Fall 1986), pp. 369–420.

INDEX